W9-CZB-824

Engendering Judaism

Engendering Judaism:

An Inclusive
Theology and Ethics

Rachel Adler

The Jewish Publication Society
Philadelphia • Jerusalem

Manufactured in the United States of America

Library of Congress Cataloging in Publication Data
Adler, Rachel.
    Engendering Judaism: an inclusive theology and ethics / Rachel
    Adler.
        p.   cm.
    Includes bibliographical references and index.
    ISBN 0–8276–0584–6
        1. Feminism—Religious aspects—Judaism.   2. Judaism—
    Doctrines.   3. Women in Judaism.   4. Jewish Women—Religious
    Life.   5. Women—Legal status, laws, etc. (Jewish law)   I. Title.
    BM729.W6A29   1997
    296.3'082—dc21   97–18944
                                                             CIP
                                                             r97
Designed by Bill Frambes Typesetting
Typeset by Bill Frambes Typesetting

To David, *haveri v'ish briti.*

Contents

Preface

by David Ellenson

Jewish tradition holds language to be both powerful and holy. Judaism identifies speech—the word—as the agent of creation. The Psalmist, in words included in the daily liturgy of the Jewish prayer book, proclaims, "Blessed is the one who *spoke,* and the world came to be." Words are also the means of revelation. God speaks to Israel at Sinai, and The Ten Commandments are referred to in rabbinic tradition as *Asseret ha-Dibberot*—The Ten Words. Indeed, words are so precious that Genesis asserts that the uniqueness and elevation of the human species reside in the gift of language with which God distinguished humanity from all other forms of life. The vocabulary of the medieval Jewish philosophical tradition recognizes these sacred roles assigned to language and speech in Judaism by identifying the human being as *ha-Medabber*—he who speaks. Through speech, all of us offer that which is ours alone to the Other. Speech affirms the existence of the self. At the same time, speech seeks a response from the Other. Words provide the basis for community, for they permit and allow for dialogue among people.

When a community accords an individual or group the privilege of public speech, it is a mark that the community has conferred equal status upon such persons. Conversely, when a community silences or excludes an individual or a group, when it views them as beings who are neither qualified nor capable of addressing the Other, then that community diminishes their humanity. Words, in the end, possess the power of conferring personhood. The ability to speak—to address Others and to be addressed—is that which signifies that we are fully human. Language and speech are primordially ethical.

Engendering Judaism is based upon these observations concerning the power of silence and speech. In these pages, Rachel Adler argues that Judaism must be conceptualized as an extended conversation, one in which the lips of participants long since dead move and inform the present. Many of these voices are recorded in classical texts like the Bible and Talmud, and they form a core element in the ground of Jewish religious tradition. As a Jewish theologian, Adler does not exclude these voices from the Jewish conversation. To do so, in her opinion, would be to display bad faith with a past that has shaped the identity of men and women as Jews for generations.

At the same time, *Engendering Judaism* passionately contends that the conversation must not be confined to these voices alone, for the Jewish conversation, as presented in these classical sources, has been an exclusionary one. In these pages, Rachel Adler rejects a Judaism that limits the speech of women. The voices and concerns of women have been silenced in the classical texts and religious conversations of our people for too long. *Engendering Judaism* seeks to redress this wrong.

Adler here grants full public expression to her own voice as a religious Jewish woman. She cites the ethical teachings contained in Jewish tradition itself as providing sufficient warrants for protesting the subordination of women in the Jewish public arena. Decrying the manner in which all too many Jewish terms and texts have obliterated or denied public expression to the voices and experiences of women, Adler adopts a perspective that begins with a commitment to the full inclusion of women in the Jewish conversation. She condemns as morally unacceptable any Judaism that would deny women their rightful public voice, and she demands that Judaism acknowledge the complete humanity of women by accepting women as dialogical partners in the public conversations of the Jewish people.

Adler anchors her conversation in the *ketubbah*, the Jewish wedding contract. She argues that the traditional Jewish legal concept of *kinyan* (acquisition) in the area of Jewish marriage law identifies the act of marriage as nothing more than a commercial transaction. In other words, the marriage contract conveys the woman as an object from the domain of one male—generally the father—to a new one—the husband. Indeed, viewed this way, traditional Jewish marriage law reduces the woman to a position of sexual chattel. For these reasons, she advocates that the institution of the *ketubbah* and the concepts of property and acquisition that undergird and inform it be discarded in the area of marriage. She proposes that the metaphor of *b'rit* (covenant) be substituted for *kinyan* (acquisition). This metaphor possesses layers of meaning that more appropriately represent the mutuality of intimate relationship involved in a marriage.

Engendering Judaism is a work of *jurisgenesis*. Instead of abandoning Jewish law, it reconstructs the law. It aims at a transformation of Jewish law and life in keeping with a vision of reality that women inhabit interdependently with men. As a work of feminist Jewish theology,

Engendering Judaism will be compared to the pathbreaking theological work of Judith Plaskow in *Standing Again At Sinai*. At the same time, *Engendering Judaism* moves beyond the realm of expository theology into the worlds of ritual and liturgy and this will cause the reader to compare elements of Adler's book to *The Book of Blessings*, written by the sensitive and inspired Jewish poet Marcia Falk. By writing *Engendering Judaism*, Adler contributes mightily to the task of constructing a Jewish theology for our time and situates herself at the center of contemporary Jewish theological-liturgical discourse.

Above all, *Engendering Judaism* reflects the distinctive voice and sensibility of its author. In this book, Adler demonstrates her command of diverse academic disciplines and fields—feminist theory, contemporary ethical writings, modern religious thought, literary criticism, and present-day legal theory. And, at the same time, she displays her mastery of and love for classical Jewish texts and liturgy. In *Engendering Judaism*, Adler demonstrates that she is an exegete par excellence of traditional Jewish writings. Although formally my student, Rachel Adler has, in truth, been my teacher and my friend. I have learned much from her, not the least of which is that it is both appropriate and necessary to include a personal voice in the Jewish story. In that spirit, I would conclude my remarks with a story from my childhood that explains why I believe her work to be of such import and significance.

Every Saturday morning of my boyhood, I, like countless numbers of Jewish boys throughout the world who attended and continue to attend Orthodox synagogues, would, at the end of services, chant the lines of *Shir ha-Kavod* (The Hymn of Glory). It was always a special moment for me, for my voice was at the center of the service, and I was being prepared for the public role I would assume in the community as an adult.

During the summer months of my boyhood, when I would travel from my native Newport News, Virginia, and spend my vacation with my maternal grandparents in Cambridge, Massachusetts, I would walk every week with my great-uncle Harry to the synagogue. There, as in Newport News, I would ascend the *bimah* (prayer platform) at the end of the service and chant the words, *"Anim Zmirot,"* with which *Shir ha-Kavod* begins. As I did so, I would scan the *Ezrat Nashim*, the balcony where the women sat, and seek out my *bubbe* (grandmother). She would always be sitting right at the edge of the *Ezrat Nashim*, and I would experience a slight fear that, in her eagerness to hear every word, she would lean too far over the side of the balcony and come tumbling down onto the floor of the synagogue. Fortunately, this never happened. However, each week, as I would sing the words of *Shir ha-Kavod,* I would see tears rolling down her cheeks. These tears never failed to startle me, though my *bubbe* and I never spoke of them directly. I simply assumed that her tears reflected the *naches* (pride) she experienced through my participation in the service and the happiness she must have felt because my chanting demonstrated that the Jewish tradition she so loved was successfully being transplanted from the soil of eastern Europe to American shores.

However, now I am not so certain that this view is the only explanation for my grandmother's tears. After all, my *bubbe* was an intelligent and articulate woman. And her daughter, my mother, was a wonderful Hebraist. Their voices were lovely, and I still smile as I recall the cadence and lilt of their words. Yet, there was one place—the synagogue—where their voices were condemned to silence. They, and my sister, unlike my brother or myself, could not ascend the *bimah.* Their glory, unlike mine, was confined to the domestic realm alone. Perhaps this is why my grandmother cried, and why she leaned so far over the balcony. It may be that she desired a simple right that ought to have been extended to her—she wanted to be a participant in the conversation of her community.

Engendering Judaism will not be without its critics. Some will surely argue with its propositions. However, none will mistake the Jewish passion that informs its pages. And none will deny the intelligence, knowledge, and creativity of Rachel Adler. In writing this volume, she has added her voice to those of other contemporary women and men who would construct and redirect the Jewish conversation in our day. In offering us this work, Adler has shown us that the human being is not only *ha-Medabber*—he who speaks. The human being is *ha-Medabberet*—she who speaks—as well. *Engendering Judaism* offers a vision of *tikkun*—repair and redemption—that lies at the heart of Jewish faith. It is an expression of that which is best in Jewish tradition.

Acknowledgments

This work was concomitantly a book and a dissertation. It was under contract with the Jewish Publication Society from the prospectus stage onward. Whereas dissertations usually inaugurate a life of scholarship, this book builds upon the work of a lifetime, twenty-five years of shaping a Jewish feminist theology and ethics. I thank everyone who has taught me, helped me, or been a partner with me in the task. A special thanks to Michael Goldberg, who first taught me that what I was trying to write was called theology and whose own work on narrative theology has profoundly influenced my thought.

A joint committee from the University of Southern California and Hebrew Union College gave me the benefit of their impressive intellectual resources and the warmth of their friendship: David Ellenson and Donald Miller, co-chairs, and Sheila Briggs, Tamara Eskenazi, and Ruth Weisberg. A special thanks to David Ellenson, who took time from his frenetic schedule to comment painstakingly on chapter after chapter and to write the introduction to this book. I am also grateful to the National Foundation for Jewish Culture for a fellowship that supported a year of writing. Dr. Yaffa Weisman, Judaica librarian at Hebrew Union College, and the entire llibrary staff were loyal and tireless friends to my project, finding obscure references, burrowing through unbound periodicals in the basement, and scouring CD-Roms and the Internet for requested information.

My mainstay during seven long years of writing has been the Women's Hevra Shas, a group of academic women and rabbis who meet weekly around my table for tea and Talmud, using a multidisciplinary feminist methodology. These dear study companions critiqued and applauded draft after draft. How can I ever sufficiently thank Tamara Eskenazi and Maeera Shreiber, who recommended sources, performed surgery on refractory chapters, and wiped my tears? I have also benefited from the good counsel of Shoshanna Gershenzon, Laura Geller, Bridget Wynn, Sue Levi Elwell, Isa Aron, and Jacqueline Ellenson.

Others also lavished time and energy on me. Over several years' time, Barbara Dalton-Taylor read three chapters aloud, making me clarify every esoteric reference or murky phrase. Another exacting critic, my son Amitai Adler, who has a particular distaste for postmodernist cultural-critical jargon, read heroically and ultimately pronounced the manuscript intelligible. Friends from afar who enriched my work with their critiques and suggestions include Judith Plaskow, Marcia Falk, Riv-Ellen

Prell, Marcia Lind, and Moshe Zemer. Finally, Ellen Frankel, Editor-in-Chief at the Jewish Publication Society, gave me many hours of her own superlative editing and her exquisite patience.

I could not have written this book without my husband, David Schulman, who has devoted his life to establishing right relations among members of society and who believes, as I do, that the purpose of law is to empower and heal. We married during my second year of doctoral work. For our ceremony, we engendered a new legal model for right relations between husbands and wives, the *B'rit Ahuvim,* described in my final chapter. Without David's tender encouragement, meticulous editing, and visionary legal imagination, the struggle to produce would have been lonely and arduous indeed.

This book will be issued just in time to celebrate my mother's eightieth birthday. I hope she will approve it, for it was she who first taught me to write and to read a literary text.

Thank you all, kind friends. May we continue to teach and delight one another.

Rachel Adler

Introduction

What does it mean to *engender* Judaism? Non-Orthodox Judaisms distinguish themselves from Orthodoxy by their belief that Jews beget Judaism; they reshape and renew Judaism in the various times and places they inhabit. If we accept this premise, it will lead us to a new sense in which Judaism needs to be engendered. Jews in the Western world live in societies where the ethical ideal is for women to be full and equal social participants. But Judaism has only just begun to reflect and to address the questions, understandings, and obligations of both Jewish women and Jewish men. It is not yet fully attentive to the impact of gender and sexuality either on the classical texts or on the lived experiences of the people Israel. Until progressive Judaisms engender themselves in this second sense, they cannot engender fully adequate Judaisms in the first sense. In this book, I propose a theology for engendering Judaism in both senses: a way of thinking about and practicing Judaism that men and women recreate and renew together as equals.

Engendering: Not For Women Only

All of us must participate in both kinds of engendering. Relegating gender issues to women alone perpetuates a fallacy about the nature of Judaism. It presumes that Judaism is a body of gender-neutral texts and traditions and that women constitute a special gendered addendum to the community of its transmitters.[1] It further presumes that while women are represented in Jewish tradition they are separate from it. Scholarship about their representation is classified as "Women in . . ." or "Women and . . ." and is regarded as nonessential knowledge of interest only to women. Men do not need to consider these special topics; they can simply study "Judaism." The truth is that, to paraphrase an old spiritual, all God's chillun got gender. There is not and never was a Judaism unaffected by the gendered perspectives of its transmitters and augmenters. If, as progressive Judaisms argue, social and historical factors affect Judaism, then it is hardly tenable to argue that gender is the only variable to which this rule does not apply. The impact of gender on Judaism, then, is not a women's issue; it is an issue for everyone who seeks to understand Judaism.

Engendering Judaism requires two tasks. The *critical task* is to demonstrate that historical understandings of gender affect all Jewish texts and contexts and hence require the attention of all Jews. But this is only the first step. There is also an *ethical task*. That gender categories and distinctions have changed in the past tells us nothing about what sorts of changes we ought to make in the future. These changes must be negotiated in conversations where participants invoke and reexamine the values and priorities enunciated in Jewish tradition in the light of the current needs, injuries, or aspirations demanding to be addressed.

Every aspect of this undertaking is complex: applying traditional values and priorities while remaining conscious of their historical contingency and their possible gender biases; conducting conversations among Jews whose beliefs, institutional affiliations, and experiences (including gender) differ widely; identifying needs, wounds, and aspirations, now full-time enterprises for social scientists, jurists, philosophers, cultural critics, and psychologists; and, finally, characterizing an elusive "present time" in rapidly mutating, pluralistic, postindustrial societies. The method for engendering Judaism, then, will have to be as complex as the Jewish people and the world they inhabit.

People who undertake ethical tasks do not come as blank slates. We bring our lives and memories, our abilities and interests, our commitments and dreams. I bring my own complex identity and commitments to this book. I am a woman descended from five generations of Reform Jews. I lived as an Orthodox Jew for many years and learned both to love and to struggle with traditional texts and praxis. I brought these concerns with me when I returned to Reform Judaism.

I am also a feminist. That is, I believe that being a woman or a man is an intricate blend of biological predispositions and social constructions that varies greatly according to time and culture. Regardless of its cultural specifics, gender has been used to justify unequal distributions of social power and privilege. Feminists view these power disparities as a moral wrong and an obstacle to human flourishing. This moral evil can be overcome only with great effort because its distortions pervade social institutions, personal relationships, and systems of knowledge and belief, including religious traditions. My commitment to feminism is based on both objective and subjective factors. I find its analysis intellectually convincing, but it also profoundly affects how I value myself as a person and what impact I believe I can have upon those around me. If I were not a feminist, I would not feel entitled to make theology. Accepting feminism's premises leads me directly to the critical and ethical obligations to engender Jewish theology. Judaism, like most cultural and religious systems, assigns men the lion's share of social and religious goods. Yet, as I argue during the course of this book, Judaism's commitment to justice obligates it to understand and to redress gender inequity. By engendering theology and ethics, Judaism takes feminism to heart. But how are theologies engendered?

The Problem of Theology as a Jewish Form

The most fundamental of all problems for feminist Jewish theology has been its very definition as theology. Whereas, from its beginning, Christian feminism has defined the transformation of theology as a major goal, the nature and boundaries of the Jewish feminist project have been more amorphous. In part, this is because the theological tradition to which Christian feminists react is highly systematized. The nature and methodology of theology are more open questions in Judaism. Biblical and rabbinic Judaisms embody a variety of theologies in forms that do not call themselves theology: narrative, prayer, law, and textual exegesis. Although in every period of postbiblical Judaism there have been influential theologies utilizing philosophical forms and categories, as Christian theologies do, there is no standard way of systematizing their Jewish content. That is because Jewish philosophical theologies serve dual purposes.

Whereas Christian theologies are principally conversations within the faith community constructing and clarifying the content of accepted rubrics, Jewish philosophical theologies are both intracommunal and intercommunal conversations. As internal conversation, philosophical theologies extend, defend, and negotiate the boundaries of normative Jewish discourse. As intercommunal and interfaith conversations, they respond to challenges from the larger social environment and its impact upon Jewish thinking and practice by examining Jewish concepts and categories in the light of this larger discussion. At worst, the result is polemics and apologetics. At best, constructive, not merely reactive, theology emerges.

Jewish feminist theology, then, shares some patterns and motifs with other Jewish philosophical theologies. It responds to transformative events in the larger social environment that present a challenge to the thought and practice of Judaism. It is addressed to both internal and external audiences: feminist Jews seeking to critique and to reconstruct Judaism, nonfeminist Jews whose concerns must be addressed, and non-Jewish feminists with whom both common language and crucial differences must be clarified. It, too, in the absence of standardized rubrics to reformulate or react against, has had to carve out its theological categories afresh. In consequence, the opponents of Jewish feminism in the 1970s and 1980s classified its writings as sociopolitical polemic rather than theology. Even today, few feminist Jewish scholars identify themselves as theologians, although their work may be covertly or even overtly theological. Yet Jewish feminist thought has had an immense impact on every variety of modern Judaism. Like the theological upheaval that produced Reform Judaism in response to the Enlightenment and Emancipation, it has produced major changes in Jewish thought and praxis.

Historical Context of Jewish Feminist Theology

The feminist critique of society and culture initiated in the 1960s and 1970s posed profound challenges to every branch of Judaism. Before this time, in no form of Judaism did women have equal access to communal participation, leadership, or religious education. Liberal Judaisms influenced by Enlightenment universalism made women invisible by regarding them as "honorary men," but did not, in fact, give them the religious opportunities afforded men.[2] Discrimination against women on halakhic (Jewish legal) grounds was common, not only in Orthodoxy but in all the other branches of Judaism. Halakhic discrimination is considerable. Women may not be included in the minyan and hence may not lead worship. They may not be called to the Torah. Their credibility as witnesses is severely limited.[3] Moreover, they are powerless to effect changes in their own marital status. Orthodoxy, which affects not only its own practitioners but also all Jewish Israeli citizens, does not permit women to initiate divorce. Women whose husbands are untraceable, insane, or simply unwilling may not free themselves to remarry. If these women remarry civilly and bear children from the second relationship, those children bear the status of bastardy and are barred by halakhah from marrying other Jews.

At the core of Judaism is the devotion to sacred text and to the interpretive process that continually recreates the text. Yet women were excluded from the interpretive process both by Orthodox and non-Orthodox Judaisms, nor did interpreters note how the texts themselves ignored or marginalized women.

Traditionally, the main duty of women was to enable the Jewish observance of men. Modern Judaisms, reeling from post-Enlightenment assimilation and from the loss of one-third of the world Jewish population in the Holocaust, augmented women's responsibilities for enabling Jewish survival. They were to repopulate the Jewish people, maintain a warm and inviting Jewish domestic environment, and be the volunteer labor force for communal projects and institutions. Early feminist Judaism, then, was depicted by its opponents not only as unfeminine and unnatural but as selfish, syncretistic, and threatening to Jewish survival.

Despite opposition, Jewish feminist thought and practice succeeded in changing modern Judaism profoundly. Between 1973 and 1983, the Reform, Reconstructionist, and Conservative movements all began ordaining women as rabbis. In *all* branches of Judaism, access to religious participation, communal leadership, and higher Jewish education took a quantum leap. New rituals were advanced to address previously ignored events in women's life cycles. The prayerbooks of the Reconstructionist and Reform movements began to address problems of inclusive language in liturgy. New academic research on the construction of gender and new evidence regarding women's activities in different periods have affected scholarship on the Bible and Talmud. All these enterprises are germane to theology, but engendering theology continues to be the slipperiest and most amorphous of these projects. Theologians disagree about its proper subject matter, its sources, and its method and categories.

Category Trouble: Polarizing Experience and Tradition

In its fledgling stage, feminist Judaism set up two primitive opposing categories: "women's experience" and "authentic Judaism." The great conundrum was to discover methods and categories to bridge the unbridgeable gap between the two. In a 1973 paper, Judith Plaskow asks, "What are the new words and how will we speak who we are?" as if the expression of women's realities and the expression of Jewish identity were in conflict.[4] Her question concerns both content and methodology. Plaskow models a solution in this article by appropriating and refashioning a midrashic tradition about Adam's rebellious first wife, Lilith. In Plaskow's retelling, Lilith and Eve bond in sisterhood. They ask each other the distinguishing questions of the new theology: "Who are you? What is your story?"

Both "women's experience" and "authentic Judaism" proved to be untenable categories, however. Monolithic notions of "women's experience" were effectively debunked by poststructuralist feminist critiques, which charged that the term privileged white, middle-class, Western women's experience and erased cultural and historical differences.[5] The term also incorporated the dubious assumption that there was such a thing as raw experience, unmediated by language and socialization. "Authentic Judaism" proved equally troublesome. There are and were many versions of Judaism. How can one argue that one is more authentic than another without enunciating criteria for authenticity?

Ellen Umansky, in a 1984 article, renounces the task of reconciling the dichotomy between these two troubled categories.[6] Instead she proposes a theology that *responds to* Jewish sources and traditional norms.[7] The feminist theologian's commitment, she declares, is not to the norms of tradition but "to the sources and to the fundamental categories of God, Torah and Israel."[8]

Jewish feminist deviations from the categories, methods, and concerns of Christian and post-Christian feminist theologians were sufficiently noticeable by 1979 to require an explanation from the co-editors of the anthology *Womanspirit Rising:*

> Since Judaism is a religion of ritual, law, and study rather than theology, creed, and doctrine, Jewish feminists have devoted their efforts not so much to defining and overcoming the patriarchal structures of Jewish thought as to criticizing specific attitudes toward women and to working for the full incorporation of women into Jewish religious life. Feminist contributions to the reconstruction of tradition most often focus on the creation of new rituals.... Even those Jewish thinkers who are most theoretical frequently express a practical concern.[9]

There is a good reason why feminist Jews began with practical concerns. If law, ritual, and study are the constitutive activities of Judaism, women cannot be other than peripheral Jews until they are full participants in these activities. The danger is that would-be participants will become so preoccupied with the problems of inclusion that they will fail to critique and transform the androcentric texts, categories, and structures that exclude not only women themselves but also categories and questions that women may advance for which no traditional precedents exist. Some feminist scholars question whether traditional methods and categories are capable of addressing these concerns. On the other hand, if feminists reject the categories and content of the tradition, how can they claim that what they create in its place is authentically Jewish?

Halakhah as a Category Conundrum

Halakhah has been the lightning rod for these controversies from the beginning because women experience its oppression directly in communal praxis and because halakhic method and categories claim to be authoritative and are attractively well defined and systematic. In addition, halakhic texts offered precedent and categories for discussing feminist concerns such as the meanings attached to women's bodies and blood, for which no theological warrant existed. Consequently, some feminists optimistically believed that halakhic change alone would remedy gender injustice in Judaism. However, it is very difficult to argue in androcentric terms without being inexorably dragged to androcentric conclusions. Moreover, halakhah is not only a theoretical discourse but an institutional structure over which exclusively male decisors exercise authority. These decisors were not eager to correct the system that privileged them.

Whether gender justice is possible within halakhah and whether a feminist Judaism requires a halakhah at all are foundational questions for feminist Jewish theology that have no parallel in Christian feminist theology. A language for critique could not be borrowed from it. Appropriating the terms and method of halakhah itself, many feminists concluded, drew them into a game they could not win. In its infancy, Reform Judaism had embarked on a critique of halakhah, but it had simply abandoned this project, so it offered few resources for feminist critique. Halakhah became the feminists' elephant in the living room. Everyone agreed it was in the way, and no one knew how to get rid of it.

The debate over halakhah as a locus of authority and authenticity dramatically illustrates the struggle over categories and method for Jewish feminist theology. The article that initiates the debate, "The Jew Who Wasn't There," which I wrote in 1971 as an Orthodox woman, draws its examples mainly from halakhah, but its primary point is not legal and its framing terminology is not Jewish.[10] Applying Simone de Beauvoir's feminist-existentialist categories, I argue that the classical tradition classifies women as peripheral Jews, permanently confined to the status of Other. The classic ideal for women is a spirituality based on not-doing and not-being, while enabling the masculine other to do and be.

In my conclusion, I urged that halakhic authorities amend these injustices, or, if they refuse, that women take steps to amend halakhah themselves. At the time, I did not understand the enormity of what I had done: I had issued a direct threat to rabbinic authority. Not surprisingly, the most common (and quite unsolicited) response of rabbis who read "The Jew Who Wasn't There" was, "Who the hell do you think you are?" Women's status appeared problematic to me, they assured me, because of my ignorance. If I were versed in traditional learning (coincidentally inaccessible to women), I would see my errors. They accused me of imposing non-Jewish standards upon Judaism and of being influenced by secular culture, i.e., feminism. Moreover, because as a woman I sought to benefit by the proposed changes, my lack of objectivity discredited my analysis. To my further astonishment, a noted Orthodox scholar attacked my article at length in a magisterial book on women and Jewish law.[11]

Judith Plaskow revolutionized the debate over halakhah in her groundbreaking essay "The Right Question is Theological," which appears in the 1983 anthology edited by Susannah Heschel.[12] The two pieces Plaskow directly challenges, Cynthia Ozick's "Notes Toward the Right Question" and my "The Jew Who Wasn't There," are included in the anthology but not in the theology section, endorsing Plaskow's contention that halakhah is outside the boundaries of feminist theology.[13] Yet Plaskow acknowledges that Ozick and I are speaking theologically. Her charge is that we have not understood the implications of the theological categories we use, "for they tend to assume that the Otherness of women will disappear if only the community is flexible enough to rectify halakhic injustices."[14] On the contrary, Plaskow maintains, the problems extend far beyond halakhah. The otherness of women is directly linked to theological conceptions of God as male and to the male authorship of Jewish tradition, "the profound injustice of Torah itself."

In a 1983 response to both Plaskow and Ozick, I fashion a rudimentary method for formulating metahalakhic questions.[15] This metahalakhic analysis explains precisely why halakhic categories and methods as they stand cannot adequately remedy gender injustices. Using a blend of historical and anthropological analysis, post-Christian feminist critique of theological methods, halakhic data, and personal narrative, I systematize and refocus the halakhic questions raised by Blu Greenberg, Ozick, and myself and add them to the methodological questions initiated by Plaskow and the questions of God-imagery stressed by Plaskow and Rita M. Gross.[16]

Remaking Categories

In place of what Abraham J. Heschel called "pan-halakhism," the framing of all Jewish questions in halakhic terms,[17] Plaskow calls for a new understanding of the primary categories of Jewish theology, God, Torah, and Israel.[18] But are God, Torah, and Israel usable fundamental categories for feminist Jewish theology, as both Umansky and Plaskow assert? In her 1990 book *Standing Again at Sinai*, Plaskow utilizes the traditional categories, redefining them as she had promised in her earlier essay. The chapter on Torah, subtitled "Reshaping Jewish Memory," deals extensively with the recovery of noncanonical sources through feminist historiography. The chapter on Israel, subtitled "Toward a New Concept of Community," deals with gender and personhood, and the issue of hierarchy as it relates to the concept of chosenness. The chapter on God concerns feminine God-language and feminist spirituality. But these categories prove insufficient for her. Plaskow must add chapters on sexuality and on "the repair of the world" to address issues that the categories of God, Torah, and Israel do not permit her to cover.

Lori Lefkovitz has recently suggested abandoning the categories of God, Torah, and Israel in favor of categories borrowed from French feminist analysis.[19] Her suggested categories are fluids and voices, blood, milk, wells, seawater, and laughter. In contrast to earlier feminist constructions of women as Other and attempts to define womanhood as a kind of normative humanity, Lefkovitz sees woman as mysterious and indefinable, in tension with the normative. Like earlier feminist uses of halakhah, Lefkovitz's categories mine traditional texts to create a code for women's bodily experiences that standard theological categories exclude.[20] But how do Lefkovitz's categories translate into praxis? By theorizing "woman" as a counternormative category, does she potentially justify denying women the social rights and privileges of normative personhood? Do Lefkovitz's categories construct one more world dichotomized by gender?

Praxis is the issue that suffuses all theological categories; a theology requires a method that can connect what we believe with what we do. Such a method has to situate itself in time. It needs to inform itself with lived realities and yet commit its adherents to a moral vision in which these realities are contingent and open to transformation. Because it is so difficult to extricate thought from praxis in a living Judaism, the method must mirror the fluid boundaries that exist among theology, halakhah and ethics, liturgy, and textual exegesis. The special problem for an engendered theology of Judaism is how to construct such a method in conversation with a tradition compromised by gender injustice.

An engendered Judaism needs the materials of the tradition to make credible theology. It will have to critique halakhah, and yet it must not leave itself without a basis for a praxis. It must rigorously interrogate the theological languages of the past while illuminating vocabularies of metaphor and devotion through which God and the people Israel can continue to reveal themselves to one another. It must also be able to interpret classical texts without rejecting them, apologizing for them, or merging with them. In other words, we will have to make the theological project as complicated as the world from which we launch it. This requires not *a* method but an entire repertory of methods for thinking, for reading, for describing, and for imagining how diversely situated and gendered people have lived, do live, and could live Jewish lives. In short, the method must be multidisciplinary. How are we to imagine such a method?

The Shit Method: A Grandmotherly Heuristic

Eastern European Jewish grandmothers used to joke that they cooked by the "*shit*" method: *men shit arein a bissel mehl, men shit arein a bissel zukker* . . . (You throw in a little flour, you throw in a little sugar . . .). The joke rests on a bilingual pun—the Yiddish word *shit*, throw, is in fact cognate to the Anglo-Saxon root that provides English its oldest, baldest word for excrement.[21] The joke is, on one level, self-deprecating. In comparison to the precise measurements and ingredient lists of American cookbooks, says *bubbe*, my methods are haphazard, messy, and worthless. On another level, grandma's naivete is an ironic con. I haven't got a cooking method at all, she says. This delicious result? I just threw some stuff in the direction of the pot.

In reality, the "*shit*" method has little to do with dumb luck. It is a carefully crafted heuristic originally designed for cooking in environments where resources are scarce and undependable. Take a kugel, for example. Kugel can be made with noodles, potatoes, rice, or matzah or even with yams or zucchini. If sugar and raisins are available, kugel can be sweet. If there are only onions, it can be savory. If eggs are plentiful, a kugel can be almost as light as a souffle. If scarce, it can be flat and substantial.

Yet a kugel is neither a hodgepodge nor a culinary masquerade like mock duck made of tofu. A rice kugel is not a mock potato kugel, but a rice kugel. The true measure of the practitioner's skill is not how ingeniously she disguises what is there or compensates for what is lacking, but how well she chooses and honors the resources at hand. That is what makes the *"shit"* method as adaptable to plenitude as it is to dearth.

All these features make the *"shit"* method a handy analogy for a feminist method. Like the shtetl cook, the feminist theologian confronts resources that are scarce and sometimes downright indigestible: a legal tradition that privileges men and disadvantages women; historical and textual materials that foreground the experiences and achievements of men and obscure those of women; a spiritual tradition that impedes women from seeing themselves as part of the divine image while impeding men from seeing past their partial reflection of the divine. Methodological "recipes" patterned on the Western philosophical tradition or on the categories and system of classical exegesis or halakhah demand resources or tools we lack while ignoring or rejecting those we have. For both the shtetl cook and the feminist theologian, to be usable the method must be heuristic: attentive to potential resources in its immediate environment, imaginative about combinations, and flexible about the structure of the recipe.

From its beginnings, feminist Jewish theology gravitated toward heuristic and multidisciplinary methods, partly in reflection of the conflicts it was mediating between secular and Jewish worlds, but also because its writers approached the tradition both as insiders and outsiders. Judith Plaskow was trained in theology in a Protestant divinity school, Ellen Umansky's field was Jewish intellectual history, and Marcia Falk, Lori Lefkovitz, and I were scholars of English literature.[22]

Multidisciplinarity turned out to be one of the most powerful tools of feminist analysis. In one essay, I describe how using a traditional method to learn legal texts about rape or divorce can seduce me to assume the text's perspectives and objectives so completely that I temporarily forget my own identity and investments as a woman. Multidisciplinary methods provide a hedge against the seductions and assumptions of texts and their worlds. By breaking the hegemony of any single code for deciphering a text, these methods allow difference and dissonance to trouble the interpretive process.[23] They allow us to maintain the otherness to approach critically an androcentric tradition in which we are nevertheless passionately invested. Equally important, they provide a way to organize the immense body of potential sources for feminist Jewish theology so they can address, rather than obscure, the theological questions.

Multidisciplinary methods and wide boundaries for what may be considered theology characterize some of the most brilliant Jewish feminist work. Marcia Falk correlates her practical concerns with remaking Jewish liturgy to theological questions about the appropriateness of any anthropomorphic language and about the boundaries between God and community and God and world.[24] T. Drorah Setel's essay on Hosea, "Prophets and Pornography," is a feminist literary critical study, but it also embodies a powerful theological challenge.[25]

For the most part, however, the hermeneutics of classical texts has been strangely neglected as a component of Jewish feminist theology.[26] Mine is very much a text-bound theology, however, because, like Umansky, I believe that is where Jewish conversation takes place. As I understand it, theology's task is to allow the texts of the tradition and the lived experiences of religious communities to keep revealing themselves to one another so the sacred meanings both of text and of experience can be renewed. In the course of this process, God becomes present in our midst.

What distinguishes my textual study from that of academics who study Judaica with the aid of secular disciplines is a difference in goals. Consequently, I am concerned not only with critiquing androcentric structures, categories, and motifs and constructing feminist theory and interpretation, but also with mending and healing Judaism by encountering, renewing, and reclaiming the holiness in texts. The theological questions I ask of a text are designed to interrogate its moral universe, to hold the text accountable, and to redeem the text by learning Torah from it. I ask:

> What is God telling us through the story? What are we telling God through the story? Having wrestled the story for a blessing, what meanings have we wrested from it? How does the story shape our collective memory as a people? What demands does it make upon us that we must integrate into the way we live our lives? How will we transmit the story?[27]

The very shape of this book constitutes a theological statement. The design is not linear. All the chapters deal in some way with the relations between God and the gendered individual, God and the community, and the self and the other. The prelude chapter that opens the book and the praxis chapter that closes it apply the methods the body of the book will set forth. The prelude chapter, "The Female Rapist and Other Inversions," demonstrates a multidisciplinary method for confronting theological problems raised by the gender code in rabbinic hero tales. Bringing feminist literary analysis and object-relations psychology to bear upon these stories, I trace two motifs that arise out of gender polarization in the world of these stories: inversions of conventional power relations between women and men and mutilation in order to preserve or recover the autonomous masculine self.

The three large chapters that follow do not claim to fit the conventional theological categories of Torah, God, and Israel. Instead, they explore the distinctive issues an engendered Judaism must confront: law, liturgy, and the ethics of sexuality and relationship. I would resist identifying the second chapter, "Here Comes Skotsl: Renewing Halakhah," with the category of Torah because I do not want to restrict the definition of Torah to halakhah. This chapter offers a feminist critique of both traditional and liberal halakhic methodologies and proposes a framework for halakhah that breaks the classical tradition's monopoly upon rules, categories, and the transmission of authority. This framework for an engendered halakhah draws upon the work of American legal theorists and upon the discussions between feminist and nonfeminist narrative ethicists and theologians.

Both chapters 3 and 4, dealing respectively with liturgy and sexuality, discuss God, the people Israel, and their relationships. Because one chapter does not logically precede the other, their sequence is purely arbitrary. I wish they could be heard in unison like the variant versions of the fourth commandment that, according to a talmudic midrash, were proclaimed simultaneously from Mount Sinai.[28]

Chapter 3, "And Not be Silent: Toward Inclusive Worship," addresses the problems of engendering the language with which we speak to and about God. It tries to describe what it is about liturgy that makes some of us so intent upon change and others so resistant to it. The chapter explores the nature of religious metaphor and identifies some difficulties in the quest for feminine God language. Here my methodology is literary, anthropological, and theological, but I also make reference to the history of Jewish liturgical change. I rely heavily on the work of Victor Turner, Barbara Myerhoff, Riv-Ellen Prell, and Lawrence Hoffman and deal extensively with the most thoughtful and accomplished of feminist liturgists, Marcia Falk.

Chapter 4, entitled "Justice and Peace Shall Kiss: An Ethics of Sexuality and Relationship," builds upon the psychological framework established in the prelude chapter. It proposes an ethic of intersubjectivity between self and other in place of an ethic that regulates relations of domination and subordination, and it tries to fashion a discourse that does not conceal the power of erotic experience. Analyses of the sexual code of Leviticus supplemented by rabbinic texts and historical materials demonstrate that sexual boundaries are influenced by social context. Intersubjectivity in the Song of Songs is contrasted with rabbinic use of the Song to legislate anti-eroticism. Eroticism alone is an insufficient basis for an ethic, I contend. It must be augmented by generosity, *hesed*, as exemplified by the Book of Ruth. In the final section, I show how the prophetic metaphor of covenantal marriage dramatizes the tension between two irreconcilable desires: that the wife be both a sexual possession and a freely committed partner.

Chapter 5, *"B'rit Ahuvim: A Covenant for Lovers,"* brings my theoretical arguments to bear upon a specific case: the wedding ceremony. I argue that the traditional ceremony is based upon two mutually exclusive definitions of marital relationship: one grounded in property law and the other in metaphors of covenant. Mordecai Friedman's research on Palestinian *ketubbot* from the Cairo *Geniza* offers a precedent for viewing Jewish marriage as a partnership.[29] I propose relocating the legal basis for the ceremony from property law to partnership law. Then I show what that would look like in terms of the document that would replace the *ketubbah* (marriage contract) and the liturgical changes that would replace the espousal blessing and spousal acquisition in the ceremony. The book concludes with a brief epilogue.

A final observation about this book concerns its audience. This book is intended to participate in various conversations. It addresses textual scholars who study the Judaisms of the past by offering critiques of the gender component in Jewish law, liturgy, and in some biblical and rabbinic texts. It addresses theologians and rabbis by modeling a method and a process for engendering future Judaisms. It also participates in a conversation with non-Jewish scholars of religion who are also engaged in talking their way into conversations where gender has been used to oppress or exclude. Another audience I want to invite in are the thoughtful and committed Jewish women and men who constitute the communities of living Judaism. They have as much at stake in this discussion as any scholarly elite. To accommodate these various audiences with their different expertises, I have tried to write a book that any educated person could follow, avoiding professional jargon wherever possible.

Engendering the Jewish conversation is a project that will occupy many generations of Jews. I am grateful for the many conversations that have enriched this book—even those where the decibel level was rather high. Every one of them is precious. Speech creates the biblical world, and every part of the creation has something to say. The hills shout, the heavens and earth give testimony, and the days and nights speak to one another. May we too speak words of truth and joy.

Engendering Judaism

Chapter 1

Prelude: The Female Rapist and Other Inversions

I am going to tell you a story.

These are the oldest and most magical words we know. We turn toward the storyteller like plants toward the sun. We are ready, we are asking to be taken into the world of the story, wherever, whenever it may be, "to project into it," as Paul Ricoeur says, "our ownmost possibilities."[1] Even more powerful yearnings are aroused by stories that have been transmitted as part of our religious traditions. As a committed Jew, I come to ancient canonical stories, biblical, midrashic, or aggadic, with an assumption that I belong to them and they belong to me. I encounter them searching for Torah, that is, for redemptive teaching, and for *zikaron*, for the collective memory that completes me, that binds me to all who ever have or will claim or been claimed by these stories. What happens, however, when I reach out to stories whose worlds do not permit me to enter, that exclude me or distort me? This is the first problem that confronts anyone who attempts to construct a theology of Judaism that includes *all* the people Israel, men and women. How do we face a story that de/faces some of us and thereby diminishes all of us?

One solution, of course, is not to face it at all. Redemptive teaching can be found in other sources, including uncanonical stories, *bubbemeises*, "grandmother-tales," not merely the canonical *zaydemeises*, "grandfather-tales."[2] But I am not willing to relinquish these problematic grandfather-tales. Like Esau, I cry out to them, "Have you only one blessing, father? Bless me too, father." It is precisely because I believe that these texts have blessings yet to bestow that, like another member of Esau's blessing-starved family, I will not let them go until they bless me. I will not abandon traditional texts, and I will not absolve them of moral responsibility.

As the saying goes, "Faced with two alternatives, always choose the third." Through the stories I examine in this chapter, I introduce both some of the problems raised by the project of a feminist theology of

1

Judaism and a third way of resolving them. The stories I have chosen depict the rabbi as holy hero.[3] Either they have roots in Talmud, or they are medieval embroideries upon the careers of well-known talmudic figures. Dramatic and engaging, they have been told and retold, transmitting ideals of holiness coded by gender.

There are no feminine correlatives for these hagiographic tales, no Judaic analogue of Teresa of Avila or Hildegarde of Bingen to model spiritual creativity and holy living for Jewish women. The way Jewish women and men have seen themselves represented and the way they have seen holiness represented in these stories cannot but affect their own sense of women's capacity for holiness, and the danger they present to the holiness of men. My third way to face these de/facing texts brings them to judgment, utilizing feminist elaborations of object relations and psychoanalytic theory as tools for understanding the psychology of their depiction of the feminine other.

But the ultimate goal of my third way is not judgment but restoration. I propose to restore these texts as sources of a trajectory toward holiness by reframing them as comedies. "The resolution of comedy," Northrop Frye observes, "comes from the audience's side of the stage."[4] Imagine these stories as continuous performances, unbounded by time. A storyteller narrates them, surrounded by an audience of men and a shadowy outer audience of eavesdropping women. Gradually, more and more women join this second audience, drawing increasingly closer to the inner circle, becoming increasingly substantial as subjects facing the story. What happens to the story as the two circles become one, when all the hearers look into each other's faces? I imagine the shock of illumination in that moment issuing forth around the circle in a great flood of purifying laughter.

"The movement of comedy," says Frye, "is from one kind of society to another."[5] The original society and those in charge of it are somehow flawed. Some rigidity impeding freedom and the fullness of life is removed and resolved as the new society crystallizes around the hero and heroine. In the rabbinic hero-tale as comedy, however, this movement toward the new and restorative society has to take place outside the narrative frame within the world of the audience as its two circles join. In place of the definitive resolution with which classical comedy concludes we must posit a trajectory, a continuous movement toward the transformation of the audience's moral universe, a practical vision of how we are going to get from here to there. It is by means of this movement and this laughter that our texts are redeemed and become redemptive.

Rabbinic Hero-Tales and the De/facing of Women

For the feminist reader, the most problematic characteristics of the rabbinic hero-tales we examine here are their tactics for the de/facing of women: silence and invisibility on the one hand and on the other what I have called dis/remembering. Invisibility is the hiding of women. Silence is their exile from discourse, their erasure from the surface of the text. An androcentric hermeneutic conspires with the text to perpetuate and normalize its silence about women. A feminist hermeneutic focuses upon the silence. Silence, in a violent cleaving, creates for women two worlds, both of which they must inhabit. Between the two worlds lies silence. Adrienne Rich has expressed this well:

> *Could you imagine a world of women only,*
> the interviewer asked. *Can you imagine*
>
> *a world where women are absent.* (he believed
> he was joking.) Yet I have to imagine
>
> at one and the same moment, both. Because
> I live in both.[6]

Dis/remembering is a different kind of rending. If re/membering is the restoration of wholeness, then in every act of dis/remembering inheres a dis/membering.[7] A dismembering is a mutilation. A dis/remembering is a particular kind of mutilation through language—a de/facing, a tearing away of the face of the other.[8] Naming and telling are the means whereby the memory of our faces is preserved. The most terrible of rabbinic curses is *yimaḥ sh'mo v'zikhro*, "may his name and memory be erased."

Dis/remembering perpetrates a distortion and a deception. A deception is not identical with a fiction. As Elie Wiesel observes, "Some events do take place but are not true; others are—although they never occurred."[9] A deception is a representation which is morally untrue. If re/presentation is the construction in language of the world as it presents itself to a subject,[10] then mis/representation is a construction in bad faith, a construction that is at the same time a destruction. The goal of deception is theft of one sort or another. It is a con that enables the deceiver to appropriate, with the acquiescence of the deceived, something that would otherwise have been inaccessible: money or property, sexual consent, or labor. What is appropriated, however, as any victim of a con artist will attest, is only a secondary theft. The first theft is a theft of consciousness about the deception being practiced. This is the crime Jewish legal tradition calls *genevat da'at*, literally, "the theft of knowledge." *Genevat da'at* in a text steals the memory of the true face of the other.

Not only narratives but hermeneutical theories as well can be guilty of such thefts. Hermes was not only the patron of messengers but also of thieves. Androcentric hermeneutics compound the thefts of consciousness perpetrated by androcentric texts. A feminist hermeneutic must identify these thefts and attempt to restore what has been stolen. A religious feminist hermeneutic must judge the thefts and provide a feminist reframing that heals the wounds inflicted upon the relationships between transmitters and receivers of Torah.

Yet judging the worlds of the past is a risky business. If we are not absolute relativists, if we do not believe that all moral universes are equally good, we bring to a text and its world the value system within which we are situated, which some future moral universe may find wanting in ways to which we ourselves are oblivious. Moreover, even if we tried to be perfectly objective about the thinking and values of these past worlds, we would distort them by bringing to our task concerns, categories, and methodologies these worlds did not know. Given that human moral insight is constrained by a host of contextual factors—social, economic, technological—it would be unfair of us to blame these worlds for not knowing what we know or acting as we act. At the same time, just because they themselves saw them as just, we cannot very well condone their brutalities or injustices.

I am going to use feminist psychological theories concerning object relations to highlight two outstanding motifs I identify in some rabbinic and postrabbinic dis/remembering narratives. These two motifs depict the reversal of power relations between women and men and the endurance of mutilation in order to preserve or recover the autonomous masculine self.

Feminist Object-Relations Theory and the Problem of Domination

It would be helpful at this point to give a brief summary of feminist object-relations theory. These psychologists note that all human beings begin life totally dependent on their mothers, and all must differentiate from the mother to become independent selves.[11] But males, especially in contexts where masculinity confers a privileged and authoritative status, achieve independent selfhood by definitively sundering themselves from the mother, denying all commonality with her and, hence, with the feminine. This abrupt and definitive separation can be experienced as a wound, a kind of mutilation that the boy sustains in order to attain the coveted autonomous self. He guards against the danger of merging once more with the maternal figure by developing a rigid boundary between "me" and "not-me." Encouraged to deny both dependency upon and identification with the desired and renounced mother, he is encouraged to perceive her solely as an undifferentiated object, an instrument for fulfilling needs, rather than as a subject different from himself with desires and powers of her own.

In a provocative book on gender and domination, Jessica Benjamin argues that this is where the problem of domination begins.[12] Benjamin contends that all human beings have both a need to control what is outside the self and a need for freely conferred recognition from an other.[13] A robot programmed to tell its owner "You're terrific" gives recognition that is worthless, because the robot could not have chosen to say "You're contemptible."

Domination and submission are faulty attempts to mediate the tension between these two desires for omnipotence and for recognition. Fully differentiated selves in relationship are able to sustain the tension between the two desires. They seek and extend recognition while negotiating desires for power and control. But for dominators and submitters, mutuality is impossible. The best they can achieve is an unequal complementarity: the dominator reserves recognition for himself while the submitter offers recognition without expecting it in return.[14] Domination is a relationship in which complementarity substitutes for mutuality, and hence, according to Benjamin, "the underlying wish to interact with someone truly outside, with an equivalent center of desire, does not emerge."[15]

Feminist object-relations theory provides a useful model for explaining how relations between the sexes are depicted in the highly patriarchalized world of rabbinic Judaism's scholarly elite in which masculinity and femininity are polarities. Boys graduate from babyhood by withdrawing decisively from the world of women. They encounter women thereafter only under special conditions hedged with rite and taboo. Women complement men rather than being equals or friends. They are praiseworthy when they enhance men's lives and advance men's goals while remaining discreetly in the background. In a variety of legal cases, women are regarded as extensions of their husbands, as exemplified by the talmudic legal principle *ishto k'gufo*, "His wife is like his own body."[16]

To polarize by gender is to deny that, bone for bone and synapse for synapse, human beings are much more alike than unlike. Gender variations are meaningful only within the context of human sameness.[17] Social strategies that exaggerate women's difference end by attempting to expunge it. Women must be subordinated or annexed. Their difference must be hidden under veils and segregated in women's quarters or ignored by law and policy and thereby expelled from the public sector. The extensive justification, legislation, and enforcement these acts require creates a masculine discourse about women's difference whose presence replaces that of actual women. Hence, women are banished from most rabbinic texts, although women's difference is a basic component of rabbinic discourse. Where are the women who cleaned and clothed and fed the inhabitants of these rabbinic worlds of "pure" spirit?[18] Why are there not more female characters like Beruriah and Yalta, whose infrequent depictions hint that some women may have presented an intellectual challenge? When women are depicted, the feminine ideal is the self-abnegating woman who consents to being objectified, instrumentalized, and eventually booted out of the world of the text.

The Homosocial Milieu

In rabbinic narratives, the classical milieu from which difference is eradicated is the study house, the *beit midrash*. Like the polarized worlds in Adrienne Rich's poem, it is a world without women. The natural habitat of sainthood, it is a world of mind and spirit. In hero-tales, as opposed to more mundane accounts, its holiest inhabitants reject all dependency not only upon women, but also upon the body, locus of human commonality. Famous scholars announce their potential for greatness in exemplary acts of self-denial.[19] Eliezer ben Hyrcanus is discovered to have fasted all of his first eight days at the *beit midrash*.[20] Hillel, too poor to pay his entrance fee, is found buried in snow on the study-house roof, absorbed in the Torah he is overhearing, oblivious of all desire for animal warmth.[21]

The *beit midrash* is not a place but a state of mind. It is what Eve Kosofsky Sedgewick has termed a homosocial environment, a world whose social economy is given over to the service of masculine emotional sustenance, where the masculine psyche and its imaginings are the coin of the realm, indeed the only legal tender.[22] Our opportunities both for judgment and for comedy arise out of our ability to see not only what this world encloses but what is exiled from it, concealed by it, unknown to it.

The substructure that holds this homosocial world together is a magnetic framework of opposed dominations and dependencies. Elements of this substructure surface in rabbinic fantasy, charged with forbidden fears and desires. On the one hand, dependency is the patriarch's nightmare. The slave or the woman can be viewed as the mirror in which the dominator sees his own repressed and rejected dependency. Yet in certain midrashic narratives, recognition from the feminine other is the powerful catalyst that urges the masculine self toward its apotheosis of self-actualization. Some of these narratives depict men who are initially dependent upon powerful women to fulfill their survival needs. The stories then describe how the men extricate themselves from this abject or physically dangerous state and are restored to normality and righteousness—i.e., patriarchal dominance.

Gender and Power: The Wife of Rabbi Akiba

The most commonly known examples of this motif are the stories about Rabbi Akiba's introduction to the world of Torah. All the versions of this story emphasize the enormous power discrepancy between the impoverished shepherd, Akiba, and the wealthy aristocratic daughter of Kalba Savua, identified in one version as Rachel.[23] In all three versions, she initiates their marriage. In two of the three, she initiates his Torah study, advising him to study in one version and compelling him by oath in another.[24]

Version one, originating in the talmudic tractate Nedarim, foreshadows Akiba's ultimate triumph by having him comfort his wife after her father has disinherited her. Although she has not been depicted as distressed by their poverty, Akiba promises her a piece of jewelry, "a Jerusalem of gold." This promise of a precious trinket, a spectacularly inappropriate reimbursement for a woman who has spurned material wealth for her husband's sake, serves to comfort, not Akiba's wife, but rather the original male audience of the story. They can be reassured that a woman so spiritually insightful that she sees a future *tzaddik* where everyone else sees a poor ignoramus, so self-willed that she chooses her own husband, and so steadfast that she embraces a life of privation for the sake of his studies will ultimately be reduced to an ordinary wife, awed and delighted by a golden bauble. The princess will become Cinderella so the shepherd can become a prince.[25]

In the middle of the narratives is a lengthy period during which Akiba is away at yeshivah but financially dependent on the self-sacrificial labor of his wife, a state that Louis Finkelstein terms "married monasticism."[26] Indeed, celibacy, whether fictional or reflective of social reality, is identified by David Biale as one pole of a profound rabbinic ambivalence about sexuality.[27] In the Akiba narratives, this period reflects the masculine fantasy of retaining autonomy and separateness while consuming the mother's nurturing. The more Akiba is able to depend upon Rachel's sustenance, the less need there is to regard her as an independent subject who might have needs or demands regarding him.[28]

Several incidents show how Rachel is annihilated as a self and transformed into an instrument for Akiba's sustenance. In one version, her friends urge her to borrow less ragged clothing to greet the triumphant Akiba, but she replies with the proverb "The righteous man knows the nature of his beast" (Prov. 14:10).[29]

By the end of the stories, it has become safe for Akiba to acknowledge his previous dependency on his wife, because not only is he no longer dependent on her, but she must now be dependent upon him. No longer powerful and imposing, she is in several accounts abject, a ragged crone kissing the master's feet, while the revolted students try to throw her out. At this point the great man can magnanimously raise her up and credit her with making him what he is today.[30]

Gender and Power Redux: Natan D'Tzutzita and the Lady Evangelist

The late medieval story of Natan D' Tzutzita, Natan "with the ray of light," also relies on this motif of the protagonist's rise out of dependency on a woman to rabbinic heroism.[31] A wealthy roué, Natan, is lovesick to the point of death over a married woman named Ḥana, whose impecunious husband is in debtors' prison. Refusing even to see her affluent admirer, she toils "day and night" to earn money to feed her man. Like Natan, the imprisoned husband becomes deathly ill. Both depend upon Ḥana for survival, and both ask her to violate her own integrity for their benefit. At first, Ḥana is obdurate. When her husband asks her to borrow from Natan, she snaps:

> Don't you know? Haven't you heard? He's sick and dying on account of me. Every day his messengers come to me with lots of money, and I don't accept it from them, and I say to them that he'll never see my face. So how am I going to go to him to borrow money? If you had any sense, you wouldn't say such a thing to me. Maybe the length of your imprisonment has damaged your wits.

When he threatens that God will hold her guilty of his death, she bluntly counters the manipulation: "This man says to me, 'go and commit adultery and defile yourself.'" Yet a constant refrain in the text is *vatahmol alav*, "she pitied him." Like a mother who is unconditionally responsible for her child's life, Hana resists, refuses, but ultimately takes pity upon the demanding dependent by sacrificing her own limits.

As Hana prepares to go to the house of Natan, the text begins implicitly to compare her with other Jewish heroines. Like Hannah in the Book of Samuel, she prays. Her supplication is introduced by the exact words that open the biblical Hannah's song of praise: *va-titpallel Hana va'-tomar*, "and Hannah prayed and said." Her arrival at the house of Natan is like the arrival of a queen. Slaves are freed in celebration of her arrival. Echoing the words of Ahashuerus to Esther, Natan asks, "What is your wish? It shall be granted you. And what is your request? It shall be done." Hana's request, like that of Esther, is to save the life of others. Like Esther, she has taken a risk upon herself to do so. But in this story two languishing men have desires that are mutually exclusive. Hana's husband begs her to save his life, but does not wish to be cuckolded. Natan gives Hana the money to free her husband but wants sex to cure his lovesickness: *Hehiyani*, he pleads, "give me life."

The rabbis regarded both the biblical Hannah and Esther as prophets.[32] The Hana of this story also has quasi-prophetic abilities, but they resemble those of Rabbi Akiba's wife: the ability to see in a man his spiritual potential and the capacity to orient him to it like a spiritual compass by means of her *eitzah*, her good counsel. Thus, Hana is able to save both lives. She saves her husband physically, and she informs Natan what only the great Rabbi Akiba will later be able to perceive and confirm: that this is the hour in which Natan will earn eternal life. Hana's call to Natan to renounce lust and repent succeeds. He prostrates himself in tears, prays, and is transformed.

> Some time later, Rabbi Akiba was looking out his window, and he saw a man riding a horse and on his head a great splendor shedding radiance like the sun. He called one of his disciples to him and asked, "Who is that man riding on the horse?" And he said, "That's Natan the whoremaster." Akiba said to his disciples, "Do you see anything on his head?" And they said, "No." And he said, "Quick, bring him to me."

But while Natan ascends into the spiritual world of the *beit midrash* where he is received with honor and becomes the most illustrious disciple of Rabbi Akiba, Ḥana, who has hastened to redeem her husband from prison, experiences an abrupt descent into powerlessness. She who was able to convince a desperately lovesick man to abjure her and repent cannot convince her husband that she did not commit the adultery that he implicitly and repeatedly urged upon her. Her status becomes that of a *sotah*, a suspected adulteress, and her husband banishes her from his household as a pious Jewish husband should.

In the stories of both Rachel and Akiba and Ḥana and Natan, the reversal of power relations follows the same pattern: While the men who have been dependent cycle upwards until they reach the apex of autonomous self-realization and social acclaim through their embrace of Torah, the women who sustained them and led them into that sacral embrace cycle downward to the nadir of their personal well-being and social respectability. Ultimately the women are restored to comfortable mediocrity through the reflected glory of the men whose development they have enabled. Never again do they exercise their own spiritual gifts.

The narrative drops Ḥana completely as it enlarges upon Natan's spiritual triumphs, but then resolves her fate in a few rapid final sentences. Eventually, Ḥana's husband sees the rehabilitated Natan in his full glory at the *beit midrash* and learns how Natan came to renounce the evil impulse. Recounting the story in this holy environment serves as the functional equivalent of the biblical ordeal for resolving the suspicions of the jealous husband. The narrative underlines this by echoing the words of Numbers 5: "*the spirit of jealousy which had passed over him* and forbidden her, quieted."

Ḥana's reward is to be cleared of suspicion and reunited with her husband. Her mollified spouse kisses her on the head and apologizes, concluding: "May the Holy One double and redouble your reward because" (and here we might anticipate some statement about Ḥana's extraordinary integrity and loyalty or her formidable evangelical gifts, but we would be wrong) "*I* have been greatly worried in my soul until the Holy One saved *me* by this thing that was revealed to me today" [italics mine].

Why don't women get haloes? Why don't crowds acclaim their deeds or heavenly voices assure them of their portion in the world to come? Object relations theorists would explain that it is because women are not perceived as autonomous subjects in these narratives. Rather, they are undifferentiated mother-objects from whom their males crave simultaneously nurture and autonomy and who demand not merely recognition but the whole of Mommy's attention and regard.

The emphasis on right reason in Ḥana's discourse and the narrative discourse about her links her with another divine Daddy's girl, Lady Wisdom, as depicted in the Book of Proverbs and other wisdom literature. This wisdom is not wise for herself any more than a muse is poetic for herself. She is an instrument for the homosocial world. Hence though the repentant Natan tells Ḥana, "Blessed be your good sense," it is Natan whom God endows with a halo to advertise his spiritual inheritance. The question of Ḥana's spiritual reward does not even arise, because feminine spirituality serves only as a tool for the realization of masculine spirituality. Once that has been attained, the text can right the inversion by which women become powerful and authoritative. Having served their purpose, powerful women like Akiba's Rachel and Ḥana can revert to being ordinary.

Cutting Loose

As I have said previously, in contexts where masculinity and femininity are regarded as antithetical, boys can experience their separation from the mother as a mutilation necessary to create an autonomous self. The great danger, then, is the danger of merging once more. Men must prevent boundary dissolution because it would unmake both patriarchal self and world. That threat is the subtext of many rabbinic texts whenever women attempt to be fully visible. The males of these narratives experience the visibility of women as a temptation to merge. The righteous man may resist this temptation by reenacting the mutilation that established him as a differentiated masculine self.[33]

Temptation narratives set up an opposition between woman and holy text.[34] Both women and texts may be known, but one represents the knowledge of the body and its passions, while the other represents the knowledge of the spirit, of reason, and of commandment that rules the passions. Women are the source of the life of the body—and hence of death. Holy text is a source of eternal life. A good woman, one who accepts her proper role in the dichotomized worlds of women and of no-women, resigns her claim to visibility in deference to the superior claim of holy text. She may even, like Akiba's wife, actively promote the claim of the text over her own and collaborate in her own ensuing invisibility. A bad woman is one who makes herself a rival of the text.

This theme emerges powerfully in the first of two stories I am going to analyze, both of which come from a postrabbinic collection called *Midrash*

Aseret Ha-Dibrot, the Midrash of the Ten Commandments. This midrash was composed between the seventh and eleventh centuries.[35] (As a point of reference, the Babylonian Talmud is complete by about 750 C.E.) Each of the stories in the collection illustrates one of the Ten Commandments. *Midrash Aseret Ha-Dibrot* shows a predilection for extreme examples. The two stories I have selected, accordingly, present motifs about the otherness and dangerousness of women in an extreme form. I have chosen these texts not to exemplify all aggadic texts nor to suggest that all texts exhibit these motifs with equal virulence, but to take advantage of these texts' naked revelation of what Freudians call the primary processes of the authors. Exaggeration, like magnification, can clarify what it enlarges.

Matiyah ben Ḥeresh: The Eyes Have It

The story of Matiyah ben Ḥeresh focuses upon a psychic struggle between woman and holy text for the scholar's attention. This psychomachia is dramatically externalized, and its threat to the autonomous masculine self is resolved in shockingly literal terms.[36] The story is set in the *beit midrash*, the paradisical world without women.

> R. Matiyah ben Ḥeresh used to sit and immerse himself in the Torah. The radiance of his face was like the sun and the moon. His face was as beautiful as an angel's for he had never lifted his eyes to look at another man's wife or at any woman. Once he was sitting absorbed in the Torah in the *beit midrash*. Satan passed and saw him and envied him. He said, "Is it possible that a man like this does not sin?" . . . In that very hour he ascended to heaven and stood before the Holy One. . . . Satan said, "Lord of the Universe, permit me to test him."

To tempt Matiyah, whose purity is reflected in his angelic beauty, Satan takes the form of Naamah, sister of Tubal-cain, whose evil is embodied as beauty so great it caused the fall of the angels. Male beauty as a reflection of moral and spiritual perfection is a recognized motif in midrashic and aggadic literature.[37] Female beauty, on the other hand, is regarded as devoid of any spiritual dimension and indeed is considered to have great potential for evil because it heightens the possibility of female visibility and, hence, rivalry with the text.

Satan's temptation of Matiyah is a ballet of confrontation and evasion: the succulent succubus vies for the scholar's attention while he tries frantically not to see her:

Satan came and stood before R. Matiyah. When he saw her, he turned away his face. Satan returned and came up on his left side. When he saw that he [she] was surrounding him from every side, he said, "'I am afraid lest the evil impulse overpower me *(mitgaber alai)* and cause me to sin."

Deliberate female visibility, then, is represented as an act of war: first ambush and then the deployment of a weapon that can neither be overcome nor eluded. Female visibility is not even female: it is Satan in drag, the personified evil impulse whose power will *mitgaber*, "overman," rise, swell, dominate its object. Satan outmans man because desire feminizes, placing man, like Eve, at the mercy of her own desire and thus dooming him to be ruled over.

Sexual sin is here defined as the wish for merger that threatens to undo autonomous selfhood by restoring the original identity with woman. The painful first differentiation from mother is recalled and invoked to counter subsequent desires. Mutilation, paradoxically, preserves integrity. In the narrative of Matiyah ben Ḥeresh, the act is concretized as a physical mutilation at whose price the self escapes intact. "He called to the student who served him and said, 'Bring me nails.'... He put the nails in the fire until they glowed and then put them in his eyes." The destruction of the eyes is the counterattack that vanquishes forever the magnetic power of female visibility.

Witnessing this mutilation, Satan, who personifies here not only appetite but also body-knowledge or sensuous experience, is "dismayed": "He shuddered and fell before him." The Holy One then dispatches Rafael, the angel of healing, but Matiyah refuses to have his sight restored until the Holy One promises him that the evil impulse will have no subsequent power over him. At the story's happy ending, Matiyah is healed both of the mutilation and of all desire to merge with the feminine.

The Female Rapist: Rabbi Meir Gets Ribbed

The second story from *Midrash Aseret Ha-Dibrot* combines both motifs: the reversal of power relations and the mutilation that preserves selfhood. In this astonishing story, the illustrious tannaitic authority Rabbi Meir is seduced by the wife of his host. The distinguished scholar has a friend whom he visits every year. One year, when he arrives, he discovers that his friend's wife has died and been replaced by a new wife. In his role as honored guest, he is served and waited upon by the attentive hostess. Her ministrations enable her to invert the roles of dominator and

13

dependent. The code of hospitality permits her to speak, to invite the guest within, to show herself before him, to render the tended male passive and vulnerable, and finally, not only to be seen, but to look. Milan Kundera in *The Book of Laughter and Forgetting* describes the destructive potential of an instrument who seizes her own subjectivity by looking at the master:

> The male glance has often been described. It is commonly said to rest coldly on a woman . . . turning her into an object.
>
> What is less commonly known is that a woman is not completely defenseless against that glance. If it turns her into an object, then she looks back at a man with the eyes of an object. It is as though a hammer had suddenly grown eyes and stared up at the worker pounding a nail with it. When the worker sees the evil eye of the hammer, he loses his self-assurance and slams it on his thumb. . . . The ability to see transforms the hammer into a living being, but a good worker must be able to bear up under its insolent glance and, with a firm hand, turn it back into an object. It would therefore seem that a woman undergoes cosmic transformation in two directions: up from object to being, down from being to object.[38]

In our midrash, the hostess-as-hospitality-tool grows eyes and gazes desirously upon her guest, causing him, as it were, to slam his thumb on her. As she acquires this gaze, the narrator assumes her point of view: "Rabbi Meir was beautiful, surpassingly attractive." Becoming an object of the female gaze feminizes Meir, depriving him of power.[39] His impairment is so great that he loses not only will but consciousness. Consequently, without any resistance from Meir, the woman is able to make him so drunk that "he did not know his left from his right."

The phrase *ad she'lo yad'a*, "so that he did not know," evokes the other rabbinic context in which this phrase is linked to drunkenness: "Raba said, a man is obligated to imbibe on Purim until he does not know *(ad she'lo yad'a)* the difference between 'cursed be Haman and blessed be Mordecai'" (Megillah 7a). The narrator renders Meir's intemperance not only credible but commendable by adding, "And that night was Purim."

Purim commemorates a redemption by means of ironic reversal and hence is celebrated by turning communal norms upside down: drunkenness replaces sobriety, frivolity replaces gravity, a burlesque of Torah study replaces the real thing.[40] As such, Purim is a one-day excursion into chaos, undoing some of the laws and boundaries that create the social universe.

It should not surprise us, then, that Rabbi Meir's undoer learns her modus operandi from the daughters of Lot, who, believing that the entire world has been destroyed and that they must repopulate it, make their father drunk, and (in defiance of time-honored observations about the potency of the intoxicated male) manage to have forbidden sexual intercourse with him. In this story, our narrator presents an analogous case of the female rapist at work. Like Lot, Rabbi Meir "did not know either of her lying down or her arising," *lo yad'a b'shikhvah u'v'kumah* (Gen. 19:34). By causing her victim not to know, the female rapist uncreates the world. To know is first of all to be conscious of selfhood, to be distinct from that first world of not-self: the flesh and nurturance of mother. Not knowing dissolves this first differentiation, returning the world to chaos. Returning to consciousness, Rabbi Meir confronts a devastated world.

In the Lot story, the narrator is not interested in how Lot felt upon becoming aware of his nocturnal activities. Plausibly, the narrator's intent was to tell his audience exactly how the Ammonites and the Moabites came to be the misbegotten bastards they are today. But in this story, the revelations of the morning after are crucial. What alerts Rabbi Meir that something is very wrong is that the woman is making herself visible to him. "She spoke with him and sported before him." Averting his gaze from her, he focuses, ironically, upon the bed, the scene of the crime of which he is as yet unaware. Reproaching him for his coolness, she assures him that he lay with her "many times" the previous night. (Even when transgressive, the rabbinic hero's capacities are heroic!) The stunned and incredulous rabbi is finally convinced when she describes to him a particular anatomical detail.

Meir flees at once, weeping and casting dust on his head. "Woe is me," he cries, "for I have lost my world. . . . Is this the reward of the Torah I have learned?" The question seems to reproach God for having allowed this catastrophe to befall him, rather than to reflect any sense of his own culpability in the matter. Yet when his relatives argue that because the adultery was unwitting God will forgive him without further ado, Meir rejects their words.

Meir appears to experience his sin as a defilement rather than as a moral wrong. His sexual union with the woman represents an undoing of masculine differentiation. The world he has lost is the homosocial world of the spirit, not only *olam ha-ba*, the World to Come, but the world of the *beit midrash*, the world in which women are invisible and silent, instrumentalities for the accomplishment of homosocial ends, and not pursuers of their own wishes. Defilement best describes Meir's sense of himself as a rape victim. "Robbers came on me and forced from me all that I had," he tells a neighbor he has met on the road *(Ba'u alai v'ansu kol mah she'hayah li)*. The sexual connotations of the verbs are even more explicit in Hebrew.

If the sin is defilement through violation, what is the remedy? Meir makes a pilgrimage to the Babylonian yeshivah to have his question answered: *Akhshav mah takanah yesh li?* "What remedy have I now?" but also "what penance will restore me?" and "What sentence do I deserve?" Meir is sentenced not to a punishment but to a heroic ordeal. He is bound hand and foot and taken to a place frequented by lions. On the third night of his ordeal a legalistically precise lion tears out a single one of his ribs and eats from it a single *k'zayyit* (an olive-sized bite), the minimum quantity constituting a meal in rabbinic law. After this, Meir is ordered released, healed of his wound and completely exonerated.

What has been removed from Rabbi Meir is his merger with the woman who raped him. Her invasion, indeed her reappropriation of him, undid the primal separation of woman and man. The feminine rib is extracted by the lion in a bloody recapitulation of creation. The mutilation excises the place where woman has come back in. Miraculously, Meir is reborn, motherless, sinless, and whole as Adam before the advent of Eve.

Redeeming Laughter

When I first read these midrashim, what startled me most was that I found them hilarious. Was this perception perverse on my part? Could it be integrated into my framework for a feminist hermeneutic of these texts: the exposure of silence and dis/remembering and the two motifs of mutilation and reversal of power relations that object relations theory so effectively lays bare? But when I read a version of my analysis to a group, others also rocked with laughter. A classically trained male scholar said rather wistfully, "You know, I was taught these stories from childhood and, although I have long understood that they were misogynistic, I never found them funny before. Now, how will I ever read them again without laughing?" Then I understood at last: I told him, "That is a gift to you from feminist Torah."

In judgment and in laughter, the audience to whom the story was directed and the unintended audience outside the storyteller's circle are finally made one. Our feminist hermeneutic re/members the storytellers and their homosocial world, their frantic scramble to preserve a patriarchal power they saw as infinitely fragile, their own sense of mutilation as patriarchs, their reconstruction of their own longings for the outcast Other as a terrifying appetite the Other turns upon them. All that was initially concealed and repressed and reversed is naked here, all that was banished and yet haunted them unceasingly. And we laugh.

Judgment, we know, is a holy act. God judges. The *bet din*, the law court, judges. We judge our society, our community. How is it fulfilling its obligations? How is it progressing toward the righteous and fructifying social vision transmitted to us by the prophets? In our secret depths we judge ourselves. We seek the courage to assume responsibility for what we do. We ask ourselves if we are becoming the people we are supposed to become. But can laughter be a holy act? Its reputation both in biblical and rabbinic texts is checkered: a euphemism for sexual play, associated with scoffing and skepticism, even idolatry. Yet it too has a sacred function, not apart from judgment but intertwined with it. We learn this lesson from the observance of the two antithetical holy days of the Jewish year.

A hasidic saying declares in a paradoxical pun: *yom kippurim yom k'Purim*.[41] Yom Kippur, the solemn day of atonement, is like Purim, the most roisterous of Jewish feasts. But in what way do these holy days resemble one another? The business of Yom Kippur is the confession of sin. Individually and communally, over and over we beat our breasts and recite exhaustive alphabetical lists of malefactions—everything from arrogance to xenophobia. We abstain from food, water, and sex from sundown to sundown. Late in the day, at the afternoon service, however, the carnivalesque bursts into our liturgy.[42] With blood sugar at low ebb, and self-congratulation for our asceticism on the rise, we read what may be the funniest book of the Bible, Jonah: a whale that can swallow people but can't digest them, animals that repent in sackcloth and ashes, a plant that grows like Jack's magic beanstalk equipped with a worm that can chomp it down at one go, and in its midst, the world's briefest, most effective, most reluctant prophet, the prophet who does not want his hearers to repent. This book, Arnold Band suggests, is a parody, burlesquing other biblical stories and punning outrageously.[43] And where is our first written source for the custom of reading Jonah on Yom Kippur? It is in Megillah 31b, the tractate of the Babylonian Talmud whose major topic is the laws of Purim.[44]

On Purim, on the other hand, while we are joking and freely imbibing and wearing silly costumes, we read the Book of Esther, whose laughter is frequently undercut by mourning, dread, and violence. Traditionally, at certain points in the narration, its lively cantillation slides into the haunting melody in which the Book of Lamentations is chanted, suggesting the tenuousness of all escapes. Texts, as Ricoeur says, "explode the worlds of their authors."[45] Our judgment and our laughter are dynamic responses altered by changes in the world, the community, and the self we bring to every reading or ritual enactment. Because of this, the text of Esther is changed for us by memories of the Holocaust, the story in which Haman won. Purim of 1994 and 1996 have changed our encounter with the text yet again. We now bring with us new memories, new massacres of innocents: the terrible celebration at the Cave of Machpelah in Hebron, where Baruch Goldstein reenacted upon the bodies of praying Muslims the revenge of the Jews of Persia upon their enemies; and the retaliatory murders of Israeli children costumed for Purim—two new manifestations of Yom Kippur in the midst of Purim. During the last bloody chapters of the megillah, the laughter that accompanies public readings of this bawdy book is silenced. Amid the uproar of the carnival, we are forced to recall the reality and finality of death, the danger of vengeance, and the terrible repetition compulsion to which it shackles both victor and vanquished.[46]

What kind of laughter will unite and transform us as audience and inheritors of classical texts? Not the laughter of separation and superiority, the laughter that says, "I could not be a fool like you." Not ungenerous laughter. It would be ungenerous to regard the struggle for holiness, which was the conscious motivation of our storytellers, merely as a cloak for their unconscious struggle for hegemony. Surely the desire for the good, the desire for closeness to God, is as real and irreducible as the desire for power, even if we have a lot of trouble telling them apart. Simply holding the stories up to ridicule, stripping them of redemptive potential, does not effect the holy comedy we as audience must bring about.

Our understanding of judgment is challenged by every new discovery into human accountability. The more adept we become with our richer psychological language, and the more we appreciate all the subtle contingencies—biochemical, genetic, social, anthropological, psychological, and historical—that both constrain and enlarge our choices, the more bitter our tears and the deeper our indignation about the violence we have done and continue to do to those who are both like us and utterly other than ourselves. Our understanding of comedy must deepen as well. Being human, none of us can see very far. Our choices in this predicament are to help one another to clearer vision and to discover a delight in the absurdity of our errors or to break our hearts alone in the darkness. I choose to walk through stories searching for the waters of salvation: the hidden springs of laughter that well up once we are willing to relinquish the suffocating security of the dominator or the smoldering grudge of the victim. After all, in rabbinic midrash even God, outmaneuvered and ruled out of court, laughs at the joke on himself and his Torah: "My children have defeated me!" He exclaims in delight. "My children have defeated me!"[47]

Chapter 2
Here Comes Skotsl:
Renewing Halakhah

For most of Jewish history, the lives of Jewish women have been controlled by a legal system whose categories and concerns they have not helped to shape and from whose authority structure they have been excluded. The rulings of classical Jewish law, halakhah, made women a subordinate group within Judaism. One of the first understandings of modern feminist Jewish theology was that it must delineate a feminist perspective from which to confront halakhah. Some scholars proposed ways to fix halakhah, alleviating its worst injustices toward women.[1] Others saw it as unfixable, an intrinsically oppressive structure[2] The only attempt that has not yet been made is to exercise our own covenantal authority to redefine and refashion halakhah fundamentally so that contemporary Jewish women and men can live it out with integrity.[3] Yet, if we define halakhah not as a closed system of obsolete and unjust rules, but as a way for communities of Jews to generate and embody their Jewish moral visions, that is exactly what we would do.

Halakhah comes from the root HLKh, to walk or to go. Halakhah is the act of going forward, of making one's way. A halakhah, a path-making, translates the stories and values of Judaism into ongoing action. That makes it an integral component not merely of Orthodoxy, but of any kind of Judaism. Such a definition of halakhah breaks the traditionalist monopoly on the word halakhah but risks some confusion about which system and ground rules I am discussing. In this chapter, therefore, I use the term "classical halakhah" when referring to the traditional system and "a halakhah" when hypothesizing about potential legal systems through which Judaism could be lived out.

Orienting Ourselves Through Stories

In this chapter, I would like to point us toward a potential halakhah. To determine where we ought to go, we must reflect on where we have been. We do this best by storytelling. As individuals, we continually rework and

21

relate our life stories to ourselves and to others and project ourselves into possible futures through dreams and fantasies. We also lay claim as members of groups to the collective memories of the group. Transmitted from generation to generation, they help to constitute our sense of who we are and to shape our future actions.[4] The ethicist Alasdair MacIntyre says, "I can only answer the question, 'What am I to do?' if I can answer the prior question, 'Of what story or stories do I find myself a part?'"[5] Commitments emerge out of stories and are refashioned in stories.[6] I would like to begin, then, by retelling a Yiddish folktale in which some women act upon their dissatisfaction with halakhah in the version of the Jewish story they inhabit.[7]

Here Comes Skotsl

Once upon a time, women began to resent that men seemed to own the world. Men got to read from the Torah and had all the interesting mitzvot and all the privileges. The women decided to present their grievance directly to God. They appointed Skotsl, a clever woman and a good speaker, as their representative. But how was the messenger to be dispatched? They decided to make a human tower. Skotsl was to scale the tower and then pull herself into heaven.

They scrambled up on one another's shoulders, and Skotsl began to climb. But somebody shrugged or shifted, and women tumbled every which way. When the commotion died down, Skotsl had disappeared. Men went on ruling the world, and nothing changed. But still, the women are hopeful, and that is why, when a woman walks into a house, the other women say, "Look, here comes Skotsl." And someday, it might really be she.

"Here Comes Skotsl" plays ironically upon several traditional motifs, but I am going to read it specifically as a story about women's relationship with the law. In this story, women reject the halakhah as it stands and search for a way to recreate it. The ironies in the story reflect both the inadequacies of the tradition for addressing women as participants and the women's own feelings of inadequacy in confronting the law and its guardians.

The name Skotsl reflects these ambivalences. The ironic greeting *skotsl kumt* is reserved for women.[8] People roll their eyes and mutter "*skotsl kumt*" when a kvetch or a gossip arrives. But is the joke in this tale on the kvetches or on the tradition that gave them something to kvetch about? In the upside-down world of the story, the loquacity that makes "Skotsl" a social disaster marks her as leadership material, in fact, as a prospective savior. Traditionally, heaven promises earth a messiah, because, from the divine point of view, the world has a problem, but in this story the messiah is dispatched from earth to heaven because the divine point of view *is* the problem.

The storyteller slyly implies that it will be easier to climb into heaven and talk to God than to try to get a hearing from the tradition's human representatives. Hence, the rebels decide to negotiate with the Boss. To reach the inaccessible top of The authority structure, they construct themselves into a parody of the tower of Babel. The tower, like its prototype, topples in confusion, but the builders remain optimistic. The story is left open-ended, awaiting Skotsl's return.

The World That Was

The world Skotsl departed is now dead. Enlightenment thought, prizing objectivity, rationality, and universalism, estranged thinking Jews from their tradition and attenuated their links with the sacred stories that shape Jewish identity. Emancipation dismantled the Jewish community as a corporate sociopolitical entity. The Holocaust delivered the coup de grâce to the remnants of shtetl culture. The Judaism in which Skotsl and her peers sought new standing is itself a lot less steady on its legs.

What is supposed to happen when Skotsl comes? Will Jewish women simply obtain what Jewish men have? Or will the mitzvot we do and the Torah we learn be themselves transformed when women become fully visible and fully audible in Judaism? In non-Orthodox Judaisms, women have been given equal access, at least theoretically. But equal access to what? If Skotsl came today, she would confront fragmented Jewish communities in which only the merest threads of a communal praxis have survived. The Jewish discourse in which God and God's law really matter has become difficult and unconvincing, Arnold Eisen suggests, because of "the loss of sustaining experiences" that would give these words referents in a lived reality.[9] Will Skotsl arrive just in time to endow Jewish women with one-half of nothing?

Modernity has punched holes in the thought and practice of Judaism, and its practitioners have had to improvise to stanch the resultant hemorrhage of Jewish meaning. The effectiveness of these improvisations varies. Some relieve and restore us while others compound our unease. It is this discomfort that fertilizes Jewish theology. The more seriously Jews think about their Judaisms, the more likely they are to find them wanting. If Skotsl came today she might be astonished to discover that it is *men's* dissatisfactions with Judaism that dominate the field known as "modern Jewish thought." The problems Judaism presents for and about women are all too frequently ghettoized as "women's issues" and exiled from general discussion.[10]

One of the major philosophical projects of Jewish feminism has been to relocate Skotsl's problem within the context of pervasive modern Jewish discomfort. What the Yiddish folktale poses as a "women's problem" feminist theologians reframe as *the* paradigmatic Jewish problem, the exemplar par excellence that exposes the failures of all the branches and varieties of Judaism to engender a Jewish tradition for modernity.[11] The problem of Jewish women calls into question the operation of all the processes by which Judaism is reinterpreted and renewed.

Engendering Judaism

There is a double sense in which one can say that Judaism needs to be engendered. Progressive Jews understand Judaism as an evolving system, constantly reshaped and renewed through its relations with its changing historical contexts. Consequently, they would agree that a truly progressive Judaism must be one that consciously and continuously re-engenders itself. In the second sense, however, Judaism has hardly begun to be engendered. The progressive branches of Judaism have hardly begun to reflect and to address the questions, understandings, and obligations of both Jewish women and Jewish men. They are not yet fully attentive to the impact of gender on the texts and lived experiences of the people Israel. Until progressive Judaisms engender themselves in this second sense, they cannot engender adequate Judaisms in the first sense. That attempt has already been made, and it has failed.

Riv-Ellen Prell, an anthropologist of religion, describes how classical Reformers used the universalist, Enlightenment model of their host culture to eradicate the special status assigned women in Orthodoxy.[12] Because "all men are created equal," Reform Judaism included women by categorizing them as "honorary men." But making women honorary men made them deviant men. It required viewing their differences from men as defects in their masculinity. As Prell demonstrates, this definition of equality not only hid discrimination that blocked women's full participation: it barred women from articulating experiences and concerns that men did not share. To enforce equality, it abolished the few women's mitzvot prescribed by Orthodoxy, making women even less visible than before. The experience of classical Reform illustrates a defect that feminist legal critiques have identified in the universalist understanding of equality. An equality predicated on ignoring the differences that constitute distinctive selves both conceals and legitimates injustice.[13] An institution or enterprise is fully inclusive only if it includes people as the kind of people they really are.

Legal and philosophical critiques, not only by feminists, but by communitarians, both progressive and conservative, civil libertarians, and poststructuralists of every sort, ask us to reevaluate the Enlightenment universalist values of equality, autonomy, rights, and justice, values in which progressive Judaisms have invested heavily. These critiques suggest that universalist values that fail to recognize crucial differences among people create inadequate understandings of what it means to be human and, consequently, make poor guides for how human beings may live in community.[14]

When we reassess the impact of these values on modern Judaism, Skotsl's problem emerges as the prime indicator of a larger problem caused by inadequacies in the very modernity progressive Judaisms embraced so fervently. The problem of Jewish women, then, cannot be ghettoized so that women can discuss and solve "their" problem unilaterally. As a key to the problems of modern Judaisms themselves, this issue affects all of us, women and men. Engendering Judaism, like other kinds of human engendering, requires women and men to act cooperatively.

If Judaism cannot be engendered without solving the problem of women, it is equally true that it cannot be engendered without solving the problem of halakhah. Without a means through which the stories and the values of Judaism can be embodied in communal praxis, how are they to be sustained by experiences? Values and stories are empty and meaningless if we lack ways to act upon them. Without concrete, sensuous, substantial experiences that bind us to live out our Judaisms together, there is nothing real to engender.

The difficulty about proposing a halakhah to progressive Jews is their presumption that the term, its definition, and its practice belong to Orthodoxy. We urgently need to reclaim this term because it is the authentic Jewish language for articulating the system of obligations that constitute the content of the covenant.

Halakhah belongs to liberal Jews no less than to Orthodox Jews because the stories of Judaism belong to us all. A halakhah is a communal praxis grounded in Jewish stories.[15] Ethicists, theologians, and lawyers who stress the centrality of narrative would argue that all normative systems rest upon stories. Whether the story is the Exodus from Egypt or the crucifixion and resurrection of Jesus or the forging of American independence, if we claim it as our own, we commit ourselves to be the kind of people that story demands, to translate its norms and values into a living praxis.[16]

A praxis is more than the sum of the various practices that constitute it. *A praxis is a holistic embodiment in action at a particular time of the values and commitments inherent to a particular story.*[17] Orthodoxy cannot have a monopoly on halakhah, because no form of Judaism can endure without one; there would be no way to live it out.

What happened to Judaism in modernity was that its praxis became both impoverished and fragmented. Some communal practices were taken over by the secular state. Other practices were jettisoned by congregations because they appeared foreign and "Oriental."[18] Still others were abandoned by individuals because they had come to see themselves as "private citizens" with minimal obligations to other private citizens. It became impossible to imagine a unified way to live as a human being, a citizen, and a Jew.

A contemporary Jewish praxis would reduce our sense of fragmentation. If we had a praxis rather than a grab bag of practices, we would experience making love, making *kiddush,* recycling paper used at our workplace, cooking a pot of soup for a person with AIDS, dancing at a wedding, and making medical treatment decisions for a dying loved one as integrated parts of the same project: the holy transformation of our everyday reality. Furthermore, we would experience ourselves less as fragmented enactors of divergent roles in disparate spheres—public/private, ritual/ethical, religious/secular, duty/pleasure—and more as coherent Jewish personalities.

We cannot simply resurrect the old premodern praxis, because it no longer fits us in the world we now inhabit. Some of its elements are fundamentally incompatible with participation in postindustrial, democratic societies.[19] The old praxis can be preserved intact only if we schizophrenically split off our religious lives from our secular lives and live two separate existences with two different sets of values and commitments. But the obligation to be truthful and the yearning to be whole are what made us progressive Jews in the first place. To be faithful to the covenant requires that we infuse the whole of our existence with our religious commitments. How is that to be done in our specific situation?

The secular values of equal respect, inclusivity, diversity, and plural-ism obligate citizens to recognize and protect one another's integrity and well-being. Jews have obvious cause to espouse these values. At the same time, classical halakhah is committed to the subordination and exclusion of women in communal life. The inability of classical halakhah to resolve this dissonance is the paradigmatic example of its inadequacy as a praxis for Jews in modernity and leads inexorably toward challenges from Skotsl's modern incarnations.

What Authority? Whose Halakhah?

Yet, as its proponents are quick to acknowledge, the formulation of a progressive halakhah presents complex difficulties. What are to be its sources? What is its authority? For fundamentalist Orthodoxy, halakhah originates in the Written Law of the Pentateuch and in the Oral Law pre-served in the Talmud. Both are believed to have been communicated directly by God to Moses. Both are regarded as infallible and immutable. All subsequent halakhic developments, such as codes and responsa, are viewed as implicit in these divine revelations. It is not that the law does not change in different situations, but that the change has already been decreed in a single atemporal revelatory event. "Whatever a disciple of the wise may propound by way of explaining a law in the most distant future was already revealed to Moses on Mount Sinai."[20]

The crucial difference between traditional halakhists and modernists is that modernists accept the premises of modern historiography: that soci-eties are human constructions that exist in time and change over time, that ideas and institutions inhabit specific historical and cultural contexts, and that they cannot be adequately understood without reference to con-text.[21] These premises are incompatible with the belief that halakhah was divinely revealed in a single event and reflects an eternal and immutable divine will. Rejecting the supernatural account of halakhah in favor of his-torical and naturalistic explanations raises fundamental theological ques-tions about the place of halakhah in Judaism. If halakhah evolved histori-cally and reflects the cultures through which it passed, then what makes it holy? Why should it be obeyed? And what makes its rules and cate-gories appropriate for contexts so different from those for which they were formulated?

When the response to these questions is to discard halakhah entirely, the ability of individuals and communities to live out their Judaism is dealt a crippling blow. The early history of Reform Judaism is a testimonial to how quickly and how devastatingly the deconstruction of halakhah can disembody everyday Judaism. Painfully conscious of the vulnerability of a halakhah unfortified by traditional absolutes, liberal halakhists are understandably protective of their fragile enterprise and apprehensive of the withering force of the theological questions raised by their own premises.[22] Rather than facing these questions head-on, then, liberal halakhists tend to evade or disarm them through formalist or positivist legal strategies. These strategies make it impossible for the core questions of feminist critique to be articulated. By translating the critique into terms classical halakhah has in its conceptual vocabulary, liberal halakhists distort the questions. The system's own terms and categories are taken as a given. The feminist critique of them is restated as "women's desire for equal access or equal obligation" and pasted onto a basically intact halakhic system, like a Band-Aid covering a superficial cut.

The Feminist Critique of Halakhah

The problems actually raised in the feminist critique, however, are *systemic* wounds too deep for liberal Band-Aids. As one of the originators of this critique, I have contended that members of a Jewish male elite constructed the categories and method of classical halakhah to reflect their own perspectives and social goals and have held a monopoly on their application.[23] Borrowing a term from the post-Christian theologian Mary Daly, I have called classical halakhah a methodolatrous system.[24] The method becomes a kind of false god. It determines the choice of questions, rather than the questions determining the choice of method. Questions that do not conform to the system's method and categories are simply reclassified as non-data and dumped out.

Jacob Neusner shows how, in Mishnah, one of the foundational documents of classical halakhah, the presumptions regarding the status and function of women determine the selection principles.[25] What is important to the framers of the Mishnah about women is the orderly transfer of women and property from one patriarchal domain to another.[26] As Judith Wegner demonstrates, women's sexuality is a legal commodity, and, in cases where it is at issue, women are treated not as persons but as chattel.[27] Moreover, women are themselves ineligible to be normative members of the community. Their role is to be "a focus of the sacred" rather than to be active participants in the processes of sanctification.[28] Halakhic data about women favors those questions about women that are of interest to the rabbinic elite. Hence, there is much information on questions of marital status, women's tasks and obligations vis-à-vis husbands and fathers, the disposition of property women brought into marriage or subsequently acquired. Regarding women's activity in the masculine realms of Torah study, juridical activity, and public prayer, however, the Talmud's characteristic question is "How do we know that they are excluded?"[29]

The presumptions select the questions. The categories shape them. Adjudication creates precedents that reinforce the form future questions must take. By this means, Torah, Mishnah, Gemara, codes, and responsa amass huge bodies of data on their favored topics, whereas other issues are condemned to haunt the outer darkness. Hence, when women advance topics that do not affect preestablished legal concerns, the system either rejects them because it has no information on them or attempts to restate them in distortive androcentric terms that would allow it to apply its own categories and advance its own goals. At worst, it attempts to limit discourse to the topics on which it has the most information: the status problems of marriage, divorce, and desertion, and the participation problems of witnessing, judging, and liturgical performance—problems the system and its presumptions created.

The critique I have outlined here is not confined to Orthodox legal processes. Indeed, its implications are far more powerful for non-Orthodox revisions of halakhah because it suggests that liberal halakhists have failed to pursue the implications of their positions. If the source-texts of halakhah are not timeless or absolute but shaped within social contexts, if its categories must exclude much of our gendered modern life experiences as non-data, and if its authority structure is neither democratic nor inclusive, then adapting its content to modernity is an inadequate solution. To argue that the system requires no systemic critique, a liberal halakhist must ignore or discount that halakhic rules, categories, and precedents were constructed and applied without the participation of women, that they reflect perceptions of women as a commodified subclass, and that they are often inadequate or inimical to concerns that women themselves possibly would raise if they were legal subjects rather than legal objects.[30]

Liberal halakhah, then, requires a separate critique to illuminate how it has attempted to adjust halakhah to modernity while evading more searching questions about its authority and structure. The two philosophies of jurisprudence liberal halakhists have adopted as theoretical grounding for this project are legal formalism and legal realism.

Legal formalism asserts that what is definitive about law is its form. A legal outcome is valid if the system's rules and categories are correctly applied. Because the rules and categories that constitute the law's form are taken as givens about which there can be no argument, a formalist approach makes an end-run around questions about the sociohistorical contexts these forms may reflect. The only possible arguments concern whether the formal applications are valid or invalid. Although legal formalism can result in extremely repressive decision making, it can also open up tremendous freedom for new and ingenious applications of legal categories, because any application, however unprecedented, can be proposed, as long as it is formally defensible.

Legal realism, a theory of jurisprudence influential during the first half of the twentieth century, maintains that law is determined not by the language of legal texts and enactments but rather by the discretionary power of judges. This power, the legal realists have argued, is appropriately employed to shape social policy. The judge's decisions are "realistic" because they adapt the law to address social realities. The problem with legal realism is its tendency to reinforce the power of the already powerful. If the wording or intent of legal texts or the existence of legal precedents does not present curbs or boundaries for judicial decisions, the discretionary power of judges will be unrestrained. Given that decisors are chosen by the dominant group, who is likely to be selected to wield power, and whose social investments do such persons protect?[31]

Versions of liberal halakhah attempt to synthesize these apparently antithetical theories, one radically atemporal and the other radically context-dependent, because both are essential to the liberal project. What the theories have in common is that each offers a means of overriding the component of jurisprudence that is most resistant to change: the power of precedent.[32] In tandem, the two theories serve to authorize and to derive changes that run counter to all legal precedent. Legal realism allows the decisor to predetermine the outcomes he or she deems most appropriate to the time and place. Legal formalism provides the means to validate those outcomes as long as the categories are tenably applied.

Each theory supplements some lack in the other. Legal formalism has no intrinsic impetus toward legal change. As long as legal outcomes are formally valid, it is satisfied. Legal realism is predicated upon the necessity that law continually adjust to changing social contexts, but it lacks any formal criteria for validity. Its sole criterion, the discretion of the individual judge, is nakedly subjective and potentially unlimited. The combination of the two maximizes the impetus for legal change while specifying and objectifying the criteria by which change is justified.[33] In this way, the contextualized power of the decisor is reinforced with the atemporal validity of the system's formal reasoning process.

A Feminist's Gallery of Liberal Halakhists

Both for formalism and for legal realism, an ultimate question remains. What is the source of their authority? In the case of legal formalism, what claim has halakhah's formal structure upon our obedience? The only liberal halakhist for whom the question presents no problem is Eliezer Berkovits, whose legal liberalism is undergirded by an Orthodox theology affirming the Torah as the revealed word of God.[34] This theology does not lead to legal fundamentalism for Berkovits, however. Implicit within Torah, according to Berkovits, is a set of ethical values that did not have to be divinely revealed. They are independently knowable through divinely endowed human reason and human social experience. These values ought to guide the interpretation of texts and the application of formal halakhic mechanisms.[35]

Louis Jacobs, the theorist who emphasizes most heavily the role of historical context in shaping Jewish law, forthrightly acknowledges the liberal problem.[36] If the Torah is an historically evolved composite document and not a verbatim record of what God told Moses on Mount Sinai, what obligates Jews to obey, and how are they to sort out what they are to do? "The ultimate authority for determining which practices are binding upon the faithful Jew," Jacobs declares, " is the historical experience of the people Israel."[37] However, Jacobs rejects as "ancestor worship" the Kaplanian answer that the people Israel itself is the source of commandment.[38] He would maintain that the will of a transcendent Deity is revealed in the historical adaptations of the halakhah. This view is a variant of the Progressive Jewish doctrine of "continuing revelation." In Jacobs' account, halakhah's evolution, its creativity in adapting to historical context, is a history of progress.

This approach has certain pitfalls. It tends to underemphasize the extent to which the struggles of rival factions for dominance and power determine the establishment or suppression of halakhic positions, nor does it take into consideration that the evolution of halakhah may not correspond to what we think of as progress. A diligent historian can unearth any number of embarrassing and objectionable developments in the various stages of halakhah. For example, S. M. Passamaneck traces a trend in medieval halakhah not merely to arrest on reasonable cause but to punish, even by flogging, on reasonable cause without conclusive proof of guilt.[39]

Another great danger in the doctrine of revelation through history is that history itself will be sacralized. If we made history its own ethical arbiter, injustices of the past, like slavery or the subordination of women, could not be condemned, because within their historical contexts, they were not viewed as wrong. At its most conservative, sacralizing history begets a kind of moral conventionalism that makes moral initiative superfluous, because, "whatever is, is right."[40] Attributing change to the invisible hand of history would relieve us of responsibility for consciously and reflectively shaping the future of Judaism. We could simply wait for history to drag us in its wake. Conventionalism is a perversion of the doctrine of revelation through history, but it suggests a cautionary lesson: God may speak to us through history, but what God is saying may be less than obvious.

One way to sidestep the challenge of history to the authority of halakhah is to make the system formally self-sufficient. The Conservative halakhist Joel Roth borrows from secular legal formalism the concept of a *grundnorm*, a presumption that grounds the legal system proceeding from it.[41] Roth offers two versions of this *grundnorm*.

> The document called the Torah embodies the word and will of God, which it behooves man to obey, as mediated through the agency of J, E, P, and D, and is, therefore, authoritative. An alternative possible formulation might be: The document called the Torah embodies the constitution promulgated by J, E, P, and D, which it behooves man to obey, and is therefore authoritative.[42]

Theoretically, the *grundnorm* could justify all of classical halakhah's exclusions and subjugations of women, but Roth employs it instead in attempting to remedy inequities. Roth takes the authority invested in the *grundnorm* and confers it upon the halakhic principle *ein lo ladayyan ella mah she-einav ro'ot,* "a judge can only rely on what his own eyes see." Judicial discretion becomes the fundamental means by which halakhic inequities toward women are to be amended.[43] Obligations from which they were previously excluded could be conferred upon women, and their disadvantages in marriage and divorce law alleviated. Judicial discretion, in other words, could enable halakhic authorities to redefine women as honorary men.[44]

The *grundnorm* is not an unmixed blessing for feminists. It poses uncomfortable theological problems. Do the passages concerning the trial by ordeal of the suspected adulteress or the characterization of homosexuality as an abomination and a capital crime really embody the word and will of God? Alternatively, if we leave God out of it and attribute the documents solely to J, E, P, and D, we are still left with texts whose androcentrism and patriarchal bias disadvantage and peripheralize one-half of the people Israel. What makes J, E, P, and D deserving of our unconditional obedience?

Moreover, what is the *grundnorm* for? Does it have any behavioral consequences of its own, or does it merely legitimate the judicial discretion that really drives the system? "As the sole normative interpreters of the meaning of the Torah," Roth declares, "Torah means whatever the rabbis say it means."[45] As David Ellenson points out, "Given the principle of [judicial discretion] and the assent to the *grundnorm* . . . it is almost logically impossible to imagine what might be an infringement of principle in the halakhic system."[46] If judges can remake the law at will, the *grundnorm* is legally irrelevant.

Leaving aside the question of how such unrestricted authority could be ethically justified, what would qualify a decisor to wield it? In Roth's adaptation of traditional criteria, the prerequisites would be a rabbinic education and ordination and a theological loyalty oath affirming the divine origin of the *grundnorm* and the authority of the sages as its sole, legitimate interpreters.[47] In other words, those who currently hold a monopoly on the halakhic process would also monopolize both the admission process and the interpretive process. Adherence to Roth's *grundnorm* would preclude a metacritique of the halakhic system. Formulating such a critique would automatically disqualify an entrant. Critique from outside the ranks is illegitimate by definition and can be ignored, since only the rabbis are legitimate interpreters. Skotsl and her peers would be immediately escorted to the door.

Halakhic authority, as Roth envisions it, is a closed system with benevolent intentions. Hence, women rabbis could also become authorities—as long as they committed themselves not only to the traditional halakhic process but to the stipulated theological underpinnings. These would implicitly require women rabbis to reject the feminist critique and to sign on as honorary men.

In the absence of the feminist critique, however, there would be no reason to engender new halakhah addressing women's distinctive experiences, much less any conceptual vocabulary to articulate such concerns.

Redefining the Game: Toward A Proactive Halakhah

The presumption liberal halakhists share is that modern halakhah must be a version of traditional halakhah adapted for a modern context by bringing formalist or positivist legal strategies to bear upon traditional texts. Decision making would remain in the hands of a rabbinical elite whose prescriptions are to be handed down to hypothetically obedient communities. The goal of liberal halakhah is to repair inadequacies of classical halakhah exposed by modernity while leaving the system basically intact.

Liberal halakhah believes itself to be modern because it is reactive to classical halakhah. To be truly progressive, however, a halakhah would have to be *proactive*. The place to begin is not with the principles we need to preserve or the content we may need to adapt but with what we mean by halakhah altogether. An understanding of law that lends itself to such a project can be found in the work of an American legal theorist, Robert Cover. Using Cover's understanding of what is meant by law, it is possible to explain how the feminist project qualifies as a lawmaking enterprise. Cover's account of the constitution and transformation of legal meanings could provide sufficient common ground to enable representatives of classical and liberal versions of halakhah and their feminist critics to enter into conversation. It offers a basis upon which feminist hermeneutics, praxis, and commitments can make defensible claims to authenticity.

Law is not reducible to formal lawmaking, Cover maintains, because it is generated by a *nomos*, a universe of meanings, values, and rules, embedded in stories. A *nomos* is not a body of data to master and adapt, but a world to inhabit. Knowing how to live in a nomic world means being able to envision the possibilities implicit in its stories and norms and being willing to live some of them out in praxis.[48]

Cover characterizes the genesis and the maintenance of law as two distinct elements in legal development. He calls these the *paidaic* or world-creating mode and the *imperial* or world-maintaining mode. Paidaic activity effects *jurisgenesis*, the creation of a *nomos*, a universe of meaning, out of a shared body of precepts and narratives that individuals in community commit themselves to learn and to interpret. This generative

34

mode is unstable and impermanent, but without its creative and revitalizing force, societies could not sustain the sense of meaning and shared purpose essential to social survival.

The paidaic mode can create worlds, but it cannot maintain them. Inevitably, the single unified vision that all social actors share in a paidaic period splinters into multiple nomic worlds holding differing interpretations. To coordinate and maintain these diverse worlds within a coexistent whole, there is a need to enforce standard social practices among them. The imperial mode universalizes the norms created by jurisgenesis and empowers institutions to reinforce them by coercion, if necessary. However, institutionalization and coercion are not the only means by which the imperial mode maintains the stability of law. Because the imperial world view does not strive for unanimity, but harmonious coordination of its differing parts, it can admit as an adaptive mechanism some tolerance for pluralism, a value foreign to the paidaic ethos.[49] Cover imagines these two legal moments, the paidaic and the imperial, coexisting in dynamic equilibrium.

Our modern problem with halakhah is reflected in the failure of this equilibrium, in the unmediated gap between the impoverished imperial world we inhabit and the richer and more vital worlds that could be. It is into this "paidaic vacuum" that Skotsl and her mission vanished. By means of feminist jurisgenesis, we can bridge that gap and regenerate a *nomos*, a world of legal meaning in which the stories, dreams, and revelations of Jewish women and men are fully and complexly integrated.

Cover offers the image of the bridge to express the dynamism of the meaning-making component that both constitutes and propels law. Law-as-bridge is a tension system strung between "reality," our present world of norms and behavioral responses to norms, and "alternity," the other normative worlds we may choose to imagine. In other words, the bridge is what connects maintenance-law to jurisgenerative potentiality. Law is neither reality nor alternity but what bridges the gap between them: "the committed social behavior which constitutes the way a group of people will attempt to get from here to there."[50] Ultimately, law is maintained or remade not by orthodoxies or visions but by commitments of communities either to obey the law as it stands or to resist and reject it in order to live out some alternative legal vision.

Cover's image of the bridge built of committed praxis grounded in story reinforces the necessity of a halakhah, for only by means of halakhah can Judaism embody its sacred stories and values in communal praxis. At the same time, Cover's bridge image makes it possible to think freshly about halakhah, because it counters precisely those features that progressive Jews, and progressive feminists in particular, find repressive in halakhah's traditional formulations. It is dynamic rather than static, visionary rather than conservative, open to the outside rather than closed, arising communally, cooperatively, covenantally, rather than being externally imposed and passively obeyed. The metaphor of the bridge also expresses what it is like to inhabit a modern *nomos*. Bridges are generally open rather than enclosed. They span gaps and connect disparate entities, functions that reflect the needs of open, democratic societies populated by diverse groups of highly individuated modern selves.[51]

I have said that Cover's image of law as a bridge offers progressive Jews a representation of halakhah harmonious with their dynamic understanding of Judaism. Now juxtapose to Cover's image the classic metaphor of protective confinement that R. Ḥiyyah bar Abba attributes to his teacher Ulla: "From the time that the Temple was destroyed, the Holy One has had nothing in His world but the four cubits of the halakhah" (B. Berakhot 8a). This metaphor eloquently expresses the constriction of God's earthly holdings from the grandeur of the Temple to this austere and narrow cell that is both prison and refuge.

The walls of the Diaspora cubicle are, at the same time, externally imposed barriers and internally established boundaries protecting it from engulfment by rival systems of meaning. The metaphor recalls Peter Berger's description of how structures of religious meaning in premodern times made sense of the world and fought off the chaotic emptiness of unmediated reality. Berger depicts these constructed universes of meaning as rickety, jerry-built fortresses reinforced by "plausibility structures" whose function is to wall out the howling wilderness of meaninglessness all around.[52] The metaphor of the cube is static as well as closed. It lacks a means of extending itself toward alternity.

Like Cover's bridge builders, Skotsl and her cohorts also build toward an envisioned alternity: a way out of halakhah-as-cube. But the only way they can imagine effecting change is vertically, rather than horizontally. They offer themselves as a ladder so that one gifted individual may climb outside the human realm to request a recreated Torah from the very top of the hierarchy and bring it back down to the bottom. Implicit in this image is the women's assumption of their profound powerlessness to grasp, appropriate, and refashion the law. Their sense of impotence and subjugation is reminiscent of Kafka's parable "The Problem of Our Laws":

> Our laws are not generally known; they are kept secret by the small group of nobles who rule us. We are convinced that these ancient laws are scrupulously administered; nevertheless, it is an extremely painful thing to be ruled by laws that one does not know. I am not thinking of possible discrepancies that may arise in the interpretation of the laws, or of the disadvantages involved when only a few and not the whole people are allowed to have a say in their interpretation. These disadvantages are perhaps of no great importance. For the laws are very ancient . . . and though there is still a possible freedom of interpretation left, it has now become very restricted. Moreover, the nobles have obviously no cause to be influenced in their interpretation by personal interests inimical to us, for the laws were made to the advantage of the nobles from the very beginning, they themselves stand above the laws, and that seems to be why the laws were entrusted exclusively into their hands.[53]

Like Kafka's narrator, the women in the folktale perceive authority as remote and inaccessible. Rather than seeing themselves as sharers in the covenantal authority through which the people Israel translate the Torah into communal praxis, they are so desperately estranged from the sources of justice that they attempt a feat Scripture has already declared unnecessary:

> It is not in the heavens, that you should say, "Who among us can go up to the heavens and get it for us and impart it to us, so that we may observe it? . . . No, the thing is very close to you in your mouth and in your heart to observe it" (Deut. 30:12, 14).[54]

Because the Torah is no longer in heaven, mistakes cannot be rectified by building a tower from history into eternity. Instead, we must discover within ourselves the competence and good faith through which to repair and renew the Torah within time. We must *extend* Torah as we extend ourselves by reaching ahead. The aptest metaphor for that constructive task is that of the bridge we build from the present to possible futures.

Down to Work: The Tools for Bridge Building

A bridge needs to be built, and Jewish women and men will have to build it together. The task requires us to look afresh at our sacred texts, at other revelatory stories about Jewish lives, and at the moral imperatives in our own lives that impel us to constitute a new interpretive community. What are the special resources feminists can contribute to building the

37

bridge? What have we learned in articulating feminist questions and feminist methodologies that will transform the world of Jewish meaning?

One crucial contribution will be the methodologies feminists have developed for understanding and using narrative. Narrative will be central to any Jewish nomic project because Jewish tradition is itself a sedimentation of stories and stories about stories. But not all methods of interpreting and augmenting the stories of tradition include women, whether as readers, storytellers, or interpreters. Feminist scholars of law and philosophy have pioneered in using narrative both as a method of vision and as a tool of legal and philosophical critique.[55] As a method of vision, feminist narratives draw upon fantasies and desires, prophecies and prayers to imagine possible worlds in which both women and men could flourish. As a tool of critique, narrative can expose within abstract theories assumptions about the nature and experience of being human, what people know, how they live, what they want, and what they fear.

These assumptions inform the highly particular stories with which universalizing theories are pregnant. Bringing out the story within the abstraction allows us to see which human characteristics, experiences, desires, and fears a theory has chosen to address and how it has understood them. For example, as Seyla Benhabib points out, in the social contract theory of Thomas Hobbes, the denizens of the state of nature are adult males who have sprung up "like mushrooms." The story excises the primal experiences of dependency and nurturing, childhood and motherhood from its account of the human condition.[56] Once its story is exposed, a defective theory can be challenged with counternarratives embodying previously excluded experiences and perspectives.

A related tool feminists can bring to nomic bridge building is an awareness of the importance of context in evaluating human understandings, obligations, and intentions.[57] A foundational principle of all progressive feminisms is that women's roles are not biologically determined and unchanging.[58] They are consequences of social structures and social experiences that differ significantly from one time and place to another. Human lives and human understanding are shaped within contexts, but human beings also possess the ability to reshape and restructure those contexts. Because narratives testify so powerfully to the impact of context, they are capable of reflecting the context-bound nature of human existence more accurately than abstract theories that claim to express truths unrestricted by time and place.

Contexts narrow the range of possibilities in narratives and provide boundaries for both history and fiction. At the same time, because contexts are conditional rather than inevitable, there is always a possibility of bursting their boundaries, of breaking and remaking contexts. The mutability of contexts is related to the capacity for change in human beings themselves. Human beings in their contexts create the need and the potential for structural transformations.

Another characteristic of contexts that makes them important for the renewal of law is their particularity. Because law requires applying general categories to specific situations, it can be hostile to particularities, regarding them as irrelevant details that, if stripped away, would reveal the situation's conformance to an existing legal category. But some particularities are not irrelevant. They may be the features that give settings and situations their distinguishing character. Removing them from consideration may distort the meaning of a situation and lead to injustice. Injustice is even more apt to result if categories reflecting one group's understanding of which particularities are important are then imposed on differing groups. Feminist legal scholars are expanding the concept of legal relevance in American law by insisting that more richly particularized contexts with wider temporal boundaries be considered as evidence.[59]

Understanding people as legal subjects requires more than an understanding of contexts, however. We need richer language in which to describe human desires and human motivations. One source for this language is the conceptual vocabulary of modern psychological theory. Secular feminist jurisprudence has begun to explore its potential for providing richer and more complex accounts of motivation in legal stories.[60] Psychological theories can delineate the impact upon human development of gender, of kinship and other social relationships, and of the larger social environment and its possibilities. Psychological theories can account not only for rational human calculation but for what is irrational or arational in human beings. They can express ambivalences, ambiguities, and subtle gradations in states of mind. The ability of psychological theories to provide accounts of gendered human identity and action that are both deeply contextualized and deeply individualized renders them powerful and convincing as components of feminist analysis and critique. Jean Bethke Elshtain identifies this use of psychoanalytic language for feminist ends as a major desideratum of feminist discourse. She explains:

> The feminist ends I have in mind include the articulation of a philoso-
> phy of mind which replaces the old dualism with which we are still
> saddled in favor of an account which unites mind and body, reason
> and passion, into a compelling account of human subjectivity and
> identity, and the creation of a feminist theory of action that compli-
> catedly invokes both inner and outer realities. A third feminist end to
> which psychoanalysis could [contribute] is the amplification of a theo-
> ry of language as meaning . . . to articulate an interpretive story of
> female experience.[61]

The Jewish worlds we create, like all nomic worlds, will be shaped by
our understanding of what is entailed in being human. The range of
human possibilities depends upon the depth and complexity of this philosophical anthropology. What it means to be human in a world of meaning
determines that world's conception of justice, for notions of justice are
predicated upon understandings of the needs and duties of humankind,
and particular visions of human flourishing. For the task of formulating
an enriched Jewish conception of human nature, then, psychological language alone will not be adequate. New understandings of Jewish narratives and Jewish values will be needed.

With its profusion and variety of narratives, codes, and prophecies,
Judaism has resources for subtle and multifaceted conceptions of human
nature. However, the conceptions of human nature that predominate in
Jewish thought, as in Western philosophy and law, are unitary. Feminist
legal theorists and philosophers have shown how this conception of a single human nature is inadequate and distortive. It sets up as a norm one
particular variant of male human nature from whom all others are
regarded as deviant. Instead, human nature needs to be understood as a
spectrum of meaningful human differences.

In addition, difference itself needs to be redefined as *variation,* rather
than *deviation.* The constitutional scholar Martha Minow observes, "For
both legal difference and difference in general, a difference 'discovered' is
more aptly a statement of a relationship expressing one person's deviation
from an unstated norm assumed by the other."[62] To remove the stigma
from gender difference, we would have to identify unstated standards that
assume that maleness is normative and replace them with norms that
reflect gendered existences. Narratives of women's subjective experiences
will be useful sources for such new norms. They can help to delineate
experiences differing from men's or those not experienced by men at all.[63]

How can we make law reflect the human differences that condition people's choices and decisions without unfairly favoring particular differences? Minow argues that a single strategy for the legal treatment of difference is inadequate, because injustice can result either from noticing difference or from ignoring it.[64] Just as singling others out negatively constructs their difference as deviance, so does refusal to acknowledge and accommodate difference in a world tailored to the specifications of some groups and not others. Sometimes it is the recognition of difference and sometimes the refusal to recognize difference that enables people to be included in the larger community.

Minow's analysis is representative of a reexamination in political philosophy of how societies composed of diverse members can treat one another equally and fairly. In the highly stratified societies that preceded the Enlightenment, treatment was contingent upon status. A philosophical and legal legacy of the Enlightenment in democratic societies has been the assumption that treating people equally requires ignoring differences and emphasizing commonalities. The most rigorous modern reformulation of an egalitarian theory of justice is that of John Rawls.[65] Rawls replaces the fable of "the state of nature" with what he calls "the original position," a hypothetical Nowheresville where we are to imagine the participants in the social contract stripped of all their particularities behind what Rawls calls "the veil of ignorance." The principles upon which contractors would agree in ignorance of their own social roles and interests could be presumed to be universally fair.[66] The two principles upon which Rawlsian justice rests are a principle of equal liberty for all and a "difference principle" which stipulates that social and economic inequalities must work to the advantage of the most disadvantaged members of society and requires open access to social and economic rewards.[67]

Feminist political philosophers differ about whether and to what extent Rawls's theory of justice could provide justice for women. Susan Moller Okin finds Rawls's theory a promising one for feminists.[68] Although she readily concedes that Rawls fails to address problems of gender injustice and that he evades discussing justice within the family, she argues that, using his two principles of justice, it is possible to develop a feminist reading of Rawls that would identify all social constructions of gender as sources of injustice.[69] Okin believes that Rawls' original position with its veil of ignorance about social roles and statuses is an adequate way to motivate people to provide fairness for gender conditions as they would for race or class.[70] Taking the original position, she argues, does not mean assuming the perspective of nobody, but rather assuming successively the perspectives of every member of society. But Okin would supplement what Rawls allows social contractors to know with information of a very different character: richly particularized information about actual human lives and the impact of social injustice upon them. Okin also rejects the ahistoricity of Rawls's theory.[71] In addition to the "general facts about human society" with which Rawls would equip contractors, she would include historical accounts of social oppression and its structures. In a sense, however, Okin would universalize these particularized, contextualized stories, because she would give all of them to all contractors rather than allowing particular participants to own and articulate them in give and take with others different from them.

For Seyla Benhabib, Rawls's theory is more problematic. She argues that the abstracted "moral geometry" undergirding the liberal principles of fairness and equality obscures crucial existential differences of gender and banishes them from consideration as justice problems.[72] By dichotomizing justice and the good life, she contends, liberal ethical theory builds in gender injustice. When justice is characterized as rational and public while the good life is regarded as the sphere of purely private, affective preferences, areas such as sexual and family relationships in which women have experienced great injustice are exempted from meeting any standard of justice.[73]

Although Rawls's ethics purports to make no claims about the nature of the contracting parties and minimal claims about their primary goods (their highest values and desires), Benhabib argues that the kind of human being whose characteristics, concerns, and investments are reflected in Rawls's underlying assumptions is the privileged majority male. He is the one for whom rights, autonomy, and privacy are red-flagged issues. Benhabib would replace this limited philosophical anthropology with one in which our relationships with others are constitutive of our selfhood.

For Benhabib, social contracting requires actual conversations rather than hypothetical ones. She would replace Rawlsian ethics of justice with a "communicative ethic of need interpretation." The participants in Rawls's original position cannot talk about their needs because they don't know what they are. They cannot engage in conversational give and take because they are indistinguishable from one another.[74] Instead, Benhabib proposes real dialogues between real people diversified by gender and culture located in specific times and places, what she calls "embodied and embedded selves." Unlike Rawls or Okin, Benhabib believes that it will help, not hurt, the dialogue to know who we and the other are.

In Benhabib's dialogues there would be no privileged subject matter. Not merely a thin list of primary goods compiled by "the male behind the veil," but whatever goods or desires the participants chose to introduce would be relevant. Finally, her ground rules for dialogue would permit metadiscourse about the conditions, rules, and definitions presupposed in contracting.

Some of these proposals are as relevant to a covenantal community as to a contractual one. Caught between Orthodox-existentialist conceptions of "halakhic man"[75] and liberal formulations of universalist ethics, we have yet to frame a Jewish discourse that makes it possible for both sexes of the people Israel to be covenantally present or to actualize a communal praxis that expresses the commitments of both men and women. Drawing upon Benhabib's stipulations, we could open up halakhic discourse and shape it to address the needs, desires, and obligations of diverse, gendered people inhabiting specific times and places. A provision allowing for metadiscourse would enable us to avoid the methodolatry that uses rules, definitions, and theological loyalty oaths to exclude the data and perspectives of women from the conversation. It would make possible a communal discourse in which neither primary goods and values nor assumptions or legal methodologies were closed off from discussion. Any vital concern in the lives of community members could be articulated and heard.

A metadiscourse provision would democratize the process of halakhic discourse without compromising the distinctive features that constitute, according to the historian of halakhah David Ellenson, its major attraction for traditionalist progressives. Like feminists, this constituency is critical both of the content of halakhah and of its traditionally elite authority structure. What they value is "the framework of the halakhah, the dialectic between halakhic interpreter and text, and the implications this holds for the community."[76] These features of halakhic process provide boundaries for Jewish normative discourse. A metadiscourse provision would allow us to examine and renegotiate framework components, to reassess questions of textual authority and interpretation, and to reevaluate who are included in the definition of community. The result would be more flexible boundaries permitting a more inclusive and expansive halakhic discourse.

Opening up halakhic discourse will enable us to fulfill more deeply than ever before the first covenantal promise of the people Israel: *na'aseh v'nishma,* "we will do and we will listen" (Exod. 24:7). If *na'aseh,* "we will do," is a commitment to a communal praxis, it cannot be realized without the commitment *nishma,* "we will listen." To live out the commandments of God together we must listen not only to God but to one another as interpreters and transformers of Torah.

There are some ways however, in which Judaism is already far ahead of the liberal justice ethics critiqued by Benhabib. Our tradition has never regarded the good life as a matter of private preference. Instead of a thin fairness doled out to others we think resemble us and a mingy list of primary goods, our prophetic and legal traditions offer us narratively rooted understandings of *tzedek,* the justice that knows the heart of the stranger, and visions of the just society where harmony and wholeness flourish.

Backtalk: Feminist Objections to Law

Even though this project of engendering an inclusive contemporary halakhah incorporates a feminist critique and brings feminist tools and goals to its task, its legitimacy as a feminist undertaking may be challenged on two accounts. Both law and traditional narratives have been the subjects of powerful feminist critiques, characterizing them as patriarchal constructions and denying that these structures have anything to offer women. Both critiques derive from secular feminist thought and have been assimilated, in varying degrees, by Jewish and Christian feminisms.

An influential and widely debated assertion is that law is a modality foreign to women's thinking. Carol Gilligan's influential work on women's moral reasoning maintains that systems of abstract rules for governing behavior are both alien and irrelevant to women.[77] Gilligan postulates an ideal-typology of masculine and feminine ethical modes. She contends that in masculine ethics the categories of thought are hierarchical, and the central concern is to protect rights and boundaries, whereas in feminine ethics the world is experienced as a web of interconnecting relationships, and the central concern is to nurture these connections through responsible caring. In its most antinomian application, Gilligan's theory is utilized by the philosopher Nell Noddings in support of an ethics of caring.[78] This ethics rejects rules and laws, principles, and notions of justice in favor of the guidance of an ideal caring self. It is in the light of this ideal image of the caring self that conduct toward the other is evaluated.

This critique is not problematic for law-rejecting feminist sects such as Wicca,[79] nor for Christian feminists, since Christianity defines itself as a law-transcending religion. At worst, the critique has given rise to ugly anti-Judaic smears. Some Christians and goddess feminists have accused Judaism and its legal tradition of originating patriarchy.[80] Reviving an ancient anti-legal polemic, some Christian feminists have portrayed early Christianity as a feminist religion in contrast to misogynistic rabbinism.[81] At their best, feminist theologies have explained that Jewish feminism's emphasis on the reconstruction of law and ritual reflect distinctive Jewish concerns not shared by other religions.[82]

The halakhic concerns of feminist Jews, then, reflect crucial Jewish investments for which secular feminists and feminists of other faiths have no parallel and which they may even regard as incompatible with feminism. To maintain that the very concept of religious law, even reduced to a repertoire of selected practices, is incapable of addressing Jewish women requires, in effect, a rejection of covenant, a repudiation of what is central to Jewish tradition, and a denial of common ground with Jewish men. At the same time, because halakhah has been the major means by which Jewish women have been oppressed and marginalized, even the most traditional of feminist Jews approach it with a hermeneutics of suspicion that distinguishes them from the men in their Jewish communities.[83] Like Skotsl and her peers, feminist Jews agree that a halakhic system in which "the men get to do everything and the women get nothing at all" requires alteration. They disagree about the extent of the alteration and about how it is accomplished.

"In some very real ways," Blu Greenberg asserts, "halakhic parameters limit women's growth, both as Jews and as human beings."[84] Greenberg, the most optimistic and the most traditional of the feminist critics of halakhah, is a liberal halakhist, committed to liberal halakhah's blend of historicism and formalism. She believes that "the techniques for reinterpretation are built right into the system" and that a gradual social evolution toward egalitarianism will result in their implementation.[85]

Darker, more anguished questions are raised by Cynthia Ozick, who dares to examine the theological implications of the Torah's injustice toward women. By sanctioning women's subordination, she argues, the Torah conspires with the social context in which it was revealed to sacralize injustice. Alleviating the disabilities with which women are burdened by halakhah does not solve this problem. We still lack a sacred text proclaiming that the dehumanization always was and always will be evil.[86]

She asks, "Where is the Commandment that will say from the beginning of history until now, *Thou shalt not lessen the humanity of women?*"[87] Ozick's proposed solution is "a new Yavneh," a radical reconstruction of Jewish tradition like the reconstruction of biblical Judaism by rabbinic Judaism, which will read the full humanity of women into the Torah.[88] She does not elaborate, however, upon how or by whom this new Yavneh is to be established nor upon the structural implications for the entire halakhic system of establishing this single precept upholding the full humanity of women.

Of all the Jewish feminist theologians, it is Judith Plaskow who has confronted the feminist critique of law most explicitly.[89] She points out that the antinomian challenge of non-Jewish feminisms rests on two dubious propositions. First, to question whether law is a female form seems to presuppose that there is such a thing as an essential feminine nature that remains constant despite history and culture. Second, the tendency of the question is to regard law as an unnecessary masculine invention, rather than as a norm-defining function all human cultures share in common.

Yet Plaskow is profoundly ambivalent about halakhah. In her response to Cynthia Ozick, "The Right Question Is Theological," she argues that the Otherness of women is a defining feature of halakhah, which suggests that nothing about halakhah merits salvage or transformation.[90] In *Standing Again at Sinai*, however, she reconsiders halakhah, offering various stipulations for its reconstruction.[91] Because the categories of halakhah reflect exclusively male interests and perceptions, Plaskow emphasizes that an effective critique must be systemic. Moreover, any future community of lawmakers must include women, and they must co-determine with men both legal content and legal process. Nevertheless, Plaskow remains divided about the usefulness of any halakhic system. She sees halakhah as an enemy of charismatic spiritualities stressing spontaneity, fluidity, and sensitivity to human relationships. On the other hand, she acknowledges that feminist Jews also desire and create law, in the form of new communal norms concerning women's access to ritual roles, their equal legal entitlements in marriage, and their fitness as witnesses.

"Perhaps what distinguishes feminist Judaism from traditional rabbinic Judaism," Plaskow concludes, "is not so much the absence of law in the former as a conception of rule making as a shared communal process."[92] All that Plaskow lacks is a frame of reference in which she can identify this feminist lawmaking as the inception of a legitimate and authoritative halakhic process.[93] This is where the work of Robert Cover is so helpful. Not only for feminists, but for all moderns who cherish democratic values, lawmaking requires a communal component. Cover reminds us that all law, including rabbinic law itself, originates in a paidaic community. Its understandings as embodied and institutionalized in the law are revised and revitalized when they are challenged by interpretive communities claiming a place in it. That is how African-Americans such as Frederick Douglass could contend that the core values of the Constitution are not compatible with slavery.[94] Feminist Jews are forming precisely such an interpretive community within Judaism.

In contrast to Plaskow's discomfort with halakhah, Ellen Umansky, a feminist Reform theologian who draws upon the Reconstructionist thought of Mordecai Kaplan, views halakhah as an often authentic source of authority whose history and continuity as "a record of the Jewish experience of the divine" give it a claim upon us.[95] Umansky acknowledges halakhah's pervasive androcentric distortions, but she argues that they may be corrected by "a feminist lens." She advocates "retaining those teachings, indeed, those commandments, that address us—men and women—as God's chosen people."[96] The criterion Umansky appears to invoke here has been formulated most rigorously by Rosemary Radford Ruether as the critical principle of feminist theology.

> Whatever diminishes or denies the full humanity of women must be presumed not to reflect the divine or an authentic relation to the divine, or to reflect the authentic nature of things, or to be the message or work of an authentic community of redemption.[97]

In her analysis of feminist attitudes toward halakhah, Umansky polarizes the positions of non-Orthodox feminists who advocate systemic reconstruction of halakhah or innovate completely nonhalakhic Judaisms and those of Orthodox feminists, whom she portrays as advocating only the amelioration of particular laws. This account, however, obscures much more subtle gradations of similarities and differences among feminist Jews, which cannot be correlated merely with their denominational affiliations. For example, the traditionalist Cynthia Ozick specifically rejects the amelioration of specific halakhic injustices as a sufficient remedy. Her appeal for a new Yavneh can only mean a call for foundational halakhic change. Orthodox feminists as well as non-Orthodox ones innovate in areas traditional halakhah did not address. Their creation of a proliferating international network of women's prayer groups institutionalizing distinctive ceremonial differences from male Orthodox services is perfectly consonant with activities among the non-Orthodox feminist poets, midrashists, and ritual innovators Umansky characterizes as nonhalakhic.[98] Moreover, using Cover's framework, so-called nonhalakhic groups are more properly identified as incipient paidaic communities attempting to establish differing nomic visions. The norms they establish for living out the implications of the poems and stories they create will be a halakhah.

In any case, the fears feminist theologians express about the dangerous precedents for oppression in halakhah seem to be counterbalanced by an acknowledgment that halakhah also cannot be easily dismissed. Any authentic modern Jewish theology has to account for the norms and praxis of Judaism. Our task, then, is to engender a Jewish tradition for modernity that would inform and be informed by a diverse but unified communal praxis and an inclusive, pluralistic communal discourse rooted in Jewish narratives.

More Backtalk: The Critique of Narrative Traditions

Narrative traditions, however, are the focus of another strong feminist critique. Although narrative approaches have strong resonances for many feminist theologians and ethicists, some post-Christian and secular feminists argue that the androcentric bias of biblical or Greek narrative traditions invalidates theologies and ethics that draw upon them. This charge embraces the work of conservative ethicists such as Alasdair MacIntyre and Stanley Hauerwas who do not question traditional gender structures and of progressive ethicists such as Charles Taylor and Michael Walzer who acknowledge the presence of gender injustice in their sources and attempt to move beyond it.[99]

Feminists who take this position argue that traditional narratives cannot be reconstructed or redeemed, because they are predicated upon the subordination and exclusion of women. Elizabeth Say contends that narrative in Western civilization has functioned mainly to transmit and preserve the great patriarchal traditions and to legitimate a vision of community from which women are excluded.[100] Susan Moller Okin demonstrates compellingly how MacIntyre appropriates an Aristotelian vision of the good life that not only excludes women but requires their servitude to support it.[101] Without an inferior caste to whom maintenance and nurturance functions may be relegated, she notes, discussions of the good life are radically transformed.

Once "the good life" is really understood to mean the good *human*
life, it must be seen to encompass vast aspects of life that are not considered even a part of the subject matter of an ethics that still rests
on sexist and elitist assumptions. It must, in the absence of slaves
and largely dehumanized workers, discuss how the products and services necessary for human life can be provided in the context of the
good life. Likewise, with women not functionally defined by their
biology, the raising of children to the point where, and in a way that,
they will be able to lead good lives becomes itself necessarily a part of
discussion of the good life.[102]

From any feminist perspective, MacIntyre's use of the classical Greek
and Christian traditions disadvantages women. The question is whether
these traditions (or that of Judaism or Islam, for example) are inherently
incapable of gender justice. MacIntyre himself would deny that merely
because traditions have historically excluded women, they are incapable of
including them. Because traditions are fluid and multivocal, he contends
that "when a tradition is in good order it is always partially constituted by
an argument about the goods, the pursuit of which gives to that tradition
its particular point and purpose."[103] To deny that the good of women *could*
be addressed, one would have to argue, as do the feminist critics of narrative traditions, that the good of women is inimical to the goods and purposes valued by the tradition.[104] One would have to claim about Judaism, for
example, that patriarchy is one of its constitutive goods, and that the full
humanity of women is not discussible because it is inimical to Judaism's
core values. Feminists committed to these faith traditions would deny that
the dehumanization of women is an integral and unalterable element in
them. Like MacIntyre, they would maintain that traditions are capable of
fluidity and can admit diverse perspectives, but they would contend that
traditions whose conversations exclude the voices of women regarding
their own good cannot be said to be "in good order."

As this chapter itself demonstrates, feminists who view themselves as
participants in traditions are willing to go to considerable trouble to join
the conversation and put the tradition into good order. Feminist critics of
tradition see this as a pointless enterprise. How, they ask, can women justify any investment in traditions written and formulated to dispossess
them? Instead, both Say and Okin recommend allegiance to women's traditions. Say, following post-Christian theologians such as Carol Christ,
presents women's literature as a textual tradition and a source of spiritual
illumination more appropriate to women than classical narratives.[105] Okin

also contends that feminism is a tradition. For Okin, however, feminism is a political and philosophical tradition, rather than a literary and spiritual one. By tradition she means, not a body of texts but "a living argument," although the participants in that argument are known to her through a great range of texts, from Wollstonecraft to Choderow, spanning nearly two centuries.[106]

But a tradition cannot be reduced to a shelf of books or an argument. It is a way groups of people live out stories and arguments in relationships, in ritual, in play, in work, and in love. Feminist adherents to traditional faiths and feminists of color may question this bland assumption that gender, all by itself, can provide a tradition, a language, a basis for shared understandings that transcends and replaces the bonds of religious and cultural heritages preserved in collective memories and etched into our lullabies and feasts, our jokes and curses and ancient sorrows. The feminist tradition by which other traditions and loyalties are to be replaced is, in fact, the hegemonic feminism of white, middle-class, liberal, secularist women, reproducing the same contempt for difference that characterizes their male counterparts. Audre Lorde cries out against it in her reproach to Mary Daly: "I am used to having my archetypal experience distorted and trivialized, but it is terribly painful to feel it being done by a woman whose knowledge so much touches my own."[107] As a Jew, I ask, what is it that should impel me to turn away from the seder table saying, "That has nothing to do with me," and say instead to Mary Wollstonecraft and Doris Lessing, "You are my people and my heritage"?

Feminist Jews, like other minority feminists, live with multiple loyalties that are difficult to reconcile and impossible to relinquish. We have refused to disavow the sacred stories of Jewish tradition, to cease to converse with them or attempt to appropriate them. We have refused to reject summarily elements of our practice that other feminist theologians regard as patriarchal and dichotomizing: our sense of distinctness as a people, for example, or religious behavior affirming separation such as kashrut, Shabbat or *havdalah*.[108] At the same time, we have confronted resolutely the fact that the tradition in which we are fighting to take our place has been dominated and shaped by men and for men. There are meanings and experiences we share with participants in other traditions and cultures and some that are ours alone. But that is true of most lives in diverse, pluralistic societies. We inhabit not one, but many intersecting spheres.[109] Simplistic accounts of traditions and loyalties not only divide us, they mutilate us; as the Chicano feminist Gloria Anzaldua charges, "They would chop me up into little fragments and tag each piece with a label."[110]

Talking Our Way In

We now find ourselves in the ironic position of having fought mightily to justify our attempts to converse with a tradition that has not, as yet, evinced a desire to converse with us. Like the women who built themselves into a human tower, having worked so hard to arrange the conversation, we now have to figure out how to begin it. What should Skotsl say when she pulls herself into heaven? Perhaps the folktale leaves her at the point when she is pulling herself in because that is the part of the story the storytellers cannot yet imagine. But if we are to extend the story, we will have to imagine it, and in order to do so we will once more draw upon the legal hermeneutics of Robert Cover. His advice to Skotsl would be to tell stories about law.

The task requires a skillful speaker, but it is by no means impossible. However primitive their attempts and however incomplete their story, Skotsl and her peers have a sense of legal purpose. Skotsl does not go up to heaven empty and helpless. She has been sent with a message. Implicit in the message is a different vision of what halakhah should be. If, as Cover contends, this implicit vision must be made explicit in narrative, then, ironically, Skotsl will have to do in heaven exactly what she would have had to do on earth: delineate and defend her vision by telling stories.

As the messiah dispatched from earth, she must bring revelations to heaven, disclosing stories unknown to the tradition, the stories of its female claimants. It is equally important, however, that Skotsl tell the tradition its own stories in a new way. The alternative tradition she presents must assert its authenticity by grounding itself in narratives the tradition believes it owns and understands. Out of the multipotentiality of those narratives, she must draw meanings that contest the tradition's legal meanings. She must make the law her accomplice in its own destabilization.

The subversive potential in law's foundational narratives renders it vulnerable at its root. "Every legal order," Cover observes, "must conceive of itself as emerging out of that which is itself unlawful."[111] An obvious example is the American legal system, which is grounded in a colonial rebellion against the authority of the British crown. The narratives of transgression upon which legal systems are founded, Cover argues, remain potentially lawless because they are precedents both for law and for the transgression of law. Consequently, there is always the threat that they may burst their restraints and challenge the very systems they authorize.[112] A feminist could note how many of these foundational transgressions are violations of patriarchal sexual boundaries. Tamar tricks her father-in-law Judah to free herself from a levirate limbo. David's son born from his tainted relationship with Bathsheba is his chosen heir. Hosea's God, violating all legal precedent, promises to reconcile with His promiscuous mate. A Skotsl challenging traditional halakhah's attitudes regarding sexuality and relationship could argue that its code, applied to the narratives that ground it, would delegitimate the people Israel and abrogate their covenant.

Even without reference to foundational stories, law can be made to abet its own critique, Cover argues, because its dependence upon narrative as a component inherently divides law against itself. The alliance binding legal precepts designed to control to uncontrollable narratives upon which their legitimation depends is inherently unstable:

> There is a radical dichotomy between the social organization of law as power and the organization of law as meaning. . . . The uncontrolled character of meaning exercises a destabilizing influence upon power. Precepts must "have meaning," but they must necessarily borrow it from materials created by social activity that is not subject to the strictures of provenance that characterize what we call formal lawmaking.[113]

Raw coercion is insufficient to authorize law. It must claim legitimating moral qualities, which it locates in its constitutive narratives. But narratives are generated within the bounds of space, time, and culture. Their resonances echo within these social contexts, always unstable, always open to the possibility of transformation.[114] This circumstance alone destabilizes the meanings upon which law relies. In addition, the multiple layers of meaning, the ambiguities and contradictions of sacred narratives, cannot be contained by systems of precept. Consequently, it is always possible that the meaning-component upon which law depends will rise to accuse it, and that the thickness[115] of its narratives will enable interpretations that will call into question its favored interpretations.

If law is constitutionally vulnerable to re-vision and reinterpretation because it depends on narrative, the obvious next step for potential revisors is to examine just how narratives can upset the legal enterprises within which they are enshrined. Cover refers to "sacred narratives of jurisdiction that . . . ground judicial commitments."[116] By the same token, however, some narratives may ground critiques and re-visions of judicial commitments. By retelling these narratives, we can destabilize the accepted meanings of law. Skotsl's gambit could be to retell and reinterpret stories like these.

Two good candidates for Skotsl's purposes are provocative narratives about the woman the rabbis love to hate, Yalta, the wife of R. Naḥman, the aristocratic and wealthy daughter of the Exilarch R. Huna.[117] Let us see how a feminist Jew could read these as destabilizing narratives concerning women and the making of halakhah and use them to claim an alternative hermeneutic for reading the tradition's texts.

> Ulla once happened to be a guest at R. Naḥman's house. He ate a meal, led the grace after meals, and passed the cup of blessing to R. Naḥman. R. Naḥman said to him, "Please pass the cup of blessing *[kasa d'virkhata]* to Yalta, sir." He replied, "This is what R. Yoḥanan said: 'The issue of a woman's belly *[bitna]* is blessed only through the issue of a man's belly *[bitno]*,' as the Bible says, 'He will bless the issue of your [masc. sing.] belly *[p'ri bitnkha]*' (Deut. 7:13). It does not say 'her belly' but 'your belly.' "
>
> So too a *baraita* [an earlier Tannaitic text] teaches: R. Natan said: "Where is the prooftext in Scripture that the issue of a woman's belly is blessed only through the issue of a man's belly? As the Bible says, 'He will bless the issue of your [masc. sing.] belly *[p'ri bitnkha]*.' It does not say 'her belly' but 'your belly.' "
>
> When Yalta heard this, she got up in venomous anger *[zihara]*, went to the wine storeroom and smashed four hundred jars of wine. R. Naḥman said to Ulla, "Please send her another cup." He sent [it to her with the message]: "All of this is a goblet of blessing *[navga d'virkhata]*." She sent [in reply]: "From travelers come tall tales and from ragpickers lice."[118]

At first glance, the story is bewildering. What is the meaning of the scene at the table? What is the point of Ulla's prooftexts, and why is Yalta so offended? Traditional interpreters read this as a story about a man who insults his host by refusing to follow the custom of the household, incurring the enmity of his spoiled and arrogant hostess.[119]

This story occurs in a chapter of Talmud concerning with the collective recitation of grace after meals. If three or more have eaten together, one calls the others to prayer and leads the blessing. Women's participation is a controversial issue. It is quickly established that women may not be counted in the quorum of three. But may they call other women or slaves to a collective grace? How may they participate if they are at the table with men?

Our text follows a talmudic discussion enumerating ten rules about the cup of blessing over which the master of the house or an honored guest recites the grace after meals. The tenth rule directs, "He sends it around to the members of his household as a gift, so that his household will be blessed." Juxtaposed to this teaching is this story in which Ulla withholds the cup from his hostess.

The exegeses Ulla quotes, first from his teacher, Yohanan b. Nappaha, and then from an earlier tannaitic source, appear at first to be theological rather than legal. They do not mention the cup of blessing, much less conclude that it may not be passed to women. But when the legal scholar Ulla cites them to justify his act, they acquire a practical legal application. Ulla uses his sources to argue that women may be excluded solely on the basis of biological inferiority, even in a case where the law has not specifically mandated their exclusion.

What is at issue, according to Ulla, is what the cup of blessing means. He produces a biblical prooftext that seems implicitly to define blessing as fertility. The recipient of blessing in this prooftext is a masculine singular "you." Hence, Ulla maintains, the Bible itself asserts that fertility belongs exclusively to men:

> He will favor you [masc. sing.] and bless you [masc. sing.] and multiply you [masc. sing.]: He will bless the issue of your [masc. sing.] womb *[p'ri bitnkha]* and the produce of your [masc. sing.] soil, your [masc. sing] new grain and wine and oil; the calving of your [masc. sing.] herd and the lambing of your [masc. sing.] flock in the land He swore to your fathers to assign to you. (Deut. 7:13)

Ulla and his rabbinic sources use this prooftext to assert that the primary actor in human fertility is the male, whereas the woman's role is only secondary and derivative.[120] If men are the ultimate source of the blessing of fertility, then the cup of blessing may be said to rest exclusively in their domain, and women can have only indirect access to it. In Ulla's biological metaphor, male potency is conflated both with spiritual blessing and with social dominance. By analogy, just as women cannot be fertile through any act of their own, so too they cannot be blessed through any act of their own but only through the agency of men acting for and upon them.

Ulla's biological interpretation strips the cup of its nuances. For in the original ten rules text, the cup's blessing is linked to a variety of spiritual and material blessings. Ulla reduces the meaning of blessing to fertility alone, just as he reduces the multivocal symbolism of the cup to a single symbolic representation: the womb, the human receptacle into which a sanctifiable liquid is poured, resulting in the blessing of fertility. Similarly, Ulla narrows the meaning of the ceremony of passing of the cup. The inclusive version of the ceremony affirms that everyone present at the table is a recipient of God's bounty and a petitioner for future blessings. In Ulla's ritual, however, women may only watch while men pass the blessing to other men. Ulla's reformulation symbolically enacts not the universal sharing of God's abundance but the transferal of ownership over wombs from patriarch to patriarch.[121]

Clearly Ulla's custom is unknown to R. Naḥman. Since a version of the custom exists that does not exclude women, we may wonder why Ulla insists upon imposing his own custom at his host's table and why he defends it at such length. Why, in other words, is he bent upon reducing his hostess to a womb? Perhaps he is compensating for other disparities. Yalta, daughter of the fabulously wealthy leader of the Jews of Babylonia, is Ulla's superior both in affluence and in lineage. The only thing Ulla has that Yalta does not is that appendage around which he and his sources have been creating a justificatory structure. Small wonder that Yalta heads for the wine storage to preempt Ulla four hundred times, shattering the containers and spilling out the sanctifiable liquid whose blessing Ulla has reserved for men alone.

In the final incident of the story, Ulla, urged by R. Naḥman, sends Yalta another cup with the message "All this is a goblet *[navga]* of blessing," which Rashi paraphrases: "all the wine in the pitcher is like a cup of blessing; drink from it." Yalta, daughter of a scholarly family, recognizes this as chicanery. Ulla betrays the lesser holiness of this cup by terminology that is never used in any other context to signify the cup of blessing, an Aramaic word not cognate with the Hebrew *kos*. A *navga* of blessing bears the same resemblance to a *kasa* of blessing as a "holy cabinet" does to a "holy ark." It is the same object with the mystery of sanctity removed from it.

Decoding this manipulation just as she had decoded the original insult, Yalta mocks its perpetrator: Ulla, the traveler between the Palestinian and Babylonian academies, must be telling her a traveler's tall tale! She flings his insult back in his face, declaring that it is Ulla himself who is disgusting. His offer of wine from the unsanctified pitcher is like a beggar offering his lice, a worthless and repulsive gift from a giver with nothing to give.

For the engenderer of law, this is a story about law as power. Ulla, a traveling rabbi unremarkable for wealth or ancestry, is able to humiliate an affluent and clever aristocrat because he is a member of the exclusively male group that shapes and enforces laws, a group Yalta is ineligible to join. This single advantage trumps all Yalta's advantages of birth, wealth, learning, and wit. Without it, she may as well be a verminous beggar. Even in her own house, she can be placed at the mercy of Ulla's (and her husband's) dubious alms.

But, while Yalta cannot shape law-as-power, she can challenge law-as-meaning. As a destabilizer of law, she exposes its hidden meanings and debunks its mystifications. Rather than accept her exclusion quietly, she chooses to make the ceremony impossible for everyone. We are told what "blessing" means both for the writers of the ten rules text and for Ulla. We do not know what Yalta understands the blessing to be, because that was of no interest to the text's transmitters. But we know that she wanted to drink from the cup of blessing herself, and that she knew a phony cup of blessing when she saw one.

In the previous narrative, Yalta was the victim of legal chicanery; in another story from a different tractate, Yalta turns the tables on the rabbis. In this story, Yalta asks for a rabbinic decision about whether the vaginal secretion that has stained her garment is to be considered menstruous. The rabbi, using prescribed tests and descriptions, must rule whether or not the spot is uterine blood and consequently whether the woman from whom it came is pure or impure. If impure, she is subject to the restrictions upon conjugal sex and intimate contact incumbent upon menstruants.

> Yalta brought blood to Rabbah b. Bar Ḥana, and he ruled that it was impure. Then she turned around and brought it to R. Yitzḥak b. R. Yehudah, and he ruled that it was pure. How could he do such a thing when a *baraita* [an earlier tannaitic text] teaches: "If a sage ruled it impure, his colleague is not permitted to rule it pure. If he ruled it forbidden, the colleague may not rule it permitted"? At first, [R. Yitzḥak] ruled that it was impure. When she told him, "Every other time [Rabbah] has ruled for me that [blood] just like this was pure, and today he has a pain in his eye," R. Yitzḥak then ruled it pure.[122]

The first unusual element in the story is that it presents the woman not merely as an object in a legal problem, but as a person with her own investment in the decision and its consequences. The story reveals to us her desire not to be declared a menstruant. The first judge renders a disappointing decision: Yalta's blood is ruled impure. Since rabbinic law lacks an appellate court, Yalta resourcefully sets up her own. She seeks out the second opinion, which the *baraita* wishes to forbid because it undermines the solidarity of the judges. In justification, she explains demurely that the first judge was temporarily incompetent to deliver an accurate opinion.

There are two ways of reading the narrative, one of which is considerably less destabilizing than the other. One could argue that Yalta is merely asking for accurate assessment of evidence and consistency in judgment; her evidence has been misassessed, because of the judge's indisposition. Consequently, his ruling must be considered inconsistent with other rulings on the same evidence and therefore arbitrary and unjust. This reading affirms the system's rules and categories and the proper positions of judge and judged within them. It portrays Yalta's recourse to a second authority as an exceptional response to unusual circumstances and hence a poor basis for a precedent. This would be the tradition's preferred reading of the story.

But a darker, more ironic reading results if we assume that Yalta's account of Rabbah Bar Ḥana's judicial record and indisposition is a calculated attempt to manipulate the system and that her motivation for turning to a second judge is not an intellectual distaste for legal inconsistency but a desire to avoid the stigma of impurity. That is how we would read this story if we regarded it as "a folktale of justice"[123] and viewed Yalta as the trickster in the tale, the folkloric prankster who incarnates and unmasks what is arbitrary, chaotic, or unjust in our universe.[124]

Traditionally, tricksters are disreputable types. Zestfully pursuing their con games and dirty deals, they expose to public derision a world with its pants down, where authority is not really just, wisdom is not really wise, and there's no percentage in playing by the rules. In the trickster's laughter, then, there is an implicit social critique. When the pretensions of the powerful to justice and purity are deflated, the legitimacy of their human authority is called into question. At that moment, the rules are up for grabs.

As a distinctively rabbinic trickster, Yalta is a kind of legal guerrilla.

She exposes the hidden relativity of the law and the hidden fallibility of its interpreters. The purportedly divine Torah must be translated into human authority. The *baraita* seeks to protect rabbinic authority and its appearance of objectivity through a policy of judicial solidarity. But as soon as Yalta can expose dissent beneath this solidarity, she demonstrates that authority is not infallible; two disagreeing authorities cannot both be right.

If authority is divisible, it is potentially manipulable. If it is fallible, it is open to critique. If authority is human, it is vulnerable; if the judge's human pain may distort his judgment, perhaps his particular human perspective may also skew his rulings. The authority passing judgment on women's blood, Yalta slyly suggests, has a pain in its eye, and that is why it mistakenly rules that blood impure.

Yalta's legal guerrilla tactics are predicated upon her skepticism that the authorities are dispensing justice. A legal realist could argue that the law is whatever a duly appointed authority says it is, and indeed, this appears to be the position of the *baraita*. A legal formalist could argue that whether the blood was declared pure or impure is immaterial. The decision is valid as long as the jurist used the system's processual rules and content categories in a defensible way. Yalta reminds us that what grounds authority is power, and power has social investments. Power can use authority to include and empower broadly. But power can also exercise authority to stigmatize, to subordinate, and to exclude. Yalta as legal guerrilla strips away the mask of justice, revealing the cruel face beneath.

Skotsl as legal guerrilla retells Yalta's stories. Applying her feminist hermeneutic, she finds a mirror within the story and holds this mirror up to the tradition's face. The purpose of a feminist Jewish hermeneutic is not to reject either text or law but to seek ways of claiming them and living them out with integrity. It keeps faith with texts by refusing to absolve them of moral responsibility. It honors halakhah by affirming its inexhaustible capacity to be created anew.

By renewing halakhah we bridge the gap between the impoverished world of meaning we currently inhabit and the richer and more vital worlds that might be. Our mission, like Skotsl's, is to make connections where there has been a rift, to make conversation where there has been silence, to engender a new world.

Engendering Judaism, like other kinds of human engendering, is a project that women and men must undertake together. We must converse, tell stories, play, and know one another if we are finally to inhabit a single *nomos* as partners and friends.[125] Together we can regenerate a world of legal meaning that fully, complexly, and inclusively integrates the stories and revelations, the duties and commitments of Jewish women and men. Then, when Skotsl returns, we can welcome her together. "Come on," we'll tell her, "we have a bridge we want to show you."

Chapter 3
And Not Be Silent: Toward Inclusive Worship

A talmudic story attributed to Rabbi Yehoshua ben Levi (B. Yoma 69b) deals with liturgical change and restoration:

> Rabbi Yehoshua ben Levi said, "Why were they called members of the *Great* Assembly?[1] Because they restored the divine crown to its ancient wholeness. For Moses came and said, 'great, mighty and awesome God' (Deut. 10:17). But then came Jeremiah who said, 'if strangers are destroying his temple, where is his awesomeness?' so [in his prayer (Jer. 32:17)] he omitted the attribute 'awesome' [and said, 'great and mighty God']. Then came Daniel, who said, 'if strangers are enslaving his children, where is his might?' So [in his prayer (Dan. 9:4)] he omitted the attribute 'mighty' [and said, 'great and awesome God']. Then came the members of the Great Assembly who said, 'on the contrary! This shows his might: that he restrains his anger and is patient with evildoers. And this shows his awesomeness: if it were not for the awe of him, how could a distinctive nation survive in the midst of other nations?'"

The text goes on to ask what could pass as a halakhic question: How was it permissible for Jeremiah and Daniel to abolish God-language established by Moses? Rabbi Eliezer explains, "since they knew that the Holy One is truthful *(amitti)*, they would not lie to him."[2]

I want to juxtapose to this story another told by Rabbi Laura Geller.

> One day when I sat in a class in my Rabbinical seminary . . . we studied the tradition of *berakhot*—blessings, blessings of enjoyment, blessings relating to the performance of mizvot (commandments) and blessings of praise and thanksgiving. My teacher explained . . . "There is no important moment in the lifetime of a Jew for which there is no blessing." Suddenly I realized that it was not true. There had been important moments in my life for which there was no blessing. One such moment was when I . . . first got my period.[3]

Both passages I have quoted presume that words we say to God are grounded in our personal integrity. A prayer that belies or misrepresents our experience or understandings violates integrity and insults God. In the first story of the Great Assembly, a legendary Sanhedrin from the time of Ezra rebuts the objections raised by Jeremiah and Daniel by reframing the meanings of the disputed divine attributes. In the light of new experiences of exile and restoration, God's might is understood more darkly, more ambivalently than before: it is the power to refrain from meeting human violence with violence, even when God's own people are victimized. God's awesomeness is now attested by Israel's endurance, despite the voracity of empires and the assimilatory pressures of exile. God is still to be addressed as "great, mighty and awesome," but that no longer means what Moses meant by it.

In the second story, reframing a canonized terminology is not an option. No canonical language exists for the experiences Geller seeks to acknowledge, because they are outside the experience of the people by whom and for whom canonical prayer was framed. By the standards of the canon, Geller's experiences are aberrant and unimportant.

Geller's story depicts a paradoxical situation. She appears to be a full participant in an egalitarian Judaism. She is even a rabbinical student. But her internal experience is of exclusion: vital components of her personhood have been ignored. What is more, her invisibility is invisible. Her teacher and her male classmates do not know that they do not see her.

What, then, does it mean to include women in prayer? For the past two hundred years, men and women professing liberal Judaisms have slowly been learning what is entailed. At the Hamburg Temple in 1818, inclusion meant allowing women's voices to be heard in the choir.[4] At Isaac Mayer Wise's congregation in 1851, it meant relocating women from the peripheralized women's gallery to "the family pew," alongside their male relatives.[5] For Mordecai Kaplan in 1922, it meant instituting for his own daughter a bat mitzvah ceremony analogous to the ceremonies for American Jewish boys.[6] For the Reform, Reconstructionist, and Conservative Judaisms of the 1970s and 1980s, it meant beginning to ordain women as rabbis. For many Conservative congregations, counting women in the minyan and calling them up to the Torah are recent innovations. But as Geller's story suggests, egalitarian Judaisms may integrate women as participants by ignoring their distinctive experiences and concerns as women.

It has been argued that early Reform Judaism began this process.[7] Obedient to the tenets of Enlightenment universalism, it abolished the rules that excluded women and instead subsumed women within the congregation as "honorary men." Deprived both of the Orthodox practices that had distinguished them as women and of the education and leadership opportunities still reserved for men, women in liberal Judaisms became even more invisible than they had been before.

In fact, the primary motivation for integrating women into the male congregation was not a sense of justice but a desire for a more "Western," more seemly synagogue decorum. Milton Himmelfarb transparently expresses this motive.

> In my wanderings I have discovered an argument, new to me, against the Orthodox segregation of the sexes. It is still true that when women sit by themselves they talk, and in *shul* they have to be shushed. . . . When . . . *dispersed among the men* [italics mine], the same women seem to talk less. . . . After one deafening Sabbath morning . . . I could appreciate the answer of the great Rabbi Israel Salanter . . . when he was asked what should be done with some bricks left over from repair work on a synagogue: "Use them to wall up the entrance to the women's gallery." In a way, that is what Conservative and Reform Judaism have done.[8]

Why do women talk in *shul*? *Why* do they seem so uninvested in the service? Such questions do not interest Himmelfarb. His problem is easily solved by dispersing the disrupters, the way naughty children are separated from each other in an orderly classroom. The message conveyed by the women in the gallery need not be addressed: it need only be suppressed.

Real inclusion can occur only when women cease to be invisible as women. It will not suffice for progressive Judaisms merely to make good on their promise to treat honorary men like real ones. Adrienne Rich explains compellingly why invisibility is so devastating and what is required to resist it.

> When someone with the authority of a teacher, say, describes the world and you are not in it, there is a moment of psychic disequilibrium, as if you looked into a mirror and saw nothing. . . . It takes some strength of soul—not just individual strength but collective understanding—to resist this void, this non-being, into which you are thrust and to stand up demanding to be seen and heard . . . to make yourself visible, to claim that your experience is just as real and normative as any other.[9]

It is not only in the women's gallery, then, that women are invisible. And it is not only at the Western Wall that, after six years of court battles, women must still pray in silence.[10] Including women in prayer requires including not only their bodies but their prayers. When congregations pray only prayers written exclusively by men for men, prayers that invoke forefathers but never foremothers, prayers that address the God whose image both women and men are said to bear in exclusively masculine forms and metaphors, prayers that express only the hopes of men, prayers that confess only the sins of men, then women are both invisible and silent.[11]

Hannah: Rabbinic Exemplar of *Kavvanah*

To pray without being fully present is highly problematic for rabbinic Judaism. A recurring talmudic controversy rages about the extent to which commandments in general and prayer in particular require *kavvanah*, the intentionality and attention with which a fully aware and situated self orients itself toward God and performs a holy act.[12] *Kavvanah* is both internally and externally manifested. It is both a proper frame of mind and a proper demeanor.

The biblical narrative that exemplifies for the rabbis the *kavvanah* with which their own liturgy ought to be prayed occurs in the first chapter of 1 Samuel. Surprisingly, this paradigmatic prayer is articulated by a woman. Hannah, a pilgrim at the Shilo sanctuary, prays there silently and desperately for a child. The High Priest Eli scolds her, mistaking her voiceless prayer for the ravings of a drunk. "No my lord," she replies. "I am a tormented woman. I have drunk no wine or other strong drink, but I have been pouring out my heart to God." Reproved, Eli blesses her. God answers Hannah's prayer and she becomes the mother of the prophet Samuel.

It is this story that the rabbis of the Talmud select to illustrate the laws of the *Amidah*, which they call *ha-tefillah*, the Prayer.[13] But why *this* story? Why should Hannah be acclaimed as the originator of prayer when she is not the first character in the Bible either to entreat or to thank God? It is because only the Hannah narrative addresses the particular concerns of the rabbis about the nature and authenticity of rabbinic prayer. This narrative is the only instance recorded in the Bible in which a private individual prays in a sanctuary where sacrifices are offered. As such, it affirms for rabbinic Judaism its own continuity with tradition, the continuity between prayer and sacrifice, ritual word and ritual deed, between the synagogue liturgies and the ancient rites of Tabernacle and Temple.

In the person of Hannah confronting the High Priest Eli, moreover, rabbinic Judaism confronts the Judaism of the Temple cult. To the imagined priestly challenge "Do you call this unprecedented behavior worship? Isn't this sacrilege?" rabbinic Judaism responds with its exegesis on Hannah's defiant "No, my lord." "Ulla or, as some say, R. Yose ben Ḥanina, said, 'You are no lord [no authority] in this matter and the holy spirit does not rest upon you'" (B. Berakhot 31b).

Yet after deriving so many norms about the spirit and decorum of communal prayer from the private prayer of Hannah, no rabbinic exegete attempts to draw the logical conclusion that women ought to be included in communal prayer. Although the interpreters can all imagine themselves as Hannah, they cannot see the Hannahs all around them.

Women's liturgical invisibility has persisted throughout many centuries of liturgical development. However radically Judaism has changed, and however radically its prayerbooks have changed, one requirement that never altered was that women temporarily abandon the selves they really are in order to pray in the words of the community, that they fundamentally disorient themselves in order to orient their hearts. Now, faced with new demands for inclusive liturgy, the traditional guardians of the prayerbooks are perplexed. Like Laura Geller's missing blessing, some of the unprecedented concerns that women bring to prayer cannot be incorporated simply through reframing. The prayers for articulating them must be newly created. Proposed new texts and modes of prayer may break existing rules or undermine existing texts and customs. When the scandalized guardians of established prayer exclaim, "Do you call this unprecedented behavior worship?" the challengers may well give the traditional reply, "You are no authority in this matter and the holy spirit does not rest upon you."

Prerequisite to the project of remaking liturgy is a recognition that the language of prayerbooks is indeed masculine. This point is often opaque to the compilers and users of prayerbooks. Some argue that masculine language is generic, that "mankind," includes women by extension, "God of our fathers," can be broadly construed as "God of our ancestors." Others argue that masculine gender in prayer is conventional, and abstract.[14] It is the addition of feminine language that would sexualize God and thus be blasphemous. Masculine imagery, they say, is not really masculine, because it is not to be taken literally, as if metaphor served to empty language of meaning instead of intensifying its meanings. Yet the God who is depicted as wronged husband, pastoral lover, judge, father, and king certainly has both gender and sexuality. As the comparative religion scholar Rita Gross wryly notes, "God has been exalted above female sexuality only."[15] If women and men made prayerbooks together, we would affirm that our maleness or femaleness is a vital component of the self we bring to worship. At the same time, we would constantly be reminded that attributing gender to God is metaphoric and not literal.

The irony is that the process by which androcentric prayerbooks normalize masculinity as a sacred metaphor is invisible to their male makers and users. The cultural anthropologist Renato Rosaldo describes how dominant groups can become vividly aware of the differences and exotic cultural content of minorities, while viewing themselves as cultureless, detached, and neutral.[16] What they have hidden from themselves is their own institutional power. That is what makes their culture seem not to be a culture but simply part of ordinary reality. Ironically, it is not only the oppressed who look into the mirror and do not see their own reflection. If men and women were to share the institutional power to make prayerbooks, in the process we would become fully visible not only to one another but to ourselves.

Three Tasks for the Making of Inclusive Liturgy

What would have to happen for liturgies to become fully inclusive of women as well as men? First of all, we would have to acknowledge women as well as men as members of the praying community. Classical Judaism, along with counting only men in the community of worshippers, based its liturgies exclusively on stories about male ancestors and described the people Israel as if all of them were male. Women's inclusion would necessitate supplying the missing ancestral memories, the missing language about the people Israel, and the missing human experiences about which prayer speaks. Second, we would have to involve women along with men in the creation and transformation of the prayers and in the compilation of the liturgies that all of us will recite together.

Third, in order to begin to create truly inclusive worship, we would have to acknowledge the extent to which our current services reflect masculine sensibilities, styles, and gestures and androcentric language and theologies. We would have to admit that the exclusively masculine language with which we currently refer to God is a metaphoric language that has been *totalized*. That is, selected metaphors have been taken to represent the totality of the God toward whom they point. Such an understanding is, at the least, inadequate and distortive. To correct this totalization, we would have to enrich and diversify the language in our present prayer-

66

books with feminine forms and imagery. But substituting words is not enough. We would have to make room for new genres, new gestures, new styles of prayer. This third task is complicated by so many considerations—theological, anthropological, psychological, and aesthetic—that it is really incommensurate with the other two. Its complexities are sorted out in a separate discussion further on, but first we need to consider (and reject) some easier answers before we enter that thicket.

History as a Source for Women's Prayers

Even if we agree that both women and men ought to be fully present in the texts and contexts of communal prayer and that some prayers and ritual events ought to articulate spiritual concerns and longings distinctive to women, how is this to be accomplished? Are there any precedents for such participation or for such prayers? One suggestion has been to turn to Jewish history and ethnography to uncover and rediscover previously ignored or misinterpreted evidence of women's rituals and prayer activities.

Rabbinic texts present an idealized portrait of the study house *(beit midrash)* and the synagogue as men's turf, although it is difficult to determine whether these texts reflect reality or rabbinic fantasy. In some synagogues of the talmudic period, however, persuasive evidence exists that women were there. Bernadette Brooten, historian of the ancient synagogue, cites a dozen inscriptions from various nonrabbinite synagogues[17] from Italy to North Africa referring to women as "Head of the Synagogue."[18] How did people pray in such synagogues? What did they say? We do not know.

The canonical prayers that have been transmitted, however, are not the only forms of spiritual expression that ever existed in Judaism. They are just the forms endorsed by officialdom, recorded and formally transmitted. The problem is not that women never engaged in spiritual expression in Judaism, but that their expressions generally went unrecognized and unpreserved. Lawrence Hoffman illustrates this point with a wonderful metaphor:

> Imagine a continuum of spiritual behavior, with the normative men's prayers at one end. The official Jewish record of spiritual striving, that is the rabbinic literary corpus, records only that end of the spectrum. But the rules largely prohibit women from operating there. . . . On the other hand, the more they agree to behave only at the other end of the line, the more their behavior escapes detection. It is as if women walked through history carrying spiritual flashlights from which there emanated only infrared wavelengths, in a world where

an automatic light detector recorded only ultraviolet. Whenever the flashlight threatened to reach the ultraviolet spectrum, it was deemed as malfunctioning and taken away by the light keepers in charge of ultraviolet transmitters. Meanwhile, a detached observer of social behavior in general would record (from time to time) traces of infrared radiation; but having defined light according to the other end of the spectrum, it would never occur to anyone to call it light, record it in detail and treat it seriously.[19]

Clearly, one project for the recovery of Jewish women's obliterated memory is to scrutinize historical records and ethnographies for Hoffman's "infrared radiation": ignored or mislabeled religious and ritual behavior.[20] But there is no guarantee we will want to reappropriate what we find. For instance, as Laura Geller notes, there is a ritual gesture commemorating first menstruation among Ashkenazic women. Upon announcing her menstruation, the girl is slapped across the face.[21] The gesture may be an authentic example of women's folk religion, but do we want to inflict it upon our daughters in the name of tradition?

Another example of rediscoveries that augment our historical record is that of the Yiddish *tkhines*, prayers written for and perhaps sometimes by women during the sixteenth through nineteenth centuries. Scholars of the elite tradition look down their noses at the *tkhines*, but Chava Weissler, who pioneered research in this area, argues that this literature is as worthy of attention as classical sources.[22] Having so little information about women's lives, we cannot afford to disdain sources that they actually used and that reflect some of their social realities.[23] What may be interesting as history or anthropology, however, may not be usable as prayer. Many of the *tkhines* only reflect and reinforce a Judaism in which women are subordinate to men. For example, one *tkhine* quoted by Weissler uses the language of *tzidduk ha-din*, the justification of God's justice, in linking childbirth and menstruation to the punishment of Eve. The *tkhine* declares, "I have had my period with a heavy heart and with sadness, and I thank your Holy Name and your judgment, and I have received it with great love . . . as a punishment."[24]

If women were impervious to historical and cultural change, rediscovering prayers of Jewish women in the past would suffice to furnish us with a repertoire of prayers for the present. However, the ruptures and discontinuities between premodern and modern experiences and sensibilities are as real and problematic for Jewish women as they are for Jewish men. Tensions between the need to speak to God from within traditions and the need to speak to God out of a felt truth tear at us all.

Inventing Women's Prayer

If traditions prove inaccessible or inappropriate, where are we to turn? Feminists have taken to heart the admonition of the novelist Monique Wittig: "Make an effort to remember. Or failing that, invent."[25] During the past twenty years, feminist Jews have invented religious ceremonies and religious language to fill the gaps. Many commemorate previously unacknowledged life cycle events.[26] A plethora of b'rit bat (sometimes called simhat bat) ceremonies initiate baby girls into the covenant of Israel. New blessings and new rituals celebrate first menstruation. Simhat Hokhma ceremonies honor women's entrance into age and wisdom.[27] A variety of liturgical events draw upon rabbinic references to women's celebration of Rosh Hodesh, the New Moon.[28] Many women's groups also celebrate an additional Passover seder with haggadot focusing upon redemption from the bondage of sexism.[29] In addition, women have constituted Shabbat worship communities, both to participate in traditional prayer and to explore new forms of spiritual expression.

The innovations are valuable because they articulate the possibility for holiness in women's experiences and concerns and because, as Riv-Ellen Prell observes, they provide opportunities for Jewish women to mirror for one another what Jewish women could be.[30] Their settings are forums not only for new rituals and rites, but also for new language and imagery about God and about the praying community.

Many of these inventions fill a vacuum, rather than replacing some preexisting liturgical form.[31] Some are separate events for women only. Others involve both women and men but inhabit an intermediate space between private and public, where attendees are invited guests rather than the community at large. Often they are one-time events whose words and gestures are not subsequently reproduced. Attendance is optional. These innovations have occasioned minimal communal conflict, because they do not compete with institutionalized liturgies or ritual events, nor do they seek to invade the sphere of public synagogue worship. However, where women's inclusion would require altering the language and customs of public worship, resistance is profound. This resistance expresses itself in a variety of proposed alternatives whose aim is to evade the problem of women's inclusion rather than confronting its full complexity.

Strategies for Evading the Full Inclusion of Women in Worship

The simplest defense against inclusive worship is to expect that women will articulate new prayer words by themselves in women's prayer communities and then go on saying them there. In the long term (a time toward which its proponents never seem to look), this solution produces a Judaism of Jewish women entirely foreign to that of Jewish men. In the short term, however, marginalizing women's prayer enables exclusionary liturgies, the "real" liturgies, to go on unchanged.

A less radical version of this solution is to embed segregation by gender within the liturgies women and men pray together. Women can turn to page 362 to address God in the feminine and mention the matriarchs while men turn to page 355 to pray in the masculine and mention only the patriarchs. A related strategy is to fetishize one specific addition to the service, such as the inclusion of the matriarchs in the first blessing of the *Amidah,* as if this addition alone could counteract an otherwise androcentric liturgy. If enough attention can be focused upon this single addition, all other discussions of liturgical innovation can be shut down.

A variation on this strategy is to neutralize masculine language or even to introduce some inclusive language in the English translations of prayers, while reproducing the original Hebrew passage untouched.[32] Both the Reform *Gates of Prayer* and the Conservative *Siddur Sim Shalom* employ this strategy. *Gates of Prayer* translates the Hebrew phrase "God of our Fathers" as "God of all generations."[33] *Sim Shalom* translates it as "God of our ancestors."[34] To accompany a Hebrew prayer beginning "Help us, our Father, to lie down in peace," *Sim Shalom* offers optional interpretative readings, one of which begins "As a mother comforts her children so I Myself will comfort you, says the Lord."[35] A service in *Gates of Prayer* containing an English paragraph that says, "Our God and God of our mothers, God of Sarah, Rebekah, Leah, and Rachel, Deborah, Hannah and Ruth" actually mentions only Abraham, Isaac, and Jacob in the Hebrew version.[36] Similarly, *Sim Shalom* offers an alternative *Amidah* in English that names both patriarchs and matriarchs, but no such choice is offered in Hebrew.[37]

The juxtaposition of neutral English translation and masculine Hebrew dramatically illustrates the feminist contention that neutered prayer language conceals within it a notion of maleness as normative. Moreover, the unacknowledged clash between English texts that include female ancestors and feminine imagery and Hebrew texts that exclude them can be viewed as an institutionally sanctioned deception: Words of lesser sacredness and power are altered, while the most powerful words remain unchanged. The assumption seems to be that only the most ignorant worshippers would desire inclusive language; those learned enough to understand Hebrew would embrace androcentrism as a religious norm. Suddenly, when it comes to inclusive language, the liturgical innovators of Conservative Judaism who radically reformulated the *Musaf* service by eliminating its plea for the restoration of animal sacrifice and the Reform liturgists who rewrote the second blessing of the *Tefillah* to reflect their rejection of the doctrine of resurrection become guardians of the liturgical tradition. Their reluctance to extend inclusivity into the Hebrew liturgy implies that it is either irreverent or impossible to articulate a feminine language for holiness in the holy tongue.[38]

But inclusion and tradition need not be enemies. Some pioneering efforts to coordinate the two goals can be found in the following: the new Reconstructionist prayerbook *Kol Haneshama, Siddur V'taher Libenu* of Reform congregation Beth El of the Sudbury River Valley, Massachusetts; *Siddur Birkat Shalom* of Havurat Shalom in Somerville, Massachusetts; and the prayerbook of the Jewish Renewal *havurah*, *P'nai or*. All these prayerbooks combine a highly traditional liturgical structure with gender-inclusive and feminized language and imagery. For all these books, women participated in writing, translating, compiling, and providing commentary.

The most rigid defense against inclusive worship is to *absolutize* the texts and traditions of prayer, that is, to render their authority absolute and unchanging, thus relocating responsibility for them onto other times and cultures. Once traditional liturgy has been absolutized, no one in the present can be blamed for its androcentrism. This is simply how the Torah said it or how the rabbis decreed it. Once liturgy is presented as unchanging and unchangeable, we are left no choice but to preserve it, however troubling it may be.

Historically, of course, this picture is inaccurate. Synagogue liturgies, both modern and classical, have occasionally taken liberties with traditional texts.[39] In Isaiah 45:7, God says, "I form light and create darkness, I make peace and create evil." Yet the morning blessing *Yotzer* euphemistically restates this as "who forms light and creates darkness, who makes peace and creates all things."[40] Although the euphemism seems to have been created to prevent gnostic dualism from entering the service, it also renders the quotation more appropriate for liturgical use.[41] Divine responsibility for evil is difficult enough to grasp theologically without requiring worshippers to bless God for it before breakfast every morning.

Even in public scriptural reading, where faithfulness to the text is mandated, adaptations have been made when the material is deeply disturbing. For instance, Deuteronomy 28:30 contains a curse that is euphemized to read, "you shall pay the bride-price for a wife and *aḥer tishkavena* (another man shall lie with her)," so that when the verse is read publicly, the ears of the congregation will not be affronted. In the exact biblical phrasing that is not read, *aḥer tishgalena*, what another man shall do to her is best translated by an Anglo-Saxon verb familiar to us all. Ironically, it is just those guardians of the synagogue who meticulously enforce traditional emendations who are likeliest to argue that, because "God of Abraham, Isaac, and Jacob" is a biblical allusion (Exod. 3:6), it is forbidden to emend it in liturgy by including the matriarchs.

Even where the exact language of Scripture is preserved, traditional interpretive devices have developed that reflect attitudes and opinions about what is being read. On the festivals of Purim and Simḥat Torah, for example, Ashkenazic readers clown, using inappropriate tropes or even secular melodies for comic effect. The two catalogues of punishments destined to befall Israel if it violates the covenant (Lev. 26:4–38 and Deut. 28) are considered so ill-omened that, in Ashkenazic congregations, they are read in a hurried undertone. Whoever has that *aliyah* is not called to the Torah by name, perhaps in response to a shortage of volunteers. On the Sabbath before the Ninth of Av, the prophetic reading is chanted in Lamentations trope, to shock and sober the congregation.

If, instead of fetishizing these customs, we were to understand them as commentaries intended to draw the hearers into conversation with what is read, we would view them as precedents for inclusive Scriptural reading. For instance, by chanting in an undertone or using special cantillation for passages like the ordeal of the woman suspected of adultery (Num. 5:11–29) or the punishment of Miriam (Num. 12), we would heighten what is disturbing about these passages and signal the need for commentary and critique.

If to absolutize liturgy is one strategy of exclusion, to relativize it produces the opposite result. When theological commitments are relativized and reduced to mere preferences, it becomes easy to make their proponents consumers of liturgy rather than communities who together create and negotiate liturgies. If the aim is to satisfy consumer preferences, a single religious movement can manufacture an assortment of liturgies articulating many different values, beliefs, and prayer aesthetics. Inclusive liturgies could fill one of these market niches and be offered as choices along with hasidic-flavored, Zionist, rationalist, and unaltered traditional liturgies. Congregations could then be asked to pray these liturgies in turn as if theological commitments were costumes one could put on and take off. Or if people have a strong preference for one liturgy, they could come to services only when it is offered.

The strategy of a liturgical smorgasbord defines gender inclusivity, and other theological and ethical issues as well, simply as matters of individual taste. This presumption makes it unnecessary to seek a communal conversation, much less a communal consensus about these issues. Liturgical diversification, then, while it evades communal conflict about the language of prayer, also fragments groups who possibly would otherwise be strongly motivated to negotiate a way to pray together.

Like law, liturgy undergoes adaptations and transformations in response to shifts in its nomic environment. Even in Orthodox liturgies, new prayers continue to be introduced, sparsely, it is true.[42] But too much change, too many options could radically change the character of Jewish prayer by abolishing what the rabbis call *keva*. *Keva* includes both the fixed rubrics from which worshippers may not deviate and, in the larger sense, the routinization of prayer.[43] Dependent upon *keva* and yet in tension with it is *kavvanah*, the intentionality of prayer. Although repetition without focus and attention is mechanical and dead, without repetition, liturgies cannot be inscribed upon the heart. To use a distinction propounded by George Steiner, customized liturgies can only be consumed; they cannot be ingested. "The danger is," he writes, "that the text or music will lose what physics calls its critical mass, its implosive powers within the echo chamber of the self."[44] Thus, even if some among the "marketed" new liturgies resonated with the multiple layers of meaning that constitute a critical mass, unless they were recited repeatedly, their resonances could not be heard.

The obstructions that prevent us from developing truly inclusive prayer emerge less from reasoned consideration than from deeply felt fears. To dismiss such fears with ideological lecturing or to brand those who voice them as sexists or sellouts will not only fail to solve the problem, but will rob us all of an unprecedented opportunity to understand what it is we do, individually and collectively, when we pray. Precisely because the fears are linked to fundamental questions about liturgical language, about theology, and about the nature of ritual behavior, we need to address them seriously and respectfully. Otherwise, we will not be able to build diverse and lively prayer communities that would enrich us all.

The Fears

In her observations of an egalitarian *havurah* minyan, sociologist Riv-Ellen Prell pinpoints how women's desires for services that normalized and made visible their gendered experiences threatened the *havurah's* fragile balance between changing Judaism and preserving it through ritual.[45] Participants, especially knowledgeable male participants for whom the tradition was a patrimony, an inheritance with which they felt very much at home, "feared becoming part of an unrecognizable Judaism."[46] This fear has to do, in part, with the loss of power, but to view it solely in those terms is reductive, as I will demonstrate.

Human beings live in a peculiar tension. To be human is to be aware. We know our own fragility and changefulness, and we know that a vast and mutable world is living and dying all around us. At this same time, it is human to resist disruption. In order to reconcile our desire for stability with our destabilizing awareness, human beings cultivate a selective obliviousness. As T. S. Eliot observes, "human kind / cannot bear very much reality."[47] Hence, we sometimes shut out what is screaming to be heard, and when we do, its drumming against the wall of our denial evokes in us an outsized sense of dread. The narrator in George Eliot's *Middlemarch* articulates both this repressed curiosity and the dread of succumbing to it:

> If we had a keen vision and feeling of all ordinary life, it would be like hearing the grass grow and the squirrel's heart beat, and we should die of that roar which lies on the other side of silence.[48]

All ordinary life, all the ordinary women's lives that have been barred from the life and language of holiness can be imagined as an impending roar battering the closed ear of establishment Judaisms. The terrified traditionalist wonders: will we die of it? The fantasy of the roar on the other side of silence imagines that women possess and repress words of destructive power, killing words. The fantasy expresses the fear that, if fully included, women will create an unrecognizable Judaism, an exile from which there is no going home.

74

The Thicket

These fears cannot be trivialized, nor can they be answered without pursuing complex and intertwined questions about the language and theology of liturgy and about the nature of ritual and ritual change. Let me state the fears, not in any particular order but deeply entangled as we first confront them.

What is the service of the heart? To whom is it addressed? What is the force of its words and why do they arouse such passions in us? Given that prayer words are not about ordinary reality, do they have truth constraints? Will we feel loss for the words we no longer say? What is the force of the metaphors with which we reach toward God? Can feminine metaphors be applied to the God of Israel? What does "woman" mean, and how will its meanings be reflected in the language of prayer? How will we discover the new words and how will we write them on our hearts?

I picture these questions as a thorny thicket through which we must fight our way. The image occurs to me partly because the Hebrew word "complex," *mesubakh,* is related to the word *s'vakh,* "thicket." And *s'vakh,* in turn, evokes the biblical story in which a thicket figures, the dreadful and perplexing story about the binding of Isaac. By plunging into the thicket, we will avert the human murder, the murder of the Jewish future. We will find the ram that is its substitute, understanding that in order to go on, violence must be done. Something has to die.

As we approach the thicket, we can begin to distinguish the different varieties within its tangle of questions. Some questions deal with the nature of the words we use in prayer and some with the nature and meaning of ritual for individuals and communities. Others address the theology we seek to embody in prayer, and yet others the impact of the construction of gender upon that theology and those prayers. All the questions, about human language and human nature and about divine presence and human language about the divine, are deeply interwoven, nor is there any obvious starting place. But since we must begin somewhere, let us begin by trying to understand as broadly as we can, not merely words, or theology, but the experience of worship as a whole.

Prayer Is an Enactment, Not a Text

As both Christian and Jewish liturgists have begun to emphasize, prayer cannot be reduced to the words in prayerbooks.[49] It is a living reality whose effects upon worshippers vary from enactment to enactment.

75

Much of what we experience in worship is not in the prayerbook at all: the body language of prayer, the sights, smells, and sounds. We stand, bow, sway, kiss *tzitzit* or the Torah scroll, walk in procession, dance. We register visual symbols: the Torah scrolls themselves in their ceremonial dress; the Ark, decked with greenery for Shavuot or shrouded for Tisha b'Av; and smells: cloves or rosewater at *havdalah; lulav* and *etrog* at Sukkot. We respond to music: congregational singing, cantorial music, the hum of *davvening,* cantillation. Some of our associations are purely personal: melodies from childhood, sitting in an accustomed seat,[50] the presence of particular others around us, evocations of holy times.[51] All these factors constitute what Reform liturgist Lawrence Hoffman has called "the liturgical field," an interrelated system of relationships worshippers have with their community, their worship texts, and God, expressed in worship styles unique to their particular time and place.[52]

Rehearsing Identity Through Prayer

What does worship do and what does it mean? Some answers to these questions can be found in anthropological understandings of ritual. Rituals, according to Clifford Geertz, are special events during which the categories of a culture, its concepts, symbols, and norms, are rehearsed, offering an interpretive model to be superimposed upon everyday reality.[53] Worship, then, can be categorized as a ritual event, and worship communities can be identified as the major loci for the rehearsal of cultural categories. As Riv-Ellen Prell demonstrates, the meaning and intent of these rehearsals has been a generational battleground upon which first-generation immigrants, Americanized Jews bent upon acculturation, and *havurah* Jews have refashioned contesting versions of American-Jewish identity, mediated through differing styles of decorum and worship aesthetics.[54] By means of communal prayer, Jews rehearse and authenticate their formulations of Jewish identity and sustain and refashion religious meanings. Meanwhile, distinctive identities and meanings are constantly endangered by the homogenization of American culture.[55] If communal prayer is how the precarious Jewish identity of American Jews is transmitted and authenticated, then it is not surprising that what prayer should be and how it should be performed would matter so urgently to people. Indeed, Prell observes that the community she studied negotiated easily about their divergent kashrut and Sabbath practices, but they fought incessantly about prayer.[56] What we can extricate from this place in the thicket is an understanding that people fight about prayer with desperate energy because they regard it as a matter of communal life or death.

Sensuousness and Predictability as Traditionalizers

Barbara Myerhoff suggests that practitioners of ritual are conservative about ritual change because they are trying to preserve the components of ritual that affect them most.[57] Ritual is attractive, she argues, because it counterposes the pattern, coherence, and predictability of a transcendent timeless plane to the unpredictability, chaos, and death that characterize ordinary existence.[58] This emotionally charged combination of rich patterning and sensuous appeal characterizes the evocative, poetic language of ritual, its choreography of movements and gestures, its music, and its concrete symbols. Ritual moves people powerfully and nonrationally, independent of the intellectual content of its prayer texts. Its sensuousness and predictability make us yearn for future performances. Woe to the theologian who tries to reason people out of beloved ritual behaviors or prayers on theological or rational grounds!

A case in point is the *Kol Nidre* prayer, which begins the service for Yom Kippur. Because of its content—the annulling of vows and promises—*Kol Nidre* has been in trouble with rabbis periodically throughout its career. Several of the Babylonian gaonic authorities opposed it during the eighth and ninth centuries.[59] One great authority called it "a nonsensical custom."[60] Later, nineteenth-century Reform Judaism frowned upon it for making Jews appear slippery and untrustworthy and began omitting it from prayerbooks as early as 1817.[61] Yet for more than a hundred and fifty years, cantors continued to insist on singing it, and congregants continued to insist on hearing it. Finally, in *Gates of Repentance* (1978) the Aramaic text was restored to print, preceded by a series of relentlessly edifying interpretive readings emphasizing that only commitments addressed to God were eligible for annulment and that it is sinful not to honor one's obligations.[62]

Congregations refused to relinquish *Kol Nidre*, Hoffman contends, because cantors had made its haunting melody beloved all over the Ashkenazic world.[63] Yet he notes that attempts to set other words to the same melody did not meet with success. Congregations without Aramaic fluency or halakhic sophistication clung tenaciously to the traditional words. Their enunciation, independent of dictionary meanings, appears to carry its own ritual messages. A similar case is the mourners' *Kaddish*. Reform efforts to reword its content to conform to its theology have failed resoundingly.[64] It is unlikely that a feminist effort to replace *Kaddish* would be any better received. An abundance of feminist writings about saying *Kaddish* testify to the continuing devotion to this prayer despite masculine imagery and an eschatological vision most feminists would repudiate.[65]

In this area of the thicket, we begin to understand that there is more to the meaning of prayer than its conceptual content. For feminists to advocate the complete replacement of traditional liturgical language is to accept the same narrow understanding of meaning as that espoused by earlier Reform Judaism, which also held that all that was important about prayer was its intellectual dimension. This assumption was consistent with Reform's theological anthropology, which considered rationality the definitive human attribute and, consequently, regarded ritual as sensual and senseless. I do not recall, in my Reform childhood, ever hearing the word "ritual" when it was not preceded by the word "meaningless."

In contrast, feminist philosophical and theological anthropologies assume that human beings are defined by bodily experience, by emotions, and by sociality, and not merely by their rationality. Most feminist Jews turn to ritual to sacralize their experiences and insights precisely because they value its sensuous and emotive qualities. But although they have appropriated the sanctifying power of ritual for liturgical innovation, they have been strangely reluctant to accord legitimacy and importance to the nonrational meanings attached to traditional prayers and rituals and, consequently, have failed to account respectfully and sympathetically for the traditionalizing effects of ritual on its practitioners.[66] From this place in the thicket we learn that we cannot ask people to alter or replace traditional rituals until we can fully acknowledge with them what we are asking them to relinquish.

Performatives and Words of Power

Prayers like *Kaddish, Kol Nidre,* and *Shema,* just to name a few, may be characterized as inherited words of power, whose very syllables are filled with spiritual meaning for worshippers. They are imbued with preciousness and power also because they are ancient words handed down to us, because we associate them with ancient tales of trial and struggle or mythic times when God's face was less hidden, or because they invoke deeply rooted metaphors, memories, or commitments.[67]

The power of liturgical words can also be understood by regarding them as what the philosopher of language J. L. Austin has called performative utterances.[68] Austin makes a distinction between *constantive* language, which makes statements and conveys information, and *performative* language, which *proclaims*, rather than describes, thereby creating a condition or impelling an action. The performative character of liturgical language (a notion that Reform Judaism in particular has found difficult to grasp) explains why "Holy, holy, holy is the Lord of Hosts" is effective as liturgy while "Through prayer we struggle to experience the Presence of God," however morally edifying, is liturgically inert.[69] In the performative "Holy, holy, holy," the congregation has the power to *make* God's holiness present by naming it in a threefold incantation. "Through prayer we struggle to experience the Presence of God" rationally describes the goal of prayer, but offers no process for achieving it.

Another illustration of liturgical performatives are *berakhot*, "blessings," a prayer genre invented by the rabbis, which constitute basic elements of rabbinic liturgy. Traditional Jewish services are structured as chains of interlinked *berakhot*. A *berakhah* is not a description or a factual statement, but a special kind of speech act that proclaims the holiness inherent in ordinary reality.[70] Hoffman argues that, for rabbinic Judaism, a *berakhah* is the means by which the holy resources created by God are released for profane human use.[71] The holiness of the resources rests with God; human beings do not make them holy. Although this reasoning credibly explains *berakhot* for the creation of foods, it is less convincing regarding blessings for natural wonders such as rainbows or thunder and lightning. In these latter cases, the function of the blessing is to acknowledge the phenomenon as a sign of God's transfiguring presence in nature. The explanation seems least convincing in reference to such *berakhot* as *kiddush* or *havdalah*, through which human beings share God's power to demarcate time.[72]

A *berakhah* is an acknowledgment of God's creative power, but it is also a unique reciprocation of it. That reciprocation is the performative content of the *berakhah*. Only God can make a tree, but only a human being can make a *berakhah* upon it. In return for God's action upon the world, the worshipper creates a corresponding act of meaning for God. I return to this category of prayers when I consider the work of the only feminist liturgist who demonstrates an understanding of the performative character of *berakhot*, Marcia Falk.

Like other performative speech acts, liturgical proclamations cause something to be by saying it is so, or commit people to make it so in the future.[73] As words of power, performatives are acts of creation or binding. Their pronouncement, especially if they entail serious social or theological consequences, may be hedged about by rules detailing how, where, and by whom they may be said. Their meanings, powers, and effects are agreed upon and often enforced by communities. An oath in court commits one legally to tell "the truth, the whole truth, and nothing but the truth." Similarly, in Jewish communities a declaration of espousal before witnesses ("Behold you are set aside for me with this ring") establishes a marriage, not just in the eyes of the bride and groom, but in law.[74] *Kol Nidre* can be recited only on the evening of Yom Kippur, and the Torah scrolls must first be taken out of the Ark.

Some performative utterances are effective only when pronounced by properly empowered persons. Thus, a case is dismissed only when the judge has said so. A minor cannot enter into a contract. Classical Judaism has a category of liturgical utterances called *devarim she-bi-kedushah,* "statements-in-holiness," which only a minyan is empowered to pronounce. They include such prayers as *Barekhu, Kedushah,* and *Kaddish.* Classical halakhah holds that no gathering of women, no matter how large, is entitled to recite them.[75] This example reminds us that words of power sometimes *dis*empower. We will need to keep that in mind when we discuss why and how liturgical language can and should be changed. For the religious purpose of words of power is not to stock an arsenal for oppression, but to touch all of us with God's power to illuminate and transfigure us, to give us words to write upon our hearts.

Not all words of power are ancient, and not all ancient words are experienced as powerful. Moreover, just because the lexical content of words does not exhaust their liturgical meaning, cognitive content is hardly irrelevant. Some words have tremendous power precisely because they illuminate for us the place where we now stand. Others, like an arc of electricity, make some unprecedented connection from the present to words of power from the past. It is also true that words of power are not invariably powerful. If they were, no one would ever have to be shushed in *shul.* Some words wear out and become empty. For others, new contexts render their power malign and not redemptive. Our present situation suggests, however, that the passing of old words of power and the birth of new ones is like the *hevlei mashiah,* the birth pangs portending the messianic time; people of good will hope for its coming, but would rather be there before or after and not during the messy part.

This part of the thicket leads us to further conclusions about meanings carried by liturgical language. The language of liturgy is compelling because it is performative. No exposition, or instruction, however theologically correct or socially responsible, can assume the power of performatives. Because traditional prayer language is performative, and because it is embedded in communal norms and deeply rooted traditions, such words of power are not easily replaced. On the other hand, it is encouraging that not all words of power are inherited. If they were, women would never become contributors to the communal stock of these words of power. Until women make such contributions, they will never be full members of the people Israel at prayer.

The Power of Hebrew

The Hebrew language is a distinctive source of liturgical power for Jews, even though the tradition permits prayer in the vernacular.[76] Jakob Petuchowski observes, "Few items in the wide range of Jewish liturgy are spelled out as clearly as the permission—indeed the mandate—to pray in the language which one understands."[77] It was ironic, he goes on to say, that the early Reformers who took this legal permission seriously were attacked by their law-abiding Orthodox opponents.[78] A second irony, however, is that their successors in modern Reform are industriously restoring Hebrew to the service. As Reform Judaism learned to its cost, eradicating Hebrew eradicates the visual and auditory cues that remind Jews that their prayer is Jewish. When prayer is entirely in the vernacular, the boundary between Judaism and the surrounding culture collapses. The thick blocks of square black letters set into pages of English text embody a vital message: you are not wholly a part of the culture in which you are immersed. The divided language of the prayerbook page both mirrors and sustains the alienated cultural experience that keeps Jews Jewish.

For many Jews, this alienation is a double-edged sword. If the writing that makes Jews different is writing they cannot decode, it alienates them not only from the non-Jewish world beyond the boundary, but also from the Jewish world within it. For these Jews, the Hebrew text serves as a Jewish museum, preserving ancient words of power. While its words can be recited in the performance of prayer, and, as we have seen, may carry powerful meanings even to those to whom they are linguistically unintelligible, the written text is indecipherable. It can only be exhibited, like a crumbling pair of tefillin or an old Torah mantle in a glass case, too fragile to touch and too antiquated to use, a holy relic whose preservation links us to vital and ancient memories. A museum is not a home. In some sense, the Jew without Hebrew is always on tiptoe in the world of Jewish prayer.

In previous generations women were more apt to experience Hebrew in this way, because traditionally girls were less likely to receive even the rudiments of Hebrew education. In our generation Hebrew illiteracy is more evenly distributed but not less disabling. The language that distinguishes Jews as Jewish arouses in these Jews a shameful sense of inauthenticity and incompetence. Those who cannot understand Hebrew words of power can hardly locate in themselves the authority to change them. It is no coincidence, then, that until recently, feminist liturgical innovation has occurred mainly in the vernacular and has had minimal effects upon Hebrew liturgical language. A major exception to this tendency is the work of Marcia Falk, whose blessings and prayers introduce a radiantly beautiful feminist liturgical Hebrew.[79]

As Falk's liturgical compositions demonstrate, the Hebrew language, because it is such a powerful carrier of Jewish identity and authenticity, can help to authenticate new liturgical forms. Perhaps, too, the authentication of a liturgical Hebrew in which women have ceased to be invisible will motivate those who are not Hebrew-literate to learn and appropriate a Jewish language that welcomes their presence. Not only does Hebrew competence mitigate alienation and empower those who attain it, but also the liturgical use of Hebrew enables a continuity with traditional terminology and metaphor that may serve as a bridge between traditionalists and innovators.

Change and Continuity as Bearers of Covenant

As Hoffman demonstrates, liturgical fields vary widely with time and culture. These differences affect even the favored images of God and how those images are translated into prayer language, decorum, music, and synagogue art and architecture.[80] For practitioners, however, it is not liturgy's dynamism but its continuity that characterizes their prayer experience. It is this sense of continuity that allows practitioners, according to their capacities, to weave themselves into webs of covenant with God, with Jews at prayer throughout history, with their immediate community and with family.[81] How is this seeming contradiction between the reality of liturgical change and the impression of liturgical continuity mediated?

One mediating structure is embedded in the liturgy itself, as newer and older materials are assimilated to one another in its texts, music, and iconography. Jewish liturgy is not like sedimentary rock in which discrete strata are neatly laid down in historical order. It is more like conglomerate or "pudding stone," in which chunks and globules of various earlier rocks are suspended like nuts and raisins in a cake. A new liturgical field does not cover over its predecessor and deposit a completely new layer. Instead, it breaks up and reassimilates shards and snatches of previous liturgies, cementing them into a new formation. So, for example, I open my prayerbook and say Israelite psalms from the sixth century B.C.E. and a *Kedushah* crafted by *merkava* mystics in Roman Palestine.[82] Or I bless the new month with the words of a Babylonian talmudic master in the musical setting of an Eastern European cantor.[83] I greet the Sabbath with a hymn by a sixteenth-century Kabbalist set to a nineteenth-century Hasidic folk melody.[84] I approach my conglomerate liturgy not just as an individual inhabiting a particular time and place, but as a conglomerate Jew. I take into myself all I can hold of the twenty-seven hundred years of Judaism and proto-Judaism suspended in my contemporary liturgical frame, and they pray themselves anew through me and my minyan. It is through conglomerate liturgies prayed by conglomerate Jews that time-transcending webs of covenant are preserved and extended.

The dilemma for feminist Jews is that virtually all the chunks in the conglomerate were created exclusively by and for men. Yet rejecting conglomeration as a liturgical process and creating totally new liturgies representing the spiritual insights of our own time and gender entail sweeping away the accumulated webs of covenant made possible by conglomerate liturgy without offering an alternative means of fulfilling its covenant-maintaining function. It is impossible to imagine how feminist liturgies could be effective as communal Jewish prayer if they were to obliterate the Jewish memories embodied in past liturgies or in their historical frames or if they cut participants off from their ancestors.

We can find an answer to the feminist dilemma in the nature of the ritual process. The most effective innovations in liturgical ritual transmute familiar and deeply embedded meanings, metaphors, and forms through processes that unify the communities to which they belong.[85] In his pioneering studies of ritual processes, Victor Turner offers a conceptual vocabulary describing how this occurs. Turner locates the meanings expressed in ritual not above or transcendent to but underneath ordinary reality on a metamorphic core of meanings over which social structures are built.[86] Within this core, which Turner calls *antistructure*, float the culture's foundational symbols, root-meanings, metaphors, and concepts. But rather than being one-dimensional or static, these elements are multivocal and liquid, filled with possibilities for transformation.[87] Opportunities for renewal and transformation occur in special events, such as liturgical rituals, which open access to the antistructure. These events are characterized by *liminality;* that is, they happen away from or on the edges of the usual order of social structure. These "places-apart" offer participants a unique vantage point from which to see afresh the life and values of the community. They are bound to other participants by a feeling Turner calls *communitas,* a human bond more fundamental than those of status and role without which other social relationships and obligations could not endure. For Jews who pray, it is *kavvanah,* prayerful intention/attention, that opens access to the antistructure, transporting the worshipper to realms of meanings that are fundamental and yet suddenly new and revelatory.

Ritual, then, seems to mediate between antithetical poles: it both preserves traditions and transforms them; it is highly patterned and predictable, yet changeful and surprising; it is both an expression and an experience; what it presents as true we may doubt or even disbelieve, while at the same time we are gripped by something that feels unalterably true as we are engaged in it. Myerhoff observes that although ritual actually changes all the time, convincing rituals make us feel as if they have always been done this way.[88] The extent and nature of leadership and participation, the formality or informality of services, and their physical settings, music, and gestures all testify to our struggle to achieve a perfect balance between preserving a precious and fragile continuity and making the changes that make worship intelligible within mutable social contexts. What we disagree about most passionately are the proportions of tradition and innovation that will accomplish that balance.

Given the power of ritual both to innovate and to mediate, it is small wonder that Jewish feminism has produced floods of women's ritual. Yet in the majority of their theoretical writings, feminist Jews' focus is fixed firmly upon, rather than beyond, the text. There are several reasons for this. The first is that texts are the central loci of exclusionary masculine power in the synagogue and in the day-to-day prayer life of Jews, and they are the most difficult to change. It is far easier for synagogues to accord women full participation in the service than to change the prayerbook from which the service is conducted. The second reason is that the project of birthing a Jewish language that will reflect and refine the spiritual experiences and yearnings of Jewish women and will integrate them into communal prayer is unprecedented. We are still puzzling out how to be midwives to it. The effort leads us into the densest parts of the thicket, the tangled debates about what God is and what we ourselves are.

God and Metaphor

The language for speaking to and about God is metaphoric. It points toward truths and encounters that can never be wholly captured in words. Metaphor is expressly suited to be the language of prayer because prayer is not a rational or an analytical process. Instead, it creates an altered reality through its dramatic presentation of patterned and repeated forms and symbols.[89] Liturgical events need metaphor because they deal in condensations and metamorphoses of reality as poetry does, as dreams do, and because, like poetry and dreams, they are charged with emotion and require language that evokes feelings.

Metaphoric language is suited for prayer because it is, as Victor Turner says, complex, multivocal, full of resonances, because it is the language of discovery and metamorphosis, the language that points toward the unknown, the language that lights up the darkness.[90] It bridges the gap between presence and absence, between substance and no/thing.[91] Moreover, as Karsten Harries observes, it is a language of humility: "The refusal of metaphor is inseparably connected with the project of pride, the dream of an unmediated vision, a vision that is not marred by lack, that does not refer to something beyond it that would fulfill it."[92]

Feminist theologians contend that the arrogance of asserting that one's God-language expresses some literal datum is connected not only with a "project," but also with a projection. Such speakers project their own gendered, culture-bound identities into their God-language, reify it, and so deify themselves.[93] Accordingly, feminist theologians argue that exclusively masculine God-language is idolatrous. Rita Gross asks, *"If we do not mean that God is male when we use masculine pronouns and imagery, then, why should there be any objections to using feminine imagery and pronouns as well?"*[94] To answer this question, Judith Plaskow applies the analytical model of the anthropologist Clifford Geertz, who argues that religious systems are templates for reality that provide both *models of* how the world is and *models for* how the world ought to be.[95] Thus, the pervasive male God-images of Jewish tradition function as models of and models for, Plaskow contends, mirroring and constructing a world in which women are subordinate to men "They both claim to tell us about the divine nature, and they justify a human community that reserves power and authority to men."[96]

While Geertz's understanding of religion's symbolic language usefully describes the social process by which God-language abets the construction of social injustice, it does not demonstrate a *spiritual* necessity for feminine God-language. One could argue, at best, that feminine God-language would promote better social engineering, or that God-language as a social resource should be distributed more evenly, so that women get their fair share of the God-language pie. But one could not infer from Geertz's model that feminine God-language has intrinsic value for illuminating aspects of Deity.

It is largely philosophers and theologians who concern themselves with the mysterious powers of sacred language. Paul Ricoeur talks about how the analogical and associative properties of symbolic language make it open-ended and potentially revelatory.[97] Metaphor invests religious language with the ability to grow and change. Nelle Morton, a post-Christian feminist theologian, describes metaphor's capacity for dynamism within time:

> Metaphor is not a static word or a frozen image. An image cannot become metaphorical until it is on its way—like a meteor. Where it explodes, or how soon, when it burns out, how long or how far it journeys, are unknowns. That is why metaphor can never be subsumed under analogy. In an analogy, there are two knowns; in a metaphor, only one—the concreteness of its beginning. . . . The final metaphoric action is always a surprise, for the new reality it ushers in is like a revelation.[98]

A metaphor, then, has a trajectory, during which it may accumulate meanings unanticipated (or even undesired) by its originators. For example, the metaphor of covenant originates in transactions between a superior and an inferior, but during its trajectory it has been picking up layers of meaning about intimate relationships between partners that subvert some of its older constructions of power relations.[99] In contrast, the metaphor of God's kingship, which originally asserted Israel's freedom from subjugation to foreign political powers, has become problematic in modernity because it no longer picks up new resonances.

Yet even archaic metaphors can continue to move us, as long as we keep responding to them as metaphors, that is, as pointing beyond themselves and as incomplete. Incompleteness preserves metaphor's truthfulness; rhetorical processes that distort metaphor are those that hide or deny its incompleteness. This happens, for instance, through *reification.* When we reify, instead of claiming that human characteristic X or situation X points toward God or that there are resonances in God that X illuminates, we claim that X in all its human dimensions and details truly characterizes God.[100] We maintain that God really is a punitive father or a warrior or a nurturant mother to whom we should respond exactly the way we respond to the human correspondent. When a metaphor is reified, frozen into a single category or framework, it is destroyed, first by having its meanings reduced to one, and second, by being perfected. A reified metaphor can no longer be polysemous—literally, many-seeded—because its significations have been reduced, its other possible meanings, associations, resonances, winnowed out and discarded. A reified metaphor is perfected by disregarding the *dissimilarities* that always exist between two terms of a metaphor. My love may be a red, red rose in some ways but not in every way. (He probably does not photosynthesize or need to be fertilized with horse manure.) But when we fill in the gaps that keep metaphors incomplete, we make them appear identical to some concrete reality.

If a metaphor is perfectly congruent with what it describes, why bother using supplementary metaphors? This reasoning leads to another process that denies the incompleteness of metaphor. That process is *totalization,* a rhetorical move that favors some metaphors with monopolies. The image of *God as patriarchal male* is just such a totalized metaphor. In prayerbooks and theologies, any metaphors incongruent with this image, such as God as Mother, or female lover, have been censured and erased. Instead of a diversity of metaphors, we restrict ourselves to this single one, repeating "God the Father" and "God the King" until we forget that other metaphors are possible.

Tikva Frymer-Kensky uses the analogy of computerized "morphing" of images to illustrate how multiple facets of divinity can be represented :

> Morphing images dissolves them into each other in what looks like a seamless way, compiling a visual image of transformation. A morphed image of God could incorporate all metaphors and genders into a constantly changing image of God—the rock-the tree-the father-the mother-the lover-the judge-the male warrior-the woman warrior.[101]

The flow of diverse images in literary texts can be viewed as a linguistic equivalent of computerized morphing. In Moses' farewell poem in Deuteronomy 32, for example, God is imaged in rapid succession as a rock, a father, a mother eagle, a birth giver, and a warrior. As long as we are simply receptive and allow the diverse images to flow past, we experience no contradictions. But when we stop the flow and try to reconcile the images logically, we run into trouble. If, instead of morphing from God the lion to God the judge, we try to amalgamate the two into a consistent image, we will wind up with a judge with a long mane and a lot of teeth or a lion with a robe and gavel. This misguided desire for consistency leads people to totalize the few images that amalgamate easily. These images, coincidentally, are precisely the ones that pack a patriarchal wallop: God the father is consistent with God the judge and God the man of war. Resistance to morphing is not only an affliction of the literal-minded, moreover. Even those who use diverse images can betray unwillingness to relinquish some characteristic associated with a particular image. In Bible and liturgy, that characteristic is likely to be God's maleness. Thus, in Deuteronomy 32, God as mother eagle and birth-giving rock retains grammatical masculinity. Morphing, then, can only be as diverse as its inputs allow. If the images entered are all masculine, the output will be a totalized masculinity. Morphing alone will not prevent the incursion of totalizing metaphors that reinforce particular theologies and exclude others.

Enter Theology

It is important, I think, to speak of theology when we are speaking about liturgy because theologies are implicit in the God-language we choose or reject. At the same time, God-language overflows the confines of particular theologies just as narratives overflow the boundaries of legal or normative systems. Both theologies and narratives lend themselves to be claimed, recast, recontextualized by other interpretive communities. Moreover, theologies themselves are suspect when they are too complete, too clear, too coherent. Perhaps a God who hides (el mistater) and a correspondingly complex and elusive humanity are best reflected in the gaps—a riddling theology riddled with fissures. My theological discussion here will be mostly gaps, because I want to take up only one question and explore only one family of metaphors.

A central conflict underlying God-language controversies in feminist theologies, and indeed in all contemporary theologies, concerns whether or not personality is to be ascribed to God. Reconstructionist theology's response to this problem has shaped all contemporary conversation about this issue. The cornerstone of Reconstructionist theology is its assertion that God is an impersonal dynamic rather than a personality. But how can Judaism continue to link with its past without affirming a personal God? The founder of Reconstructionism, Mordecai Kaplan, understands God to be that power or process in the universe that supports human fulfillment.[102] Any language used to personalize or anthropomorphize God is merely a rhetorical device. However, the impersonality of God does not obviate prayer for Kaplan. Rather, he regards prayer as one of the most impressive ways Jewish civilization speaks to itself, perpetuating the mores and folkways that express its identity. Prayer serves a variety of useful social functions. It encourages group cohesion, instills moral values, offers uplifting spiritual and aesthetic experiences, and heightens awareness of the wonders of nature.[103]

Reconstructionists are therefore genuinely motivated to pray, and even to embrace Hebrew text and traditional liturgy, because these function to sustain identity and continuity. At the same time, as Richard Hirsh points out, traditional liturgy explicitly undermines Reconstructionist theology by addressing a supernatural being, using anthropomorphic imagery, and recounting improbable mythic events.[104]

Because they share some problems about how God is to be named and imaged, feminists and Reconstructionists have much to say to one another. Feminists fear the reifying power of particular images of God because, invariably, what is reified is God's masculinity. For Reconstructionists, in addition, the very attribution of personality to God is a reification. Hence, both feminist and Reconstructionist theologies are critical of the traditional language of transcendence. Reconstructionist suspicions of supernaturalism find their parallel in feminist charges that theologies of transcendence reject the human domain—the physical, the sensuous, the immanent—by relegating it to women.

The solution in some contemporary Reconstructionist theologies, notably that of Arthur Green, is to reconstruct spirituality by drawing a metaphoric language from mysticism.[105] The resulting theology is also profoundly attractive to some feminist theologians. Green identifies the quintessential spiritual experience as the mystical union with the divine. This fusion experience, dissolving boundaries that separate self, world, and God, can barely be articulated. Its most common anthropomorphic metaphor is sexual intercourse, but images connected with water, light, and fire abound as well.[106] Of course, the experience of merging is not confined to traditional religions. It can also be recognized in William James' "cosmic consciousness"[107] or the "oceanic feeling" that Romain Rolland described to Freud.[108] The universality of unitive mysticism, its appearance even among secularists or the "unchurched," is one of several features that make it harmonious with Reconstructionism. Although Green wishes to maintain personal address as a religious metaphor, some versions of unitive mysticism do not address God personally or depend on religious narratives that specify and concretize the ineffable. Unitive spirituality thus relieves the frigid rationalism of classical Reconstructionism without actually conflicting with it, since flexible boundaries between self and world are already a feature of Kaplanian theology.

Unitive spirituality also resolves some knotty theological and liturgical problems for feminists. Here is a spirituality in which metaphors of hierarchical relations are inapplicable and gender differentiation is irrelevant. Moreover, it is unnecessary to prove that anthropomorphism is inadequate. That has already been acknowledged, and alternatives are welcome. A feminist liturgist whose work embodies a distinctively feminist and implicitly Reconstructionist approach to unitive spirituality is Marcia Falk.[109] "My relationship to the divine," Falk says, "is about a loss of otherness, a merging, a breaking down of boundaries and a (momentary) release into the Wholeness."[110] The function of prayer for Falk is to evoke this experience.

Many feminist thinkers have revived interest in traditional images drawn from nature—God as rock, lion, or tree.[111] But these images have inspired Falk to create new images, often based upon phrases or concepts from earlier Judaisms, which imbue her prayer language with an uncannily traditional flavor. She explains:

> I create and use new images—images such as *eyn ha-ḥayyim*, "wellspring or source of life," *nishmat kol khai*, "breath of all living things," and *nitzotzot ha-nefesh*, "sparks of the inner, unseen self"— to serve as fresh metaphors for Divinity. With these images and still others, composed of all the basic elements of creation—earth, water, wind and fire—I hope to help construct a theology of immanence that will both affirm the sanctity of the world and shatter the idolatrous reign of the lord/God/king.[112]

Falk's unique innovation is to incorporate this theology of immanence into the primary forms of Jewish liturgy. She has coined a *berakhah* formula that counters traditional theologies of transcendence by collapsing God into nature and community. What is revolutionary in Falk's blessing formula is that it replaces the rabbinically ordained formula *Barukh atah Adonai Eloheynu melekh ha-olam,* "Blessed are you, Adonai/Lord our God, king of the universe," whose essential components are known as *shem umalkhut,* "name and kingship."[113] In the classical formula, the divine name *Adonai,* Lord, stands in for YHVH, from the Hebrew root HVH, Being, the name that is not pronounced, and God's kingship is acknowledged with the words "king of the universe." Falk begins her new blessing formula with *nevorekh,* "let us bless," instead of the traditional "Blessed are You." By addressing not God but the community, she evades the problem of having to address God as either masculine or feminine. One appellation she substitutes for *Adonai* is *eyn ha-ḥayyim,* "source [or spring] of life," echoing the imagery of many Psalms that praise God as a life giver or a water source. "My soul thirsts for you," the Psalmist says (Ps. 63). God "turns the rock into a pool of water, the flint into a fountain" (Ps. 114). Grammatically, like all Hebrew terms, the phrase *eyn ha-ḥayyim* has gender, but as an image it is gender neutral.

Falk's blessings have been criticized for rejecting the ancient and universal formula. Some find it unacceptable that God is not addressed directly. Others raise the halakhic objection that Falk's blessing does not acknowledge God's kingship. But even traditional blessings come in variant forms, not all of which obey the ex post facto rules established by the *Amoraim.*[114] Both the *Tefillah* and the wedding blessings, for instance, deviate from these rules. For Falk, because God is radically immanent, within us individually and communally, kingship would be an unsatisfactory metaphor even if its emphasis on hierarchy did not render it objectionable.[115] Her solution challenges those who would retain the ancient formula to ask what the rabbis meant by calling God a king and whether those are meanings we can either appropriate or reframe.

The larger question both Falk and the Reconstructionists raise is whether God should be imaged as an Other at all, since the imagery of otherness is particularly vulnerable to reification. In the traditional texts where it originates, it is largely masculine. Why continue to use imagery so easily abused? For me, the chief reason is that the otherness of God is compellingly real and infinitely precious. Eradicating otherness, breaking down all boundaries between self and other, self and God, God and world simultaneously eradicates relatedness. How is it possible to have a covenant without an Other? If God is not distinct from self and community, why use a theological language of partnership at all? Moreover, given how bitterly feminists have resisted being subsumed or swallowed up, how hard we have fought for integrity of selfhood, why embrace the experience of fusion in our spirituality? Opposite Falk's unitive spirituality, then, I would set a spirituality of otherness.

God's Otherness, God's difference from us, is what makes possible relationship and exchange. God's is the primary Otherness in a world where, as Emmanuel Levinas teaches, self constantly raises its face to the other.[116] An other carried us in her belly, cut the cord that made us one, and embraced us as her other. An other fed us from her own body. Otherness is the mother of human language: because of the other, we are moved to speak. Others teach us and are taught by us. Others work and build the world with us. Others heal our loneliness. Others befriend us. Female or male, straight or gay, we seek the body of the other to cohabit, to be interpenetrated. Because God is Other, God creates a world filled with difference. Because God is Partner, all difference is filled with holy possibility.

Only if there is an Other can there be mirroring and reciprocity. Some of the tenderest rabbinic metaphors and stories describe how we see ourselves reflected in the responses of the other. In the first chapter of tractate Berakhot, a series of exegeses declare that God goes to synagogue, that God wears tefillin, and that God prays.

> Rabbi Nahman bar Yitzhak asked Rabbi Hiyya bar Avin, "What is written in the tefillin of the Master of the Universe?" He replied, "Who is like your people Israel one unique nation in the world [goy ehad ba-aretz]" (1 Chron. 17:21). . . . The Holy One said to Israel, You have made me the unique object of your love (hativa) in the world and I have made you the unique object of my love in the world. You have made me the unique object of your love in the world, as it says in Scripture, 'Hear O Israel, the Lord our God, the Lord is One' (Deut. 6:4). I have made you the unique object of my love in the world, as it says in Scripture, 'Who is like your people Israel one unique nation in the world' (1 Chron. 17:21)."[117]

In this passage, Israel's proclamation of God's Oneness and God's proclamation of Israel's oneness mirror one another. They are reciprocal declarations of devotion. Neither is an ontological statement. They are testimonies to the way the other is experienced relationally.

Mirroring and reciprocity reach across the boundaries of difference, but do not dissolve it. God creates and upholds the distinctness of all things one from another. The Psalmist depicts a God who not only numbers the stars, but "calls each one by name" (Ps. 147:4). We matter not only collectively, but also individually. Because we are utterly distinct from all others, we can make ourselves mysterious. We can hide, leaving the Other to cry out, "*ayyeka*, Where are you?"[118] Or we can make ourselves transparent to the Other, illuminate our mystery, allow ourselves to be known.

The premise of relationship grounds metaphors in which we and God are interdependent: friends, lovers, co-creators of the world. Mutual commitments and shared projects bridge the boundary of difference and open opportunities to redistribute power. When these metaphors are woven into stories, they cease to be static ideals, because relationships are filled with tensions and conflicts as well as harmonies and coalescences. Friends may be insensitive, lovers may betray, co-workers may clash. Relationship potentiates abandonment, violence, enigma.

Sin, in the context of relationship, is not a transgression of an abstract norm but an injury toward an Other rendered vulnerable by his/her trust. *Teshuvah* is turning again to face the Other, not to annul what has occurred, but to sew up the wounds and determine how to go on. Relationships bear scars because they have memory. As memories accumulate, they carry consequences that bind us. They retell how we have come to be related in the way we are, but they also point us toward what we must become, what we must recreate, what we must repay. Without memory, there can be no covenants.

In a theology of relationship where there are flexible boundaries between God and others, both unity with and separation from God are possible. Imagine God as continually pregnant with, delivering, rearing, and separating from the world, like a tree at once bearing blossoms, unripe fruit, ripe fruit, and the stems and scars from fruit that has fallen from the tree. The world is inside God, outside God, part of God as in halakhah the unborn infant is "part of its mother's body," and separate from God, as the emancipated child is separate from a parent who still watches its story unfold, sometimes with pride, sometimes with pain.[119]

Metaphors of Power

To acknowledge God as Other than ourselves, as creator of the universe, as the covenant partner with whom we co-create a world of law, raises questions of power, authority, and responsibility. These are questions of particular moment in a feminist theology, because theologies can be used to enforce and validate distributions of power by gender, status, and class in the social world and to teach people to perceive themselves as helpless, incompetent, or irremediably flawed.[120] Metaphors of power and authority are particularly problematic if we believe they endorse absolutism or create castes, because, in democratic societies, we reject power distributions that disenfranchise people or that do not entitle them to equal respect.[121]

We need to ask ourselves whether disparities of power and authority are inherently oppressive or whether it is the abuse of these disparities that is unjust. I would like to suggest several categories of relationships that necessarily involve disparities but do not require disadvantaging or degrading the less powerful or less authoritative participant. These include relationships in which one participant with specialized competence helps the other to heal, to acquire learning or skill, or to gain self-understanding or spiritual illumination. Such relationships are ethical when recipients are made partners in the process and when the goal is to benefit and empower. Indeed, if the helper were to regard the recipient as passive and incompetent, it would make it impossible for the goal to be achieved.

Other relationships where disparities exist but need not degrade or infantilize are mentoring and parenting. Good mentors and good parents take pride in the developing powers of those in whom they have invested themselves and look forward eagerly to their full flowering. When maturation is complete, a generational boundary still remains in place between parent and child, mentor and disciple. They may respect each other deeply and yet not be peers. Obligations will still bind the guided and the guide to one another, but they will have come to share a language in which they can discuss how particular obligations fit into the overall pattern of what now are shared projects and values. Their history together invests the good mentor or parent with continuing influence and respect, without any presumption of incompetence on the part of the disciple or grown child.

Images of God as experienced helper show us to ourselves as attainers of competence. What they do not reflect are our limits, our gaps, our constraints, our regrets. We act, we make things happen, but things also happen to us. As storytellers together, we and God write our lives. God presents us with inevitabilities, with opportunities and constraints. We present God with our choices and responses. Because of our power to choose, things also, as it were, happen to God. God as powerful Other, as the one who perceives beyond the bounded perspective, who permits into our stories elements we experience as disruptive, as agonizing, is the lightning rod for our rage and fear, awe and dependency. To continue to affirm that we are in relationship with this God is not to affirm God-as-power or God-as-patterner in some abstract sense, but rather to assert that we as actors have moral weight: we matter to God. This does not necessarily require from us passive acceptance of God's will. Our indignation is an equally powerful act of trust: it presumes that our covenant partner can be held accountable in relationship.

Affirming God as Other, however, still leaves the problem of gender unresolved. Some who would grant that God reveals Godself to us as an Other argue that a more truthful language would purify itself of gendered imagery entirely, presenting the divine Other in neuter terminology. This is clearly impossible in Hebrew, which has no neuter gender. Even in English, however, objections arise. Used in reference to human roles and attributes, neuter language is more abstract and hence less emotionally charged. Vivid images and powerful feelings accompany the words *mother* or *father* but do not attend the word *parent*. Moreover, in a male-dominated society, neuter language is still assumed to refer to males. If the referent is female, it is customary to signify this difference through a modifier: "a woman rabbi," or "a woman judge." God can, of course, be compared to gender-free aspects of the creation, such as rocks, hills, wells, and fountains, but anthropomorphic imagery inevitably entails gender, because the human beings reflected in it are sexually differentiated creatures.

Should anthropomorphism then be discarded as a language of theology or prayer? Marcia Falk accuses it of facilitating "liturgical idolatry."

> It is not just the exclusive maleness of our God-language that needs correction, but its anthropocentrism in *all* its ramifications. For as long as we image divinity exclusively as a person, whether female or male, we tend to forget that human beings are not the sole, not even the "primary" life-bearing creatures on the planet. We allow our intelligence and our unique linguistic capabilities to deceive us into believing that we are "godlier" than the rest of creation.[122]

Yet I would argue that expunging anthropomorphism from the language of prayer, even if it were possible, would be undesirable. We can still include the beautiful images of God as bird or rock or water. But these images alone are not sufficient to sustain relatedness. Anthropomorphism is necessary because stories are necessary. We know God from the stories we and God inhabit together. Stories are a human genre. For God to step into story with us, God must clothe Godself in metaphor, and especially in anthropomorphic metaphor, because the most powerful language for God's *engagement* with us is our human language of relationship.

We and God are characters in the foundational narratives that constitute the *nomos*, the universe of meaning in which we live as Jews, like the Exodus story, and in the interpretations, visions, biographies, and memories that augment them or transform them. Without stories, there is no Judaism, because without stories, there is neither the God of Israel nor Israel itself. We cannot talk about ourselves as a people without telling the stories of Egypt and Canaan, Babylon and Baghdad, Vilna and New York, stories of exile and return, of matriarchs, patriarchs, midwives, prophets, tricksters, scholars, martyrs, and rebels. We cannot talk about the God of Israel without talking about the creator, dweller in the thornbush, liberator, covenanter, nursing mother, adversary, voice in the whirlwind, scribe, judge, and exiled Shekhinah. Allegorizing the stories or abstracting them flattens all their meanings into a single layer, closes them off to further interpretation, surgically extracts their emotional content, censors all their ambivalences, contradictions, mysteries, and scandals. Only through stories can we glimpse the wildness of God, of infinite and untrammeled possibility, untamable within the confines of any systematic theology.

Story conveys the moral heft and heat that differentiates God as a living presence from the bodiless, passionless abstraction of the philosophers: *A story is a body for God.* The dilemma to which feminism points is not caused by the nature of stories but by a paucity of certain kinds of stories. Most of the stories transmitted to us clothe God in a male body. Only a few embedded metaphors ascribe to God feminine roles or attributes. That dilemma will not be solved by rejecting or dismissing stories but by telling more stories, clothing the nakedness of God as we become aware of it.

Investing God with bodies is admittedly a dangerous enterprise. How badly does God need bodies? In liturgy especially, I would maintain, very badly indeed. It is frequently suggested that because God is not literally male or female, the most appropriate God-language is neuter. But

Hebrew has no neuter gender; all words must be grammatically masculine or feminine. There are, however, appellations and images that are *conceptually* gender neutral. Nevertheless, a God-language restricted to gender-free vocabulary presents difficulties. The Reconstructionist prayerbook *Kol Haneshama* attempts to mediate among the differing God-languages of feminism, classical Reconstructionism, and Reconstructionist mysticism by offering a wide range of translations, commentaries, and interpretive readings using feminine, masculine, and gender-neutral language.[123] In addition, *Kol Haneshama* offers both gender-neutral and grammatically feminine versions of the *berakhah* formula.[124] These options are located in the commentary, however. The Hebrew text uses the traditional masculine *berakhah* formula, although it translates *Adonai* in gender-free terms according to the theme of the prayer: "the Infinite," "Eternal One," "Compassionate One."

For a dedicated antisupernaturalist, however, the gender inclusiveness and gender neutrality of *Kol Haneshama* do not go far enough. Richard Hirsh would use English text to restate the themes of Hebrew prayers in nonpersonal and nonsupernatural terms.[125] Hirsh's solution illustrates the dangers of gender-free liturgy. Not only does it conceal the gendered nature of the Hebrew text, but in the process, it drains and deadens the language of prayer by translating the myths and metaphors of the original into moral and rational language. To use J. L. Austin's terminology, Hirsh replaces performative language with constative language. Hirsh's treatment of the *Geulah* (Redemption) blessing of the *Tefillah* is a convincing demonstration. The Hebrew *berakhah*, "Blessed (masc.) are you (masc.) *Adonai* (masc.) Redeemer (masc.) of Israel," culminates a vivid account of the liberation from Egypt and the parting of the waters. Hirsh's restatement, "In moments of redemption, we become witnesses to and partners in the work of freedom," is a Kaplanian yawner.[126] As a liturgical statement, it replaces a performative with a moral observation. It makes no reference to the narrative it seeks to transvalue, and, hence, to the gendered nature of that narrative, and, by banishing imagery in favor of abstractions, disembodies both its subject matter and the liturgical community who are supposed to identify with the statement.

Addressing God-She: A Conundrum

Embracing a gendered God-language still leaves us with the question of what kinds of stories and metaphors can constitute a feminine body for

God. To answer, one must ask, what does it mean to be a woman? Before feminism gave women voices, it was men who defined women. Philosophical definitions of women by male philosophers presupposed an essential feminine nature based upon women's biological characteristics that determines women's behavior, interests, and limits.[127]

In an early phase of contemporary feminism's development, many feminists enthusiastically embraced this idea of an essential feminine nature, although they rejected masculinist philosophical valuations of it. Instead, on the basis of women's shared biological characteristics and history of patriarchal oppression, they postulated a universal women's culture whose common experience transcended historical context, cultural difference, class, and politics. Biological processes were understood as universals whose meaning was not mediated by culture. The assumption was that, by menstruating, birthing, and nursing, middle-class white American women were having the same experience as Ndembu women in Zambian villages or nomadic Israelite women in ancient Canaan, experiences belonging to a timeless "women's culture."[128] The supporters of this cultural feminism catalogued and embraced indiscriminately a melange of feminine symbols and stories from world religions.[129] They used this cross-cultural stew of women's roles and functions both to discover options that differed from those in modern Western societies and to revalorize the traditional roles of mother and homemaker. Amid the clashes and diversities of pluralistic society, cultural feminists promoted a nostalgic vision of universal sisterhood.

For Jewish women, cultural feminism provided ways to affirm the holiness of bodies that do not have "the covenant sealed in our flesh,"[130] bodies that menstruate, bodies that lactate. Confronting a tradition from which women have seemed so absent, it was hard to know how to begin to generate a feminine language. Cultural feminism offered rich and readily accessible sources for feminine imagery. Moreover, because many of its images were archaic, they appeared superficially to be harmonious with traditional language. Some women looked particularly at the writings of Jung and his disciples because they seemed to offer a diverse and systematically organized feminine symbology. They searched out examples of these Jungian feminine images in classical midrashic texts and in Kabbalah and built upon them new rituals, new midrash, and new prayers. This influence is apparent in the liturgical and midrashic work of Lynn Gottlieb and in several alternative prayerbooks.[131] It is the philosophical bedrock upon which women's Rosh Ḥodesh rituals are constructed.[132]

For a variety of reasons, however, feminist philosophers are critical of essentialism. Essentialism conflates sexual differentiation, which is biological, with gender, which is socially constructed. It also ignores differences among cultures in the assignment of gender roles and the impact of sociohistorical contexts in shaping or changing them. Once we admit that gender roles and values attached to them are *constructed*, we also acknowledge that they are *contingent*. Then we must ask ourselves how we would wish to change them or whether we would wish to construct them at all.[133]

The extent to which biologically or culturally assigned roles could or should limit the roles and values women may embrace in the future is a matter of much debate. What is clear is that, because essentialist imagery reinforces gender stereotypes, it confines rather than throws open the significations of what it means to be a woman. Jungian accounts of the Feminine provide a prime illustration of how essentialism, while purporting to describe femininity, can enforce existing versions of it. Not only do Jungian accounts reify socially assigned gender roles and characteristics, representing them as innate sexual qualities, but they also uphold these descriptions as standards to which psychologically healthy women ought to conform.[134]

As feminist theory matures, bringing with it a more rigorous analysis of the category of gender, some of feminist Judaism's early attempts at feminine prayer language appear simplistic. It is no longer credible that a feminist Judaism can be achieved merely by including more moon and water imagery in our liturgies, by sitting in a circle, or by depicting God with essentialist imagery.[135] If we reject reducing human possibilities to the terms of gender constructs, essentialist God-language becomes doubly problematic. Depicting God-She exclusively as hushed, modest, helpful, and receptive: restricting femininity to images of parenting and domestic concern—the nursing mother, the nesting bird, the midwife, the busy *hausfrau*—limits both God and women.[136] If reductive or stereotyped imagery is inadequate to express human complexities, then how can it reflect a God who is, ultimately, beyond all human attempts at description? The issue here is not to censor out any experiences or activities of women as inappropriate to God-She, but to widen their diversity.

How, then, do we name God-She? Is it inauthentic to borrow language about goddesses from other religions?[137] Do we risk paganism by endowing God with a Canaanite goddess's title such as "Queen of Heaven"?[138] In the Bible, God is called *el,* even though that is the name of the chief god of the Canaanite pantheon. Is gendered borrowing of names and titles somehow different from or worse than other borrowings? Specifically, is it blasphemous to feminize the generic term for God, changing *el* to *elah,* a term currently restricted to pagan deities? (My question is specifically about *elah.* The other feminine biblical term, *elilah,* is inherently contemptuous, for the doubled root letter forms a diminutive: an *elilah* is not a goddess but a female godlet.) Ellen Umansky, viewing *elah* as irrevocably idolatrous, warns that "the feminist theologian who [reclaims] the word *Elah* does so at the risk of breaking with the community of Israel."[139] Umansky's apprehension is puzzling. What kind of syncretism does she fear? There is no other deity in our social environment to whom the term *elah* commonly refers. *El* became identified with YHWH in ancient Judaism under far more dangerous conditions.

Feminine images and ascriptions from earlier Jewish traditions present a different set of problems. The ancient term Shekhinah is a prime example. Is it possible to extricate Shekhinah from the essentialist meanings with which it was endowed in Jewish mysticism? Plaskow embraces the term: "[T]he image of Shekhinah . . . like the term God itself, cuts across the layers of anthropomorphic and non-personal language. Addressed in myriad personal guises, the Shekhinah is also the presence of God in the place called the world and the one who rests in a unique way in the midst of community."[140] Frymer-Kensky objects that "Shekhinah has become almost the female deity, rather than a female facet of God. This presents the real danger that a message of God's duality will be delivered subliminally, in much the way that the maleness of God is currently conveyed."[141]

In place of *elah,* Ellen Umansky has recommended the abstract noun *elohut,* "Divinity," as a term untainted by past or present associations with idolatry.[142] But while *elohut,* like all nouns with the *-ut* ending, is grammatically feminine, its abstraction seems more suitable for metaphysics (or science or sociology) than for liturgy. In modern Hebrew, these abstract nouns abound in political and administrative discourse, which makes me fear that addressing *elohut* would feel like addressing the Israeli bureaucracy; one would anticipate the same level of responsiveness.

A new name current among some Jewish feminists is *Raḥamema,* a feminine coinage from Hebrew *raḥaman,* or Babylonian Aramaic *raḥmana,* "merciful one."[143] Because the Hebrew word for mercy is derived from *reḥem,* "womb," *Raḥamema* represents a powerful melding of physicality and moral force. The name also has a punning, Joycean charm, combining the word for mercy with the intimate *ima,* "mama." At the same time, however, the term raises all the questions about essentialism. Frymer-Kensky asks, "Does using *raḥamema* as a name reinforce the idea that mercy is a female quality? If so, does that give human males the right or the obligation to act without compassion?"[144] Yet given the long history of *raḥaman* as a masculine appellation for God, it is difficult to see how the addition of a feminine equivalent would promote gender stereotyping.

One source of fresh and contemporary imagery that can be imported into theology and prayer can be found in literature created by Jewish women and men. I hesitate to call this literature secular, first, because I think the dichotomy between sacred and secular art is generally false, and second, because I believe that Jews, and Jewish women in particular, often turn to secular forms and contexts to articulate what are really Jewish concerns. If, as George Steiner argues, all art presupposes the presence of a transcendent Other whom the artist mirrors by creating moral universes, there is no secular art.[145] Art and prayer alike are acts of creation and of bearing witness, framed in revelatory metaphors.

In a special sense, however, many works by women poets in Hebrew and Yiddish cannot be considered secular. Poetry such as that by Zelda, Kadia Molodowsky, Malka Heifetz Tussman, and Leah Goldberg is engaged in a conversation with Jewish tradition. Like Rachel stealing the household gods, these poets steal the language of tradition, wresting it away from masculine theologies of spirit and transcendence and resituating it in embodied, sensuous, gendered experience. Some of these poems were originally conceived as acts of rebellion against a tradition that seemed to have no room for the perceptions and concerns of women or the riddles and ambiguities of modernity itself. It would be an act of *tikkun,* a mending of the shattered world, to make liturgies that could embrace these poems and say to them: "You can bring your stolen language home now."[146]

Feminine God-Language and the Specter of Inauthenticity

Any discussion of feminine God-language is invariably haunted by the fear of inauthenticity. Some critics have argued that introducing feminine images automatically places feminist theologies and the gender-inclusive God-languages they articulate beyond the pale of Jewish tradition.[147] But this objection misrepresents the stringency of Judaism's theological boundaries. Those boundaries are, in fact, immensely broad: wide enough to embrace the literature of *Shi'ur Komah,* descriptions of the dimensions of God as a cosmic body, complete with limb-by-limb statistics calculated in parasangs;[148] wide enough to incorporate the strict incorporeality and *via negativa* of Maimonides;[149] wide enough to include the elaboration of multiple personalities, male and female, within the Godhead in Lurianic Kabbalah.[150]

When I assert that these theologies are within Jewish boundaries, I do not mean that they occasioned no controversy when first propounded, but rather that neither the texts nor their proponents were thrust out of Judaism. Similarly, in our own time, Reconstructionist Judaism is in conflict but also in conversation with other Judaisms, and its followers are free to marry other Jews. (An example of a theological community extruded by Judaism is that of Messianic Jews, who believe that God is Christ and who are both doctrinally and structurally interlinked with Christian ecclesiastical organizations.) Given the range of theologies within these boundaries, there is no credible reason why feminist theologies whose God-language includes both feminine and masculine metaphors and invokes traditional Jewish language and texts should not be included as well, although they may, for a time, be locked in bitter dispute with androcentric theologies.

Struggling Toward a Praxis

One can become so bored and weary with the entire controversy over inclusive prayer language that one is tempted to dismiss it as liturgical nit-picking. Does it really matter that much? Given how adaptable human beings are, why can't we adapt to any liturgy, old or new? Perhaps we can. Perhaps we can make ourselves oblivious to tradition or to context or to the women praying beside us. Perhaps we can teach ourselves to pray blind and deaf and with hearts of stone. But, as the prophet asks: "Is this the service God requires of us?"

The task before us is both inspiring and daunting. We are experienced at making words of analysis and words of persuasion, but we are novices at shaping words filled with religious power. There are no recipes, no formulas, no blueprints for such words. They cannot be manufactured. They can only be grown, and the soil in which they are grown is communal prayer. For feminist Jews, it is clear that prayers develop out of a praxis of prayer. This praxis is prior to any recipes for prayer it may employ. We pray, mainly in groups. We think and talk about what and how we have prayed.

It seems simple and obvious to assert that prayers grow out of a communal prayer-praxis, but that is not the way rabbinic associations currently create prayerbooks. A friend of mine on a liturgical committee suggested that the committee pray together as part of its work. The other members, he confided, were nonplussed or annoyed at the inefficiency and subjectivity of his approach. But if our service is to be the service of the heart, we can only make new prayers by reaching within for the moral courage to speak to God with integrity—and that is no light task if one believes there really is a God and that God can be addressed.

To grow a prayer language that is authentic and inclusive and powerful, we will have to work hard at the new task of praying together. Sacrifices will be demanded of us. We will have to relinquish some familiar forms and language and try to write upon our hearts some language that is strange to us. Some of the prayers we make will be raw and clumsy and ugly, and yet we may need to pray them on the way to better ones.

Two points are fundamental: prayer is not for lying to God, and prayer is not for hurting or excluding members of our community. In Psalm 30, the ability to pray is what distinguishes the living from the dead. "What is the good of my blood, *dami*," asks the Psalmist, punning on *dumah* (silence) and *dima* (weeping), "in my going down into the pit?" The Psalmist prays for life and restoration: *Lema'an yezmerkha khavod velo yidom*, "so that my whole being may sing your praise and not be silent." Our task is to work together so that, when we pray, none of us is dead and none of us is silent.

Chapter 4
Justice and Peace Shall Kiss: An Ethics of Sexuality and Relationship

At the very beginning of our people's story, our foremother Sarah has a misunderstanding with an angel about sex. Three divine messengers appear before Sarah and Abraham's tent by the terebinths of Mamre, as we are told:

> Then one said, "I will return to you when life is due, and your wife Sarah shall have a son." Sarah was listening at the entrance of the tent, which was behind him. Now Abraham and Sarah were old, advanced in years; Sarah had stopped having the periods of women. And Sarah laughed to herself, saying, "Now that I am withered, am I to have enjoyment [ednah]—with my husband so old?" And YHWH said to Abraham, "Why did Sarah laugh, saying, 'Shall I in truth bear a child, old as I am?' Is anything too wondrous for YHWH? I will return to you at the time when life is due, and Sarah shall have a son." Sarah dissembled, saying, "I did not laugh," for she was frightened. He replied, "But you did laugh." (Gen. 18:10–15)

This story exemplifies what Robert Alter has called a "type-scene," in this case, an annunciation scene, in which, through a series of conventional narrative motifs, it is announced that a previously barren woman will miraculously bear a son.[1] Usually, in the Bible, the woman herself is the recipient of the news. Sarah's situation is atypical and even comical: she eavesdrops on her own annunciation scene. Moreover, her reaction to the announcement is less than demure. Instead of being properly awed by this miraculous gift of fertility, Sarah's imagination moves immediately to the act by which the child will be begotten, and she laughs at the prospect of again having *ednah.* Now the word *ednah* is from the same root as the word Eden. It means not simply pleasure, but physical pleasure, erotic pleasure.[2] "So the old man and I are going to do it again!" she thinks to herself. And the picture of their fragile old bodies shaken by fierce young pleasures evokes from her a bawdy and delighted guffaw.

"Why did Sarah laugh?" the divine messenger asks.[3] But he does not wait for an answer, nor does Sarah offer one. The angel's attention is riveted upon the necessary outcome: the divine plan requires that Abraham have an heir, and Sarah is slated to bear him. The mechanics by which this is to be accomplished are of no interest to the angel.

Laughter, moreover, is a physical spasm as mysterious to him as sex. Indeed, laughter, from the Hebrew root *tzahak*, is sometimes associated with biblical sex. The king of the Philistines sees Isaac *mitzahek*, "playing" with his wife (Gen. 8). Potiphar's wife accuses, "That Hebrew slave, whom you brought into our house came to me *l'tzahek bi* [to dally with me]" (Gen. 39:17). Its use in Exodus 32:6 in connection with the feast for the Golden Calf where the people "sat down to eat and drink and then rose *l'tzahek*, "to make merry," leads the classical commentators to envision an orgy. Laughter is erotic, spontaneous, and anarchic, a powerful disturber of plans and no respecter of persons. How then do you go about explaining to an angelic herald that you were laughing about getting laid? Sarah does not even attempt it. Intimidated and alarmed, she denies her laughter and swallows the angel's theology lecture. The encounter is never resolved. "You did laugh," the angel insists. But Sarah is silent and will not explain.

The classical commentators take their cues from the angel. They all assume that Sarah's incredulity is about the miracle of birth, ignoring the miracle-for-two that must precede conception. Sarah's allusion to *ednah* is either misconstrued or forgotten. To construct a feminist Jewish theology/ethics of sexuality, we must return to that original miscommunication and retrieve the meaning of Sarah's laughter.

Laughter has not figured very prominently in Jewish theologies or ethics of sexuality, nor has appreciation of the erotic. Instead, sages and philosophers have concentrated their concern on how sexuality is to be controlled and channeled. Their texts require us to talk about bodies and passion in an exclusively rational manner, as if principles and paradigms, rules and consequences were sufficient to reflect all that shapes us and all that impels us as sexual beings. This juiceless discourse is so wildly incongruent with the explosive sensuality of its subject matter that with every word it undermines its own credibility.

The truth is that we learn different languages for talking about sexuality: a formal language spoken rationally and solemnly in school, in synagogue, in the courtroom, in the doctor's office, or the scientist's laboratory and, flowing steadily beneath it, a subterranean language whispered in bedrooms and daydreams, burlesqued and boasted among laughing friends, growled from alleyways over a loaded gun. This language is itself a sexual experience, a kind of "oral sex." I will call it the language *of* sexuality, or for short, *language-of*.

Formal language, on the other hand, is language *about* sexuality, distanced from the experience of it. Laughter and eroticism have been banished from its precincts. Abstract, rational, and objective, fluently polysyllabic, syntactically intricate, it is the language spoken by authorities and professionals. In it, speakers present themselves as utterly detached from bodies, including their own bodies, their maleness or femaleness, their vulnerabilities, hungers, and delights. This *language-about* both disembodies and depersonalizes. Descriptive statements such as "subsequent to arousal, the penis is introduced into the vagina," or "penetration was effectuated digitally" separate sexual body parts and acts from whole bodies and from the selves that inhabit them.

The educational filmstrips that used to be shown in junior high school exemplify for many adults an early encounter with *language-about*. Using diagrams, the films depicted heterosexual genital intercourse (the only kind of sexual act ever mentioned) as a mechanical operation whereby "tab A" is inserted into "slot B." Possible motivations for engaging in this extraordinary procedure were not discussed. Other early exposures to *language-about* may have been the cautionary lectures on sexual hygiene or sexual morality delivered in high school classrooms or synagogue youth groups by teachers or rabbis unimaginable without their clothes on. At a more mature stage, such language may have been encountered in sex manuals, whose instructions attempt to program acts that are uniquely resistant to systematization.

The language *of* sexuality, is, in contrast, a language of wants, pleasures, repulsions, and obsessions. Stammering and elliptic, or raw and outrageous, it is the vehicle for our tenderness, our delight, our hungers, our laughter, our violence: a language of unrestraint. The only thing we are unable to do in this language is to reflect upon what sexual feelings and experiences mean and how we want to live as sexual beings. These topics require a different language, a *language-about*, because it is impossible to reflect upon our sexual being and our sexual acts in the language that stirs our blood and exposes our nakedness.

"Reflection" means seeing not the object itself but an image of it thrown back to us from some other surface. We can only reflect at a distance. If we were unable to draw back and reflect, we would be creatures entirely of impulse. Our capacity for reflection allows us to become participants in cultures and to place ourselves and our actions within larger patterns of social meaning. Our capacity to reflect upon our impact upon others and their impact upon us also contributes largely to our differentiation as unique selves. A distanced sexual language, then, is part of what makes us fully human. We want it as a touchstone for ourselves and also as a boundary between ourselves and those with whom we must not or do not wish to strip ourselves naked.

We cannot do without a *language-about*. But I wish to argue that the one we currently employ is inadequate. A *language-about* must distance us from the immediacy of sexual experience, but if it purges itself of all sensuousness and carnality, it disables our efforts to reflect upon the meaning and ethics of what we feel and do as embodied creatures. What we need is a way of talking about sexuality that *distances* us from sexual experience without *estranging* us from it.

The *language-about* most frequently employed in instruction, ethics, and policy making concerning sexuality is not merely a language of distance but a language of alienation. It maintains a gap that makes it impossible to draw upon embodied experience for reflection. To see the effects of the gap, let us return to one of our earlier examples: the teenagers at the lecture on morality or sexual hygiene. Many of the young men and women listening already know the prohibited touches and penetrations to which the lecturer alludes so circuitously. Some, craving solace for loneliness or stability amid chaotic family situations or simply relief for raging hormones, have reached for one another's forbidden bodies. Others have surrendered not to passion but to peer group coercion; dutifully and without relish, they have handed over their bodies and have proved themselves cool. Still others have experienced or fantasized desires for their own sex. If women, the lecture will tell them nothing, except that their desires for other women are so anomalous as to be unmentionable. If men, the only thing they are likely to learn is that such desires lead to a horrible death. Some students in the audience could give a lecture very different from the one they are hearing. A relative, teacher, or family friend, some grown-up with a façade perhaps as gray and asexual as the lecturer's own, has violently intruded or continues to intrude upon their young bodies. Terrible things are threatened if the secret is told, and besides they doubt that anyone would believe them. These students listen cynically. The act that has been forced upon them does not resemble the one depicted in the diagrams or pious slogans, but of course, all adults are liars.

In all these cases, there is a dissonance between language and experience. An alienating *language-about* with its chosen topics and its deliberate silences belies the realities the students inhabit while at the same time excluding these realities from discussion. Everyone has been hurt by the existence of the gap, even those who never expected truth from the lecture or endowed the lecturer with authority. Everyone has been short-changed. None have been addressed as the people they really are. None have learned how to make sense of their sexual realities, much less how to change these realities or what obligations are congruent with them or how such obligations can be fulfilled.

The task of a theological ethics of sexuality is to bridge the chasm between what is and what ought to be. To take up this task, we will have to remake our language about sexuality so that it is distanced enough for reflection but flexible enough to evoke for us the bodily experiences and feelings that so greatly affect our inner and outer worlds. Literature, because it has a unique ability to mediate sensuous experience and reflection upon it, can be used to concretize and enrich theological language. Stories and poems can allow us to witness sensuous experiences imaginatively from the perspectives of the characters or speakers within the world depicted, as well as from the perspectives we bring from our own life experiences and social world.[4] Because literature can vividly evoke embodied experience without plunging us into the experience portrayed, it allows us to imagine not just laws and values but also the moral universes where they would be at home. The multidimensionality of literary moral universes, like the multidimensionality of real human ones, cannot be compassed by one-dimensional rules. Both demand of us that we understand complexly before proceeding to judgment.

Other disciplines can also contribute language and understandings about sexuality to the theological enterprise. The newly developing studies of the psychology, sociology, and anthropology of gender help to explain how power imbalances between women and men and differences in their socialization affect perceptions and constrain actions and choices. Psychological theories may also offer us some accounts of human sexual motivation to help us understand sexual behavior that is ethically problematic: predatory, manipulative, self-degrading, or unfaithful.[5] Histories attentive to questions of sexuality and gender allow us to see how sexual attitudes and behavior are framed by events and assumptions belonging to specific times and places.[6]

To engender an inclusive Jewish theology of sexuality, we will have to bring all these resources to our tradition's stories and laws about sexuality and to the ways these teachings have been lived out by Jewish communities, past and present. The resources offered by history and the social sciences may be particularly unsettling. By acknowledging that Jewish attitudes and praxis concerning sexuality differ according to historical context, that they are not untouched by time, we will be opening ourselves to some of the same theological dilemmas that we faced in our examination of Jewish law in "Here Comes Skotsl." Incorporating a sociohistorical dimension into our theology of sexuality may permit us to recover long-forgotten beliefs and practices, but we may also be forced to relinquish cherished popular beliefs about Jewish attitudes toward sexuality. We will find, for example, that it is not true that Judaism has always disapproved of asceticism or that sexual pleasure has always been regarded as a good.[7] These are misapprehensions that occur when Judaism is viewed not just ahistorically but also monolithically, as a single continuous entity taking on accretions through time in an orderly and harmonious evolution.

The most popular modern version of Jewish social history, one from which even certain scholars are not immune, sets up a sentimental account of pre-Holocaust Eastern European Judaism as a norm against which later Judaisms are measured and a frame through which earlier Judaisms are viewed. In this story, the Jewish world consists of cozy, preindustrial shtetls populated by pious scholars and bustling housewives. Pogroms intervene as occasional tragedies perpetrated by drunken peasants, but within the shtetl, harmony prevails. No class struggle divides the merchants and the water carriers. There are no smugglers, no government informers, no child laborers, let alone wife batterers or rapists. The fierce battles between Hasidism and its opponents, the challenges of Enlightenment philosophy and science, and the steady growth of Reform Judaism among urban Jews are only a distant rumor.[8] Interpreted through the master image of this Yiddish world that never was, the Judaisms of the First Temple or of the Babylonian academies, of tenth-century Cairo or Baghdad, of twelfth-century Toledo, or of sixteenth-century Florence become mere variants of idealized shtetl

Judaism in different costumes. Among the casualties of this historical kitsch are context-specific norms related to sexuality and gender.

If we are to make theologies with integrity, we will have to acknowledge that all these Jewish worlds are very different from one another, and that even within individual worlds there are tensions and controversies, attested both by texts and interpretations and by behavior within communities. Often, too, we will reencounter the gap we have spoken of previously between what existed in those worlds of embodied experience and what was believed ought to exist. But as we have learned, what bridges this gap is the human willingness to recreate the world so that what we hold sacred is expressed in all our institutions and relationships. Precisely *because* sexual values and relations are contextual, and not merely instinctual, *because* they have varied according to place and time, we have the capacity to create them anew over and over, along with ourselves and our worlds.

If, then, the Jewish tradition to which we look for guidance is not one but many traditions, it follows that we, like all who have ever sought to build a world of Jewish meaning, must recover and reclaim *some*, but not *all*, of its multitude of memories and stories, laws, and values. Our vision of a new *nomos* will call forth stories and memories that have been repressed or have lain fallow. It will gather and disseminate stories our traditions have yet to tell. As for those texts and traditions that most threaten to refute the new vision and forbid its realization, they must be not merely disarmed but transfigured, re-formed, so that they, too, can belong to the new world.

If the new *nomos* is one that engenders a truly inclusive Judaism, what stories, laws, and values concerning sexuality could be represented in it, and how might they be illuminated by the hermeneutical tools discussed? In this chapter, I examine a variety of canonical and noncanonical texts. Challenging texts include the two accounts of humanity's creation in Genesis and the laws of forbidden sexual relations in Leviticus. The Song of Songs and the Book of Ruth are textual sources for a Jewish sexual ethic valuing both sensuous delight and recognition of the other's subjectivity. A final challenge to this sexual ethic is presented by the prophetic metaphor of adultery. I examine its use in Hosea 1 and 2.

The Creation of Humanity: Two Accounts[9]

If we needed to prove that scripture can affect the real world, Genesis 1 and 2 would be chief among the prooftexts. Creation stories would seem to invite speculations about theological anthropology: What are we? What is our place in the scheme of things? What links us to our creator and to the rest of creation? Of all the human capacities that can be inferred from these stories, the one that has riveted the attention of traditional commentators is power. There is hardly a detail of these two accounts that has not been a prooftext for man's power over woman, over the earth and its creatures, in favor of or against some system of human government.[10] One imagines the two chapters buckling under the slagheap of human and geophysical suffering piled upon them by interpreters.

This mass of interpretation also weighs us down as readers, for it overdetermines our experience of the texts. How can we fail to be affected by their lengthy history as prooftexts for the subjugation of women and ecological dominance? What we are about to read has been used by past generations of interpreters to legislate circumscribed definitions of humanness, maleness, and femaleness and to justify privilege on the basis of gender.

More recently, these creation texts have become battlegrounds for feminist countercommentary.[11] Counterreadings employing literary, philosophical, and historical methods have been used by feminist scholars to expose and critique ideologies of sexuality and power. One influential version of this critique argues that opposition and subjugation particularly characterize patriarchal modes of making categories and making sense, and that, consequently, in patriarchal cultures, the structure of thought itself predisposes us to split and separate rather than to perceive interconnections and interdependencies.[12] At the heart of this universe carved into dualisms is a definition of normative humanity as maleness and irreducible otherness as femaleness. According to this account, woman is the first stranger.

The critique goes on to argue that from patriarchal man's alienation from woman proceeds an infinite series of dualisms. In each, the superior term is associated with patriarchal man, while the inferior and opposed term is associated with woman. Heaven and earth, light and darkness, spirit and body, cleanliness and filth, good and evil, freedom and slavery all are made to mirror the estrangement of patriarchal man from the woman he has cast out. These dichotomies then justify the subordination and exclusion of all those consigned to the feminized category of the other, for the ramifications of patriarchal dualism are political as well as psychological.

Feminist process theologian Catherine Keller traces these themes of hostility to the other throughout the history of Western theology and philosophy.[13] In Keller's account, patriarchal man, pained by the fragmentation of self and world that he has engineered, longs for unity. He conceives of it, however, not as the reunion of all he has driven apart, but as the conquest and incorporation of the realms of the other. As in the later philosophical works through which Keller traces this theme, selfhood is attained aggressively, by opposing and subjugating the other. The resulting separative masculine self is complemented by a soluble feminine self, the object of opposition and subjugation whose feeble boundaries collapse into his.[14] Like Jessica Benjamin, whose feminist object-relations theory also describes a pathological complementarity of dominator and dominated, Keller proposes the dissolution of gender polarity and its ensuing structures of domination. Keller's solution is to regard selves and world as related processes rather than separate stable entities.

The exemplary texts of patriarchal domination, according to Keller, are the Genesis creation stories.[15] Genesis 1, Keller argues, incorporates but abstracts the violent fragmentation of the body of the mother by which the world is created in the Mesopotamian creation myth upon which the Genesis creation is modeled. Behind the demythologized deity of monotheism, she contends, the antimatriarchal warrior gods and heroes of polytheism still lurk. The monotheistic deity of the creation accounts is a projection of the dualizing, autonomy-worshipping, patriarchal consciousness. This god-projection serves both as a model and as a justification for all patriarchy's tyrannies and exclusions, as well as for its militarism. YHWH's ethicized battles, His concern for social justice, is a mere façade, masking the objectifying violence beneath.[16]

This critique raises serious questions for Judaism and for other monotheistic traditions. Does worshipping God as One inevitably entail sexism and separatism? Does it require characterizing all relations between self and other in terms of dominance and submission? Is the primordial category making and establishment of boundaries that the creation stories depict understandable only as a normalization of patriarchal fragmentation and opposition?

If the answer to all these questions were yes, how could one avoid concluding that Judaism is an evil and destructive belief system? This is not to say that there is no truth in the critiques and that patriarchal oppositions cannot be found in our sacred texts and in our traditions. But

Keller's argument is reductive. She writes as if the Bible were a unitary text that represents God or men or women in a single consistent way and as if the Bible alone defined Judaism. But after the Bible, Judaism continued to develop other sacred texts and exegetical traditions which it does not share with Christianity and whose importance is sometimes discounted by scholars who are primarily interested in Judaism's impact on Christianity. Because the influential rereadings of texts or shifts of emphasis that have shaped later versions of Judaism are not noted in Keller's analysis, her presentation of Judaism is both static and one dimensional.

It is not necessary to discard Judaism or its texts to make a world of meaning in which women and men are equal subjects. Instead, our task is theological: to read these texts as believing Jewish women and men today without evading or denying their patriarchal past and to seek in them redemptive meanings to propel us toward a more just and loving future.

Progressive theologians read Scripture both as human constructions framed by time and as sacred text whose interpretive possibilities transcend any single historical time. We begin by learning what we can about our texts as historical entities. Historical critics assign the authorship of Genesis 1 and 2 to different documentary sources, Genesis 1 to P, the priestly document, and Genesis 2 to J, the Yahwist source. They explain differences in the chapters by pointing to the particular interests and emphases of these two authorial groups. This information helps us to separate the two stories and to account for their discrepancies. But although source criticism is necessary, it is theologically insufficient. Without obliterating their differences, we must illuminate both stories as Torah, as sacred text, to hear what they can teach us about what we are and what we ought to become and yet bring to them our own insights about where we have been and what we hope to be. To do such a reading, we must keep returning to the questions of boundary making and power distribution and how they affect our understandings of sexuality and gender.

Genesis 1: The Beginning of Boundaries

In the beginning, we are told, there was *tohu va-vohu,* a formless void. Creation both fills the void and gives it shape. Shaping is accomplished by means of boundaries, which differentiate the primeval wholeness into a multitude of entities, defining their contours and extent, what is inside and what is out. Boundaries maintain the integrity of entities, preserving them from inundation and restraining them from dribbling out into everything else. Without a boundary there can be no I and no other. Setting one's own boundaries, setting the boundaries of other entities, and placing them in categories are ways for societies and individuals to draw relationships among the components of a vast and various world. But while bounding and categorizing are acts of relation, they are also acts of power.[17] Power determines who draws the boundary and how and who makes the categories and for what reasons. Both boundary making and the exercise of power are basic human activities. They have no intrinsic moral valence. Boundaries are not intrinsically divisive any more than power is intrinsically oppressive. Indeed, as we shall see in our Genesis and Leviticus readings, both are indispensable for the creation of just societies and just relations between the self and the other. But acts of distinction and acts of power are morally charged. They carry implications for how members of categories are to behave and how others are to behave toward them. Hence, acts of definition are vulnerable to abuse.

Some boundaries are purely barricades—chainlink fences patrolled by Dobermans, borders scoured by searchlights, trenches, bastions, stockades, outposts of the Hobbesian war of all against all. Other boundaries are not primarily barriers but loci of interaction. A cell membrane, for instance, is part of the living substance of the cell. It is the perimeter at which the cell conducts its interchanges with other cells, the contacts, the flowings in and out that maintain its life within its environment. Human beings begin life with flexible, rather than rigid, boundaries. Born tiny and helpless, we are from the start profoundly interdependent. Only through perceiving our impact upon others and their impact upon us do we become distinct and particular beings. Intimacy with others is a survival need for our species. Even if they are fed and cleaned, babies who lack a caring other die in alarming numbers from a syndrome known simply as "failure to thrive." We affect and are affected by nonhuman others as well. From birth to death, we inhabit a great network of living things whose existence is interwoven with our own and to whom we are therefore responsible.

Physically, emotionally, ethically, we are best served by boundaries that acknowledge the integrity of both self and other yet are flexible enough to allow for creativity and communion. These are the boundaries advocated by feminist object-relations theorists. Benjamin, relying upon Winnicott, traces the origins of these flexible boundaries to the development of a holding environment between mother and infant in which the child reaches out to play and explore unhindered and yet unabandoned by the other.[18]

> Winnicott often quoted a line of poetry from Tagore to express the quality of the holding environment and the child's transitional area: "on the seashore of endless worlds children play." The image suggests a place that forms a boundary and yet opens up into unbounded possibility; it evokes a particular kind of holding, a feeling of safety without confinement.[19]

According to Benjamin, the mature version of this combination of mutual attunement and freedom to know one's own desires is enacted in the erotic space two people create who recognize one another as subjects. In such a union, she observes, "receptivity and self-expression, the sense of losing the self in the other and the sense of being truly known for oneself all coalesce."[20]

This boundary fluidity, these delicate calibrations of closeness and distance, interpenetration and distinctness characterize relations in Genesis 1 between God and humanity, between humanity and world, and between man and woman. As we shall see in Genesis 2 and 3, however, boundaries undergo a terrible transformation. In the world of these texts, closeness can only be imaged as fusion and distance as estrangement. Rather than creating distinctions, boundaries set up oppositions.

In contrast, both distinctions and similarities constitute the harmonious world of Genesis 1. Although the sequence of creation exactly parallels the Mesopotamian creation story, there is a crucial difference. In Genesis 1, creation is not the aftermath of war. The primeval watery chaos (tehom) is not imaged as an enemy of God, nor is it annihilated by the creation. Instead, God distinguishes various elements of the watery chaos and establishes their boundaries by naming them. Juxtaposed verses underline the parallels among these created elements. Stretched over the kindred waters above and below are kindred solid expanses, sky and earth.[21] The earth is sown with trees and grasses. The sky is sown with lights. The sea and air bring forth their many kinds of creatures. The earth brings forth its many beasts. The creation of humankind continues the themes of both the uniqueness of created things and their similitude with some differing other.

The Creation of Adam and the Boundary of Sexuality

> God said, "Let us make *adam* in our image, after our likeness. They shall rule the fish of the sea, the birds of the sky, the cattle, the whole earth, and all the creeping things that creep upon the earth." God created *adam* in his own image; in the image of God he created him [it]; male and female he created them. God blessed them and God said to them, "Be fertile and increase, fill the earth and master it; and rule the fish of the sea, the birds of the sky, and all the living things that creep upon the earth" (Gen. 1: 26–27).[22]

Adam is the Bible's first name for humankind. It is derived from the Hebrew root 'DM, the root associated with redness.[23] Red is the color of the clayey earth *(adamah)*, of blood *(dam)*, of raw flesh. *Adam* is the red-earth creature, a continent of flesh reticulated by rivers of blood. *Adam* is God's conundrum: an earthy, fleshy, bloody being resembling *(domeh)* God.[24] The text dwells insistently upon the linkage. In the space of two verses, the likeness between God and *adam* is reiterated four times. Two terms, image, *tzelem,* and likeness, *d'mut,* describe the relation of *adam* to God. *Tzelem,* in its primary sense, means a physical representation, often a statue or an idol.[25] *D'mut,* from the root *DMH,* to resemble, is a more generalized word for similitude. Both terms are used in verse 26: "God said, 'Let us make *adam* in our image *[tzelem],* after our likeness *[d'mut],*'" leaving the nature of *adam's* likeness to God delicately poised between the substantial and the insubstantial. But in verse 27, the more abstract term *d'mut* is dropped; likeness to God is realized in the flesh: "God created *adam* in his own image *[tzelem],* in the image *[tzelem]* of God he created him [it], male and female he created them" (Gen. 1:27).[26] *The one piece of new information in this verse is adam's embodiment as male and female.*

Human sexuality is presented as unique, Phyllis Trible notes. None of the animals have been specifically designated as male and female.[27] But what does it mean to link this unique sexuality with the divine image, as the text does? The metaphor of the divine image conferred upon male and female, Trible argues, preserves not only likeness to God but also the dissimilarity between a God who transcends sexuality and creatures endowed with it.[28] Both males and females bear in common a likeness to God, but their maleness and femaleness are not signifiers of this likeness but of unlikeness.

Yet by its placement of the creation of sexual difference, the text suggests precisely the contrary. Had the text set the creation of maleness and femaleness off by itself in a separate verse, or had it linked them to verse 28 in which God bestows the blessings of fertility and dominion, that would suggest that these characteristics mark a dissimilarity to God. Instead, the creation of sexual difference climaxes verses wholly devoted to establishing human similarity to God. Genesis 5:1–3 reiterates the link between likeness to God and gendered humanity: "This is the record of *adam's* line. When God created *adam*, he made him [it] in the likeness of God; male and female he created them *(bar'am)*. And when they were created, he blessed them and called them *adam.*"

I want to turn Trible's argument upside down and argue that in Genesis 1 human sexuality is itself a metaphor for some element of the divine nature.[29] Something in God seeks to restate itself in flesh and blood. Perhaps it is God's creativity, or delight, or the ingrained yearning for communion with the other that serves as impetus for creation and for covenant.[30] But something in God, in seeking its human mirror, reveals itself as both infinitely varied and utterly whole. That something is, as it were, God's sexuality, which our own sexuality was created to reflect.

Genesis 1 refers to God both in the singular and in the plural and, like Genesis 5, attributes both singularity and plurality to *adam. Adam's* plurality is its sexual diversity. We are incalculably various, and the most basic of our variations are sexual. We are capable of unity, and our desire for sexual union adumbrates this gift. Sexuality, the most primary way in which humankind is at once many and one, is a metaphor for the infinitude and unity of God.

Our sexuality marks us both as boundaried and boundary-transcending. It is at once personal and transpersonal, private and public. Within ourselves, all by ourselves, is the capacity for eroticism. It is in our skin, our muscles, forested with twining nerves, our blood gusting through us like rising and falling winds, our genitals raining their fluids, our senses all alive to joy. Yet sexuality also turns us toward the other. Overriding the physical and emotional boundaries that keep human beings distinct from one another, it urges us to open our portals, to extend ourselves, to create places of co/habitation where we and the other are interlinked. They are "the seashore of endless worlds" upon which we play, rapt in our desire, ever aware of the desire and the presence of the other. These places of communion we establish with our bodies, dissolving the boundaries of inside-outside, yours-mine, giver-getter, haver-holder, bespeak our likeness to the God the rabbis called *Ha-Makom,* the Place. The capacity to create intersubjective space, which we and God share, is what makes covenant possible.

Humanity and the Conferral of Power

The other Godlike characteristic bestowed upon the different forms of *adam* in Genesis 1:28 is power, specifically the capacity for power over the earth and its creatures. In Judaism's exegetical history, this verse has been used as a justification for the interconnected subordinations of woman and nature (although it was not easy making the verse cooperate). Extracting a proof for male supremacy from a verse enjoining humanity in plural imperatives to "be fertile and increase and fill the earth and master it" is a difficult proposition. Rabbinic tradition accomplished it by seizing upon a variant spelling in the Masoretic text as an exegetical hint of women's exclusion from mastery. The word *kibshuha,* "master it [lit. her]," lacks the vav of the plural form, making it possible to read the word as a command in the masculine singular "master it [her]."[31]

This missing vav is perhaps the most influential spelling error in the history of theology. In a legal dispute in the talmudic tractate Yebamot, it provides ammunition for the majority opinion that only men have the obligation to procreate.[32] Talmudic and midrashic[33] explanations of the missing vav are welded together by the eleventh-century exegete Rashi into a comprehensive justification for the subjugation of women: "The missing vav is to teach you that the male masters the female, so that she should not be a gadabout and it also teaches you that man whose disposition *(derekh)* is to master is commanded concerning procreation and not woman."[34]

Some feminist critics have charged that Genesis 1:28 endorses the pillage of the environment and the alienation of humanity from the rest of the natural world.[35] Interpreting mastery as a license for destruction, however, ignores the limitation on its use established in verse 29, where humans are assigned only the seed-bearing grasses and the fruit-bearing trees for food. Since humanity is implicitly forbidden to prey upon the fishes, birds, and cattle over which they have mastery, mastery in Genesis 1 cannot mean the right to tyrannize over other creatures.[36] Permission to eat flesh is not given until after the Flood, and its price is estrangement from other creatures: "The fear and the dread of you shall be upon all the beasts of the earth and upon all of the birds of the sky" (Gen. 9:2).

For the text's ancient readers, the promise of mastery was probably understood as a promise of survival in a perilous and unpredictable world.[37] Droughts, famines, epidemics, cattle plagues, earthquakes, floods, and incursions of wild animals haunt their stories, their psalms, and their supplications. Mastery is, at best, a temporary blessing, for human beings share the same needs and terrors as other living creatures.

> *All of them look to You*
> *to give them their food when it is due.*
> *Give it to them, they gather it up;*
> *Open Your hand, they are well satisfied;*
> *hide Your face, they are terrified:*
> *take away their breath, they perish*
> *and turn again into dust.*
> *(Ps. 104:27–29)*

For many Americans, power has become disreputable. In comparison with its atrocities and its deceits, its good deeds seem weak and unmemorable. In the news, on the talk shows, in discussions of political and social policy, power is too often confused with abuse, and victimization is valorized as if it were a moral position. Actually, victimization cannot be a moral stance, because a victim is a person under constraint, a person who has been robbed of choice. Choices require some degree of power. But instead of determining what power we do have or could acquire together with others, instead of organizing to maximize our power and share it more broadly, we vie with one another in a kind of moral poor-mouthing, as if denying our power relieved us of the obligation of sharing it and exercising it responsibly. Confronted with evidence of our destructive impact on the earth and our fellow creatures, we confess ourselves overwhelmed and go right on polluting, wasting, and destroying. It is significant that, in Genesis 1, where humanity is created and empowered coequally, power is conferred as a blessing. As we shall see, in Genesis 2 and 3, power is part of a curse. The injunction to master the earth, then, carries with it the potential for sin, the possibility of abusing power.

Two other forboding terms are the words that distinguish male and female, *zakhar* and *nekeva*. In Genesis 1, and in its reiteration in Genesis 5, *adam* is an inclusive term for a sexually diverse humankind. *Zakhar* and *nekeva* merely specify *adam's* sexual variations. But the roots of these words, laden with the connotations of doer and done-to, foreshadow situations in which *zakhar* and *nekeva* are not equally called *adam*.

The Hebrew word *zakhar* means the creature with the male member.[38] Female is *nekeva*, the pierced one. In these two terms the entire history of patriarchy is distilled. It is probably more than the coincidence of homophony that the *zakhar* is also the *zokher* and the *zakhur*, the rememberer and the remembered. The only memory in patriarchies is male memory because the only members are male members. They are the rememberers and the remembered because they are the recipients and transmitters of tradition, law, ritual, and story, the authorized interpreters of experience.

Zakhar names as his Other *nekeva*, the pierced one, the one whose boundaries are penetrated. He sets her up as his antithesis. His name for her declares that she and only she is permeable; despite all evidence to the contrary, he sees himself as impenetrably sealed. He is the invader and the conqueror. She is the invaded, the subjugated. He is the remembered. She is the forgotten. What she called herself, what tales she told, what wisdom she imparted, have fallen into silence. In drawing the boundary between himself and her, *zakhar* did not concern himself with what she was; only with what she was not. Through his memories she may be glimpsed dim and distant behind the rigid boundary of gender polarity. Genesis 2 and 3 hints at the earliest of these memories.

Genesis 2: The Closing of the Borders between Woman and Man

> When YHWH God *(elohim)* made earth and heaven—when no shrub of the field was yet on earth and no grasses of the field had yet sprouted, because YHWH God had not sent rain upon the earth and there was no *adam* to till the soil . . . . YHWH God formed *adam* from clods of earth.[39] He blew into his nostrils the breath of life, and *adam* became a living being. YHWH God planted a garden in Eden, in the east, and placed there the *adam* whom he had formed. (Gen. 2:4–8)

In Genesis 2, the creation of humanity is depicted as a process of opposition and segregation. *Adam* is no conundrum here. Rather than being akin to his creator, he is an artifact molded *(yatzar)* out of earth as God later forms the animals and birds (2:19). Nor is the meaning of his creation mysterious. In contrast to Genesis 1, where *adam* has no instrumental purpose, in Genesis 2, as in Mesopotamian myth, *adam* is designed for labor. His purpose is to serve the earth *(adama)* out of which he has been shaped. I say "he" because the *Adam* of this narrative is both generic human and gendered male. His maleness represents the original human condition, rather than one variety of it. Hence there is no mention of the creation of maleness, as there is in Genesis 1.

Competent and adult from the moment of his creation, endowed with language and engaged in labor, he bears a curious resemblance to the motherless asocial resident of the state of nature in liberal political theory. The creation of woman, like the creation of the social contract, is planned as an improvement on the inconveniences of the original human condition.

> YHWH God said, "It is not good for the *adam* to be alone; I will make a fitting helper for him." And YHWH formed out of the earth all the wild beasts and all the birds of the sky and brought them to the *adam* to see what he would call them . . . but for the *adam* no fitting helper was found. So YHWH God cast a deep sleep upon the *adam;* and while he slept, he took one of his ribs and closed up the flesh at that spot. And YHWH fashioned the rib that he had taken from the *adam* into a woman; and he brought her to the *adam.* (Gen. 2:18–22)

Although human sociality is recognized as a necessity, the remedy for man's isolation is the creation of an oppositional other: "I will make him a helper *k'negdo.*" The word *neged* means both "against" and "corresponding"; hence the term *k'negdo,* translated by the JPS Tanakh as "fitting," actually carries dual senses of polarity and likeness: "a helper who is his counter/part." Instead of the tension of like and other sustained in intersubjective relations, an unequal complementarity is established in which man is the subject and woman, his helper and reflection, is both counter to him and part of him.

Woman is brought into being in a manner unlike that of all other creatures. She is not created (BRH) like *adam* in Genesis 1 nor formed (YTzR) like Adam and the animals in Genesis 2; instead she is constructed (BNH). "YHWH God built the rib into a woman and brought her to the *adam.*" Adam greets her with joy. She does not seem to him to be an other at all. "This one at last / is bone of my bones / and flesh of my flesh. / This one shall be called Woman *(ishah),* / For from man *(ish)* was she taken. / Hence a man leaves his father and mother and clings to his woman *(isha),* so that they become one flesh."[40]

Unlike the P texts, Genesis 1 and 5, Genesis 2 never recognizes the woman as *adam,* only as *isha,* a creature derived from *adam,* contrasted to him and possessed by him, a construction designed to meet his specifications. In contrast, only in the wordplay that establishes woman as derivative is Adam identified by his gender. "This one shall be called

Woman *(isha)* for from man *(ish)* was she taken" (Gen. 2:23). Together they will be *ha-adam v'ishto,* "the human and his woman" (Gen. 2:25).

Whereas in Genesis 1, God declares the various features of creation intrinsically good, Genesis 2 presents earth and its living things as a collection of resources valuable insofar as man can use them. The trees of Eden are "a delight to the eye and good for eating." The rivers that branch out from Eden point to the location of gold and precious stones or mark off the territory of nations. The birds and animals are noted because *adam* names them. Woman's importance lies in the function she fulfills for man. Unlike the beasts and birds, she will serve as a suitable mate. In this world where everything is viewed extractively, the tree of the knowledge of good and evil is an anomaly, a resource whose consumption is mysteriously forbidden.

Genesis 2, then, is a description not of the creation of the universe, but of the creation of the patriarchal perspective, in which the self relates to what is external to it by subjugating or devouring. Its account of the construction of woman to alleviate man's loneliness, of the process of splitting off and opposing femininity to masculinity, and of the resulting sense of mutilation in patriarchal man resembles the theoretical account offered by feminist object-relations psychology. As I summarized in Chapter 2, these theorists view the primal severing of identification with mother as the precipitating event in the construction of oppositional masculine identity. Because the man did not differentiate by learning to regard woman as another independent subject with whom interrelation is possible, he both craves and fears the infantile merger that would heal his estrangement by obliterating his autonomy. He seeks to resolve his dilemma by annexing and reincorporating the other, obliterating her independent selfhood. In both the object-relations story and Genesis, these attempts end badly. Disaster is inevitable in an Eden founded upon fantasies of obliteration. These fantasies carry the seed of death, the ultimate loss of all autonomy and recognition from the other. They are the bridge from the patriarchal Eden to the patriarchal world beyond its boundaries.

In the world brought about in Genesis 3, domination constrains the human couple, fettering humanity to a treadmill of compulsive and futile activity. Woman's sexual desire dooms her to be subjugated by man and to painful childbirths. Man's desire is not even mentioned. His energies are to be exhausted by the unabating struggle to pull food from the dust by which he himself will be devoured. The goodness of creation and mastery conferred in Genesis 1 are complicated by pain, alienation, and defeat.

The redemptive truth offered by this grim depiction is that patriarchal social relations construct a world that cries out to be mended. Yet mending is contingent upon the healing of gender relations. Gender polarity creates a world where power is a burden both for those who wield it and for those under its foot. Compulsive toil and unrelenting watchfulness replace freedom and trust, while hierarchy and caste obstruct fellowship and communion. Boundaries become fearful places where the reciprocal enmity between the serpent and the children of woman lurks. The underling strikes at the heel of his superior, who, in turn, bruises his subordinate's head. At the top of the ladder, privileged man, facing his unrewarding labors, must doubly watch his back, first against the hostility of the serpent on the bottom and then against his nearest other, his competitor for subjectivity.

However unhappy the world of patriarchy may be, it is unnecessary to conclude that it is God's will that we continue to inhabit it.[41] Judaism provides ample precedent for reading Genesis 2 and 3 as an etiological tale about the hardships of human life rather than as a normative statement. The rabbinic tradition does not use the story as a source of legal prooftexts, nor is there any prohibition on alleviating its conditions.[42] Some antitechnological Christian sects have understood the curses following the eating of the fruit as literal prescriptions, but no Orthodox kibbutz harvests with sickles because of the verse "by the sweat of your brow shall you get bread to eat" or refrains from hydroponic gardening because "Thorns and thistles shall it sprout for you. But your food shall be the grasses of the field." When childbirth anesthesia was invented, some Victorian clergymen saw it as a rebellion against the decree "In pain shall you bear children,"[43] but Jewish law never forbade the alleviation of childbirth pain. A consistent reading of the passage would not allow singling out "Your desire shall be for your husband and he shall rule over you" and endowing it alone with prescriptive force.

Passive acceptance of conditions is not an option in the post-Edenic world of Genesis 3. Humanity must act upon its environment simply to survive. This does not necessitate making adversaries of the earth or of one another. Just as we can invent technologies that ease our farming without damaging the earth or decimating its species and techniques that ease our birthing without seizing control from birthing mothers, we can invent ways of coexisting without dominating one another.

The urge to oppose and conquer the other may ultimately be more deadly to our kind than any of its earlier hardships. Dorothy Sayers once asked, "If women are the opposite sex, then what is the neighboring sex?"[44] When woman is defined as derivative *isha* or invaded *nekeva,* a shared reality is denied. We all live deeply within one another's boundaries. The question is whether we can do so in justice.

Leviticus 18: Sexuality and Law

Sexual expression is so powerful a way of bonding with others and so devastating a way of hurting others that it can never be reduced to a mere matter of personal preferences. Sexual desires have immense capacities to order or disorder the social world. Because of this, the social meanings and expressions of sexual desire, connections, and taboos are an organizing component of human societies: Who wants whom? Who belongs with whom? Who is forbidden to whom? What do infractions mean, and what are their consequences?

The Torah delineates such a system of sexual boundary violations and their consequences in Chapter 18 of Leviticus. Documentary Bible critics identify this section as part of an ancient priestly document they call the Holiness Code.[45] Bible readers often invoke its laws in debates over contemporary sexual ethics. Can this code be used as a guide for contemporary sexual behavior, as its upholders insist? If not, must it be rejected as sacred text as its detractors demand? What is its authority over us? Essential as these questions are, they are seldom thought through with any care. In fact, many defenses of the Leviticus code rest upon assumptions to which the defenders really do not subscribe.

Modern historiography, upon which all non-Orthodox Judaisms rely, posits that societies exist in time and change over time. Ideas and institutions reflect a culture's categories, the way it divides up and labels and makes sense of the world. As contexts evolve, so do values and categories, and the laws and institutions through which people live them out. Yet disputants who would assent to all these propositions persist in reading the forbidden couplings of Leviticus 18 as if it did not matter in what kind of society they had originated and as if they ought to be understood in the same way by Jews in every time and place. Unlike the laws about isolation of lepers or flogging or capital punishment for witchcraft, some (but not all) of the laws of Leviticus 18 are upheld as timeless, absolute norms. Why?

The Leviticus code addresses the question: How can we be sexual in a holy way? Perhaps we fear that unless we keep reading these texts in fundamentalist and ahistorical ways we will eradicate whatever sexual boundaries we still possess, or that we will find no other way to affirm that it is possible to be holy while being sexual. Perhaps we fear that if we try to read them contextually, we will not be able to redeem them as sacred text. If so, we have forgotten that what makes Torah sacred is not that it has one fixed eternal meaning, but that its meanings are inexhaustible. We have forgotten how to wander in the company of the sacred, without fearing that, because we do not know where we are headed, we will be lost. This is the lesson we learn in the Book of Numbers. In the wilderness, we live by trust. We do not put down roots or plan our next destination. When the divine cloud lifts itself off the Tabernacle, we pack up and follow, until we arrive at a place where it can settle for a while.

Right now, Americans are in a time of wandering with regard to sexual ethics. The last thirty years have seen sweeping changes in sexual behavior. It is now common for unmarried people of all ages to engage in sex: adolescents in their hormonal prime, young adults who are finishing lengthy educations and are unready to make lifetime commitments, singles seeking compatible life partners, older widows and widowers wanting companionship but loath to risk their pensions or their children's inheritances. Feminism has encouraged women to demand equal power in marriages, to strive for economic independence, and to leave marriages that are unhappy or violent. More people live openly gay or lesbian lives. Unprecedented technological advances have made it possible for people to have sex without having children and to have children without having sex. There is a bewildering range of sexual options with so many lifted constraints.

We live in a highly sexualized society. Indeed, it seems that the more exhausting and the less intrinsically rewarding our work becomes, the more dangerous our environments, the more unknown our neighbors, the more impoverished our internal lives, the more we are urged to consume sex to replenish all this emptiness. Sex is the panacea hawked by movies and best sellers, diet food ads, rap, rock, and pop, fashion marketing, newscasts, plastic surgery. This obsession with the sexual has not produced a society filled either with erotic joy or with erotic tenderness. If the appointment books of psychotherapists and the police blotters are any evidence, the lifting of repressions and the relaxation of taboos have not made us either happier or less hurtful human beings. More than ever, we need to learn how holiness may be expressed through sexuality. Given the escalation of loneliness among us, our insatiable sexual longings, and our confusion about sexual ethics, it is no wonder that some of us wish for the security of unvarying "thou shalts" and "thou shalt nots," sexual boundaries that require no guesswork.

I want to suggest, however, that we have long ceased to draw the boundary lines as the original readers of the Holiness Code did. Not only have our sexual ethics been augmented and emended by rabbinic interpretation, but new and equally compelling "thou shalts" and "thou shalt nots" have emerged from gendered experience in later sociohistorical contexts. Because the Holiness Code's prohibition on homosexuality is currently the focus of dispute, we tend to behave as if the rest of its sexual ethics were unproblematic. But, as I will show, all these laws presuppose power structures and conceptual categories very different from our own. Without interpretation and augmentation, they cannot address the ethical problems that trouble us today.

First of all, sexual boundaries had a different significance in the world in which these texts originated. For the priestly framers of the Holiness Code, they were a subset of the laws of purity. Purity laws demarcate the categories that create and organize the social world: what is masculine or feminine, what is edible or not, what is plant or animal, who is classified as one's own flesh.[46] Stepping across the lines and blurring the categories cause pollution.

Pollution endangers. It threatens to unmake the world by undermining its organizing framework. The two condemnatory terms for the most dangerous of these acts of sabotage are *tevel* and *toevah*. Humans and animals, for example, inhabit different categories. Their sexual union is forbidden (Lev. 18:23) because it is *tevel*, chaos-creating, from the root *bll*, to confuse. It is the ultimate example of mixtures regarded as world-destroying. Others include weaving together linen (a plant) and wool (animal hair), grafting to create hybrids, and interbreeding animals. Behavior censured as *toevah*, "abhorrence," erases primary distinctions between the Israelite culture and those surrounding it. *Toevah* infractions, as the word is used throughout the Torah, imitate idolatrous cultic practices or undermine practices that define the ethos of Israelite culture, such as refraining from eating unclean species.

The sexual connections that undermine the categories of the priestly world are called the *arayot.* The singular, *erva,* literally means an exposure of the genitals. *Erva,* along with concerns about purity, fertility, and genealogy, is a major topic of priestly writings. Of the fifty-five biblical occurrences of the word *erva,* thirty-two are in Chapters 18 and 20 of Leviticus. Another two, in Exodus, concern priestly garb.[47] Eight times the term occurs in Ezekiel, the prophet most preoccupied with priesthood and purity.[48]

Erva both shames the exposed and opens their boundaries to invasion and conquest. It is no coincidence, then, that in forty-five of the fifty-five instances the exposed subject is imaged as female.[49] In these and many other biblical texts, with the notable exception of the Song of Songs, the sexual act is the paradigmatic enactment of dominant and submissive relations. Right relations are defined as those in which the male is entitled to expose and dominate. In disordered relations, his exposure and domination violate the way the world is supposed to be structured.

The primary category demarcation, in this society organized by patriarchal kinships, is the generational boundary between father and son through which power and authority are handed down. The first *arayot* mentioned are those that disrupt this flow: sexual breaches in which the son reaches upward toward women appropriated by the elder generation, his mother or his father's wife who is not his mother. A man is forbidden to expose his father, as in the story of Noah and his sons, or to usurp the father's exclusive right of exposure.[50] This is the sin of Reuven, who lies with his father's concubine Bilhah (Gen. 35: 22) and is consequently disinherited as firstborn (Gen. 49:3–4). David's son Absalom as well climaxes his revolt by public intercourse with his father's concubines (2 Sam. 16:21–22).[51] Taking the father's woman is a *political* act that redirects the genealogical flow. It pollutes by fundamentally disorganizing the patriarchal world.

These commandments do not refer to incest as moderns define it: the sexual victimization of younger kin by older, more powerful relatives. It is the son, not the parent, who is cautioned not to initiate sex. Moreover, father-daughter incest, the most common abuse of patriarchal power, is not even mentioned.[52] Its prohibition is inferred by the rabbis.[53]

All the *arayot* are addressed to males: sons, fathers, and brothers. All these prohibitions begin "you shall not." Women are not directly addressed even regarding the one *erva* in which they are named as perpetrators: Leviticus 18:23 reads *V'isha lo ta'amod lifnei vehemah l'riv'ah,* "let no woman stand before a beast to go down on all fours for it [my translation]."[54] What is sinful and world-polluting here is not inflicting sexual violence or betraying trust but violating the categories and statuses that define the various social actors.

In most of the cases, the lines that must not be crossed, the categories that must not be breached, enclose women who belong to other men. Adultery is defined as sexual intercourse with another man's wife, although she is equally culpable. But as long as his mistress is not some other man's possession, a husband's unfaithfulness is not an *erva*. Unlike wifehood, husbandhood is not a status and creates no status limitations.

Monogamous marriage is not a norm either in these texts or in many later texts. Biblical narratives attest to the practices of concubinage and polygyny.[55] The Babylonian talmudic tradition continued to permit polygyny.[56] Indeed, on the basis of two stories in tractate Yebamot, Isaiah M. Gafni argues that the Babylonian tradition even countenanced time-limited, temporary marriages, as did non-Jews in Sassanian Persia—a convenient arrangement for men on business trips![57] Reviewing evidence from the Cairo *Geniza* (roughly seventh to thirteenth centuries), Mordecai Friedman writes:

> whereas most marriages certainly were monogamous (as is the case in almost all polygygnous societies), polygyny and concubinage with slave girls were far from rare occurrences, and the Jewish community frequently occupied itself with the problems associated with these phenomena.[58]

Monogamy may be a primary Jewish value in our moral universe, but it did not become mandatory for Western Jews until the medieval period; for Jews from Arab countries, polygyny was finally outlawed by the State of Israel.[59]

Other sexual rules that moderns regard as fundamental to a Jewish sexual ethic need to be read back into the Torah the way the rabbis read in the prohibition on father-daughter incest or later authorities read in a prohibition on polygyny. Today, we regard child molestation as an abhorrent crime. Yet the Torah specifies no minimum age for sex with a girl-child, and the Talmud's minimum age is three. The Talmud prescribes no penalty for intercourse with a girlchild under age three, because it was believed that the hymen would regenerate at that age, and consequently she was considered to have sustained no damage (Ketubbot 11a–b). In the worlds of Torah and Talmud, fathers are entitled to marry off minor daughters without their consent (M. Yebamot 13:2).[60] They are also permitted to sell minor daughters as slaves.[61] Talmudic law presumes that former slavegirls are not virgins (M. Ketubbot 3:2), either because slaves could not protect themselves against sexual intrusion or because, as Wegner suggests, the minor had been raped prior to sale.[62] Wegner argues that the right of sale, combined with the absence of indemnity for the rape of a minor (M. Ketubbot 3:8), virtually forced the father of a minor to recoup the loss in her marital value by selling her. The Talmud also prescribes no penalty for sodomizing a very young boy. In the opinion of Rav, a very young boy is defined as less than nine years of age and, in the opinion of Shemuel, less than three (Sanhedrin 54b). This does not mean that these acts were necessarily well regarded, but it does mean that what modern Jews consider heinous sexual crimes carried no criminal penalties in these earlier Judaisms.

Another sexual crime that contemporary society regards more severely than Jewish tradition is rape. The only rapes about which the Torah legislates are destructions of virginity. The rape of an unmarried girl is viewed as a property crime against the girl's father.[63] Perpetrators must pay a fine and bride price and keep the woman (Deut. 22:28–29).[64] "He must drink from his garbage-pot," says the Mishnah.[65] The rape of an *arusa*, a woman who has been appropriated but not yet installed in her husband's home, is not merely a property crime but a socially disordering act like adultery whose perpetrators incur the death penalty.[66] To be exonerated, the woman must prove she was not complicit.[67] Other rapes, even the brutal gang rape by which the concubine of Gibeah meets her death in Judges 19, are not classified as world-disordering violations. In social contexts where women are regarded more as people than as commodities, rape is defined by the experience of the victim. Hence, contemporary thinking about rape emphasizes the terror, violation, and degradation experienced by its victims.[68] But where all sexual intercourse is viewed as an expression of dominance and submission, rape seems more normal; it is simply an improper method of acquisition.[69] It is when sexuality becomes an expression of caring and sharing, rather than just *having*, that rape becomes an atrocity.

Our discussions about child molestation and rape demonstrate how profoundly some of our values about sexuality have diverged from those of our ancestors. Now, in the context of all we have been saying, let us turn to the controversial verse, Leviticus 18:22: "Do not lie with a male as one lies with a woman; it is a *toevah.*" What could that have meant in its earliest context? What ought it to mean to us now? One proposed rationale for the prohibition is the priestly concern with fertility. Homosexual intercourse wastes the precious fluid through which the divine promise is realized: "I will make your seed as numerous as the stars of heaven" (Gen. 22:17). Hence, like sexual intercourse with menstruants, it is forbidden because it cannot lead to conception.[70] But even if this explains the prohibition in Israelite religion, it does not suffice for later Judaisms in which procreation is not the only legitimate reason for intercourse. Thus, the rabbinic tradition permits sex when women are pregnant or menopausal, when male semen is insufficiently numerous or active to enable procreation, and, in certain cases, when procreation is intentionally prevented.[71] Moreover, modern technologies such as artificial insemination and test-tube fertilization make it possible to procreate without engaging in heterosexual intercourse. Fertility, therefore, is not a credible reason for continuing to prohibit homosexual relations.

Some scholars have argued that Israelite culture knows of only two types of homosexual acts: acts of cultic prostitution, specifically forbidden in Deuteronomy 23:18; and acts of aggression against strangers, as in the Sodom story (Gen. 19), in which the Israelite practice violated is the sacredness of hospitality.[72] They conclude that only these acts were forbidden. Yet, there is no way of proving that the priestly writers shared this opinion. Moreover, even if we assume that the absence of biblical narratives about consensual and nonidolatrous same-sex relations suggests that the Bible wishes male sexual desire to be directed solely toward women, we cannot conclude that the Bible's attitude toward homosexuality is simple and obvious. Howard Eilberg-Schwartz contends that repressed homosexual desires boil beneath the Bible's surface, complicating the relations of Israelite man and his masculine deity.[73]

There is another way also in which a man lying with a man as with a woman subverts Israelite notions of order and proper assignment of power: a man declasses another man by this act. Someone socially assigned to a dominant role is forced to enact a subordinate role that degrades by feminizing.[74] That would explain why in Genesis 19 and in Judges 19 homosexual rape is so much more repugnant than heterosexual rape.

Now we are at the nub of our problem with the Leviticus laws. Some of the very boundary demarcations intended to establish right relations instead build injustices into the social fabric. The titanic struggle that feminism has initiated in our own time is a struggle to disentangle sexual relationships from power inequities, not to reinforce them. Right relations in the moral universe moderns inhabit are characterized by reciprocity, mutuality, tenderness, and equal power. Perhaps we should reread the prohibition on homosexuality with the exegetical device the rabbis call a *ribui*, an extension: Because it is forbidden for a man to force submission upon another man, it is, by extension, forbidden to subordinate any sexual partner!

We can redeem the *arayot* as foundational moral teachings if we are able to think of law in Robert Cover's terms: not as a static entity, but as a bridge between our present moral universe and the yet unrealized moral universe toward which we are reaching, a bridge we constitute through the committed social actions by which we try to get from here to there.[75] If so, the Leviticus laws are still important to us. They are part of what is holding down one end of the bridge. But we need to look not just at where they were, but at where they are pointing.

Genesis 1 teaches that we are created *b'tzelem elohim*, that our diverse sexualities reflect some element in the complex unity that is God. Leviticus demands that we manifest that likeness in our sexual lives. The Holiness Code's explanation of its laws is *kedoshim tihiyu ki kadosh YHWH elohekha*, "You shall be holy, because I YHWH your God am holy" (Lev. 19:2).

That statement is sandwiched between two lists of laws. The preceding list is that of the *arayot*, which mark off the sexual boundaries. The succeeding list specifies the basic commandments for just and loving interactions, concluding with *v'ahavta l'rei'ekha k'mokha*, "You shall love your neighbor as yourself" (Lev. 19:18). The medieval commentator Ibn Ezra contends that "you shall be holy" sums up both the list it concludes and the list it introduces. If so, holiness has to do both with setting limits and with forging bonds, with separation and with connection. If we had no boundaries and limits, we could never give one another the gift of relaxing them and welcoming a special other in.

How would we read the laws about sexual boundaries if we saw them as a subset of laws about justice to our neighbor? We could think of them as rules that make trust possible. Sexual boundaries strengthen trust within committed relationships. They bond partners uniquely to one another. But generational boundaries and status rules can also foster trust. They can ensure that elders do not abuse their influence or authority with those they should be guiding and tending, and that younger, less powerful persons need not offer their bodies in exchange for protection or regard. We could then extrapolate to helping relationships that have no parallels in the priestly world, covenants between rabbis and congregants, doctors and patients, therapists and clients, teachers and students.[76] Wherever power is unequally distributed, the sexual integrity of the less powerful party must be guarded.

To contend that sexual boundaries need to fit our moral universe is not to say that there should be no boundaries. All Jews have an obligation to express their sexuality in a holy way. But as communities, we have an obligation to keep regenerating the norms for how that is to be done. How it was done in the First Temple, in the Babylonian academies, in seventh-century Vilna must echo in our conversation, but previous generations' wrestlings with the text do not absolve us of responsibility to reapproach it here and now. It is up to us to make a world for one another where, in the words of the Psalmist, "Lovingkindness and truth will embrace; justice and peace will kiss each other" (Ps. 85:11).

The Song of Songs: Two Subjects, One Love

It is one thing to set the boundaries within which holy sexual expression may occur, but it is quite another to image the act. Are there lovers among the righteous, and if so, how do they make love? When they are intertwined, drenched, transported, are they still embodying the divine image? In much of the Bible, the physical expression of sexuality is flatly noted: "and he knew *(yad'a)* her." We are party to this information only because a manchild has come of it.

The Bible is reticent about the emotions accompanying sexual relationships. Almost always, the feelings recorded are those of men, and they are stark and unmodulated, either love or hate. Where there are several wives, the favorite is "loved" and the unfavored is "hated."[77] Revulsion can also follow on the heels of love. After Amnon's rape of his half-sister Tamar, he "hated her with a great hatred, greater than the love with which he had loved her."[78] Of the 208 occurrences of the verb "to love" in the Bible, women are subjects of the verb in only eleven. Five of these eleven instances are in the Song of Songs.

The Bible's most vivid representations of sexual love occur in the Song and in the prophets. This great metaphor of Israel's love relationship with

God, which lies at the heart of biblical literature from the Pentateuch through the prophets, is regarded by some scholars as a monotheistic transformation of the sacred marriage of god and goddess reenacted in Mesopotamian religious rites.[79] If so, the portrayal of woman's desire was badly mangled in the process. In graphic depictions of adulterous sex, the prophets equate woman's desire with the appetite for idolatry, woman's eroticism with betrayal of covenant.[80] The prophet pulls the reader into a shared voyeurism, recounting these forbidden sexual pleasures and the stripping and punishment that follow them: "Abandoning me, you have gone up / On the couch you made so wide. You have made a covenant with them. / You loved bedding with them" (Isa. 57:8–9). Chaotically indiscriminate, woman's desire appears as a monstrous inversion of assigned gender roles. "You spread your legs for every passer-by" (Ezek. 16:25). "You were the obverse of other women; soliciting instead of being solicited; paying instead of being paid" (Ezek. 16:34). That not all prophetic depictions of eroticism are demonic does not solve the problem. Ilana Pardes observes, "The prophets, who offer a profusion of detailed chastisements concerning Israel's wanton ways, become rather reticent when dealing with blissful erotic moments between God and the nation."[81]

In the Song of Songs, in contrast, we do not observe the lovers from some alien moral vantage point. We share their perspective. We experience through their consciousness. When the Shulamite proclaims her desire in her own voice, that desire is neither gross nor demonic, but joyful and appreciative. Only in the Song of Songs is woman's desire desirable.

As a dissonant text in a canon that distrusts eroticism and links it to orgiastic paganism, the Song's inclusion in the Bible was controversial.[82] Its canonization both affirms and denies the moral and spiritual possibilities of eroticism. Rabbi Akiba's passionate defense of the Song in Mishnah Yadaim 3:5 as "the holy of holies" may be a tacit recognition that the Song's canonization hangs upon its rabbinic interpretation as sacred allegory.[83] Yet the content of that allegory, which translates the passion of the two lovers into the love between God and Israel, and especially between God and the rabbis, distances itself from the erotic relations of real women and men, implicitly undermining their holiness. We are back to the questions with which we began: Do human sexuality and human sexual expression reflect the divine image?

In the rabbinic tradition, the encounter with the other is an embodied meeting. The bodily imperatives of the other are as real and as important as spiritual and emotional needs. Yet the rabbinic allegory of the Song links the bodily expression of sexuality with the stigmatized difference of women and banishes both from their moral universe. The rabbinic allegory leaves no room for women, because it reassigns the feminine role to male Jews. God assumes the role of male lover, while a male Israel, or more specifically, the students of Torah, are cast as the female lover. These acts of splitting, projection, and rejection cannot be divorced from questions of power.

To reinstate an ethics from which women are not excepted depends upon our understanding carnal love as neither domination nor debasement but as a communion of equals. This is the project that leads feminist thinkers back to the Song of Songs. Feminist scholars, both Jewish and Christian, have long identified the Songs of Songs as a dissident representation of sexual relations between men and women within the biblical canon.[84] It is the one canonical source whose perspective is unarguably antipatriarchal. First of all, one of the main characters is female, and she is of intrinsic interest, whereas in most biblical texts women are minor characters who appear because they are instrumental to some action or purpose affecting the destinies of men.

The Songs of Songs is atypical, moreover, because it celebrates mutuality. A major theme in biblical narratives where women are prominent, from Tamar and Judah to Samson and Delilah, is the violation and subsequent restoration of male sexual dominion. But in the Song of Songs, there is no sexual dominion. The man's sexual feelings and behaviors are not privileged above those of the woman, nor is her sexual subjectivity portrayed as violative. Both are subjects of desire: givers, gazers, and wooers. The lovers of the Song are a match, not because one opposes the other or complements the other or possesses the other, but because each acclaims the other. The Song of Songs has become, therefore, the wellspring of both feminist theology and feminist sexual ethics.

The Song provides both a mythic past in which the faulty relations between women and men were righted and a feminist eschatology in which justice and harmony will ultimately be restored. For Phyllis Trible, this poem about lovers in a garden redeems the love story that went awry in the Garden of Eden.[85] "In this setting," she contends, "there is no male dominance, no female subordination, and no stereotyping of either sex."[86] Marcia Falk seems to allude to this hope of ultimate restoration when she suggests that "this ancient text has something new to teach us about how to redeem sexuality and love in our fallen world."[87]

Yet if the Song of Songs is a return to Eden, it is not the Eden of which Adam and Eve were caretakers. The garden of Genesis is an Eden without *ednah*. Sensuous pleasure is not depicted there. In the garden of the Song, however, luscious fruits are sources of delight rather than temptations to sin. Flowers and spices, animals and birds, are not objects to tend or exploit, but an exuberant flowering of life contiguous with and reflective of the lovers' own. Work itself is eroticized, an opportunity for dalliance among the flocks. All the environments the lovers inhabit are settings for festivity and play: gardens and vineyards, banquets, processions, and dances.[88]

The hierarchical relations established in the Eden story are overthrown in the Song. Eden's gender polarities are inverted or dissolved. "Your desire *(teshukatekh)* shall be for your husband," Genesis 3 decrees, "and he shall rule over you." The Shulamite exults, "I am for my beloved *(ani l'dodi)* and his desire *(teshukato)* is for me" (Song of Songs 7:11).[89] For the lovers in the Song, desire and power are shared attributes.[90] Reciprocally, they praise each other's bodies in lingering detail from head to foot.[91] Reciprocally, they speak imperatives: "Sustain me," "Refresh me," "Arise," "Open to me," "Turn back," "Run away." Both are clothed in images of power, the man as a king (1:4,12), and, in a splendid subversion of gender stereotyping, the female as a triumphant army (6:10).

Some imagery in the Song overflows gender categories.[92] Both lovers liken each other to fawns browsing among the lilies; to orchard trees, to Mount Lebanon. Each attributes to the other eyes like doves and the smells of henna, nard, and myrrh. In other images, as readers have noted since the time of the Mishnah, gender is difficult to assign.[93] Even after the canonization of Masoretic voweling, some passages remain assignable to either the male or the female speaker, a remarkable feat for a poem written in a gender-inflected language.[94]

We see the lovers, as we never see Adam and Eve, playing together. Their play is physical, even childlike. "Draw me after you, let us run" (1:4); "There he comes, / Leaping over mountains, / Bounding over hills" (2:8). Whereas Adam and Eve conceal themselves in terror and shame from a punishing God, the lovers of the Song play at concealment, teasing each other with endless games of peekaboo and hide and seek. He pleads, "O my dove, in the cranny of the rocks, / Hidden by the cliff / Let me see your face" (2:14). He tells her, "You have thrilled my heart / With one of your eyes" (4:9).[95] "There he stands behind our wall," the Shulamite says, "Gazing through the window, / Peering through the lattice" (2:9), one of the few male faces in the Bible framed in a window.[96]

While for Trible the postpatriarchal world is fully realized in the Song, Ilana Pardes emphasizes the subversiveness of the lovers' bond.[97] She points out that the mutuality and eroticism of the lovers is shadowed by a backdrop of threatening patriarchal figures, the woman's brothers and the city watchmen. Gardens, fields, vineyards, or solitary wild places, mountains, and deserts are places of safety to which the lovers escape. The structures of city and family interpose between them, as do internalized patriarchal restrictions. For Pardes, the Song both challenges and accepts the authority of patriarchal law over female bodies and female eroticism. Locating these tensions in the Song itself explains how it has been used to support radically conflicting ethics of sexuality and requires that interpreters assume responsibility for their interpretations and for the ethical visions drawn from them. As I illustrate later on, by tipping the balance toward one pole, the rabbis use the Song to curb female sexuality and to attenuate female sexual subjectivity. Tipping the balance toward the other pole makes possible a moral vision in which carnal love is not an expression of power.

The structure of the Song differs from that of every other biblical book. It is not presented as a series of discrete units like the Psalms. Like a narrative, it has a setting and a cast of characters. Yet the narrative is not coherent. It is nonlinear, even dream-like; one setting fades into another, and fantasy cannot be distinguished from action. "Love is as strong as death," the woman proclaims (8:6). If death is the triumph of time, love is the triumph of timelessness. Outside the dimension of time, the lovers have enjoyed, have never enjoyed, are always enjoying one another's love. Hence, passages hinting at a consummated relationship are interspersed with passages that revert to unconsummated longings.

Time is not all that dissolves in the Song. The physical boundaries between the lovers dissolve. Formless substances and unbodied forces provide the imagery that conveys this dissolution: beverages, scents, wind, fire, and flood. The lovers themselves are liquescent, and, in contrast to the pollutant body fluids of the purity laws, the juices they drip are delectable. "Sweetness drops / from your lips, O bride; / Honey and milk / Are under your tongue" (4:11). "His lips are like lilies; /They drop flowing myrrh. / His mouth [literally *ḥiko*, his palate] is delicious / And all of him is delightful." "O for your kiss!" she exclaims, "For your love more enticing than wine."[98] Wine and pomegranate juice, the blood-dark liquids, evoke no disgust here. The lovers imbibe each other thirstily.

In the Song, genital sexuality is subsumed within an encompassing polymorphous eroticism that makes the lovers equals and connects them to their surroundings. It is this eroticism that makes the geography of the lovers' bodies contiguous with the landscape and with the animals and birds that inhabit it, that allows them to see each other in mountains, and pools, fawns, and doves, and to taste and smell each other in spices, fruit, honey, milk, and wine.[99]

The Song's capacity to give a voice to its female protagonist is directly related to its polymorphous experience of sexuality. Polymorphous eroticism, in which feelings of pleasure are distributed over the entire surface of the body, was regarded by Freud as the most primitive infantile developmental stage (oral-passive). It was to be superseded by oral-biting, anal, and ultimately, a genital stage in which sexual feelings finally settle where Freud thought they belonged—in the penis and vagina.[100] Mature sexuality requires that the female relinquish erotic independence and depend upon the phallically endowed male. Linking woman's desire to polymorphous eroticism, and to the entire playground of bodies in relationship, denies this foundational assumption of male sexual dominance. Jessica Benjamin expresses this forcefully:

> The relationship itself, or, more precisely, the exchange of gestures conveying attunement, and not the organ, serves to focus women's pleasure. . . . The dance of mutual recognition, the meeting of separate selves, is the context for their desire. When the sexual self is represented by the sensual capacities of the whole body, when the totality of space between, outside, and within our bodies becomes the site of pleasure, then desire escapes the borders of the imperial phallus and resides on the shores of endless worlds.[101]

This intertwining of whole bodies and whole selves engages the imagination as genitally focused eroticism does not.[102] Indeed, the imagination is its primary erogenous zone. In contrast to the narrowly focused specificity of the genital, polymorphous eroticism is charged with metaphor. Metaphor makes the entire universe a prism to refract human yearning and delight. Disentangling the knot of sensuous experience into iridescent threads, it reweaves them into images that point toward what is too vast and too complex ever to be wholly grasped. It is this capacity for bridging the gap between the embodied and the ineffable that befits metaphor for sacred language.

Commentators have noted that the absence of an explicit sexual consummation distances the Song from the erotica of polytheistic religions and also makes it usable for theologies in which eschatological fulfillment is yet to come.[103] That the eroticism of the Song is polymorphous rather than genital, then, makes possible its classical interpretation as an allegory of the love between God and Israel.[104] What devalues carnality and disempowers women is the rabbinic tradition's refusal to regard this eroticism as "real sex." There is no consummation in the Song if consummation means penile penetration and ejaculation. Genital intercourse, though it is not precluded by a holistic eroticism, is not the sole definition of a complete sexual encounter. According an eroticism of whole bodies and whole selves its own integrity, independent of genital intercourse, allows the Song to put on flesh once more and restores women to the world of the text.

The recognition of polymorphous eroticism as "real sex" also presents a solution to the related dilemma posed by Eilberg-Schwartz concerning the relations between the God of Jewish tradition and his male worshippers.[105] Eilberg-Schwartz argues that both biblical and rabbinic narratives assume that God has a phallus, although this portion of the divine anatomy is veiled, rather than explicitly represented. The veiling of this divine phallus, however, becomes intensely problematic because it expresses a paradox. The priestly writer of Genesis 1 insists that humanity embodies the divine image. If God has no phallus, then the human phallus is not in the divine image. But if God does have a phallus, it cannot be used, because a monotheistic God cannot have a consort. In this case, it is male sexual activity that is not in the divine image. Obviously, as Eilberg-Schwartz briefly notes, the female body is excluded from the divine image by either of these alternatives. However, he contends, the paradox also leaves males in conflict with their bodies and reproductive capacities. Traced into rabbinic literature, the paradox explains tensions between the rabbinic insistence upon procreation as a commandment and the prohibition of homosexuality on the one hand and the homoerotic electricity between student and teacher, between study partners, and between God and rabbinic man fostered by rabbinic institutions and rabbinic interpretation of the Bible on the other.

Eilberg-Schwartz's dilemma is only intensified by the traditional interpretation of the Song of Songs. The problem is that he does not interrogate the assumption of his rabbinic sources that genital equals sexual. For Eilberg-Schwartz, nonphallic eroticism is "metaphoric," by which he seems to mean *unreal* rather than *hyperreal.* I return later to the difficulties of this position.

Rabbinic attitudes toward nonphallic eroticism depend upon the gender toward which they are directed. Among males and in the environments of study and prayer, nonphallic eroticism is not problematic. I have written elsewhere about how the rabbis channel and normalize homoeroticism through the institution of study partnerships and the eroticizing of study that accompanies them.[106] Daniel Boyarin also notes homoerotic themes attached in particular to stories about the beautiful Rabbi Yoḥanan ben Nappaḥa.[107] In the spiritualized homoeroticism based upon Song of Songs, the garden is the study house, the scholars are companions in the garden, or the beloved of God. The perfumes and ornaments are words of Torah. These tropes recur pervasively in both Talmuds, in Sifre, Mekhilta, Targum, and *Song of Songs Rabba.*

In contrast, regarding the sexual relation between men and women, the rabbis deny the very possibility of an eroticism that is not genital. The talmudic passage we are going to focus upon strikingly illustrates how the rabbis use the Song's diffused eroticism to validate a sexual ethos that is its very antithesis. In Berakhot 24a–b, the erotic imagery of the Song is manufactured into prooftexts that systematically reduce women to their genitalia.

The text we are going to read deals with rabbinic anxieties about nakedness, *erva.* Interestingly, the Song of Songs itself, in which bodies are so visible and so praised, contains no words for nakedness. The principal concern of our talmudic passage, in contrast, is to determine what constitutes sexual exposure. Its starting question is whether men may recite *Shema* when they are naked in bed with others (men, women, or children). In this connection, it cites R. Huna's opinion that it is only when the vulva is visible that women are sexually exposed. According to R. Huna, therefore, a naked woman sitting and kneading dough is in a state of adequate modesty to make a blessing over the *ḥallah* offering she takes from it.

> The *baraita* says, "each one turns his face away and recites *Shema.*"
> But their buttocks are touching! This supports R. Huna who says

140

buttocks do not at all constitute *erva*, [i.e., are not erotic]. Can we say that this supports another teaching of R. Huna: A woman may sit naked [on the ground] and take the *ḥallah* offering from her dough [reciting the appropriate blessing] because her "face" [euphemism for genitals] can be covered by the earth, but a man cannot. R. Naḥman bar Yitzḥak explained, [this applies] when her "face" is plastered with earth.

The metaphor of face for vulva is not unique to the Talmud. The vagina (Latin for sheath or scabbard) must also be a mouth since it is surrounded by labia (Latin for lips). The face is our most individual body part, the one by which we are identified, the locus of our meetings with others.[108] In R. Huna's case, as elaborated by R. Naḥman bar Yitzḥak, the woman's "face" is her vulva, and it is plastered with mud.

At what age, asks the text, is a minor in bed with a man saying *Shema* an erotic distraction? It specifies signs of incipient maturation, thus leading the discussion back to its central concern: defining and delimiting the sexually arousing nakedness of the other. The view of R. Huna, that the woman's vulva is, in effect, her only sexual characteristic, is outweighed by an avalanche of prooftexts from Torah, prophets and the Song of Songs, claiming that the entire woman is a genital exposure:

R. Yitzḥak said, "a handsbreadth [exposed] of a woman is *erva*." In what legal context? If [R. Yitzḥak's pronouncement] regards the prohibition of gazing at her, here is what R. Sheshet said: "Why does Scripture include the outer ornaments with the inner ornaments [in Num. 31:50]? To tell you: Anyone who gazes at the little finger of a woman, it is as if he were gazing at the filthy place *(makom ha-toref)*. Another alternative is that the legal context [of R. Yitzḥak's pronouncement] is confined to the case of a man's own wife when he is reciting *Shema*."

R. Ḥisda said: "A woman's leg is *erva*, as it is written, 'bare your leg. Wade through rivers.' The text continues, 'Your *erva* shall be uncovered and your shame shall be seen' (Isa. 47:1–3)." Shemuel said: "A woman's voice is *erva*, as it is written 'for your voice is sweet and your face is comely' (Song of Songs 2:14–15)." R. Sheshet said: "A woman's hair is *erva*, as it is written, 'your hair is like a flock of goats' (Song of Songs 4:1)."

R. Yitzḥak's opening statement for this section is a global generalization: if a handsbreadth of the woman is visible, that constitutes total exposure. The Gemara asks whether R. Yitzḥak's pronouncement applies to the broad prohibition of gazing at a woman or only to the much narrower prohibition of gazing at one's wife while reciting *Shema* in bed. The question is not explicitly answered, but the claims and prooftexts that follow do not appear to confine themselves to the narrow case.

What is the sense of these prooftexts? What do the rabbis intend by them? Let us look first at R. Ḥisda's prooftext. "R. Ḥisda said: A woman's leg is *erva*, as it is written, 'bare your leg. Wade through rivers.'" The text continues, "Your *erva* shall be uncovered and your shame shall be seen." The prooftext cites a passage from Isaiah 47:1–3 depicting Babylon as a noblewoman enslaved when her country is defeated in war.

> *Get down, sit in the dust,*
> *Fair Maiden Babylon;*
> *Sit dethroned on the ground,*
> *O Fair Chaldea,*
> *Never more shall they call you*
> *the tender and dainty one.*
> *Grasp the handmill and grind meal*
> *Remove your veil*
> *Strip off your train, bare your leg,*
> *Wade through the rivers.*
> *Your nakedness shall be uncovered,*
> *And your shame shall be exposed.*

The images of Babylon as an enslaved captive woman sitting on the ground grinding meal for bread conflated with the images of her stripping and exposure remind us of the talmudic image offered by R. Huna and R. Naḥman: a naked Jewish woman, her vulva plastered with mud, taking the *ḥallah* portion from her dough. Whereas Isaiah depicts the humiliation of a "virgin" enemy, one never before invaded and dominated, the rabbinic legal example is a mundane episode in the work life of a Jewish woman. It is normal for this face to be smeared with mud.

The two prooftexts that follow R. Ḥisda's are from the Song of Songs: Shemuel said: "A woman's voice is *erva*, as it is written 'for your voice is sweet and your face is comely' (Song of Songs 2:14–15)." R. Sheshet said: "A woman's hair is *erva*, as it is written, 'your hair is like a flock of goats' (Song of Songs 4:1)." Let us first examine the source of Shemuel's prooftext:

> *O my dove in the cranny of the rocks,*
> *Hidden by the cliff,*
> *Let me see your face* (mar'ayikh)
> *Let me hear your voice;*

142

For your voice is sweet
And your face is comely.

In the Song of Songs passage, the dove in the cranny of the rocks hidden by the cliff suggests both the fluttering clitoris lodged between the labia and hidden by the cliff of the mons veneris and the fluttering tongue lodged in her hidden face with its dove-like eyes, and dove-like voice.[109] At the same time, however, it refers to the woman as an entity. Her *mar'eh* is not merely her face, as the JPS translates it, but her visible form, her appearance as a whole. This constellation of metaphors takes the form of a chiasmus, a parallelism in which the elements of one line are repeated in reverse order in the next line. Shemuel reduces this chiasmus which so intricately intertwines face/appearance and voice to a crude equation: voice = vulva. The Song of Songs citation becomes a means to declare that woman has no other face than this one, which the preceding legal discussion exposed to us, plastered with mud.

R. Sheshet's prooftext for his contention that a woman's hair is *erva* cites Song of Songs 4:1:

> *Ah you are fair, my darling,*
> *Ah you are fair.*
> *Your eyes are like doves behind your veil.*
> *Your hair is like a flock of goats*
> *streaming down Mount Gilead.*

In the Song itself, the male lover's appreciation, his reiterated "Ah, you are fair" *(hinakh yafa),* is balanced by the female lover's identical praise of him *hinekha yafe).* Landy describes the poem as "a giant tautology," in which repeated praises substitute for "the act of which no words can be spoken."[110] The refrain marks points of communion and of erotic stasis in the text:

> The lovers look in each other's eyes and say . . . "Behold you are
> beautiful . . . behold you are beautiful." The doves to which the eyes
> are compared fly to and fro. They are united in their love and just
> apart; there is no desire, no tension between them. At this point
> beauty is not enigmatic, for there are no questions, merely the
> unquestionable *"hinnak . . . hinneka."*[111]

What, however, is the meaning of R. Sheshet's contention that the simile comparing the woman's hair to a flock of goats streaming down a mountain proves that women's hair constitutes *erva?* We can only make sense of this by arguing that R. Sheshet is reading from the beginning of the verse, that it is the male's declaration "behold you are beautiful" that marks the characteristics that follow as *erva*. Implicitly, R. Sheshet splits the declarations of erotic appreciation echoing through the Song: only those of the male are significant in his prooftext. The refrain "Ah you are fair," rather than signifying the lovers' union in erotic stasis, points an accusing finger toward the female features that arouse the restless concupiscence of the male, in this case the woman's hair. R. Sheshet traces the effect back to its cause: the man declares, "Ah, you are fair" because he has seen the woman's unbound hair exposed. The cause of eros is *erva*.

We have not yet discussed one of the "genitalizing" prooftexts from our talmudic passage. That is R. Sheshet's earlier citation of Numbers 31:50 to claim that "Anyone who gazes at the little finger of a woman, it is as if he were gazing at the filthy place *(makom ha-toref)*." Numbers 31:50 contains a biblical account of ornaments captured from the Midianites. It is less than obvious how this proves that a woman's little finger is like her vulva. If we persevere, however, we will discover that R. Sheshet's proof is part of an extensive midrash on Numbers 31 that can be found in B. Shabbat 64a–b. Let us turn to this remarkable midrash.

The biblical passage upon which the midrash is based depicts the aftermath of a battle. Midianite priestesses have attempted to seduce the tribes into pagan fertility rites, and the Israelites have retaliated with war. At Numbers 31:48, where the midrash begins, the officers of the victorious Israelite army bring Moses the looted Midianite ornaments as an offering to God. What puzzles the midrashists is the purpose of this offering. The officers begin by reporting that no Israelite soldiers were lost in battle, which suggests that the ornaments are a thank-offering. But they conclude by saying they have brought the ornaments "to make expiation for ourselves," which indicates a sin-offering. If the offering is expiatory, what had they done? Is there any clue to be found in the catalogue of obscurely named ornaments? By explicating the biblical verses line by line, the midrash clarifies this mystery while imparting a sexual ethic to its auditors.

> And we have brought as an offering to the Lord such articles of gold as each of us came upon: armlets *(etzada)*, bracelets *(tzamid)*, signet rings *(taba'at)*, earrings *(agil)*, and pendants *(kumaz)*.[112]
>
> R. El'azar said, an *agil* is an image (or cast) *(defus)* of female breasts. A *kumaz* is an image/cast of the vulva *(bet ha-rehem*, lit. "the house of the womb").[113]
>
> R. Yosef said, "If so, that is why the Aramaic translation renders it as *mahokh*—a thing that leads to *gihukh*, obscenity or laughter.[114]

Rabba said to him, from the very letters of the word, its meaning
can be inferred: *kumaz* is an acronym for **kan makom zima,** "the
place of lustfulness is there."

In our first talmudic passage in Berakhot, the Song of Songs was
invoked to genitalize every part of a woman. Here, even her ornaments
represent a sexual iconography. And just as R. Ḥisda's prooftext equated
the enslaved Babylonian captive with the Jewish woman, this midrash
uses its prooftext about the looted jewelry of conquered Midianite women
to teach loathing for the sexuality of Jewish women. Two sets of equiva-
lences emerge from these texts: (1) the female body and all its adorn-
ments are like a vulva; and (2) the Jewish woman is like a captive
enslaved, an enemy defeated.

In contrast to the bawdy laughter of Sarah or the playfulness of the
Song, this text sniggers. A *kumaz* is a vulva, which is a *maḥokh,* something to leer at. For Rabba, the very letters of the word *kumaz* announce
it: *kan makom zima,* "there (down there) is the place of *zima.*" And what
is *zima?* Its connotations and echoes wind intricately through biblical and
talmudic vocabulary. In biblical Hebrew, the word refers to sexual
depravity or, more generally, evil intent or deed. Of its twenty-nine biblical occurrences, it is used in the sexual sense twenty-seven times, fourteen of them by the purity-obsessed prophet Ezekiel. A talmudic meaning
of the root ZMM, "to be filthy," is linked with a similar-sounding Aramaic
word *zum,* "to be greasy or filthy."[115] *Zum* is associated with yet another
root, ZHM, "to be glistening, loathsome, smelly." Its noun *zehima,* a
near-homophone of *zima,* occurs only once in the Bible,[116] but its past participle, *mezuham,* is a talmudic term meaning unchaste or lascivious.

The similarities of sounds and meanings in this constellation of terms
suggest that "the place of *zima*" expresses not only fear of the demonic
potential of sexual union, but also disgust for the odors and effluences of
female genitals. What was associated in the Song with honey, wine, and
perfumed ointments is presented in this talmudic passage as noisome
slime. The last passage of the Numbers midrash finally delivers the
punchline of our talmudic texts: R. Sheshet's prooftext with its pornographic gaze.

"Moses became angry with the commanders of the army" (Num.
31:14). R. Naḥman said that Rabbah bar Avuha said, Moses asked

Israel, "Perhaps you have returned to your first sin?" [the intercourse with the Midianite women in Num. 25]. They said, "No." "Not
a man of us was lost." "If so [Moses asked], why ask for expiation?"
They said to him, "We avoided the sin, but we did not avoid fantasizing about it *(hirhur)*. Hence we have brought an offering to the
Lord."

    The School of R. Ishmael taught, why did the Israelites of that
generation require expiation? Because they fed their eyes with *erva*.

    R. Sheshet said, "Why does Scripture include the outer orna-
ments with the inner ornaments [in Num. 31:50]? To tell you: Anyone
who gazes at the little finger of a woman, it is as if he were gazing at
the filthy place *(makom ha-toref)."*

What fascinates the midrashists about Numbers 31 is not the bloody
vengeance of the Israelites upon their seducers, but the orgiastic intercourse that preceded the war. Was the victory over pagan pleasure complete? It was not. Perfect control over the sexual impulse would be attested
by the absence even of sexual thoughts, hence the need for an expiatory
sacrifice.

The midrash itself represents both sin and expiation. By pondering its
graphic sexual iconography, the midrashist reenacts the sin for which the
offering was brought: sexual rumination, *hirhur.* Drawn into complicity,
the male reader, like the midrashists and their fantasizing army, sum-
mons up forbidden sights, ruminates on odors and outflows at once fasci-
nating and repulsive. Now, guilty as charged, he is fully vulnerable to R.
Sheshet's climactic teaching: the outer ornaments are like the inner ones.
Everything about a woman inside or outside, hollow center or outermost
extremity, is the filthy place. There is nothing about her that is not other,
that is not repugnant, that is not to be obsessively resented and desired,
nothing that does not seduce him into sin. He is trapped, imprisoned in
zima. He does not understand that it is he who has plastered her face
with mud.

The way out of this impasse is to retrace our footsteps to the way in.
We must return to the Song of Songs, reverse the rabbis' genitalization of
its feminine imagery. Once we have reconnected female eroticism with
embodied love, we can restore the women of Israel to the female lover's
role without banishing the men from the love story. What forced women
out of the rabbinic allegory was the assumption that, since maleness is
dominant, only the male lover could represent God. Out of respect for
God's dominance, male Israel was relegated to the female role. In the

Song itself, however, the lovers' relations are not characterized by dominance and submission, but by equality and reciprocity. There is no reason why either lover should not image the divine. And even in texts other than the Song, God's veiled middle, to which Eilberg-Schwartz has so brilliantly drawn our attention, may best be regarded not as an allegorical penis under wraps but as an unspecified territory full of sexual possibilities.

A reading of the Song based on these assumptions must necessarily be an allegory, a unidirectional code, cataloguing flat one-to-one correspondences between symbol and abstraction. But meaning must be more fluid, more transitive. Reading metaphorically permits the current of meaning to flow both ways: the vehicle embodies the tenor and the tenor trans/figures the vehicle.

The metaphoric reading I am proposing emphasizes the very characteristics of polymorphous eroticism that made the Song suitable for representing the relations between God and rabbinic man. Precisely because its eroticism is allusive rather than graphic, globally sensuous rather than reductively genital, the Song can become available once again as a metaphor for relations between man and woman and between God and humanity that are not predicated on differences in power. This richer metaphoric reading strategy frees the imagination, our doorway to the inner worlds of others.

The metaphoric mode out of which polymorphous eroticism operates serves as an erotic common denominator, a kinship in the sexual experience of women and men, heterosexuals and homosexuals, young people and very old people. As irreducibly distinct as their experiences of body and self are from our own, this at least we share, this longing that clothes itself in scraps of dreams and ghosts of music, this joy that blooms for us out of intimations of flesh that is not our own. And if we have not learned to hate our own longing and forbid our own joy, our commonality with the other arouses tenderness and compassion in us and a wish to be kind.

The capacity for imaginative eroticism, then, is a potentially redemptive feature of human sexuality. Just as it leaps the rift between ourselves and the other, it bridges the incalculable gap between the sexuality of humanity and the sexuality of God. We began by asking whether the divine image is manifest in us when we are making love. That is related to the two questions posed by Eilberg-Schwartz: Does God have sexuality, and if so how can God exercise sexuality? My answer is that God's sexuality, so to speak, is polymorphous. God who created hills and mountains bursting into song and trees clapping their hands, God who plays with leviathan, delights in the vibrant substantiality of the other.[117] The language in which we and God communicate is grounded in this commonality. Because of it we weave the sights and smells and textures of the created world into ritual. Because of it, the metaphors of erotic landscape pervade the Song of Songs, the prophets, and the Psalms. Suffused with eroticism, the world reveals itself as contiguous with ourselves and with God, the field, the garden, the wilderness where, fleetingly, tenuously, in hurried ecstasy, we and God co/habit.

Ruth: Of *Ḥesed* and Cutting Corners

"Love is sweet," says a Yiddish proverb, "but it tastes even better with bread." In the Song of Songs, love is all sweetness, unhampered by hardship. Emotional stress is minimal, a distant rumble of unsympathetic brothers and fragmentary run-ins with the gendarmes. In the timeless, ahistorical domain of the Song, the lovers find and lose each other repeatedly, but losses are purely temporary, "for love is stronger than death." Economic stress is absent as well; luscious fruit is plucked off the trees, and there's never a bill at the banquet hall. The lovers wander unchallenged through expensive real estate: gardens, orchards, vineyards. They are in perfect accord, and no material need disrupts their bliss. In the absence of disharmony or withdrawal, scarcity or loss, kindness and generosity are unnecessary. There is no effort in giving.

In contrast, the Book of Ruth is set in a hard world. That is established in its first verse. "In a time when the judges *(shoftim)* ruled, there was a famine in the land of Israel." The mythic time evoked in the Ruth narrative is not an idyllic one. The Judges traditions to which the post-exilic writers of Ruth would have had access are darkly shadowed, for the Book of Judges, as Mieke Bal has observed, is about death.[118] Periods of obedience to YHWH with their consequent serenity are punctuated by episodes of idolatry, carnage, and chaos.

In Ruth, it is not a people, but a single family that is threatened with destruction—first by starvation, then by the renunciation of home and land, then by absorption into the culture of Moab where the relocated family intermarries, and finally by the death of all its males, first the patriarch, Elimelekh, and then his two ill-named sons, Maḥlon (Sickness) and Kilion (Ending). From a patriarchal perspective, the story is all but finished before we have reached the fifth verse: "And so, the woman was left without her two sons and without her husband." The only remnant of the family is a childless widow in a foreign land, unable even to provide for the widowed daughters-in-law dependent on her.

One proposed etymology of the word *almanah*, widow, derives the word from 'LM, "to be unable to speak, silent, bound."[119] The man who spoke for her, who provided for her, who gave her a place in society, is dead. Her new designation depicts her as a mirror of that death, mute, helpless, adrift. Small wonder that the prophets keep reminding the people to remember the widow. Along with the stranger and the orphan, she is a disconnected person, unclaimed by any and having claims upon none. For a book whose main characters are widows, generosity is not an unpredictable theme. What is surprising is that the generosity that drives the plot originates with the characters who typify emptiness and need, the widows themselves.

There are two gifts that even the destitute can bestow. The first of these is *hesed*. The word occurs three times in the Book of Ruth and not at all in the Song of Songs. Variously translated as goodness, lovingkindness, piety, fidelity, generosity, or righteousness, *hesed* is a feeling, a character trait, and a mode of relation. Directed toward the other, it is, nevertheless, independent of the other's response. Like a plant adapted to drought, *hesed* can sustain itself when the other is too empty, too bitter, or too grieved to reciprocate. Subsisting on its stores of lovingkindnesses received and its hopes of mutuality reawakened, patiently, tenaciously, it guesses and meets the other's loneliness and need.

The second gift is *berakhah*, "blessing." In the Bible, a *berakhah* is an extemporaneous prose prayer offered by someone who has received a kindness. The *berakhah* serves both to recognize the gift and to reciprocate by commending the giver to God.[120] Sometimes, both giver and God are blessed in the same breath, acknowledging the divine grace underlying human generosity.[121] A *berakhah* is a prayerful recognition of the other's concern and attention and of the divine attentiveness it intimates. There are times when people are too demoralized to give. But to be unable to recognize that one is receiving, one must be numb indeed. Blessing the giver, then, reinvolves the detached and the destitute with the other from whom they have been estranged; the blessing provides them with something of substance to offer in return. For a blessing is more than an idle wish. In the act of blessing, the individual pours her

149

spiritual power into an invocation of God's power in order to bring about a desired result.

The plot of the Book of Ruth is strung upon a chain of *ḥesed* and blessings. The first distant hint that divine *ḥesed* has reawakened occurs in the narrator's parenthetical explanation for Naomi's proposed return: "for in the country of Moab she had heard that YHWH had fulfilled his commitment to *(paḳad)* his people and given them food" (1:6).[122] But the first act of human *ḥesed* is Naomi's. Displaced and on the road, she offers her daughters-in-law all she has left to give: release from their commitments to her, return to the protection of their own mothers, and a blessing. In giving these gifts, she divests herself of her remaining connections, leaving herself to confront all alone a difficult journey culminating in an unprovided old age.

Some critics have charged Naomi with selfishness and self-pity, yet her farewell to Ruth and Orpah shows both affection and concern.[123] She kisses them. She weeps with them. Most tellingly, she has put aside her own anguish and despair long enough to think carefully and practically about the futures of her two remaining responsibilities. Without the protection of male kin or the promise of fertility, Naomi's own future is grim enough to render the assistance of two energetic and devoted young women a temptation. But Naomi offers no false hopes. She reminds them that she is past childbearing, and that even if she were able to conceive more sons for them to marry, they would be condemned to a protracted social limbo until these mates matured.[124]

In her blessing, Naomi also acknowledges Ruth and Orpah's loving attention to her and to her dead. Unable to reciprocate herself, she transfers her obligation to God by means of the blessing and prays that God will reward their *ḥesed* with *ḥesed,* and give them *(menuḥa),* "a haven, a resting-place, in the house of a husband." This language of haven is used by Naomi again in 3:1, when she seeks *manoaḥ,* a settling place for Ruth. *Manoaḥ,* "a place to set foot," is what the dove was seeking after Noah's flood (Gen. 8:9). Barred from *manoaḥ,* the exile has no respite. "Yet even among those nations you shall find no peace," reads a Deuteronomic curse, "nor shall your foot find a place to rest *(manoaḥ)*" (Deut. 28:65). "Be at rest, once again, O my soul," says the Psalmist rescued from peril. Naomi requests for her daughters-in-law this precious commodity so unavailable to unsheltered women in a world owned by men: a haven.

If Naomi's act of generosity is to renounce her bonds with her daughters-in-law, Ruth's is to cement them irrevocably. Swearing a solemn oath with curses to befall if it is violated, she pledges herself to Naomi, to Naomi's people, to her God, and to her fate. Some commentators interpret Naomi's lack of response to Ruth's pledge as a silence born of resentment and frustration.[125] Naomi's exhaustion after her effort to break these last bonds and her inward quailing at Ruth's "clinging" (DBK) despite Naomi's depletion seem to these critics highly blameworthy. They censure Naomi for bitterness toward God and ingratitude toward Ruth implicit in her terrible cry to the women of Bethlehem: "I went away full, and YHWH has brought me back empty" (1:21). Her complaint betrays that she is cruelly oblivious that one child, at least, has not abandoned her.

The implicit assumption of these critiques is that good people, loving people always reciprocate. No expectation has destroyed more friendships or more marriages. An ethics of relationship based upon a richer account of human psychology would acknowledge that sometimes good and loving people are too depressed or too tormented to give, that sometimes they are too depleted to reciprocate when others give to them. These withholdings and withdrawals may not be character flaws, but rather the nethermost points of those deeply internal processes by which people learn to accept the unbearable. At these times, reciprocity and recognition cannot be expected. Love, like life, is not fair. Whichever friend or partner can, must manage not only to give, but to give unilaterally. Accordingly, the text records neither reproach nor discouragement from Ruth. Instead, she volunteers to exercise the prerogative of the very poor to scavenge for fallen grain behind the harvesters, the ancient equivalent of applying for welfare.

It is at this point in Ruth's story that the deficit in Naomi's giving is balanced by the beginnings of generosity in Boaz. As Trible notes, his first question about Ruth is a patriarchal one: not who is she, but *whose* is she?[126] Yet even the servant who replies sees her as more than chattel. He tries to ensure Boaz's kindness by adding the unrequested information that Ruth has worked hard.[127] Critics have noted that Boaz's benevolence has been overrated.[128] His insistence that she glean only his fields, his orders curbing his randy farmhands, and his offers of water and food are not extraordinary attentions to the destitute elderly widow and daughter-in-law of a close kinsman. But one gift Boaz does give Ruth in their first encounter is recognition of a sort no other character has accorded her.

As Pardes observes, Ruth puns on two words from the same root when she asks challengingly, "Why have you been so kind as to recognize me *(lehakireni),)* when I am a stranger *(nokhriya)*?"[129] Why, in other words, do you not go on ignoring the needy stranger? Is not estrangement the universal rule for maintaining the boundary between "us" and "them"? In meeting Ruth's challenge, Boaz is forced to acknowledge all he already knows about Ruth's own initiatives in crossing that boundary and to recall the Israelite ethic that forbids estrangement, "for you know the feelings *(nefesh)* of the stranger" (Exod. 23:9). To recognize Ruth is to value her and to accord her the blessing she deserves.

> I have been told much *(huged hugad li)* about all you did for your mother-in-law after your husband's death, how you left behind your father and mother and your birthplace, and came to a people you had never known. May YHWH requite your actions. May you be fully compensated by YHWH the God of Israel under whose wings you have sought shelter.

Trible notes Boaz's allusion to Genesis 12:1, where God commands Abraham to leave his father's house and his birthplace and resettle in an unknown land God will show him.[130] The reference confers Israelite status upon Ruth by its paradoxical acknowledgment that Boaz and his people also come of a race of strangers, of whom Abraham the Hebrew, *ha-ivri*, literally, "the crosser-over," was the progenitor.[131] Drawing upon this history, Boaz speaks, as no one else in the story does, not about how good Ruth is to Naomi, but about what Ruth's *ḥesed* has cost her.

Boaz's blessing to Ruth is an overlay upon and an elaboration of Naomi's blessing. By using the terms *yishalem*, "requite, repay," and *maskurtekh*, "your compensation, your reward," he sharpens and concretizes Naomi's prayer for divine reciprocity. Boaz's prayer, like Naomi's, alludes to the uprooted woman's need for shelter, but in his prayer this haven is already present, for Ruth has taken refuge beneath the unfailing shelter, the wings *(kenafayim)* of the God of Israel.

Just as Boaz's prayer is interlinked with Naomi's, his kindnesses are braided into the chain of human *ḥesed* by which the patterns and purposes of divine *ḥesed* are realized. Boaz's contributions feed Ruth and allow Ruth to feed Naomi. Similarly, Boaz's recognition of Ruth comforts both women. Ruth responds directly, "Thank you for comforting me. You have touched your maidservant's heart" *(dibarta al lev shifḥatekha)*. Naomi is comforted still more deeply by the news that it is Boaz, the potential redeemer *(go'el)* of patriarchal property, who has befriended Ruth. Through this first awareness of an intricate pattern in which divine ḥesed works through human agency, Naomi learns that, after all, God "has not failed in ḥesed toward the living or toward the dead" (2:20) and is galvanized to add her own efforts to the gathering momentum toward her own and Ruth's redemption. The irony Naomi previously directed toward the God who brought her back empty she ingeniously redirects toward the social institutions that conspire to keep her empty. Paradoxically, it is when Naomi rediscovers ḥesed that she becomes a trickster.

Marge Piercy complains of the Book of Ruth, "It's concerned with inheritance, / lands, men's names, how women / must wiggle and wobble to live."[132] Yet the very reason that the legal circumstances in Ruth are the subject of sustained debate is that, for three of the four chapters, they are presented not from the perspective of landowners and heirs for whom their details are endlessly absorbing, but from the perspective of the women dispossessed and constrained by them. From this vantage point, the laws promoting the continuity of patriarchal clans by encouraging kinsmen to purchase family property (including sexual property) and replace missing male heirs are of no intrinsic interest. They appear only as a vaguely sketched set of obstacles to women's well-being. Hence, although Naomi knows enough to identify Boaz as a *go'el*, she indicates no awareness that there is a closer kinsman who has priority or that she could have alleviated her poverty by liquidating her deceased husband's property. Her approach to the problem of redemption is not legal, but outrageously extralegal. Instead of ordinances and arguments, it presents the woman's body, a tempting pawn apparently unprotected—until the queen swoops down to check and mate.

Naomi's strategy for Ruth echoes that of Boaz's enterprising ancestress Tamar, another non-Israelite woman suspended in legal limbo by Israelite inheritance laws: seize the forbidden sexual initiative, and suddenly materialize in the bed where it will do the most good. Tamar, veiled and disguised as a prostitute, tricks her father-in-law, Judah (Gen. 38), into lying with her and triumphantly vindicates herself in a legal proceeding over which Judah presides. "She is more righteous than I," he admits.

Tamar sells her body outright. Naomi's instructions and Ruth's subsequent actions with Judah's descendent are more ambiguous. While no explicit sexual act is described, Ruth is to wash, anoint, and dress herself as if for a sexual encounter, to hide herself at the threshing floor, and, once Boaz is asleep, to "go to him, uncover his feet and lie down." These last details emphasize the daring reversal of gender roles accomplished by this trickery. Usually, it is the man who "goes to" a sexual partner, who uncovers nakedness, who lies with the woman. The exposed parts, *margelot*, from *regel*, "foot or leg," describe an unspecified amount of the lower body. (Legs, after all, go all the way up to X-rated regions.)

A third word in this constellation of sexual terms is *kanaf*, which refers to the wing of a bird, an edge or extremity, as in the four corners of the earth or the skirt of a robe. A *kanaf* delineates a boundary and designates as its own what is within or beneath it. Spreading the *kanaf* is an act of espousal.[133] The lifted skirt of the robe intimately reveals its owner's body to the woman over whom it is spread. In merging with the body beneath the *kanaf*, she covers her own nakedness and is invested with his; hence, a man who marries his father's former wife is said to have uncovered his father's *kanaf* (Deut. 23:1).

Images of spread wings and spread robes converge in metaphors of covenant as marriage. "I spread my robe *(kanaf)* over you and covered your nakedness, and I entered into a covenant with you by oath—declares YHWH God, thus you became mine" (Ezek. 16:8). Ruth's words to Boaz build upon the covenant imagery implicit in his blessing that she find recompense under the divine wings. "Spread your *kanaf*/robe/wing over your handmaid," she says, "for you are a *go'el*, a redeemer." Boaz identifies this proposal as Ruth's second great act of *hesed*. Not only has she gone home with Naomi, but rather than seeking a sexual connection to benefit herself alone, she has proposed one that will maintain her kinship ties with Naomi and enable her to continue protecting her. In addition, she has generously chosen the man who has been generous to her, whose recognition and respect for her are so clearly articulated: "All the elders of my town know what an impressive woman *(eshet hayil)* you are."

Boaz's respect for Ruth is mirrored in Ruth's and Naomi's trust of Boaz. Thus, the "bed trick" played on Boaz is strikingly different from Leah's impersonation of Rachel or Tamar's disguise as a prostitute. When Boaz cries, "Who are you?" Ruth tells him the truth. Unlike Jacob or Judah, Boaz is no dupe. Invited by Ruth and Naomi, he takes his place as the third accomplice in the cutting of legal corners that undermines, even while it appears to uphold, the patriarchal power to extend or withhold the *kanaf*. Boaz demonstrates his complicity in urging that Ruth stay the night, despite his admission that a closer kinsman has a prior claim upon her, and in the reassuring message he conveys to Naomi by sending Ruth home laden with grain.

In the last chapter, set in the public world of men, Boaz proves a master of lawyerly trickery. The ranking redeemer, robbed even of the dignity of a name in the narrative, is drawn in unsuspecting and unprepared, and played like a fish before a quorum of elders. Boaz informs the anonymous kinsman that Naomi is selling her husband's land. By what authority she does so is left unspecified, as well as how she came to designate Boaz as her agent rather than the closer kin. By showing his own eagerness to redeem, Boaz rushes the man into snapping at the bait and only then reveals that the sale is not unconditional. The conditions upon the sale are presented as unattractively as possible. The buyer must take "Ruth the Moabite," the alien woman, designate her male offspring as her deceased husband's heir, and relinquish the property and its profits to him. The disgruntled redeemer huffily declines, and amidst loud congratulations, Boaz acquires the estates of all three of the deceased, an opportunity he has not offered his opponent. The last blessing of the townsfolk who have witnessed this transaction, "may your house be like the house of Perez whom Tamar bore to Judah," hints wryly at their awareness that Tamar's talent for legal skullduggery has just reasserted itself in her descendant.

The last great act of *hesed* is Ruth's. Thumbing her nose at patriarchal genealogies and assignments of ownership, she gives her son to Naomi as a foster child. "A child is born to Naomi!" the chorus of women exclaims. This child will be her redeemer, they affirm, not because of patriarchal inheritance law, but because of *hesed*, because "he is born of your daughter-in-law who loves you and is better to you than seven sons."

After all this legal drama, who are, finally, the mother and father of the child Oved? Maternity in the Bible is usually not difficult to determine. But here, Ruth bears Oved, and Naomi "nurtures him in her bosom" (4:16). Has Ruth renounced her maternity in Naomi's favor or are Ruth and Naomi co-mothers? And who is Oved's father? Boaz declares that he intends "to perpetuate the name of the deceased upon his estate, that the name of the deceased may not disappear from among his kinsmen and from the gate of his home town" (4:10). But in a final ironic wink at the efficacy of law in effecting redemption, the genealogy that concludes the book identifies the child Oved not as the son of Mahlon, but as the son of Boaz. The midrash *Ruth Rabba* appears to acknowledge that, as a source for statute law, the Book of Ruth is useless. Its value lies in its teaching of *ḥesed*, without which law has no power to redeem:

> R. Ze'ira said, "This scroll [Ruth] tells us nothing either of purity or impurity, of the forbidden or the permitted. For what purpose was it written? To teach how great is the reward of those who do deeds of lovingkindness."[134]

Hosea 1 and 2: I Will Espouse You in Justice

Relationships expose our nakedness. To seek anything from another is tacitly to acknowledge that we cannot attain our desire alone. Divested of our façade of self-sufficiency, we reveal ourselves as vulnerable and wanting. Modern contracts hide this nakedness by presenting the fulfillment of needs as a reciprocal arrangement between equals, even though in actuality both parties may not benefit equally.[135]

In contrast, many biblical scholars depict the covenant of God and Israel as an ancient contract between radically unequal parties, one of them so powerful and self-sufficient as to have no need of the contract. Historical scholarship has unearthed several political prototypes for such covenants in the cultures surrounding ancient Israel.[136] There are suzerainty treaties stipulating the obligations to which a king bound his vassals, parity covenants in which two equals pledged themselves to mutual obligations, and promissory grants in which a sovereign bound himself unilaterally to confer benefits upon his inferiors. The covenants with Abraham and David are said to be modeled on promissory grants, whereas the Sinai covenants in Exodus and in Deuteronomy reflect ancient Hittite suzerainty treaties and their later Assyrian adaptations. But as Elaine J. Adler points out, the prophets barely mention these political covenants.[137] Their predominant metaphor for the covenant is not vassalage or the master-slave relation, but marriage, and their predominant metaphor for covenant breaking is adultery.

But in what sense is biblical marriage a covenant? Legislation concerning marriage categorizes it as a commercial transaction by which sexual chattel is acquired. While there appear to have been wedding festivities, the Bible records no ceremony in which the participants made mutual pledges or oaths.[138] From the legal perspective, adultery, defined as sexual intercourse of a married woman with a man other than her husband, is to be punished by death, not because the woman has made and then violated a commitment, but because in misappropriating her purchased sexuality she confuses paternity and jeopardizes the transmission of tribal inheritance. The conception of marriage as a unilateral acquisition of property, analogous to the acquisition of slaves, animals, or fields, rather than embodying commitments on the part of two participants, dominates legal thinking in rabbinic texts, especially those of the Babylonian tradition.[139] Indeed, if it were not for the prophetic metaphor of the covenant as a marriage, we would be unlikely to think of either biblical or rabbinic marriage as a covenant.[140]

But the metaphor of the covenant marriage and its elaboration in prophetic narrative deepen and expand the ethical and spiritual possibilities both in covenant and in marriage by definitively distinguishing God's covenant with Israel from a contract. A contract is an agreement by which parties obligate themselves reciprocally and concurrently to do or to refrain from specified acts. If one party breaches the contract, the other party is not obligated to fulfill its part. The relationship represented by the contract exists only insofar as both parties meet the stipulated conditions. In the marriage narratives, however, the commitment is not to an agreement with another, but to the other's self. Hence, although inconstancy and betrayal, rage, hurt, and vengefulness tear at the relationship, the covenant is never abrogated.

In recent years, feminist critics have argued that the depiction of women in these prophecies as whores and nymphomaniacs, stripped, battered, raped, humiliated, but ultimately forgiven by a magnanimous divine spouse, is too high a price to pay for a covenant. They claim that these metaphors of adulterous Israel punished for her sins against her husband construct a social reality that sanctions wife battering and reinforces patriarchal monopolies over women's bodies and women's sexuality, that they constitute a theology coded by gender to equate masculinity with divinity, holiness, and restraint and femininity with wickedness, impurity, and unrestraint.[141]

Building on this claim, David Blumenthal suggests that the God portrayed in these prophetic passages is an abuser, and that their theological interpretation, rather than evading or excusing, must come to grips with how an abusing God is to be understood and addressed.[142] But pathologizing God's violence radically narrows our options for response. We are left with a God without insight into his violence and without the capacity to integrate or assume responsibility for his behavior.[143] The metaphor of an abusing God is inherently totalizing. It overwhelms and discredits all other metaphors. If God is fundamentally and pathologically untrustworthy, then a current of distrust must flow beneath every other metaphor. There is nothing to be done with such a God but to reject him. To label the covenant marriage as a battering syndrome, then, utterly discredits the prophetic texts and the ethics of social justice derived from them.[144]

Can these texts be redeemed without condoning violence against women? With this troubling question in mind, let us examine the oldest of the prophetic covenant-marriage metaphors, in the book of the Northern Israelite prophet Hosea, who himself enacts the soured covenant marriage. We will wrestle the first two chapters of his prophecy for a blessing. The opening chapter introduces Hosea, whose name means Salvation, the wife he marries, and the children he begets.

> YHWH said to Hosea, "Go take yourself a whoring wife and get children of her whoring, for this land will whore away from YHWH." So he went and took Gomer bat Diblaim, and she conceived and bore a son (1:2–3).

Hosea names this son Jezreel because in the valley of Jezreel the bloodiest crimes of the Israelite monarchy were perpetrated, and there he prophesies that Israel will be defeated. He names his daughter Lo-ruhama, Unpitied, and his second son Lo-ami, Not-My-People. Given the allegorically freighted names of Hosea and his children, it is reasonable to suspect that his wife's name may also convey a message. Decoding the message, however, has proven difficult for scholars. Linked to the root GMR, to finish or end, Gomer's name, like the ill-omened names of her children, may prophesy the end of Israel. Alternatively, it may allude to her promiscuity, as Rav suggests in a brutally contemptuous talmudic exegesis (*Pesaḥim* 87a): "they all finish in her." The second part of Gomer's name has presented yet a greater enigma. Ordinarily, bat Diblaim would represent either Gomer's patronymic or her place of origin; however, Diblaim is recorded neither as a man's name nor as a place name. Particularly puzzling is Diblaim's dual plural ending, *aim*, which is most commonly used in naming body parts that come in two, like hands and feet. The singular form of the word, *develah*, denotes a round cake of pressed figs. One modern commentator specifically rejects any association between this meaning and Gomer's name and observes that fig cakes in the dual plural make no sense as a name.[145] A more graphic imagination and somewhat less purity of heart may suggest how a pair of fig cakes could give rise to a nickname. In addition to "son or daughter of" and "inhabitant of," *ben* or *bat* can mean "possessor of." "Bat Diblaim," then, can mean the woman with the *diblaim*, possessor of a pair of body parts associated with roundness, sweetness, and orality. Gomer bat Diblaim is Gomer-with-the-fig-cakes, a pornographic cartoon to snicker or shudder at, Death/Orgasm with the big sweet knockers.[146]

This decoding of Gomer's name emphasizes that she, too, is a metaphor rather than a historical personage. Despite the efforts of biographically inclined scholars to reconstruct it, the book of Hosea contains no narrative of Hosea's relationship with Gomer.[147] Instead, in the second chapter, Hosea's rejected children and his whorish spouse merge inextricably with the figures of the pampered child, Ephraim, and the wife from the wilderness, Israel. Renita J. Weems argues convincingly that the three chapters we are examining can best be understood not as prophetic biography, nor as a historical source about Canaanite fertility cults or Hebrew marital law, but as a *literary* text whose prophetic message is conveyed through the working out of a marriage metaphor.[148] Both structure and content reflect the conflicts and contradictions in that message. The text is shaken by manic swings between prose and poetry, narrative and prophecy, past and future, between vindictive rage and tender acceptance, violent threats and loving promises.

What is it that makes the marriage metaphor so uniquely compelling? Elaine Adler observes that the marriage metaphor has a biographical character that suits it for historical allegory, encompassing the stages of courtship, honeymoon, conflict, and reconciliation.[149] For Weems, it is the evocation of sexual intimacy and sexual bonding that gives the metaphor its inimitable emotional charge. Regina M. Schwartz traces the correspondence to an even more fundamental patriarchal theme, the drawing of boundaries between what is mine and not-mine, us and not-us. She argues that, in biblical imagery, the associations of marriage and adultery with the observance and violation of the covenant and the integrity and dissolution of national identity are deeply ingrained.[150] Tracing the homology between adultery and the subversion of covenant throughout the narrative cycle from Judges through 2 Kings, Schwartz concludes, "The biblical obsession with adultery is, at bottom, a preoccupation with monotheism. And that preoccupation with monotheism is, in turn, an effort to forge a collective identity."[151] Schwartz's functionalism reduces monotheism to an implement for constructing a distinctive national identity—a simplistic characterization of monotheism from a theologian's perspective.

However, her analysis highlights wonderfully the symbiosis between monotheistic theology and an Israel distinct from other nations. She is able to show how that symbiosis corresponds metaphorically to sexual fidelity in a marriage. Schwartz's Foucaultian concern with rupture and discontinuity makes a useful lens through which to view prophetic histories in which Israel is more often faithless than faithful. What composes Israel's identity, she argues, are the very contradictions and violations that undermine it:

> "Israel" is an inconstant, fractured, and multiple concept: a people who are bound by a law that they refuse to obey, a people who are defined by their nomadism but are promised a land to settle in and embark upon its conquest, a people who remember (or adopt) a shared history only to forget it, a people who promise fidelity to God only to go astray.[152]

What the metaphor of marriage and adultery captures so vividly about this incontestably accurate account of tensions and violations is that a fracture is an injury. Our failures at being whole and being true, however inevitable, cause pain to the other and to ourselves. They violate the guiding visions of ideal selfhood out of which our integrity and fidelity are formed. They shatter trust. To be human is to be discontinuous; times and settings affect us, our choices change us, our body/selves change, ripen, decay, are shaken by desires, revulsions, regrets. Yet paradoxically, human beings wish to trust and to be trusted, and this is impossible without accountability. Only a cynic or a nihilist disclaims responsibility for yesterday's robbery on the grounds that he was a different person then. The rest of us struggle to bridge the discontinuities between who we were and who we are, what we did and what we do now, to compose a coherent narrative with which to extend ourselves into the future. This narrative is our construction of integrity. Through it, we seek to assume responsibility for our fractures and our fracturing without relinquishing our hopes of being trustworthy and being trusted. For if all errors were fatal, we would be too paralyzed by despair to wish to assume responsibility or to desire integrity. If discontinuous selves are to be continuously responsible, our only hope is in the possibility of *teshuvah*, "return and reconciliation," the possibility that injuries can be healed.

The great innovation of the prophetic marriage metaphor is that it presents God as an injurable other enmeshed in a *danse macabre* of reciprocal injury. Unlike God the Creator or God the King, God the husband is an erotic subject who can be hurt, insulted, deceived. Endowing Israel with the power to hurt God intimately redistributes the balance of power in the divine-human relationship.[153] The terrible rage in prophetic adultery is, ultimately, a helpless rage. It acknowledges that God is dependent on the other partner for what God wants, a desire that no amount of stripping or whipping can satisfy. God's desire for sincere and unconstrained recognition from the other renders God vulnerable to disappointment and abandonment.

The common response to such injuries is rage and the desire to punish. In our society, the arena where narratives of betrayal are rehearsed and vengeance is sought is the divorce court. There, as in a shadow-play, looming silhouettes of husbands and wives are projected onto the distorting screen, where they enact monstrous dramas of menace, manipulation, and extortion. Sometimes the shadows belong to real brutes and con artists; the end of the drama finds their victims destitute, maimed, or dead. At other times, the light of day exposes ordinary men and women caught in brief unlovely spasms of rejection or revulsion, eventually resolved or at least moderated for the sake of the children or for the sake of their own souls. For the urge to punish is shocking. We dread and reprove it in others and deny or rationalize it in ourselves.

The marriage metaphor reveals an injured and infuriated God struggling with the urge to punish his unfaithful lover. Supplanted by the *ba'alim*, the lords and masters of the Canaanite pantheon, God as *ba'al*, husband/owner/master, has sustained a twofold injury.[154] He who had supposed himself unique and irreplaceable to his mate discovers that he is not, and she who was his property chose to whom she would give herself. The first injury is the loss of love. The second injury is the loss of control. Entangled with the feelings of betrayal and rejection, then, are patriarchal assumptions about marriage as the property right that constitutes the foundational boundaries of patriarchal society.[155] The book of Hosea presumes that a husband has exclusive ownership over his wife's sexuality, her desire, her very body. He can threaten to strip the unfaithful woman and leave her to die of thirst (Hos. 2:5), to cast out her children (2:6), to block her flight to her lovers by holding her prisoner (2:8), to humiliate her publicly by exposing her genitals (2:12).

The woman is never given her own voice in the narrative, because anything she could say would be indefensible. What she felt about being taken as a wife, whether she chose freely or was coerced, how she experienced the marriage, what her motive was for infidelity—all these are irrelevant. If a husband is indeed a *ba'al,* her preferences are immaterial because her desire does not belong to her.

The metaphor of marriage as patriarchal property right, however, is a mixed blessing even for the traditional theologian. On the one hand, the context of patriarchal marriage is necessary for the analogy between adultery and idolatry to have maximum weight and gravity. Only in that context is adultery a primal crime that pollutes land and society and overthrows the world order. On the other hand, if the covenant with YHWH is merely YHWH's exercise of property right complemented by Israel's passivity, is Israel's obedience freely offered or coerced? And if coerced, how can the covenant be valid? Rabbinic theology explores this question, although not in the context of the marriage metaphor.[156] A midrash on Exodus 19:17, "And they stood under the mountain," reads "under" literally and concludes: "This teaches that the Holy One bent the mountain over them like a barrel, and said, 'If you accept the Torah, fine; if not, here will be your graves'" (B. Shabbat 88a). For the two Babylonian rabbis who comment on this midrash, its coercion is problematic. The first rabbi, R. Aḥa b. Yaakov, protests, "This story seems to attest that the Torah was accepted only under duress [and is therefore an invalid contract]."[157] The second sage, Rava, must implicitly concur, for he adds, "But the generation at the time of Ahasuerus accepted [the Torah freely]."[158] Perhaps Rava is referring to diasporic communities like his own who must choose Judaism over other alternatives. In any case, it is important to both commentators that the covenant be voluntary.

Here then, is a problem at the core of the metaphor: if marriage does not embody patriarchal sex-right, then the gravity of adultery is vitiated; but if the covenant is a patriarchal marriage, where is the free consent and reciprocity that validate it as a covenant? Instead of resolving this problem, however, Hosea intensifies it. In his version of the covenant marriage, what both parties have in common is that they have been used as things rather than acknowledged as selves, and both rebel. Israel/Gomer, the wife who was from the start sexual chattel, is further objectified after reappropriating her own desire. Now she is sexual chattel gone astray. God as injured husband also resents being used. He refuses to be exploited and consumed: "I will take back my new grain in its time, / and my new wine in its season, / I will snatch away my wool and my linen" (2:11). In the most degrading objectification, the wife places him in competition with other god-things, idols of wood and stone, the local agricultural deities *(ba'alim)*, to whom she attributes his bounty (2:7, 2:10). A relationship where one party is a person and the other a thing is difficult to sustain; there is an inexorable slippage toward symmetry. What is wrong with the patriarchal marriage, then, affects both participants.[159] It cannot be put right merely by restoring asymmetrical relations. The very frame of patriarchal marriage must be broken.

To break the frame of patriarchal marriage is, as I have said, a fundamental violation of the laws that constitute patriarchal society. But to remain in covenant with a transgressive people, God, too, must violate the law. Instead of the terrible symmetry of reciprocal injury, God's law breaking makes possible reciprocal generosity. What laws, specifically, does God break? In both Leviticus 20:10 and Deuteronomy 22:22, the penalty for adultery is death. In Deuteronomy 24:1-4, a man is forbidden to remarry a woman he has divorced who has been the wife of another man, "since she has been defiled." Yet in Hosea, God reunites with the woman he has cast off after she has had many lovers.[160]

The book of Hosea then, is polarized between chapters where law and its punitive possibilities are in full force and chapters where law is nullified. In the chapters where law rules, Israel's adultery is punished by Israel's destruction. The covenant marriage and its human participants are annihilated. Salvation is impossible. In Chapter 2, by contrast, even when the right levers are pulled, law simply does not operate. Sentences are not executed. Legal formulas have no efficacy. God pronounces a divorce formula: "For she is not my wife and I am not her husband," but the formula fails to dissolve the relationship.[161] Instead, God concludes by promising a reconciliation that Deuteronomic law explicitly labels "abhorrent" (Deut. 20:4). Here, then, is the contradiction that tops all contradictions: *the metaphor that preserves the covenant breaks the law.*

Violation of the law, however, is not necessarily hostile or dismissive of law. An audacious rabbinic dictum demonstrates that sometimes law must be violated so that justice may be upheld: "It is a time to act for the Lord, therefore they have violated your Torah."[162] This sort of violation is an element of what Robert Cover would identify as a "redemptive" legal project.[163] Its intention is not merely reform, but the moral transformation of the law and the social world in which it is practiced. We may term this moment in the jurisgenerative process "constructive violation." One can read the book of Hosea as a *psychomachia* in fourteen chapters, a struggle within the divine consciousness, in which God is torn between the maintenance of law and its constructive violation.

Because the constructive violation of law is depicted metaphorically, it affects not only the law but also the metaphor that is its carrier. If the law is broken and reconstructed, then the marriage that represents it is broken and reconstructed as well. The motive for the constructive violation of law is the preservation of the covenant. Covenant, unlike contract, endures as an attachment and a commitment even when reciprocal contractual obligations have not been fulfilled. If marriage, too, can be healed when its contractual obligations are broken, then marriage is transformed from a contract to a covenant. The introduction of reconciliation into the breached covenant marriage accomplishes a constructive violation of metaphor. The vehicle of the metaphor (marriage) is radically redefined in order to bear the new growth of meaning in the metaphor's tenor (the covenant between God and Israel). Redefined marriage is based not upon ownership, but upon mutual responsiveness.

Tamara Eskenazi points out that the movement from enforcement of ownership to response and reconciliation in Hosea 2 can be traced through the three strategies proffered by God, each beginning with the word *lakhen*, "thus" or "assuredly."[164] In the first *lakhen* section (2:8–10), God plans to obstruct Israel's access to her lovers until, in despair or resignation, she returns to him. In the second *lakhen* section (2:11–15), God plans a variety of punishments for Israel: to withhold the bounty of the land which provides her nourishment, to humiliate her by public stripping, to cancel her festivities, and to destroy the works of cultivation, the vines and fig trees whose maturity takes years, returning the land to wilderness. The third *lakhen* section (2:16–17) is poised upon the ambiguous clause that begins it: *Lakhen hinei anokhi mefateha.* If this is translated "Therefore, behold, I will seduce her" the third strategy is merely another manipulation. However, this is not the only possible translation of the verb. The root meaning of PTH has to do with width and openness. Although its more common associations are with simple-mindedness, persuasion, seduction, and deceit, positive associations with receptivity, spaciousness, and simplicity or innocence do occur.[165] In our Hosea verse, the ambiguous root PTH infuses the conferral of width with eroticism, combining the meanings "I will arouse her sexually," "I will cause her to open," and "I will create openness or spaciousness for her." He continues:

I will lead her through the wilderness
And speak to her heart
I will give her vineyards from there
And the Valley of Akhor/Turmoil as a doorway of hope[166]
There she will respond as in her youthful days
When she came up from Egypt.

These verses continue to link openness or spaciousness with eroticism. In contrast to God's threat, "I will make her like a wilderness" (2:5), this wilderness is a place to wander joyfully together. There God will "speak to her heart," comfort her, touch her heart by speaking to her as another subject. The difficult places the relationship now inhabits, the wilderness, the desolate landscape of Emek Akhor, the Valley of Turmoil, will be the sites where its renewal begins. There Israel will recover the sense of freedom she had when she came up from Egypt. But is God describing renewal or merely regression to a preadulterous stage of the marriage? The verses that follow the third *lakhen* describe a profound renewal, a recreation of the universe in which God and Israel take their place amid a great community of life; the beasts of the field, the birds of the air, the heavens and the earth, all responding with generosity to one another. The first sign of this remaking of the covenant will be, God declares, "You will call me *Ishi*, 'my man,' and not my *ba'al*, 'my master/owner/patriarchal husband/idolatrous god-thing.' For I will remove the names of the *ba'alim* from her mouth and she will remember them no more."

Citing an analogous formula found in documents from the Jewish community at Elephantine, Mordecai Friedman argues that this declaration "you are my man" alludes to standard formulas for Israelite marriage ritual: a declaration by the man, "you are my wife," and a reciprocal declaration by the woman, "you are my husband *(ba'al)*."[167] Ironically, whereas Hosea's change in wording underlines the parity between the two partners, the later ceremony established by the Babylonian rabbinic tradition expunges any trace of mutuality by having the woman's silence signify her acquiescence.

In preference to a divine title that is shared with pagan gods, the text introduces an anthropomorphism so outrageous that the Aramaic Targum refuses to translate it.[168] *Ishi* and *Ishti*, "my man" and "my woman," are equivalent and nonhierarchical terms of relationship. But the shocking change from "my *ba'al*" to "my man" affects the vehicle of the metaphor as well as its theological tenor. It prophesies a time when marriage will not be a relationship of master to subordinate, owner to property, or omnipotent giver to extractive dependent. In a striking parallel to the hopes of contemporary ecofeminists, the prophesied resolution of the war between the sexes is to usher in a new covenant of universal harmony. At this time, God pledges,

> *I will espouse you forever:*
> *I will espouse you with righteousness and justice*
> *And with lovingkindness* (ḥesed) *and with compassion,*
> *And I will espouse you with faithfulness*
> *And you shall know YHWH. (2:21–22)*

Questions remain. If espousal *(erusin)* is a process by which a man unilaterally takes a wife, how can it be righteous or just? How can a process devoid of mutuality, embodying different standards of behavior for husband and wife express *ḥesed* or compassion? Only by an upheaval in the norms of patriarchal marriage. This upheaval is hinted in the gender reversals that conclude the verse. God, rather than his spouse, pledges fidelity. A female Israel is to "know" YHWH. Now, in every other biblical case where one person "knows" another sexually, the knower is male and the known is female.[169] Only here does a woman "know" her man. "On that day," God promises, "I will respond." God's response to Israel reverberates in a chain of responsivity throughout the vast community of the heavens and the earth culminating in a gender-bending pair of commitment declarations between God and Israel, the bastard son Lo-ami, (Not-My-People), modeled directly upon the marriage formulas: "And I will say to Lo-ami, 'You are my people,' and he will respond, 'You are my God.'"[170]

The book of Hosea does not resolve the tension between its polarized depictions of marriage: marriage as property right and control versus marriage as mutuality and renewal. We could think of them as alternative realities. For the latter of these alternatives, there is no place in the original social context of Hosea. But as Unger points out, since all human worlds are conditional, it is always possible to have an insight or discovery that momentarily breaks through the boundaries of the world we are inhabiting and points toward somewhere else.[171] These moments are a brief step out of the familiar into a kind of nowhere. But human beings cannot live in nowhere. Either the insight must challenge and reconstruct established structures or it must be swallowed up by them and returned to oblivion. The miracle of a prophetic metaphor like the covenant marriage envisioned in Hosea 2 is that its prophetic character preserves it. In the caulked basket of sacred text, it floats on the river of time until someone, someday, pulls redemption out of the flowing stream.

Chapter 5
B'rit Ahuvim: A Marriage Between Subjects

The book of Hosea presents a dilemma: a husband who has appropriated a wife and assumed legal ownership of her sexuality finds that he wants not merely her fidelity, but fidelity freely given out of love. Possessing her is inadequate and, as it turns out, impossible; his ownership does not preclude her infidelity. The chapters seesaw between the husband's rage at the woman as a defective possession and the painful tenderness he feels for another whose will, desire, and feelings are distinct from his own. He does not see that his two desires—the urge to possess and control absolutely and the yearning for a loving, willing partner—are irreconcilable.

These unresolved tensions between woman as possession and woman as partner are embedded in the classical liturgy upon which all modern Jewish wedding ceremonies draw. Two elements comprise this ceremony: a legal transaction in which the bride is acquired by a declaration of exclusive possession and a ring, followed by a liturgical celebration *(Sheva Berakhot)* that associates the new marriage with the covenantal reconciliation of God and Israel and depicts it as a new Eden for "loving companions" to inhabit. If we unpack the definitions of marital relationships underlying these two components, however, we find that they are mutually exclusive. The legal definition, derived from talmudic property law, anachronistically categorizes women as a special kind of chattel over which the husband has acquired rights. In contrast, the metaphors that inform the *Sheva Berakhot* characterize marriage as a covenant between partners who choose each other, fail each other, even despair of each other, and yet return and renew their commitments. The traditional wedding ceremony, first treating the bride as a piece of property and then paradoxically depicting her as a covenanter, mirrors in its very structure the irreconcilable expectations implicit in patriarchal marriage.

To treat both parties consistently as persons rather than as property, we would have to reframe the legal portion of the ceremony in terms of

169

partnership law rather than property law as it is currently categorized. Only then would the ceremony's legal component accurately reflect the kind of marriage to which egalitarian couples mean to pledge themselves.

We have now reached a critical moment in constituting the legal bridge to a new world: our rereadings of ancient sacred stories and infusions of new ones demand to be embodied in living praxis. All that was said in previous chapters about how nomic worlds are remade and how the language of holiness is renewed we now bring to bear upon a specific Jewish practice: the practice of wedding. I will demonstrate how we may engender a truly covenantal marriage. I call this commitment a lovers' covenant, *b'rit ahuvim.*

In the first section of this chapter, I explain why the traditional legal language for Jewish marriage is fundamentally incompatible with egalitarian relationships. In the second section, I examine how marriage is depicted as a covenant in the celebratory *Sheva Berakhot.* Finally, I propose a remaking of the wedding ceremony so that its legal language describes the just and caring relationship covenant partners intend: the *b'rit ahuvim.* This final section also addresses the impact of the *b'rit ahuvim* on the integrity of Jewish peoplehood. A Jewish wedding is not a private arrangement, but a commitment to establish a *bayit b'Yisra'el,* a household among the people Israel, to contribute to its continuity and well-being and to engage in its task of *tikkun olam,* repairing the world. Consequently, we have a responsibility to consider how the *b'rit ahuvim* may affect the difficult enterprise of maintaining a pluralistic Jewish peoplehood.

The process of making our way through this chapter is much like struggling through the *s'vakh,* the thicket of terror from our liturgy discussion in Chapter 3. Again, what confronts us is *mesubakh,* tangled, complex. Again, for Judaism's future to be rescued, something will have to die. We must consent to be bereaved in order to be renewed. Again, we must try to balance respect for ritual's time-honored performative language with the ethical demand that we use that language with intention and integrity. Past the thicket, along the banks, where justice flows like a mighty river, the bridge awaits us. Let us pick up our tools and start out.

The Nature of Traditional Jewish Marriage

In the Bible, the verb "to marry" is simply *lakahat,* "to take."[1] If the woman is young and still under her father's roof, the husband or his agents give her father a bride price, *mohar,* for her. Whether the bride must consent is unclear. The one biblical bride whose consent is explicitly sought is Rebekah. Her father and brother ask, "Will you go with this man?" (Gen. 24:58). Although David sends messengers to speak directly to the widowed Abigail (1 Sam. 25:40–43), it is unclear whether her consent is asked or whether she is simply informed that she is being taken. Similarly, we are not told whether Saul's daughter Michal has consented to being taken from her second husband and restored to David, who has demanded her of her male relatives, Abner and Ish-Boshet. For David, Michal is primarily a political necessity, but her second husband's feelings are captured in a haunting cameo: "Her husband walked with her as far as Bahurim, weeping as he followed her; then Abner ordered him to turn back, and he went back" (2 Sam. 3:12–16).

Deuteronomy describes a two-stage process for marriage. In an act of espousal, *erusin,* a man designates a woman to be his own.[2] After an interval, usually about a year, the process of acquisition is completed by a second act, *nissuin,* in which the man takes the woman under his own roof and consummates the marriage. Deuteronomy 22:20 stipulates that if it is discovered that the woman has slept with another man during the interval between *erusin* and *nissuin,* she is to be stoned before the doors of her father's house.

These texts depict the marriage of a young virgin as a private commercial transaction in which rights over the woman are transferred from the father to the husband. This commercial origin is reflected in the relational terminology. The word for husband is *ba'al,* the general term for an owner, master, possessor of property, bearer of responsibility, or practitioner of a skill.[3] No specialized relationship term exists for wife; she is simply *isha,* woman. The owner of a house is *ba'al ha-bayit,*[4] the man responsible for an open pit is *ba'al ha-bor,*[5] the owner of an ox is *ba'al ha-shor,*[6] the owner of a slave is *ba'al ha-eved,*[7] and the husband of a woman is *ba'al isha.* The sole signifier for marital relationship is the grammatical form of the construct *(semikhut),* which binds man and woman as subject and object of an implied preposition: *ba'al isha,* the master of a woman; *eshet ish,* the woman of a man.

At the same time, marital ownership in the Bible transcends the purely commercial. Adultery, like idolatry, incest, and murder, pollutes the land itself. These acts cause the land to vomit out its inhabitants (Lev. 18:24–28, 20:22–24). Adultery, then, is not a mere misappropriation of private property, but is an act of war against both the social order and the physical terrain. Thus, perpetrators are not fined as they would be for theft, but are executed.

As we have seen in the Hosea section of Chapter 4, the marital relationship, more than any other relationship of possession—the master and the slave, the herder and the unruly calf, the cultivator and the vineyard is the central metaphor for Israel's covenant with its God.[8] Yet, curiously, there is no evidence of any cultic ritual associated with marriage, although the social conventions of bridal processions, rejoicing, and ornamentation are mentioned in several prophetic texts.[9]

By the time of the Mishnah, however, a wedding has become a religious event of cosmic significance.[10] Taking a woman to wife is categorized as a unique kind of acquisition, blending characteristics of both purchase and the religious act of setting goods aside for sacred donation, *hekdesh.* The ceremony of taking acquires a new rabbinic name reflecting its sanctification: *kiddushin.*

But what did sanctification mean to the rabbis? What about marriage characterized it as holy? *L'kadesh* means to set aside for sacred use, and hence, implicitly, to exclude from secular use. Sanctification is a major rabbinic means of drawing boundaries and demarcations, a legal and ritual creation of the universe out of undifferentiated chaos. The rabbinic ideal is a world of sharp distinctions, of clear-cut categories in which priest and Israelite, slave and free, permitted and forbidden, holy and secular stand in fixed and eternal opposition. Yet ironically, these rabbinic categories throw into relief certain ambiguities and anomalies that the rabbis cannot adequately account for, phenomena that can be catalogued partially under several categories but wholly under none, or phenomena that remain persistently fluid, fitting sometimes one category and sometimes another.

Judith Wegner has argued that women represent such an anomaly to the rabbis.[11] She draws an analogy between rabbinic legal treatment of women and rabbinic legal treatment of the *koy,* a mythical hybrid produced by crossing a goat with a gazelle that was considered a domestic animal for some legal purposes, a wild beast for others, and for yet others, neither. As *property owners,* women have the same economic rights and powers as men. But women's *sexuality* is regarded as chattel. Once it has been acquired by a man, the woman has no rights of ownership in it.[12] Logically, then, autonomous women should be treated legally like men. But all women, autonomous or married, are excluded from the realm of public religious expression. Add to these legal features women's menstrual impurity, and you have a creature of no fixed status: alternately pure and impure, permitted and forbidden, visible and invisible, person and object, in short, a prime candidate for sanctification.

Jacob Neusner explains with devastating clarity how mishnaic sanctification functions to normalize the anomalous and to place it within a constructed order in the patriarchal mind:

> Mishnah cannot make women into men. But it can provide for a
> world in which it is normal for women to be subject to men—father
> or husband—and a system to regularize the transfer of women from
> the hand of the father to that of the husband. The regulation of the
> transfer of women is Mishnah's way of effecting the sanctification—
> that is special handling—of what, for the moment, disturbs and disor-
> ders the orderly world. The work of sanctification *becomes* necessary
> in particular at the point of danger and disorder so as to preserve the
> normal mode of creation, so that maleness may encompass all, even
> at the critical point of transfer.[13]

The danger against which the cosmically reinforced boundary of sanctification is meant to guard is the misappropriation of women. This dangerous obliteration of boundaries is the transgression called *gilui erva*, forbidden sexual exposures, which, like idolatry and murder, disorder and pollute the nomic world. Rabbinic espousal—*kiddushin*—bridges the girl's passage from her father's hands to her husband's. This transfer procedure is designed to prevent the anarchic and world-disordering expression of autonomous female sexuality that could occur during the dangerous hiatus between these two statuses of daughter and wife, when a girl might consider herself in her own independent domain.

Women in mishnaic times experienced status ambiguity only briefly; generally, they married young. Both Wegner and Neusner believe that, in the time of the Mishnah, fathers generally arranged a girl's marriage when she had grown to the age of *na'arah*, youth, between twelve years and one day and twelve and a half, or even earlier, when the girl was still a minor, *ketanah*.[14] A woman became autonomous, *bogeret*, at twelve and a half. If Wegner and Neusner are correct, adult women experienced autonomy only if they were widowed or divorced. Not to marry at all was socially unacceptable; never-married women were presumed to be disreputable. Although the marriage of minors without their consent is permissible and is discussed in the Mishnah, it was later disapproved by influential Amoraic authorities. "Rav Judah said in the name of Rav, One may not give one's daughter for espousal as a minor. Rather, she should grow up and say, 'I want so-and-so.'" (B. Kiddushin 41a). Rabbinic law requires that a woman who is not a minor must consent to marriage, but her silence suffices as evidence of consent. She need not, like Joyce's Molly Bloom, gasp an ecstatic "yes I said yes I will Yes." As long as she has not protested, "No, no, I won't!" her acquiescence is assumed.[15]

Acquisition and Espousal

The mode by which women are legally transferred from one domain to another is called *kinyan,* acquisition, an act by which a subject unilaterally acquires specified rights over an object. *Kinyan* is essential in commercial transactions. Consequently, the Mishnah (M. Kiddushin 1) posits formal parallels between the acquisition and divestiture or alienation of women, fields, and slaves, which the Gemara then explains and justifies. The basis for establishing that women are "taken" rather than reciprocally linked to men is an analogy between the language of "taking" in Abraham's purchase of the field of Ephron (Gen. 23:13) and the phrasing, "if a man takes a wife" (Deut. 22:13).[16]

The rabbis pursue the analogy still further: women and fields can both be acquired though a transfer of money. The Mishnah specifies two other effective methods of acquisition. Women can be acquired by a deed *(shtar)* attesting to their acquisition,[17] or they can be acquired through sexual intercourse, if such intercourse is for the purpose of appropriation. Analogously, slaves can be acquired by causing them to perform a service for the acquirer, and land can be acquired by cultivating it unchallenged for a three-year period, creating a presumption of acquisition by habitual use *(ḥazakah).*

Although all three methods are legally effective, monetary acquisition *(kinyan kesef)* is, for reasons I later explain, the one approved method for appropriating wives. What, precisely, is acquired by this means? Is it the woman's body, her services, or her sexual exclusivity? The rabbis themselves see the acquisition of wives as different from other commercial transactions. As a Tosafist explains, the formula of exclusive acquisition by which wives are appropriated *(kiddushin)* does not apply to the acquisition of garments or loaves of bread, because in the act of acquiring these objects they do not become forbidden to all but the purchaser.[18] One may buy a loaf of bread and share it with a neighbor, lend one's cloak to a chilled friend, sell it or give it away, but a man is not permitted to dispose of his wife in any of these ways.

The generic language of acquisition ("taking") thus fails to express precisely those characteristics of matrimony the rabbis view as definitive: the transformation of status and category and the delineation of a boundary. To remedy these deficiencies, they turn to the language of sacralization and the metaphor of *hekdesh,* property set apart and earmarked as a pledge to the temple. Just as *hekdesh* simultaneously becomes reserved for sacred use and forbidden for secular use, so marital acquisition reserves a woman for one man and forbids her to others. In this limited sense, then, *hekdesh* is analogous to marital acquisition.

By naming the entire wedding ceremony *kiddushin,* however, the rabbis demonstrate that they are using not just analogy, but also metaphor in the complex, many-voiced sense we talked about in Chapter 3. That is, rather than pointing to some particular feature or circumstance in which marriage and *hekdesh* resemble one another, they link *kiddushin* to all the performative acts through which rabbinic man constitutes and characterizes the cosmos-ordering realm of the sacred.[19] Thus, the language of *kiddushin* transmutes biblical acquisition but does not invalidate it.[20] Indeed, it affirms that the acquisition of wives is inherent in the very nature of the cosmic order. At the same time, the rabbis etherealize the commercial transaction of biblical bride purchase into a symbolic act in which, at the ceremony at least, only a token sum of money changes hands. This sum, as little as a penny *(peruta)*[21] according to the academy of Hillel, represents the biblical bride price, now transformed into a marriage settlement, written into the *ketubbah* document and paid not to the father but to the woman herself in the event of divorce or widowhood.[22] It is as if the woman were purchased with an annuity due to mature at a future time.[23] As for the token sum used for *kiddushin,* Ze'ev Falk explains, "the amount was then returned to the husband together with the other items of the wife's property, so that the 'purchase' had become a mere formality."[24]

If purchase was no longer literal, why should even a symbolic purchase be necessary? Was it a vestige of the older custom, lingering like the Cheshire Cat's grin after the rest of the beast had gone? So rabbinic scholars would have us believe. In modernity, the genteel account of rabbinic *kinyan* insists that monetary acquisition is merely a formal vehicle for effectuating marriage and implies no comparison between the ownership of women and that of fields or other property.[25] Some apologists argue that marital acquisition is merely a figure of speech and bears no relation to its literal meaning.[26] The view that literal and figurative uses of terminology are arbitrary and unconnected would have astonished the rabbis of the Talmud, for whom etymological relationships, associations, and even puns had profound theological and legal significance. Moreover, the very halakhic apologists who make this argument want to make the opposite argument as well. While denying the connection between the term "acquisition" for fields and oxen and "acquisition" for wives, they insist upon the connection between *kedushah*/holiness and *kiddushin*/ marriage.

How, then, is the metaphor of *kinyan* meaningfully linked to its literal sources? Comparing marital *kinyan* to transactional modes rejected by the rabbis clarifies why the rabbis chose to formalize and etherealize *kinyan* rather than discarding it altogether. What all the legally acceptable transactions have in common is that they are *unilateral* acts. Marriage cannot be initiated by the woman (Kiddushin 4b), nor can it result from mutual exchange (Kiddushin 3a, 6b).[27] The man cannot acquire her with a loan or a conditional gift (Kiddushin 6b). He cannot bestow himself upon the woman; he must declare "you are mine" and not "I am yours" (Kiddushin 6b). *Processes in which both parties are active participants are explicitly rejected.* The man must take, and the woman must be *taken.*[28]

It is the woman who must be acquired because only the woman undergoes a status change. She will belong exclusively to the man. The man will not belong to the woman because, in relationships, men are subjects but never objects, unless they are slaves. Hence, a man can validly declare, "be espoused to half of me," because he may divide himself among as many women as he chooses, but if he declares, "I hereby espouse half of you," no *kiddushin* has been effected, because unlike a slave who may be owned fractionally by several masters, a woman can only be espoused as the exclusive acquisition of one man (Kiddushin 7a).[29]

Thus, while the *purchase* of the bride may have dwindled to a mere formality in the rabbinic transformation of marriage, her *acquisition* is no formality. The language of acquisition still accurately reflects a relationship in which the woman has been subsumed and possessed. Moreover, the metaphor continues to resonate, because comparisons to other acquirables are still richly evocative. A woman is not a slave, but she has a master *(ba'al).* A woman is not an ox, but, like an ox, she bears man. A woman is not a field, but in her, man sows his seed and hopes for fruit. These metaphoric associations are strikingly apparent in Maurice Lamm's defense of *kinyan* as the mode of espousal. "Just as the buyer of property intends to protect it, develop it, make it productive, and cherish it, this must be the plan of those who undertake marriage."[30] The phrase "Those who undertake marriage" obscures the fact otherwise so clear in Lamm's agricultural analogy that one partner is the acquirer and the other the acquisition.

Like slaves, land, and cattle, a wife is one of the comforts and assets of the patriarchal household. These associations that link a wife with other life-enriching acquisitions are deepened and justified by the language of *kiddushin,* which seals patriarchal dominion into the very nature of cosmic coherence. Significantly, these meanings cannot be conveyed by sexual intercourse as a method of acquisition. For although a man may acquire a woman through sexual intercourse, nothing about intercourse announces that his possession of her is exclusive. Only *kiddushin* accomplishes that.

Interdicting acquisition by sexual intercourse is central to the rabbis' transformation of marriage into a public religious ceremony. The admonitory tone of the espousal blessing, instituted during the Second Temple period, may reflect how difficult it was for the rabbis to bar acquisition by intercourse. Aided by the serendipitous rhyming of the words *arayot,* "nakednesses," and *arusot,* "espoused brides," the blessing hyperbolically equates sexual relations with the espoused bride with the foundational sexual taboos catalogued in Leviticus 19–21, capital crimes such as adultery and incest.[31]

> Blessed are you, Adonai our God, ruler of the universe who has sanctified us with your commandments and commanded us concerning the forbidden sexual relations/ "nakednesses" *(arayot).* You have forbidden us the merely espoused *(arusot),* and permitted us those who have been fully wedded to us *(nesuot)* by means of the bridal chamber and holy setting-aside *(ḥuppah v'kiddushin).* Blessed are you who sanctify Israel by means of the bridal chamber and (holy) setting-aside *(ḥuppah v'kiddushin).*[32]

The expression *ḥuppah v'kiddushin* seems to mean the entire wedding process. *Kiddushin* is espousal *(erusin),* and *ḥuppah,* the rabbinic term for the bridal chamber, refers to the consummation of the marriage at *nissuin.*[33] The order of the terms is reversed, probably for euphony.

Although intercourse between the espoused couple never attained the status of a foundational sexual taboo, a tradition attributed to the third-century Babylonian authority Rav decrees that acquisition by intercourse is punishable by flogging.[34] A variant and much more permissive view is that Rav forbade espousal by intercourse only when the couple had no prior betrothal arrangements. Authorities in some communities had the power to enforce punishment for such improperly contracted liaisons.[35]

But what is it that has been made holy by *kiddushin*? Isaiah Gafni argues from the wording of the espousal blessing that the rabbis did not view marriage as intrinsically holy.[36] It was instead *instrumental* to holiness, since it offered men the opportunity to sanctify themselves by performing the (exclusively male) commandment to increase and multiply.[37] Hence, the espousal blessing does not end "Blessed are You who sanctify *huppah* and *kiddushin*," but rather, "Blessed are You who sanctify Israel by means of *huppah* and *kiddushin*." One Babylonian variant of the blessing omits all reference to *huppah* and *kiddushin* and simply reads "Blessed are You who sanctify Israel." This is the variant preferred by the eleventh-century authority Rav Hai Gaon, who explains in a responsum that it is incorrect to add *huppah* and *kiddushin* to the blessing because, "the sanctity of Israel is not dependent upon this."[38]

A caution: data on marriage from ancient texts must be taken with a grain of salt. Martha Roth points out that we know relatively little about marriage either in Jewish or non-Jewish antiquity.[39] She argues that because written records are exceptions rather than the rule, the few marriage contracts that have been discovered cannot be regarded as representative of ancient marriage in general. This caution is an important one. Especially in instructional literature like that of the Mishnah, what is depicted may be a behavioral ideal rather than a general practice. Citing evidence from an ancient archive, Tal Ilan suggests that the norms regarding premarital cohabitation may have differed considerably from place to place during the time of the Mishnah.[40] The archive, discovered in a cave in the Judean desert, contains documents belonging to a woman named Babata together with the documents of other refugees from the aftermath of the Bar Kokhba revolt.[41] A marriage contract found in this trove specifies that the couple had lived together for some time prior to the contract. Ilan combines this and another marriage contract with evidence from rabbinic sources indicating that premarital intercourse was sometimes practiced in Judea, but not in Galilee. After discussing all the possible arguments for other interpretations of the documents, Ilan suggests that we assume that they mean what they say. Citing the well-documented Judean custom of a long interval between espousal *(erusin)* and the completed nuptials *(ḥuppah)*, she concludes that some men and women cohabited during espousal. The existence of such a practice would explain the lecturing tone in the *erusin* blessing and its hyperbolic comparison of pre-*ḥuppah* relations to the Levitical forbidden sexual exposures; the vehemence of rabbinic statements is often inversely proportional to the rabbis' power to enforce them.[42] Ilan reminds us that, when our source is a prescriptive literature, we should suspect that information about contesting norms has been suppressed.

This point is further illustrated by the research of Mordecai Friedman on Palestinian *ketubbot* in the Cairo *Geniza.*[43] These records, an archive containing generations of business and family documents from the medieval Palestinian Jewish community of Old Cairo, offer a credible account of a community's matrimonial customs. By this time, documents commonly recorded the legal transactions of family and communal life. Rather than a few archaeological finds or the carefully selected examples of an instructional literature, the Cairo *Geniza* contains thousands of accumulated documents.[44] Among these documents, Friedman found some eighty *ketubbot* representing a Palestinian tradition ultimately engulfed by the dominant Babylonian tradition. These *ketubbot* differed from the Babylonian form and from one another. Even earlier *ketubbot* in the Babylonian tradition were not the unvarying boilerplate we have today, but contained tailor-made stipulations concerning such issues as the wife's possessions and her right to visit her relatives out of town. But in the Palestinian *ketubbot,* Friedman remarks, "the wife's status seems, almost, to be approaching equality with the husband."[45] The most striking of these features, a stipulation that enables both parties to initiate divorce proceedings, appears also in the second-century *ketubbah* of Babata found in a Judean cave and in papyri from the Jewish community of Elephantine from the fifth century B.C.E.[46] It was, of course, the husband who granted the divorce, as the logic of *kiddushin* necessitates. But he was enjoined to grant a divorce upon the wife's demand, regardless of his own preference. These *ketubbot* reveal an astonishing fact: *a tradition that endured more than a thousand years offered Jewish women a right Orthodox women do not have today.*

Other features of the Palestinian *ketubbot* emphasize mutuality as the Babylonian tradition does not. In contrast to the third-person reportage of the Babylonian documents, the Palestinian *ketubbot* incorporate the voices of both bridegroom and bride, delineating mutual obligations. Most strikingly, a number of Palestinian *ketubbot* (and the Palestinian Talmud itself) use a term for marriage unknown in the Babylonian Talmud: *shutafut*, partnership. As Friedman observes, the term describes a relationship, including a business relationship between equal partners, both of whom can withdraw from the partnership at will. In a Tyrian *ketubbah*, Friedman finds an example of the language of covenant as well as the language of partnership. The husband in this document, quoting Malachi 2:14, refers to his wife as "my companion and my wife in covenant" *(ḥaverati v'eshet b'riti).*[47] Friedman notes that the fragments from the Tyrian *ketubbot* unfortunately have breaks at this point in the text. Parallels to this language of covenant can be found in later Karaite marriage formulas, but whether the Karaites influenced the Rabbanites or vice-versa is inconclusive.[48]

These *ketubbot* still reflect a society in which power was not equally distributed in marital relationships. Wives promised to serve their husbands. Women's rights to go out of their houses, to visit or to attend celebrations or houses of mourning, had to be negotiated and stipulated. But it seems clear that, had the Palestinian tradition become dominant, we would have already been on the road to a more egalitarian wedding ceremony. What happened? During the Gaonic period (the mid-seventh to eleventh centuries), a great struggle for hegemony was taking place between the Palestinian and Babylonian academies. As part of this struggle, the Babylonian authorities rejected the authenticity of Palestinian legal traditions and ultimately managed to eradicate the Palestinian *ketubbah* from the practice of Jewish communities.[49] Ironically, the Babylonian rabbinic tradition, whose heirs are even now accusing feminist Judaism of "polemic," have inherited their own polemical construction of Jewish marriage embodied in a polemical ceremony.

Sheva Berakhot: The Seven Blessings

In contrast to the prosaic legal machinery that effects *kiddushin*, the second half of the Jewish wedding ceremony is poetic and allusive. It consists of a series of celebratory blessings recited over a cup of wine. The Talmud calls these *birkat ḥatanim*, the bridal blessing.[50] A later term, *Sheva Berakhot*, seven blessings, includes the introductory blessing over the wine along with six bridal blessings to add up to the sum of seven, the number of perfection. The Palestinian tradition apparently used only three blessings, but the texts that refer to them do not specify their content.[51]

Kiddushin is dependent upon the bridal blessings to make it "respectable." Their function in the traditional ceremony is to reframe the *kiddushin* acquisition as an archetype of redemptive union. As we shall see, however, the blessings are surface outcroppings of vast subterranean formations. Beneath them lie the stories, prophecies, and poems that constitute the metamorphic core of the Jewish *nomos*. Ancient, powerful, many-voiced, they can destabilize marriage-as-acquisition as easily as they can justify it. What the blessings celebrate is not "taking" but "wedding," a conjoining that, according to the prophets, supersedes the rules of acquisition-marriage. This, and not *kiddushin*, is the union from which redemption flows.

Let us then begin to probe the seven blessings. They are:

1. Blessed are You, Adonai our God, Ruler of the universe, who created the fruit of the vine.

2. Blessed are You, Adonai our God, Ruler of the universe, who created everything for your glory *(she' ha-kol bara likh'vodo).*[52]

3. Blessed are You, Adonai our God, Ruler of the universe, shaper of humanity *(yotzer ha-adam).*

4. Blessed are You, Adonai our God, Ruler of the universe, who has shaped humanity in Your image *(asher yatzar et ha-adam b'tzalmo),* patterned after Your image and likeness *(b'tzelem d'mut tavnito),* and enabled them to perpetuate this image out of their own being *(v'hitkin lo mimenu binyan adei ad).*[53] Blessed are You, Adonai, shaper of humanity *(yotzer ha-adam).*

5. May the barren one exult and be glad as her children are joyfully gathered to her *(Sos tasis v'tagel ha-akara, b'kibutz baneha l'tokha b'simha).* Blessed are You, Adonai, who gladden *(mesameah)* Zion with her children.

6. Grant great joy to these loving companions as You once gladdened Your creations in the Garden of Eden. Blessed are You, Adonai, who gladden the bridegroom and the bride *(mesameah hatan v'kallah).*[54]

7. Blessed are You, Adonai our God, Ruler of the universe, who created joy and gladness, groom and bride, merriment, song, dance and delight, love and harmony, peace and companionship *(asher bara sasson v'simha, hatan v'kallah, gila, rina, ditza, v'hedva, ahava,*

v'ahva, v' shalom v're'ut). Adonai, our God, may there soon be heard in the cities of Judah and the streets of Jerusalem the voice of joy and the voice of gladness, the voice of the bridegroom and the voice of the bride, the rapturous voices of the wedded from their bridal chambers, and of young people feasting and singing *(mehera yishama b'arei yehudah u'v'hutzot yerushalayim kol sasson v'kol simha, kol hatan v'kol kallah, kol mitzhalot hatanim me-hupatam, u'nearim mi-mishteh neginatam).* Blessed are You, Adonai, who gladden the bridegroom together with the bride *(mesameah hatan im ha-kallah).* [55]

Although they cannot be dated precisely, the bridal blessings are very old. The third-century Babylonian authority Rabbi Yehudah ben Yehezkiel cites in their entirety all six of those we use today (Ketubbot 8a) without any dissent from other authorities. Their formal irregularity indicates that the blessings were composed prior to the rabbinic rules for *berakhah* formulation. [56] Some contain one idea; others, several. Some repeat the introductory *berakhah* formula, whereas others use only a concluding *berakhah.* Moreover, the blessings are oddly repetitious. Blessings three and four are formally distinct from one another, but both use the signature "Blessed are You, Shaper of humanity." [57] The openings of blessings five and six are synonymous and syntactically parallel exhortations to joy. [58] Blessings six and seven use nearly identical signatures praising God for gladdening the bridal couple. [59] The "coupling" that occasions the celebratory blessings is echoed in their very structure.

Two Blessings of Holy Joy

A constant note of joy in the blessings braids together its twin themes of creation and redemption. A blessing over wine is the standard rabbinic vehicle for sanctification, because "wine gladdens the human heart" (Ps. 103). A blessing over wine transfigures the event and makes it holy. The second blessing, "who created everything for your glory," is another blessing of transfiguration, related to prayers of the *kedushah* genre. The paradigmatic *kedushah* verse is Isaiah's theophany with its angelic chorus exclaiming, "Holy, holy, holy! The Lord of Hosts! The whole earth is full of his glory" (Isa. 6:3). [60] By means of these prayers, the community of Israel joins a vast chorus in which all things above and below acclaim the glory of creation. A parallel to the second bridal blessing is found in a prayer the rabbis term *kedushah d'sidra:* "Blessed is our God who has created us for his glory." To perceive the created world ablaze with God's glory is to perceive it from the divine perspective. *Kedushah* prayers articulate the most precious hopes of rabbinic Judaism—consciousness of the divine presence and participation in the coming of redemption.[61] By invoking the theme of holy transfiguration, the second bridal blessing "telegraphs" the related themes of creation and redemption that will follow.

Two Blessings for the Creation of Humanity

Blessings three and four praise God for creating humanity. In contrast to the bare simplicity of the third blessing, the fourth is complex and cryptic.[62] The blessing interweaves the language of divine image from Genesis 1 with the terminology of "shaping" from Genesis 2 and adds terms that occur in neither account. In the phrase *b'tzelem d'mut tavnito,* which I translate "patterned after your likeness and image," the Genesis 1 terms "image" *(tzelem)* and "likeness" *(d'mut)* are augmented by the word *tavnit. Tavnit* can mean a figure or representation of the divine: Ezekiel uses it, along with *d'mut,* to describe his vision of the God of Israel (Ezek. 8:2–3), although it is more commonly applied to idols.[63] A *tavnit* is also a design, pattern, or prototype for a holy place such as the Tabernacle (Exod. 25:9,40).[64] The possibility of reproduction is introduced by this new word, *tavnit.* Not only is humanity endowed with God's image and likeness but also with God's ability to reproduce the divine image.

My translation of the body of the fourth blessing is: "who has shaped humanity in Your image, patterned after Your image and likeness, and enabled them to perpetuate this image out of their own being." Birnbaum's translation differs radically: "who hast created man in Thy image and didst forever form woman out of his frame to be beside him."[65] The words that occasion such widely divergent translations occur in the difficult final phrase of the blessing: *v'hitkin lo mimenu binyan adei ad.* The literal translation of the phrase is "and set up (or established) for it/him out of it/him an everlasting/infinite/continuous *binyan.*" The entity for whom the *binyan* is set up, the referent of it/him, is *adam,* which takes the masculine pronoun even where it is identified as male-and-female. It is unclear whether the referent of "out of it/him" is God, the originator of image, likeness, and *tavnit,* or the male *adam* of Genesis 2 or the dual *adam* of Genesis 1.

What, moreover, is a *binyan adei ad?* The expression occurs in rabbinic literature only in allusions to this bridal blessing. *Binyan* is itself problematic. The verb *bana* usually means "to construct an edifice," but in the second Genesis account God "builds" the rib of *adam* into a woman. The noun *binyan* occurs biblically only in the book of Ezekiel, in reference to Ezekiel's envisioned temple. In rabbinic literature, *binyan* can refer to a physical structure such as a building, or to the human frame or skeleton, but it is also commonly used to mean a standard rule or paradigm, a prototypical structure by means of which other examples can be generated.[66] In this sense, *binyan* is a synonym for *tavnit.*

And Thereby Hangs a Tale

Given the multiple possibilities for translation I have demonstrated, and the fact that the blessing does not explicitly mention woman at all, why is it that the favored interpretation of commentators from Rashi and the Rishonim onward is the one Birnbaum invokes in his translation?[67] The answer lies in an ancient debate arising out of discrepancies between the two creation accounts. Following this debate is irresistible, like pulling on a loose thread to see how much it will unravel. Our pulling will lead us into a long and revelatory digression in which we untangle some of the voices, battles, and stories knit into the third and fourth bridal blessings. The controversial question is whether woman was created simultaneously with man or as an outgrowth of him. The problem is that the disputants have two conflicting agendas: they want to prove that masculine precedence is inherent in the creation; but they also want to claim that the Torah is whole and perfect. Consequently, not a word can be discredited. All apparent discongruities between the two creation accounts must be reconciled.

The clash between these two agendas results in a convoluted debate that resurfaces periodically in Babylonian talmudic discussions.[68] Its underlying assumption is that the timing and character of woman's creation indicate not only her status in the hierarchy of creation, but also her essential nature. The debate is cast in terms of whether woman is a face (*partzuf*) or a tail (*zanav*). Those who view woman as a face see her as part of an original two-faced, male-and-female *adam*. The "operation" in Genesis 2 is her division from this entity.[69] Those who regard woman as a tail understand her to be a secondary creation derived from a male *adam*. To a modern reader, the symbolism in this terminology is shockingly transparent. Implicit in the metaphor of tail is the assumption that man is a whole to which woman is an inconsequential appendage. If the face is the location of personhood and dignity, the tail is the location of hidden genital and excretory orifices. Tails are associated with animals. Is the formation of woman from the tail an attempt to remove the animal from man and situate it in woman? However you cut it (so to speak), the metaphor of tail inscribes profound sexual dualisms.

In B. Ketubbot 8a, where the bridal blessings are enumerated, the one disagreement is whether one recites five blessings or six (excluding the blessing over wine). What is the source of the variation, the Gemara asks. Does the one who recites five blessings believe in a single creation while the one who recites six believes in two?[70] According to this talmudic theory, the proponent of five blessings would then recite only the third blessing, "Shaper of humanity," while the proponent of six blessings would recite both the third and fourth blessings, referring to the creation of man in the third blessing and the creation of woman in the fourth.

Our Gemara (B. Ketubbot 8a) explicitly rejects the dual creation theory, insisting that "everyone" believes in a single creation.[71] Instead of reiterating the entire face/tail controversy, it cites a single tradition from that debate. This tradition, attributed to R. Yehuda in our Gemara and to R. Abbahu in B. Eruvin 18a and B. Berakhot 61a, poses an apparent problem in textual references to the creation of humanity. In Genesis 1:27, God announces that he is creating two beings, but because the pronouns that refer to *adam* (Gen. 1:27 and 5:2) are masculine singular, it appears that God actually created only one (and subsequently built a second being from him).[72] R. Yehuda's solution is to distinguish between the divine intention to create two and the divine act, which was, ultimately, to create only one. Accordingly, our Gemara concludes, those who say only the third blessing commemorate the divine *act*, while those who add the fourth blessing commemorate the divine *intention.*

What does this distinction mean, and what is its point? To understand this, let us begin by examining the alleged scriptural conflict. The Eruvin prooftexts Genesis 1:27 and 5:2 use *both* masculine singular and plural pronouns to refer to *adam.* The masculine singular, which Fox translates as "it," refers to *adam* as a species: "God created humankind in his image, in the image of God did he create it," while reserving the plural to refer to its sexual variations, "male and female did he create them" (Gen. 1:27).[73] That two were created and both are called *adam,* humanity, is even harder to contest in the second Genesis prooftext (Gen. 5:1–2):

This is the record of the beginnings of adam/*Humankind.*
At the time of God's creating humankind [adam],
in the likeness of God did he then make it [masc. sing.]
male and female he created them
and gave blessing to them
and called their name Humankind [adam]!
on the day of their being created.

For this second prooftext, which is clearly a losing proposition, the defender of "tail" in Berakhot substitutes Genesis 9:6, a divine edict to Noah punning on the words *dam*, blood, and *adam*: "Whoever sheds human blood for that human shall his blood be shed *(shofekh dam ha-adam ba-adam damo yishafekh)*, for in God's image he made humankind *(adam)*." This proof is incontestable because it is tautological. It requires a prior assumption that *adam* means man in the singular, for the only masculine grammatical forms in the verse refer either to God or to "Whoever sheds."

For whom, then, is the textual problem a problem, and what agenda does it conceal? The answer to this question lies in the Berakhot and Eruvin versions of the creation debate. There we discover that this distinction between God's intention and God's act is offered by the proponents of "tail" to refute the prooftexts that form the cornerstone of the case for woman as a "face." The intention/act distinction, then, denies that woman was created as part of the original *adam*, but asserts that she was intended from the beginning.

Although the intention/act tradition is cited by the "tail" faction, it is less a "tail" argument than a compromise position between "face" and "tail," deftly avoiding some of the theological embarrassments threatened by a dual creation theory. A thoroughgoing dual creation theory would be unable to reconcile Genesis 1 with Genesis 2 and hence would be forced to desanctify some texts in favor of others. The distinction theory upholds the texts most at risk by declaring that they refer to a subsequently fulfilled divine intention. The intention/act distinction also moderates the sexual dualism implicit in dual creation theory. Because he holds that the female subsequently "built" out of the unitary *adam* was present in the original divine intention, woman is less of an afterthought or epiphenomenon for the distinction theorist than she is for the "tail" theorists. The distinction theory is less conducive to the demonization of woman. One could reason from dual creation theory that woman does not share the divine image, but the intention/act distinction will not support that argument.

However theologically advantageous it may be, the practical consequences of the distinction compromise are identical to those of the positions it attempts to harmonize. In the Talmud, all these positions ultimately are used to justify the masculine precedence from which male dominance is inferred.[74] From a feminist perspective, therefore, the entire debate looks like a case of "if it's heads, I win; if it's tails, you lose."

Building Beyond Polemics: An End Beyond the End

The importance of the debate from a feminist perspective is the question it raises about the meaning of the fourth bridal blessing: Does the blessing demand to be read as a polemic? The answer, I would argue, is no. Polemics avoid ambiguity, stating their points as baldly as possible. We noted this in the *erusin* blessing, which explicitly forbids pre-*nissuin* intercourse and brackets it with the forbidden sexual relations in Leviticus. If the fourth blessing were a polemic, would it not clearly articulate woman's secondary status? This blessing, however, does not even use the word "woman." Its final phrase, into which the rabbis of Babylonia read their creation agenda, has far too many resonances to serve as a reference to a single text or interpretation. Instead, the fourth blessing constitutes a complex and evocative metaphor.

The everlasting *binyan* may be the product of the prototypical *tavnit* mentioned in the preceding phrase: the human frame that embodies the divine image. The *binyan* itself may be prototypical, the paradigm inherent in all human bodies for infinitely reproducing the divine image. The *binyan* may also refer to the female body that shelters the fetus. *Binyan* may indeed allude to the "building" of Eve, but many midrashic readings of Genesis 2:22 do not imply a secondary creation. One such exegesis, possibly Tannaitic, suggests that God's "building" in Genesis 2 is not the creation of Eve but the construction of her body in the shape of a granary, wide below and narrow above (to contain the fetus).[75] Another much repeated Tannaitic exegesis associates the word *binyan* specifically with God's activities as a bridal attendant. It interprets "God built the rib" to mean that God braided Eve's hair for the wedding, because in the coastal towns, *binyata* (*binyan* with an Aramaic ending) means braiding.[76] A companion exegesis on "God brought her to the *adam*" suggests that God also acted as best man for *adam.* These popular midrashim may well have been standard fare at weddings. In addition, *binyan* may call to mind ancient associations of woman with house or the classical pun on *banim* (children) and *bonim* (builders).[77]

This richer reading of the fourth blessing also allows us to see the third and fourth blessings as related, rather than opposed. In the former, God is the creator and shaper of a male-and-female-humanity. In the latter, humanity mirrors God's creative ability by being able to create children out of itself and through them to extend itself toward eternity.

The Fifth Blessing: Back to the Future

The fourth blessing commemorates the trajectory from the beginnings of humankind to their creative extension toward the future. The fifth blessing locates us in the redemptive future of the collective Israel. A mosaic of prophetic allusions celebrate Zion's reconciliation with her divine husband and the restoration of her exiled children. At this festive event, Zion is at once the covenant bride, the barren wife made fruitful, and the mother reunited with her lost children. Moreover, these themes overflow into one another, so that the ingathering of the exiled children itself resembles a wedding celebration at which the children are the bride's ornaments. "Swiftly, your children are coming," says Isaiah (Isa. 49:17–19). "They are all gathered, are coming to you. Deck yourself with them like a bride."[78] The blessing opens, "May the barren one exult and be glad," echoing both Isaiah 59:1 "Sing O barren one," and Isaiah 61:10:

> *I exult and am glad in YHWH.*
> *My whole being rejoices in my God.*
> *For he has clothed me with garments of salvation*
> *Wrapped me in a robe of righteousness*
> *Like a bridegroom crowned with priestly turban*
> *Like a bride bedecked with her jewels.*[79]

This prophetic metaphor of the barren woman comforted situates us in the time of redemption but recalls the beginnings of the people Israel. The metaphor draws its power from Israel's most ancient assurances of its continuity, miraculous births out of barren matriarchs in fulfillment of the divine promise. Transmuted into the mother bereft of her children in Lamentations, the matriarch Rachel weeping for her exiled descendants in Jeremiah, the barren one is promised, "There is hope for your future. Your children shall return to their country" (Jer. 31:15–17). The signature of the blessing is placed in the present tense: "Blessed are You who gladden Zion with her children," as if the bridal couple together with their gathered friends and family embody the assembly of the redeemed.

Six and Seven: Songs for Lovers

The signature of the fifth blessing, praising God as the gladdener *(mesameaḥ)*, links it to the sixth and seventh blessings, whose nearly identical signatures praise God for gladdening *(mesameaḥ)* the bridegroom *and* or *with* the bride. In the sixth blessing, the bridal couple is compared to the primeval pair in the Garden of Eden. The couple in the garden, however, are not depicted as the worker and his helper, as in Genesis 2, but rather as "loving companions" *(re'im ahuvim)* reminiscent of the gentle egalitarian lovers in the Song of Songs. This expression, *re'im ahuvim,* does not occur in Scripture. But its vocabulary resounds in the great verse *v'ahavta l'reakha kemokha,* "You shall love *(ahav)* your companion *(re'a)* as yourself" (Lev. 19:18).[80]

The seventh blessing extends a great triumphal arch spanning the unstained world of the beginning, when joy and celebration were first created, and the redeemed world yet to come, the unending jubilee. Into its construction, the authors have poured all the words for harmony in the Hebrew language, ten of them all told, with the bride and groom enthroned in their midst. Then, shockingly, at the height of rapture, the arch passes over the archetypal landscape of destruction, and, in two stunning scriptural allusions, the destruction of Jerusalem invades the blessing. Jeremiah delivers his prophecy of joy renewed amid corpses and rubble: "Again shall be heard in this place, which you say is ruined, void of human or beast—in the cities of Judah and the streets of Jerusalem the voice of joy and the voice of gladness, the voice of the bridegroom and the voice of the bride" (Jer. 33:10–11). The singing youths to whom the blessing alludes are first encountered after the fall of the city: "The elders are gone from the [city] gate, the youths from their singing. Gone is the joy of our hearts; our dancing is turned *(hafakh)* to mourning" (Lam. 5:14–15). The blessing celebrates the inversion *(hipukh)* that turns this chaos and agony right-side up: "You turned *(hafakhta)* my wailing into dancing," the Psalmist sings, "You took off my sackcloth and girded me with joy" (Ps. 30:12).[81]

At the heart of joy, downfall, death, grief, and pain all are acknowledged. Bride, groom, and wedding guests, houses and investments, all will fall into fragments like the glass that is smashed after this last blessing has been spoken. "But I call this to mind and therefore hope," says the speaker in Lamentations, "God's kindness *(ḥesed,* pl.) is not ended nor his mercies spent. They are new every morning. How great is your faithfulness!" (Lam. 3:22–23).

Every joy is unique, freshly experienced, surprising. Joy heals us by making us new. The blessing triumphs over inexorable suffering and sorrow, proclaiming the inevitability of joy. Thus, the bridegroom and the bride in the blessing are simultaneously the human couple in their pristine innocence, still unwounded by one another, and the divine bridegroom and covenant bride, veterans of long strife and many betrayals, but healed at last, their love made new.

If *kiddushin* represents a sanctification through separation, then the *Sheva Berakhot* celebrate a sanctification through the holy coming-together that is covenant. They celebrate the cosmic process of wedding that occurs at all levels of sacred time and sacred history: making one, making joy, making new. Wedding is the beginning and end of time shaped into a circle and wreathed around the bridegroom and the bride. Wedding is creation and redemption, the origin of all bonds and their perfect mending, the first encounter of lover-equals and Zion's reconciliation with the lover she will no longer call "my *ba'al.*" This expansive metaphor of wedding strains at the limits of the *kiddushin* relationship it is meant to complement, and the strain cries out for relief. Either *kiddushin* must coopt the *Sheva Berakhot,* or the *Sheva Berakhot* must rise up and cast out *kiddushin.* This latter is the course I have chosen.

The Case for Altering *Kiddushin*

What are we to do when the words and gestures that effect marriage do not reflect but distort the event being celebrated in the life of the participants and their community? Under pressure from their constituents, nontraditional Judaisms and even modern Orthodoxy have sought to alleviate discomfort with the *erusin* portion of the wedding ceremony by liturgical innovations. These focus mainly upon the bride's silence and passivity in the traditional ceremony and the inability of the traditional *ketubbah,* the marriage settlement contract, to address the social reality of the relationship into which the participants intend to enter. These innovations include additional vows like those in Christian ceremonies, where the partners promise to cherish and protect one another.[82] Or after the legal acquisition is concluded and the *ketubbah* has been read, the bride recites a verse from Song of Songs to her husband, sometimes accompanied by the gift of a ring. Creative *ketubbot* that articulate the couple's own visions of how the marriage is to be conducted supplement or replace the standard *ketubbah* form that attests the husband's responsibility to provide food, shelter, clothing, and sexual intercourse *(onah)* and records

190

a financial settlement (now superseded by civil community property and inheritance laws) in the event of divorce or the husband's demise.[83]

These innovations, however charming and individualized, are halakhically impotent. They leave the legal structure of *kiddushin* intact, and that structure with its implicit definitions of the marital relationship legally supersedes any personal statements the bride and groom make to one another. It is as if a man purchased a slave in accordance with laws governing the institution of slavery and then promised his purchase, "I'll always treat you like an equal." The slave's treatment would depend not upon any recognized legal standard, but upon whether his legal owner was an exceptionally nice guy.

This is not to belittle the serious efforts couples have made to renovate the wedding ceremony. Their alterations reveal an instinctive understanding that a Jewish marriage is a legal ritual, and therefore it is important that the words that specify the commitments being made be words that the participants intend to honor. Even though Jewish marriages are now performed solely by rabbis, Jewish marriage is not a sacrament effected by an anointed officiant with special powers. The couple themselves accomplish marriage by pronouncing and receiving the effectuating legal formula in the presence of witnesses. For this very reason, rabbinic law is at pains to establish the actors' intent to accomplish the condition the rabbis define as marriage.

The Double-Ring Ceremony: Equal Opportunity Commodification

One innovation that does reject the classical premises of *kiddushin* is the double-ring ceremony in which both partners make the traditional declaration of acquisition. According to classical halakhah, no *kiddushin* is effected, because equal exchanges cancel each other out. It is as if each participant had given the other a five dollar bill; their circumstances are precisely what they were before the transaction. From an ethical perspective, the double-ring ceremony is a dubious amelioration. The problem with marital *kinyan* is not simply that it is unilateral, but that it commodifies human beings. The groom's commodification and acquisition of the bride is not rectified by the bride's retaliation in kind. *Kinyan* of persons violates values conscientious people have come to regard as moral goods. As the abolition of slavery and the institution of labor unionization attest, ownership of another person's body or of another's alienated labor is no longer viewed as just. The vocabulary and constitutive assumptions of *kiddushin* cannot be made to reflect a partnership of equals.

191

Partnership as a Legal Basis for Marriage

Marriage, some wit once remarked, makes man and woman one—and the man is the one. We have just reached a point in history where it is possible to envision, and sometimes to realize, marriages in which two remain two, marriages that are not incorporations but covenants. We need a wedding ceremony that embodies the partners' intentions to sustain and strive with each other all their lives, to endure like the protagonists of the stormy but ultimately redemptive covenant marriage of biblical prophecy. This intention is not reflected in an act of acquisition. It can only be expressed by an act of covenanting. Like all covenants, a marriage agreement must embody some of the characteristics of contracts, articulating standards for an ethical relation and laying out some of what the partners most need and want. The marriage agreement must specify the obligations that will form the fabric of the marriage. The partners must be able to make some promises to one another, even though promises are sometimes broken. And if a marriage loses its qualities as a *shutafut*, a partnership, people must be free to dissolve it.

For these reasons and others I will explain, partnership law, *hilkhot shutafut*, forms the legal basis for the contractual aspects of the *b'rit ahuvim*.[84] The model of a partnership reflects the undeniable fact that marriage is not only a social but an economic institution. But unlike the *ketubbah*, which presumes that most economic power and resources belong to the male, the *b'rit ahuvim* presumes communal resources and requires joint decisions about their distribution.

Partnership law embodies other desirable values as well. In halakhah, it mediates between the partners' needs for autonomy and their needs for interdependence. A partnership is formed by mutual agreement, and each party has the power to terminate it. In classical halakhah, a partnership is not an independent legal entity as a corporation is in modern Western law, nor are the identities of the partners submerged in it. They remain individually accountable. Because the laws of partnership developed out of the laws of joint ownership, the partnership is regarded as a kind of property in which the partners have invested. Consequently, each partner acquires legal obligations for maintaining the partnership and its projects.

The halakhic process of forming a partnership generally embodies three elements:

1. A partnership deed. Although from the tenth century on, verbal agreement was considered sufficient to contract partnerships, written evidence in the form of a deed seems to have been more usual.
2. A statement of personal undertaking in which partners committed themselves to certain acts on behalf of the partnership.
3. A *kinyan* or symbolic acquisition of the partnership.[85] Partnerships were first understood as joint ownerships achieved by pooling resources. "Pooling resources" in talmudic idiom is *l'hatil b'kis*, to put into one pouch, and an ancient legal gesture for partnership acquisition was for each partner to put a sum into one pouch and to lift it up together. Lifting is one of the fundamental halakhic indications of taking something into one's domain. By lifting the pouch together, contributors would signify joint acquisition both of the money in the bag and the investment it represented.[86] This special gesture was later abandoned in favor of a legal convention for ratifying all sorts of transactions, *kinyan sudar*, in which one party pulls a scarf or handkerchief out of the other's hand.[87]

I have represented all three of these elements in the formation of the *b'rit ahuvim*. There is a partnership deed, which I have called a *shtar b'rit*, a covenant document, in recognition that this special partnership has the potential to be more than a contract *(shtar)*. There is a verbal commitment by the partners during the ceremony. And, finally, there is a *kinyan* by means of which the partners symbolically acquire their partnership, not through the more common *kinyan sudar*, but through an adapted form of the more ancient pooling of resources in a pouch.

The Contractual Content of the *B'rit*: Balancing Individual Needs and Communal Standards

The *b'rit ahuvim* is not a private arrangement, but a commitment entailing communal responsibilities. While its stipulations can be tailored to the needs of particular couples, it embodies a standard of righteousness based upon how a conscientious progressive community interprets and lives out its Jewish obligations. As a *bayit b'Yisra'el*, a household among the people Israel, *b'rit* partners share with other Jewish households a responsibility for the continuity and well-being of the people Israel and for participating in its task of *tikkun olam*, repairing the world.[88]

The *b'rit ahuvim* specifies both the standards of righteousness and the desires of the partners. But, as in classical covenants, the partners are committed ultimately to one another and not merely to the terms they have promised to fulfill. To the extent that this covenantal commitment is realized in the relationship, it can survive breaches in contractual obligations. Like the covenant between God and Israel, the *b'rit ahuvim* is a promise of exclusivity. The relationships it delineates are lasting, monogamous unions, whether heterosexual or homosexual.[89]

The *b'rit* document should be written in Hebrew, because it is traditionally a language for learning, law, and sacred expression and because it is spoken as a living language by large communities of Jews in Israel and in the Diaspora. It records a commitment that affects not only individuals, but also *klal Yisra'el*, the collectivity of the Jewish people, and hence should be comprehensible anywhere Jews live. If Hebrew is not the primary language of the partners or those who will witness the wedding, the document should also be translated.

In the model of *b'rit ahuvim* I have designed, the *b'rit* document opens with two paragraphs rooting *b'rit ahuvim* in biblical covenant stories and identifying the relationship with the rabbinic ideal of holy companionship (see Appendix). The contractual stipulations follow. The specific stipulations I have recommended are: (1) a pledge of sexual exclusivity; (2) a commitment to the rights and duties of familial relationship; (3) an assumption of joint responsibility for children; (4) a pledge to live a holy life as a Jewish family; (5) a pledge to fulfill communal responsibilities; and (6) a pledge that either spouse will protect the dignity and comfort of the other in his or her dying.

Couples may wish to add or vary particular stipulations. For instance, blended families or noncustodial parents may have other arrangements about familial responsibilities. Stipulations such as these should be amendable upon mutual agreement. The stipulations must be flexible enough to accommodate changes either in external conditions or in the two parties themselves. At the same time, formulating the stipulations provides an opportunity for partners to disclose to each other their tacit assumptions and strongly held convictions about family roles, resources, and plans for the future. A partner's intention to put a child from a previous marriage through graduate school, the expectation of caring for an elderly parent at home, the yearning for many children, and a strong distaste for children are examples of obligations and desires best placed on the table at the very start.[90]

Kinyan Trouble: The Lore of the Rings

Kinyan, or symbolic acquisition of the partnership, is the third traditional element of partnership law embodied in the *b'rit ahuvim,* and it is fraught with difficulties. For reasons I will explain presently, it is essential to demonstrate that the couple intends to form a *b'rit ahuvim* and not to contract *kiddushin.* Hence it is necessary to be particularly clear about the language and gestures surrounding the transaction that establishes the relationship. Two classic tokens of *kinyan* in particular are sufficiently identified with *kiddushin* that their use in ratifying the *b'rit* transaction could create confusion about the nature of the relationship. The most troubling of these is the giving of the wedding ring, a universal symbol of espousal in Western cultures. In *kiddushin,* the woman's acceptance of a ring from the man signifies that she consents to be purchased symbolically from herself by him. There is reason to be concerned, therefore, that giving and accepting a ring in the context of a wedding ceremony could be taken as evidence that, despite the lack of any supporting declaration, the couple actually intended *kiddushin.*

The wedding ring is not just a minor detail of the ceremony; metonymically, it represents the whole affair.[91] Is a ceremony without rings likely to be as convincing as a performative ritual should be? Will the participants feel married? Will the wedding guests leap up and shout *"mazel tov!"* or will they shrug and remind one another that it's a free country? The wedding ring's power as a signifier is a good example of the points discussed in Chapter 3: ritual is profoundly conservative, and it is compelling in ways that cold reason can neither account for nor refute. It seems unlikely that most people will relinquish the ritual of giving wedding rings. Is there a way to include rings while avoiding both the possible confusion with classical *kiddushin* and the tit-for-tat commodification implicit in double-ring adaptations of *kiddushin?* I will propose several possible solutions to this problem shortly.

The other indicator of *kinyan* I have rejected is *kinyan sudar,* the exchange of the handkerchief. Although it became the common mode of ratification in later partnership law, *kinyan sudar* is also the means by which the bridegroom acquires the *ketubbah* from the officiant of the wedding. Even though in traditional ceremonies the bride does not engage in *kinyan sudar,* I have ruled out adapting this ritual for both partners in the *b'rit ahuvim,* lest this ritual's traditional associations with the *ketubbah* mislead anyone into mistaking the *b'rit* document for a "creative" *ketubbah* that both the bride and groom are acquiring. The distinction between these two documents is crucial. The *b'rit* document is one of the elements that effectuates a partnership of equals. A *ketubbah*, on the other hand, does not effectuate *kiddushin*. That is accomplished by the husband's statement "Behold you are sanctified to me" (exclusively acquired by me) and by his giving and her accepting the ring. Only then does the wife acquire the *ketubbah*, for its function is to moderate the husband's power over his acquisition. The content of the *ketubbah* thus details entitlements and duties, protects the wife's position in the household by making it expensive for the husband to divorce her, and ensures her some degree of economic security in the event of his demise or her divorce.

Even if *kinyan sudar* did not leave the *b'rit* document open to misinterpretation, it would still be unacceptable because it is aesthetically unappealing. It smells of the marketplace. Among Orthodox Jews, it remains to this day a common means of ratifying all sorts of financial transactions.

There is, however, as I have said, a form of *kinyan* that was used in ancient times exclusively for partnership acquisition: symbolically pooling resources in a bag and lifting it together. This gesture could not possibly be mistaken for an acquisition of *kiddushin*. Moreover, like the *b'rit* document and its stipulations, this ritual for acquiring pooled resources is another adaptable, expressive element of the ceremony: After the *b'rit* document has been read aloud and signed by the partners and by two witnesses, each partner places an object of some value in a bag provided for this purpose, perhaps specially designed or decorated. These may be objects that are especially eloquent of their owners' personalities: a musical instrument, a much-consulted book, a legacy from a beloved relative or teacher. Partners may choose to explain the objects' significance and the particular contribution to the relationship they represent. This ritual can also provide a solution to the ring dilemma. Along with these chosen objects, or instead of them, each partner may put the other's wedding ring into the bag. In this way, the rings are acquired specifically as tokens of partnership.[92] When the partners lift the bag together, they make a blessing, using their preferred *berakhah* formula as discussed in Chapter 3: "Blessed are you . . . who remember your covenant and is faithful to your covenant and keeps your word." This is the traditional blessing upon seeing a rainbow, and its content seems particularly appropriate to express the hope that a trustworthy covenant has been sealed.

As If it Was Always Like This: The Order of the Service

As a reformulation, the *b'rit ahuvim* has both continuities and discontinuities with tradition. Attentive to the observation of Barbara Myerhoff that ritual should seem as if it has always been this way, I have preserved as many elements of the traditional ceremony as possible. The *b'rit ahuvim* section that replaces the elements of *kiddushin* (the *erusin* blessing, declaration of acquisition, giving of the ring, and reading of the *ketubbah*) is both preceded and followed by traditional words and traditional melodies—and, of course, the ceremony is performed under a *ḥuppah.*[93] The order of the service reflects this "frame" of traditional elements:

1. *Mi adir 'al ha-kol* (traditional invocation of blessing for the couple).
2. Officiant's speech (traditional). Following the invocation is a traditional time for the officiant to speak briefly, outlining and explaining the ceremony and its meaning and speaking personally about the couple. The officiant should take this opportunity to explain what a *b'rit ahuvim* is and to distinguish it from *kiddushin.*
3. Blessing over wine (analogous to the tradition, but distinct from it). In the *kiddushin* ceremony, this blessing would be followed by the *erusin* blessing, and only the couple would drink from the cup. Here, the officiant should explain that a blessing over a cup of wine is a way to begin a holy celebration. To distinguish this cup from the *erusin* cup, it may be passed to all those around the *ḥuppah.*
4. Reading of the *b'rit* document in Hebrew and in English (analogous to the reading of the *ketubbah* but clearly distinguished from it by its contents).
5. *Kinyan,* acquisition of the partnership by placing symbols of pooled resources in the bag and lifting. This will be the most unfamiliar part of the ceremony, but it may also be powerful precisely because it is new. If the partners have put in distinctive personal objects and intend to talk about their significance for the partnership, they should do so before lifting the bag. Wedding rings can be placed in the bag at this time. The partners then lift the bag together and recite the blessing. They could then put on their rings.
6. The *Sheva Berakhot,* Seven Blessings (traditional). Gay and lesbian couples may want to replace the words "bridegroom and bride" with

re'im ahuvim, "loving companions," an expression taken from the text of the sixth blessing.

7. Shattering the glass (traditional). Despite its dubious origins in medieval European folk custom, shattering the glass has become an indispensable ritual.[94] Couples may wish to have a glass for each to shatter. A traditional explanation is that the shattered glass reminds us of the destroyed Jerusalem whose memory we are to prize above our greatest joys. A contemporary reinterpretation of the custom identifies it with the still shattered world we reenter after the Edenic space of the wedding ceremony.

8. *Yiḥud* (traditional). Immediately after the ceremony, the partners go into a room to be alone together. Traditionally this symbolized the commencement of living together. What is moving about *yiḥud* is the contrast between the raucous singing, dancing, and shouts of congratulation that greet the breaking of the glass and this sudden haven of quiet intimacy. Couples who do not put their rings into the bag of pooled resources may wish to exchange them together at this special time.

Dissolving the *B'rit Ahuvim*

The *b'rit ahuvim* reflects but does not duplicate the divine covenant-marriage. Neither of its participants is the divine partner who can heal the wounds of history. For human marriage, some wounds are fatal. Marriage begins with the celebration of humanity's divine image in the bridal blessings. It is appropriate that it end by honoring that divine image in the ways that the partners are helped to dissolve the partnership justly and generously.

The ancient Jewish community of Elephantine made divorce a public matter. The man or woman first had to announce before the congregation his or her intent to divorce.[95] In contrast, halakhic divorces exclude the community; they usually occur in a rabbi's study with only the rabbinical court and its designated witnesses and scribe in attendance. These participants are technicians, expert in the mechanics of divorce. The couple's spiritual condition is not of concern to them because it does not affect the legal validity of the divorce. But the dissolution of *b'rit ahuvim* should be different. It should reflect that a covenant, not merely a contract, has failed. The community must not distance itself from those who have experienced this catastrophe. Representatives from the couple's religious environment, or perhaps a minyan similar to a *shivah* minyan, should be present to comfort the separating partners, much as a *shivah* minyan bears witness to a death and comforts the bereaved. Similarly, the dissolution of *b'rit* might even be followed by a day of mourning, at which friends and family can support and console the two partners as *shivah* visitors do, listening to the mourner or just being quiet together.

Like the business partnerships that provide its contractual structure, the *b'rit ahuvim* may be dissolved at the initiative of either partner. This procedure should be conducted by a court of three learned Jews. If the couple has difficulty dividing their material assets or coming to agreements about custody, support, visitation, and education of children, they should resolve these matters before the final dissolution with the help of a professional mediator or a lay arbitration court of three, one arbitrator chosen by each partner and the third chosen by agreement of the other two. At the dissolution proceeding itself, the court should draw up a document in Hebrew, also translated into the vernacular, attesting to the termination of the *b'rit ahuvim,* the distribution of its assets, and arrangements for any continuing obligations. The document should be signed by two witnesses.

B'rit ahuvim, then, both is and is not a marriage. On the one hand, it formalizes a relationship between two lovers pledged to fidelity. Like any marriage agreement, it may be licensed and registered and thus recognized by the state, although at this writing that option is not yet available to gay and lesbian couples. But *b'rit ahuvim* does not meet the requirements for marriage under classical halakhah, because one party does not acquire the other in the ceremony, nor is the couple's subsequent sexual intercourse meant to effect the woman's acquisition. While the *b'rit* contractors intend an enduring, monogamous relationship, they reject the power imbalance that characterizes *kiddushin* in favor of shared power and consensual decision making about all aspects of the relationship, including its inauguration and, if required, its termination. This point is essential to establish because, as I will show, there are some halakhists who would classify any lasting intimate relationship as a de facto *kiddushin.* And because any *kiddushin* requires a *get,* a halakhic divorce, for its termination, it is important to establish that *b'rit ahuvim* is not equivalent to *kiddushin.* For if *b'rit ahuvim* is not a halakhic marriage, then it can be dissolved without a *get.*

The Anatomy of Jewish Divorce

What is a *get?* Why is it an issue regarding *b'rit ahuvim?* And why should liberal Jews care how traditionalists regard their marriages and divorces? These questions are related, but let's take them one at a time.

In *kiddushin*, the mode of dissolution parallels the mode of effectuation. Thus, because the husband was the acquirer, only he can release his acquisition.[96] At the culmination of the traditional divorce ceremony, a gesture eloquent of this inequality occurs; as the woman stands silently, the husband drops the *get* into her outstretched hands.[97] The divorce document is roughly parallel to a slave's deed of manumission,[98] and it leaves the woman with the stigmatized status of a divorcee, *gerusha* (literally, a woman who was chased away), which renders her unfit to marry a man of priestly lineage *(kohen)*. Should she remarry without having obtained a proper Jewish divorce, classical halakhah would regard her as an adulteress. The children of any subsequent relationship would be labeled *mamzerim*, bastards. This status is immutable and is communicated to offspring. They and their descendants are forever proscribed by classical halakhah from marrying legitimate Jews.

The *get* proceeding itself has little relevance to the living realities by which partners disassemble their household and undo their ties. In North America and Europe, where Orthodox courts enjoy no monopoly on regulating marital status, even Jews who insist upon a traditional *get* rely upon civil law to determine how the divorce will be lived out: distribution of assets, child custody, and continuing responsibilities. Even in Israel, the *get* is ceremonial. Standards for property division and custody are set by the state. In effect, the only reasons for the traditional ceremony are negative: to avoid stigma to future offspring and to enable future access to religious marriage.

In the traditional Jewish wedding ceremony, the power imbalance implicit in *kiddushin* is masked by the covenantal rhetoric of the *Sheva Berakhot*. But divorce exposes the full extent of the inequity and the many abuses it makes possible. Greedy husbands blackmail and extort in exchange for granting divorces. Vindictive husbands withhold divorces for years, leaving their wives in limbo.[99] At the same time, halakhah powerfully discourages women from turning to the secular courts to free themselves. Since, according to halakhah, only the husband can relinquish his acquisition, and then only by the process prescribed and administered by the religious courts, the wife's secular divorce has no effect. Any subsequent relationship will be considered adulterous, and any offspring will bear the stigma of bastardy. On these grounds, many rabbis refuse to remarry a woman without a *get.* An unfortunate marital episode may thus haunt a woman or her descendants. In our own time, religious courts research and record marriages and divorces with unprecedented assiduousness in a central computer bank. So it is that patriarchal power, armed with cutting-edge technology, avenges itself upon the rebels' children and their children's children forever.[100]

Traditionalist scholars sympathetic to the dilemma of women have proposed various ways to mitigate the grosser injustices of Jewish divorce. These consist of legal mechanisms by which prospective husbands transfer the power of divorce to the rabbinic courts.[101] While none of these innovations gives Jewish women access to divorce comparable to that of the Palestinian tradition, all offer traditional Jewish women some relief from marital limbo.[102] However, none addresses the foundational injustice of *kiddushin* itself, the commodification and *kinyan* of women that necessitates the *get.*

Reform Judaism's response to the inequities and humiliations inherent in traditional divorce was to turn the whole business over to civil authorities.[103] It declared that civil divorce alone sufficed to dissolve its marriages. Ironically, this strategy only served to intensify the sense of estrangement from community already present in traditional divorce. To be sent to secular authorities to dissolve a holy covenant is the ultimate abandonment by the Jewish community, the quintessential silent treatment. In addition, for classical halakhists, Reform's toleration of civil divorce exacerbated a problem first encountered in Muslim lands but greatly amplified by the Emancipation. The problem was sharpened still further when Reform and other non-Orthodox Jews decided to issue their own religious divorces: When Jews contract and dissolve marriages outside of classical Jewish law, how are these relationships to be categorized?[104] Are the marriages halakhically valid, and hence, do they require to be terminated by *get?*

The implications of plural versions of Jewish marriage and divorce are far reaching and bring still broader questions in their wake: What is the relationship between liberal Jews and *klal Yisra'el,* the entire collectivity of the Jewish people, and what obligations flow from that relationship? Can *klal Yisra'el* maintain its integrity without imposing a unitary standard of practice to which all must conform? For several centuries, halakhists and theologians have fought hand to hand on these questions amid barrages of flying anathemas, while plural traditions of practice con-

201

tinued to develop. At the heart of this controversy are the most basic issues of communal integrity and questions of status.

Traditionalists are alarmed at the growing number of Jews who decline to undergo a traditional divorce and who subsequently contribute to the proliferation of bastardy. They advocate that all Jews conform at least to the rabbinic laws of marriage, divorce, and conversion to avoid creating two Jewish peoples who cannot intermarry. In North America, traditionalists pressure for these standards; in Israel, where status matters are in the hands of Orthodox rabbinic courts, they actively coerce. As I have explained elsewhere, this conflict is painful but inevitable. "People who inhabit a *nomos* together cannot simply 'live and let live' because they are interdependent. Our hermeneutical commitments and their behavioral consequences affects our neighbors' lives as well as our own."[105] As soon as we live by our commitments, we affect one another's Judaism.

In order for Jews from differing communities to continue to marry one another, we need some basic agreement on standards for defining, effecting, and dissolving marriages. But what compromises must be made to achieve such an agreement, and by whom? Traditionalists protest that because classical marriage and divorce law is enormously intricate, its determination belongs in the hands of experts.[106] I would argue that classical halakhah deliberately esotericizes marriage and divorce law and gives its practitioners a monopoly on its adjudication because it believes that the orderly transmission of women from domain to domain sustains a fundamental social boundary. According to this view, if the ownership of women and of their offspring is confused or deregulated, chaos will result similar to the chaos that prevailed at the time of the Flood; that is, obliteration of these primary boundaries and the hierarchies of power and status they ensure will corrupt humankind so ineradicably that destruction will be the only remedy.[107] The orderly transmission of women under auspices designated and controlled by men is, in this view, the keystone of Jewish civilization.

Because the halakhic consequences of nontraditional marriage and divorce are so devastating to the existence of the Jewish people, traditionalists claim they trump liberal Jewish concerns about conscience, the integrity of religious expression, and the dignity, rights, and welfare of women. They argue that, even if non-Orthodox Jews have to hold their noses, they ought to leave divorce (and preferably marriage as well) in the hands of the Orthodox rabbinate.

To non-Orthodox Jews, this reasoning appears both self-serving and self-referential. From a progressive perspective, halakhah is not a time-less, divinely authored code, but a construction within time and culture for which human beings are responsible. To the progressive Jew, then, the traditionalist's demand for exclusive authority would force him or her to act in bad faith. In effect, the traditionalist is saying: "Because we believe the system has been constructed by God, not by us, and is there-fore indisputable, you ought to put aside your own deepest convictions and submit to ours."[108] These two mutually exclusive viewpoints speeding toward one another can only produce a train wreck. They cannot occupy the same track. But might they run on parallel tracks, coexisting without concurring? If traditionalists recognize precedents within halakhah that relegate some status questions and ceremonies to areas outside their jurisdiction, it is possible to bring about a detente between Orthodox and non-Orthodox world views.

Does Non-Halakhic Marriage Require a *Get?*

There are, in fact, several streams of halakhic opinion concerning the status of non-halakhic marriages.[109] The most stringent of these we may call the pan-*kiddushin* position. Authorities who embrace this view polar-ize heterosexual conjoinings into two categories: *kiddushin* and *zenut,* licentiousness. The key principle cited in defense of this position is the rabbinic generalization, "A man does not make his act of intercourse *zenut*" (B. Gittin 81a). Pan-*kiddushin* halakhists overgeneralize this prin-ciple, contending that all sexual intercourse, regardless of context or cir-cumstances, is presumed to be for the sake of establishing *kiddushin.*[110] This global generalization is then allowed to override other legal consider-ations such as the intentions of the contractors and attestation by wit-nesses. It is possible to argue from the pan-*kiddushin* perspective that, regardless of the kind of wedding ceremony a couple chooses, we assume that their practice of living as husband and wife constitutes *kiddushin* after the fact by virtue of their intimate relations, even if there are not formal witnesses to their intimacies.[111]

Other halakhists, however, consider intention and attestation to be decisive factors in determining whether *kiddushin* has been accom-plished. This position bases itself on a ruling in the Shulḥan Arukh, which declares that no *kiddushin* exists without the *intention* to contract *kid-dushin* and the attestation of qualified witnesses.[112] For these decisors, it is not enough to establish that the couple does not intend to have casual sex *(zenut).* It must further be established that they meant to contract *kiddushin* "according to the law of Moses and Israel." By this reasoning, it would be possible to establish that a civil marriage or a *b'rit ahuvim* does not qualify as *kiddushin* and does not require a *get.*

The pan-*kiddushin* position, on the other hand, is necessarily a pan-*get* position as well. In its view, all long-term connubial relationships require a *get* to terminate the relationship. For the traditionalist, this opinion has the obvious charm of validating an Orthodox monopoly on the definition (and enactment) of marriage and divorce, even though it is difficult to force compliance, even in Israel. Moreover, the inherent coerciveness of this position and the bitter resentments and resistances it arouses may prove as corrosive to the Jewish people as the issue of *mamzerut.*

Another strain in classical Jewish law, however, offers halakhic precedent for a class of intimate relationships that are neither *kiddushin* nor *zenut.* Its classic example of such a relationship is concubinage, *pilagshut.* Into this category, earlier halakhists tossed a wildly ahistorical muddle of relationships: the maidservant wives of the biblical patriarchs; the royal concubines of David and Solomon; the *hetairas, amicae,* and *concubinae* of the Greeks and Romans; and the mistresses of the medieval Spanish Jewish aristocracy.[113] These examples, in turn, served for some authorities as models for civil marriage and other nonhalakhic long-term relationships. For the progressive Jew, however, these analogies are fundamentally flawed: none of these examples describes an egalitarian relationship. For the traditionalist, however, what all these long-term relationships have in common is their claim to be other than *kiddushin.* The following halakhic questions arise concerning such relationships: (1) are they permissible according to Jewish law? and (2) are they, in fact, relationships established without "benefit of *kiddushin*"?

Only one talmudic source differentiates concubinage from wifehood. This is a brief passage explicating a verse about King David's wives and concubines (B. Sanhedrin 21a). The text asks: What is the difference between wives and concubines? R. Yehuda, citing Rav, offers a basic distinction: a wife has *kiddushin* and *ketubbah,* whereas a concubine has neither. The Talmud's question suggests that there was no common practice to consult on this matter. Moreover, little is said about concubinage in either the Babylonian or the Palestinian Talmud. By the early centuries of the common era, Jews had ceased to practice concubinage. Hence the topic was of no practical concern to the rabbis. Their few references conflate biblical practices with the quite different institution of Greco-Roman concubinage that they observed among non-Jews.[114]

In several later Jewish societies, however, affluent Jewish men kept mistresses, and the authorities who addressed these situations categorized such relationships as concubinage. Maimonides forbade them outright, declaring that only a king could have concubines.[115] Despite the Talmud's clear statement to the contrary, a few authorities argued that a concubine lacks a *ketubbah* but has *kiddushin*, in which case she would require a *get*.[116] But a number of authorities not only permitted so-called concubinage, but distinguished it conclusively from *kiddushin*, among them Ramban (Nahmanides), R. Shlomo ben Adret, and R. Yaacov Emden.[117]

One modern authority, R. Toledano, even suggested the category of concubinage as an option for non-Orthodox Jews who did not want to deal with the problematic consequences of *kiddushin*.[118] Thus, prospective couples would be given a choice between contracting *kiddushin* and participating in a ceremony that established only *pilagshut*. This proposal neatly solves the problem posed for traditionalists when people will not or cannot obtain halakhic divorces and thereby minimizes the occurrence of *mamzerut*. But the choices it offers women are insulting: would you rather be a permanent possession or a long-term lease? No matter how many halakhic problems concubinage would resolve, to impose it on people who regard their relationship in quite different terms can only incur resentment. Although concubinage may be valuable as a placeholder for relationships differentiated from *kiddushin*, such relationships need not be identified as concubinage. They could instead be identified as other non-*kiddushin* relationships for which concubinage is the first precedent in Jewish legal history. *B'rit ahuvim* belongs in this category.

Why, however, should traditionalists accept such a third category in addition to *kiddushin* and *zenut*? After all, halakhic voices that reject the validity of such a category have been in the majority for the last two centuries. A compelling reason is that the halakhic precedent for such a category provides a halakhic opportunity to save the collective of Israel, *klal Yisra'el*, from the very catastrophe traditionalists have been predicting for it. For Orthodoxy to insist upon the pan-*kiddushin*/pan-*get* position when an alternative is available is to write off all those whom it cannot control. Ruling according to a minority opinion in order to avoid fracturing *klal Yisra'el* is not really such a daring act. Some of the great rabbis of the Talmud took far more dangerous halakhic liberties, because they believed it a desecration to make God's Torah a source of torment and destruction.[119]

The most violent divisions result from efforts to impose unrelenting unity. Under the slogan "We Are One," the many ways in which we diverge fester in hiding. The problem is not how to eradicate our differences, but how to differ without breaking apart. This is the goal of religious pluralism. As the Protestant theologian David Tracy shows, pluralism is predicated on the assumption that the entire truth is not within our grasp.[120] The texts that guide us and the life situations to which we seek to apply them are ambiguous. They can be interpreted in more than one way. When we are uncertain whether our interpretation is the only correct one, whether our plan of action is the only one that will work, we are better able to hear and value the interpretations and plans of others. This is seldom easy. We want our beliefs and opinions to have an impact on reality because we have real-life investments in them that we want to protect. The only easy pluralism is, as Tracy describes, "a genial confusion in which one tries to enjoy the pleasures of difference without ever committing oneself to a particular vision of resistance and hope."[121]

Only those who are certain that they possess the whole truth and that its applications are entirely clear to them can totally reject pluralism. Intellectually responsible versions of Orthodoxy would not make such claims because halakhah is diverse rather than monolithic. To work through a problem in the Talmud, the learner takes on each opinion in turn, sees the problem through its lenses, and explores its *shitah,* the entire system within which this opinion makes sense. No opinion is assumed to be devoid of merit. Talmudic dispute, boisterous and pugnacious as it is, is like an act of prayer: it is "dispute for the sake of Heaven."

> Any dispute for the sake of Heaven will ultimately produce some lasting result. Any dispute that is not for the sake of Heaven will come to nothing. What is an example of a dispute for the sake of Heaven? The dispute of Hillel and Shammai. And a dispute not for the sake of Heaven? The dispute of Korah and his faction. (Mishnah Avot 5:17)[122]

Korah's rebellion in Numbers 16 is, for the rabbis, the paradigmatic power grab, made more heinous by its cynical distortions of religious rhetoric. But what is meant by the example of Hillel and Shammai? These two sages could be termed the mythic ancestors of rabbinic Judaism. They flourished about 20 B.C.E. during the Herodian period. Instead of being a single ancestral figure—a sort of rabbinic Abraham, they are a conflictual pair, the first of many such *zugot* or pairs of authorities. The schools of Hillel and Shammai differ on hundreds of laws, some of them having the gravest implications about marital status and legitimacy. One Mishnah lists a whole series of these status disputes, but adds:

> Nevertheless, even though one permits what the other forbids and one cancels what the other validates, the school of Shammai did not refuse to marry women from the school of Hillel and the school of Hillel did not refuse to marry those from the school of Shammai. (M. Yevamot 1:4)

This concord cannot have been easy. Following the list of disagreements in the Mishnah are pages upon pages of dispute. But somehow, given issues of the utmost seriousness regarding the composition of their society, the two schools refrained from further dividing their already fragmented Jewish world.

The *b'rit ahuvim* I have set forth in this chapter is a proposal for *tikkun*, mending, on many levels. It mends a wedding ceremony split into two mutually contradictory parts. It amends the commodification and subjugation of women inherent in *kiddushin*. It heals the corrosive effects of *kiddushin* both on women and on men by transplanting the legal definition of marriage into partnership law. There the covenant metaphor that pervades the bridal blessings can at last flourish and bear fruit. Finally, *b'rit ahuvim* offers a way to mend a widening rift in *klal Yisra'el.* It suggests a way to preserve the Jewish dispute over the definition and performance of marriage and divorce as a dispute for the sake of Heaven, to sustain our differences without ceasing to unite.

Epilogue:
On Seeds and Ruins

At the beginning of the Talmud is a story about ruins. The story is found in the first chapter of Berakhot, the tractate that heads the first of the Talmud's six orders, *Seder Zeraim*, the Order of Seeds. This is an odd place to find a story about ruins, because *berakhot* is to the Talmud what Genesis is to the Bible. Just as Genesis sets forth a cosmos, Tractate Berakhot offers the seeds of a *nomos*. The seeds that contain the *nomos* of rabbinic Judaism are the blessings, *berakhot*. Their theological content and ritual performances generate and propagate rabbinic Judaism's sustaining institutions, the synagogue and the study house. In contrast to the cosmos of Genesis, which is created out of chaos by divine fiat, the rabbinic *nomos* is evolved, as the metaphor of seed implies. Seeds contain both the past and the future. As legacies from the dead, they reproduce the world. As pledges to the future, they change it. Every seed points to some future seed that will both incorporate it and differ from it.

Ruins attest only to the past. Yet these echoes of the past are resonant with power. That is why the stones of an ancient temple wall can move us to tears. The ruins in this story come from the time when that particular ruin was made—the bitter and tumultuous years when Rome devastated the land of Israel, beating down one Jewish rebellion after another. In the time of the story's narrator, the ruins are fresh and raw. He is one of the various rabbis named Yose, active during the period between 70 C.E. when the Temple was destroyed and 200 C.E. when the tannaitic period ended. Here is his story:[1]

> It has been taught: R. Yose said, "One time I was traveling *(mehalekh)* on the road and I went into a ruin—one of the ruins of Jerusalem—to pray. Along came Elijah—may he be well remembered—and waited for me in the doorway until I had finished my prayer, he said to me, 'Peace upon you, rabbi!' And I answered, 'Peace upon you my rabbi and my teacher!' And he said to me, 'My son, why did you go into this ruin?' 'To pray!' I said. And he said to me, 'you should have prayed on the road.' 'But I was afraid,' said I, 'lest passers-by interrupt me.' And he said to me, 'You should have prayed the short prayer' *(tefillah ketzarah)*. In that moment, I learned three things from him: I learned that one should not go into a ruin, I learned that one may pray on the road, and I learned that one who prays on the road should pray the short prayer.

"Then he said to me, 'My son, what voice did you hear in that ruin?' And I said, 'I heard a divine echo *(bat kol),* and she was moaning like a dove, saying, "Alas for the children because of whose sins I have destroyed my house, and burned my sanctuary and exiled them among nations."'² 'By your life and by your living head!' he exclaimed. 'Not just this once does she say so, but three times every day she says so. And not only that, but at the time when Israel goes into the synagogues and studyhouses and responds, "May his great name be blessed" *(Yehei shemei ha-gadol [raba] mevorah),* the Holy One nods his head and says, "happy is the king who is praised in his house like this. What's to become of a father who has exiled his children and alas for the children exiled from their father's table?" ' "

We hear the story as an echo from far away. As the term *tanya,* "it is taught," indicates, an Amoraic redactor is quoting a tannaitic tradition from centuries past, now preserved in the text of the Gemara like a fly in amber; the story of a story. At the story's beginning, a rabbi is traveling on a road, a situation that often introduces a bit of transmission of case law in the Talmud: I was traveling on the road and such and such a contingency occurred and my companion Rabbi So and So taught me this law concerning it. But traveling on the road is also metaphoric of halakhah, the path-making process of Jewish law. The particular contingency about which R. Yose teaches is what to do when one is traveling and it is time to pray one of the three daily services. R. Yose decides to pray in a roadside ruin, and that is when strange things begin to happen.

It is not just any ruin R. Yose enters, but "one of the ruins of Jerusalem," an image that irresistibly evokes the destroyed Temple. In the doorway, the liminal space between "inside" and "outside," R. Yose's prayer is observed by a liminal figure: Elijah, the prophet who was carried up to heaven in a fiery chariot and never died. Elijah, the crosser of impassable boundaries, is designated to travel through time to "turn the hearts of parents to the children and the hearts of children to their parents" (Malachi 3:23), to announce the coming of redemption. Elijah's history and past make him a paradoxical figure. He is not exactly dead but not exactly alive. He is not part of the heavenly host but has no place or portion on earth. This rootless wanderer mirrors the rootless alienation of a landless people waiting to survive history, but also its hopefulness. Elijah attests to a future in which all the broken connections will be mended. The rabbis appoint him link between the biblical past and the rabbinic present and the messenger between heaven and earth, now that the destruction of the Temple has severed communication.

In our story, Elijah's first questions to R. Yose are those of a rabbi to a disciple. They teach the laws of which R. Yose is unaware: it is not permissible to go into a ruin, it is permissible to pray on the road, even at risk of interruption, but to minimize that risk, one who prays on the road should pray the short form of the *Tefillah.* This halakhic discussion of the day-to-day contingencies of prayer grounds Elijah's rabbinic authority and enhances his credibility when he questions the rabbi about the attraction of the ruin. What did R. Yose hear in the ruin?

In the Talmud, our story is preceded by a debate about how the hours of night are divided. In a tannaitic tradition, R. Eliezer has declared that night is divided into three watches, and to mark those watches in heaven, God roars like a lion. In the biblical prooftext he cites (Jeremiah 25:30), God is roaring with rage, about to destroy the first Temple and exile his people. An Amoraic tradition attributed to Rav transmutes God's roar of rage into a roar of regret: "At each watch the Holy One sits and roars, 'Alas for the children because of whose sins I have destroyed my house, and burned my sanctuary and exiled them among the nations.'"

R. Yose hears these words but identifies the voice that speaks them not as a lion's but a dove's. The rabbi identifies this voice as a *bat kol,* literally a daughter of a voice, or divine echo, another tenuous link with the upper regions once accessible to prophet and priest. In many rabbinic stories, a *bat kol* emits a proclamation. This, however, is a rather unusual *bat kol.* She is given a distinctly feminine dove-like voice, and both R. Yose and Elijah repeatedly refer to her with feminine pronouns and verbs. Her femininity undercuts the forbidding image whose words she speaks: the stern father now grieving the devastation he has wrought. Her dove-like moaning is also resonant with gendered meanings. Biblical natural history regards doves as a monogamous species and associates their cooing with erotic longing or unquenchable grief for an irreplaceable partner.[3] R. Yose, listening to a hidden dove in a ruin, evokes a happier lover playing hide-and-seek with his lady, the lover in Song of Songs who coaxes, "O my dove in the cranny of the rocks / Hidden by the cliff / Let me see your face" (Song of Songs 2:14). R. Yose's case is more poignant. His beloved appears to be inextricable from the ruin.

Elijah's reaction to R. Yose's report is vehement. He impresses upon the rabbi that no special revelation has been vouchsafed him. The *bat kol* says these words three times a day. Moreover, God is not accessible only in a ruin. The encounter with God must take place elsewhere. The settings God now calls his house are the still new rabbinic institutions of synagogue and study house, and the words that now comfort God's grief and intensify God's longing are the congregational response to the new prayer that is the trademark of these institutions: the *Kaddish.*

In directing R. Yose away from the ruin, Elijah estranges him from the feminine image of God he found there. But the prophet also transmutes the masculine image the dove depicts, softening the drama of the punishing patriarch alone with his regrets into a scene filled with familial intimacy and rueful charm. This father is not the implacable disciplinarian whose roaring Jeremiah described, but a complex and vulnerable rabbinic parent. Sitting alone after sending his children from the table, he worries about what will become of him in their absence. He understands now that he and they are interdependent.

This revelation of the interdependency of God and Israel contains the seeds of rabbinic law and rabbinic prayer. They encode the capacity for remaking justice and for tender reciprocity with the divine Other. From these seeds, God's human partners regrew their shattered *nomos* and cultivated a new world they and God could inhabit together. Out of its fructifying vision come the seeds of future nomic worlds, like the one this book seeks to engender, a world that Jewish women build together with Jewish men, a *nomos* we inhabit where we co/habit justly and generously. Over the bridge of alternity we carry the seeds to new earth. Gently, gently, we bring the dove we have freed from the ruin. Here at last she can make her nest.

Appendix

B'rit Ahuvim Lovers' Covenant

On _____ (day of week) the _____ day of _____ (month), 57___, according to Jewish reckoning (_____month____day_____year, according to secular reckoning), in the city of _____, _____(state or region), _____ (country), _____ (Hebrew name) daughter/son of _____ and _____ whose surname is _____ and _____ (Hebrew name) daughter/son of _____ and _____ whose surname is _____ confirm in the presence of witnesses a lovers' covenant between them and declare a partnership to establish a household among the people of Israel.

The agreement into which _____ and _____ are entering is a holy covenant like the ancient covenants of our people, made in faithfulness and peace to stand forever. It is a covenant of protection and hope like the covenant God swore to Noah and his descendants, saying

> "When the bow is in the clouds, I will see it and remember the everlasting covenant between God and all living creatures, all flesh that is on earth. That," God said to Noah, "shall be the sign of the covenant that I have established between me and all flesh" (Gen. 9:16–17).

It is a covenant of distinction, like the covenant God made with Israel, saying

> You shall be My people, and I shall be your God (Jer. 30:22).

It is a covenant of devotion, joining hearts like the covenant David and Jonathan made, as it is said,

> And Jonathan's soul was bound up with the soul of David. Jonathan made a covenant with David because he loved him as himself (1 Sam. 18:1–3).

It is a covenant of mutual lovingkindness like the wedding covenant between God and Zion, as it is said,

> I will espouse you forever. I will espouse you with righteousness and justice and lovingkindness and compassion. I will espouse you in faithfulness and you shall know God (Hos. 2:21–22).

Provisions of the Covenant

The following are the provisions of the lovers' covenant into which
_____ (Hebrew name) daughter/son of _____
and _____ and _____ (Hebrew
name) daughter/son of _____ and _____
now enter:

1. _____ and _____ declare that they
have chosen each other as companions, as our rabbis teach:

> Get yourself a companion. This teaches that a person should get a
> companion, to eat with, to drink with, to study Bible with, to study
> Mishnah with, to sleep with, to confide all one's secrets, secrets of
> Torah and secrets of worldly things. (Avot D'Rabbi Natan 8)

2. _____ and _____ declare that they are setting
themselves apart for each other and will take no other lover.

3. _____ and _____ hereby assume all the rights
and obligations that apply to family members: to attend, care, and provide
for one another [and for any children with which they may be blessed]
[and for _____ _____ child/children of
_____].

4. _____ and _____ commit themselves to
a life of kindness and righteousness as a Jewish family and to work
together toward the communal task of mending the world.

5. _____ and _____ pledge that one will
help the other at the time of dying, by carrying out the last rational
requests of the dying partner, protecting him/her from indignity or abandonment and by tender, faithful presence with the beloved until the end,
fulfilling what has been written:

> Set me as a seal upon your arm, for love is stronger than death.
> (Song of Songs 8:6)

To this covenant we affix our signatures.

The partners:

_____

_____

Witnessed this day the _____ day of Parashat _____
(Hebrew date).

The witnesses:

_____

_____

ברית אהובים

להלן תנאי ברית האהובים שבה יבואו _____ בן/בת _____
ו _____ בן/בת _____ ו _____ .

א. _____ ו _____ מכריזיים שבחרו זו/זה
את זו/וזה כחברים וידידים כמו ששנו רבותינו:
קנה לך חבר כצד מלמד שיקנה אדם חבר לעצמו
שיאכל עמו וישתה עמו ויקרא עמו לישנה עמו ויישן
עמו ויגלה לו כל סתריו, סתרי תורה וסתרי דרך ארץ.

ב. _____ ו _____ מקדשים את עצמם
זו/זה לזה/זו ולא יקחו אוהב אחר/ת.

ג. _____ ו _____ מקבלים עליהם את כל
החובות והזכויות השייכות לבני משפחה. [נוסף על כך הם מקבלים באהבה
אחריות לגדל ולחנך (כל בנים ובנות שיברכו בהם) (ואת _____ בן/בת
_____ של שותף אחד)]

ד. _____ ו _____ מקבלים על עצמם
לחיות חיים של חסד וצדק כמשפחה ולעבוד יחד במלאכת הצבור של תקון עולם.

ה. _____ ו _____ מתחיבים שיעזרו
זו/זה לזה/זו בשעת מותם בקיום הבקשות ההגיניות האחרונות של הנוטה למות.
שישמרו את הנוטה למות מביטול אישיות, מפגיעה בכבוד, ומעליבה, וישיארו
זו/וזה. עם זה/זו ברוך ובאמונה עד הסוף, לקיים מה שכתוב:
שימני כחותם על לבך
כחותם על זרועך
כי עזה כמות אהבה.

לברית הזאת אנו חותמים:

השותפים: _____

_____

העדים: _____

216

תנאי הברית

ב _____ בשבת (יום) _____ (חודש) _____ (שנה)
_____ לבריאת עולם למנין שאנו מונים, ב (עיר) _____ (מדינה)
_____ השותפים, _____ בן/בת _____ למשפחת
_____ ו _____ בן/בת _____ למשפחת _____
מקימים ביניהם לפני עדים ברית אהובים, ומכריזים על כוונתם להתקשר
בשותפות להקים בית בישראל.

הסכם זה שיבואו בו _____ בן/בת _____
ו _____ בן/בת _____, ברית קדושה היא כבריתות הקדומות של
עמינו העשויות באמונה ובשלום לעמוד לנצח.

ברית שמירה ותקוה היא, כברית שנשבע יי אל נוח וצאצאיו, שנאמר:
והיתה הקשת בענן וראיתיה לזכור ברית
עולם בין אלוהים ובין כל נפש חיה
בכל בשר על הארץ. ויאמר אלוהים
אל נוח זאת אות הברית אשר
הקמותי ביני ובין כל בשר אשר על הארץ.

ברית סגולה היא כברית שעשה יי עם עם ישראל, שנאמר:
והייתם לי לעם ואנוכי אהיה לאלוהים.
ברית ידידות היא המקשרת לבבות כברית שכרתו דוד ויהונתן, שנאמר:
ונפש יהונתן נקשרה בנפש דוד.
ויכרות יהונתן ודוד באהבתו אותו כנפשו.

ברית של חסד הדדי הברית הזאת, כברית נשואיהם של יי וציון, שנאמר:
וארשתיך לי לעולם. וארשתיך לי בצדק ובמשפט ובחסד
וברחמים. וארשתיך לי באמונה וידעת את יי.

217

Notes

Introduction

1. Miriam Peshowitz, "Engendering Jewish Religious History," in *Judaism Since Gender*, ed. Miriam Peskowitz and Laura Levitt (New York: Routledge, 1966).
2. Riv-Ellen Prell, "The Vision of Woman in Classical Reform Judaism," *Journal of the American Academy of Religion* 50, no. 4 (1983): 575–589.
3. Generally, women are disqualified from witnessing (B. Shevuot 30a), but there are exceptions. For example, women's testimony concerning whether they were raped when taken captive may be believed when their testimony is to their own disadvantage—for example, a wife of a kohen who acknowledges having been raped must be divorced (Ketubbot 27a–b).
4. Judith Plaskow, "The Jewish Feminist: Conflict in Identities," *Response* 18 (summer 1973). Reprinted in *The Jewish Woman: New Perspectives*, ed. Elizabeth Koltun (New York: Schocken: 1976), 3–10. I quote and cite from the Schocken anthology, because it is still easily available.
5. For a summary of these arguments, see Mary McClintock Fulkerson, *Changing the Subject: Women's Discourses and Feminist Theology* (Minneapolis: Fortress, 1994), 50–58.
6. Ellen M. Umansky, "Creating a Jewish Feminist Theology: Problems and Possibilities," in *Weaving the Visions: New Patterns in Feminist Spirituality*, ed. Judith Plaskow and Carol Christ (San Francisco: Harper and Row, 1989), 187–198. Reprinted from *Anima*, 1984.
7. Ibid., 194.
8. Ibid.
9. Carol P. Christ and Judith Plaskow, eds., *Womanspirit Rising* (San Francisco: Harper and Row, 1979), 134.
10. Rachel Adler, "The Jew Who Wasn't There: Halakha and the Jewish Woman," *Davka* (summer, 1971) reprinted in *On Being a Jewish Feminist*, ed. Susannah Heschel (New York: Schocken, 1983), 12–18.
11. Moshe Meiselman, *The Jewish Woman in Jewish Law* (New York: Ktav, 1978).
12. Judith Plaskow, "The Right Question is Theological," in *On Being a Jewish Feminist*, 226.
13. Cynthia Ozick, "Notes Toward the Right Question," in *On Being a Jewish Feminist*, 120–151.
14. Plaskow, "The Right Question Is Theological," in *On Being a Jewish Feminist*, 226.
15. Rachel Adler, "I've Had Nothing Yet, So I Can't Take More," *Moment* 8 (September, 1983): 22–26.
16. Blu Greenberg's position may be characterized as pan-halakhic. See Blu Greenberg, "Coming of Age in the Jewish Community," *Tradition* (spring 1977), and *On Women and Judaism: A View from Tradition* (Philadelphia: Jewish Publication Society, 1981). Rita M. Gross wrote several ground-breaking pieces on God-imagery. Rita M. Gross, "Female God Language in the Jewish Context," in *Womanspirit Rising*, 167–173, and "Steps Toward Feminine Imagery in Deity in Jewish Theology," in *On Being a Jewish Feminist*, 234–247.
17. Abraham Joshua Heschel, *God in Search of Man* (Philadelphia: Jewish Publication Society, 1955), 328.

18. Plaskow, "The Right Question is Theological," 231.
19. Lori Lefkovitz, "Eavesdropping on Angels and Laughing at God: Theorizing a Subversive Matriarchy," in *Gender and Judaism: The Transformation of Tradition,* ed. T. M. Rudavsky (New York: New York University Press, 1995).
20. For example, my 1973 article on menstruation and the laws of mikveh and my 1993 retraction both deal with the Jewish meanings given to women's blood and their impact on women's quest for holiness. Rachel Adler, "*Tumah* and *Taharah: -Mikveh,*" in *The Jewish Catalog,* ed. Michael Strassfeld, Sharon Strassfeld, and Richard Siegal (Philadelphia: Jewish Publication Society, 1972). Reprinted with additions as "*Tumah* and *Taharah*: Ends and Beginnings," in *Response* 18 (summer 1973): 117–127, and in *The Jewish Woman,* 63–71. Rachel Adler, "In Your Blood, Live: Re-visions of a Theology of Purity," *Tikkun* 8:1 (January/February 1993), 38–41.
21. Eric Partridge, *A Dictionary of Slang and Unconventional English,* 8th ed., ed. Paul Beale (New York: Macmillan, 1984). Uriel Weinreich, *Modern English-Yiddish Yiddish-English Dictionary* (New York: McGraw-Hill with YIVO, 1968). See also Alexander Harkavy, *Yiddish-English Dictionary,* 22nd ed. (New York: Hebrew Publishing Company, 1928).
22. Fifteen years after my first article, I went back to school for a doctorate in religion and social ethics. By that time, I sometimes found my own work on the reading lists.
23. Mieke Bal, *Murder and Difference: Gender, Genre, and Scholarship on Sisera's Death,* trans. Matthew Gumpert (Bloomington: Indiana University Press, 1988), 1–13.
24. Marcia Falk, "Notes On Composing New Blessings," in *Weaving the Visions,* 128–138.
25. T. Drorah Setel, "Prophets and Pornography: Female Sexual Imagery in Hosea," in *Feminist Interpretation of the Bible,* ed. Letty Russell (Philadelphia: Westminster Press, 1985), 86–95.
26. Scholars whose historical and literary approaches have strong theological implications include Tikva Frymer-Kensky, *In the Wake of the Goddesses: Women, Culture and the Biblical Transformation of Pagan Myth* (New York: Free Press, 1992), and Ilana Pardes, *Countertraditions in the Bible: A Feminist Approach* (Cambridge, MA: Harvard University Press, 1992).
27. Rachel Adler, "Women and Judaism: On Talking Our Way In," in *The Jewish Condition: Essays on Contemporary Judaism Honoring Alexander Schindler,* ed. Aron Hirt-Manheimer (New York: UAHC Press, 1995).
28. B. Shevuot 20b. The midrash is meant to resolve a contradiction between the two versions of the fourth commandment in Exodus 20:8 and Deuteronomy 5:12.
29. Mordecai Friedman, *Jewish Marriage in Palestine,* 2 vols. (Tel Aviv: Jewish Theological Seminary, 1980).

Chapter 1

1. Paul Ricoeur, "The Hermeneutical Function of Distanciation," in *Hermeneutics and the Human Sciences* (Cambridge: Cambridge University Press, 1981), 142.
2. I heard Lynn Gottlieb use the term *zaydemeise* at an oral presentation.
3. The technical term for such stories is aretalogy. Morton Smith, "Prolegomena to a Discussion of Aretalogies, Divine Men, and Jesus," *Journal of Biblical Literature* 90 (June 1971): 174–199.
4. Northrop Frye, "The Mythos of Spring: Comedy," in *The Anatomy of Criticism* (Princeton, NJ: Princeton University Press, 1957), 163–186. I am aware that I am using Frye in a way he himself would not approve.

5. Ibid., 163–164.

6. Adrienne Rich, "Natural Resources," in *The Dream of a Common Language* (New York: W. W. Norton, 1978), 61.

7. I want to acknowledge that Mary Daly uses the categories of deception and dismemberment in the First Passage of *Gyn/Ecology*. Mary Daly, *Gyn/Ecology: The Metaethics of Radical Feminism* (Boston: Beacon, 1978). Although I did not consciously draw upon Daly, I see in retrospect that I have been responding to her. She bears no responsibility, however, either for my category of dis/remembering or for my account of deception as *genevat da'at.*

8. I agree with Emmanuel Levinas that the face of the other is the locus of moral obligation, although I do not believe that he has followed out the implications of this notion in his treatment of women. For a thorough discussion of Levinas's use of the trope of the face, see Susan Handelman, *Fragments of Redemption: Jewish Thought and Literary Theory in Benjamin, Scholem, and Levinas* (Bloomington: Indiana University Press, 1991), 201–225.

9. Elie Wiesel, *Legends of Our Time* (New York: Avon, 1968), viii.

10. Martin Heidegger, *Being and Time*, trans. John Macquarrie and Edward Robinson (New York: Harper and Row, 1962), sect. 31–34.

11. Nancy Choderow, *The Reproduction of Mothering: Psychoanalysis and the Sociology of Gender* (Berkeley: University of California Press, 1978).

12. Jessica Benjamin, *The Bonds of Love: Psychoanalysis, Feminism and the Problem of Domination* (New York: Pantheon Books, 1988).

13. Ibid., 31–36. This argument draws upon the intersubjective psychology of Winnecott and upon Hegel's famous essay, "Master and Slave."

14. Ibid., 78–82.

15. Ibid., 73.

16. For cases in which a wife is regarded as a physical or mental extension of her husband, see B. Berakhot 24a, B. Menahot 93b, B. Ketubbot 66a, and B. Bekhorot 35b.

17. Heidegger sees this negation or repression of otherness as a consequence of the [masculine] subject's struggle for hegemony in post-Cartesian philosophy. Mark Taylor, "Cleaving: Martin Heidegger," in *Altarity* (Chicago: University of Chicago Press, 1987), 35–58. However, Catherine Keller, using a combination of Jungian and feminist object-relations theory and process philosophy, views it as a fundamental pattern throughout the history of Western cultures. Catherine Keller, *From a Broken Web: Separation, Sexism and the Self* (Boston: Beacon, 1986). Jessica Benjamin sees domination as an alienated form of differentiation that fails because the other is not allowed to "make a difference," i.e., is not experienced as an external reality outside the self. She further argues that the ostensibly gender-neutral rationalization and bureaucratization of modern societies continue to promote the eradication of difference by veiling a gender polarity that dichotomizes the world into a masculinized public sphere and a feminine private sphere. *The Bonds of Love*, 183–218.

18. On the implications of Beruriah traditions for women's education in the rabbinic period, see Robert Goodblatt, The "Beruriah Traditions," *Journal of Jewish Studies* 26 (1975): 68–86. Also, Daniel Boyarin, *Carnal Israel: Readings in Talmudic Culture* (Berkeley: University of California Press, 1993), maintains that the Palestinian tradition was significantly more tolerant of women's Torah study than the Babylonian.

19. Steven Fraade, "Ascetical Aspects of Ancient Judaism," in *Jewish Spirituality*, vol. 1, ed. Arthur Green (New York: Crossroads, 1988), 253–288. In this ground-breaking article, Fraade concludes, "Sanctification of oneself through abstinence is common to rabbinic and pre-rabbinic Judaisms." He also observes that rabbinic Judaism main-

tains an unresolved tension between sexuality and a sage's preoccupation with Torah study.

20. *Avot D'Rabbi Natan*, chap. 6

21. B. Yoma 35b.

22. Eve Kosofsky Sedgewick, *Between Men: English Literature and Male Homosocial Desire* (New York: Columbia University Press, 1985), 1–27.

23. Mikhah Yosef Bin-Goryon (Berdishevski), *MiMekor Yisrael: Ma`asiot v'Sipurei `Am* (Tel Aviv: D'vir, 1965), 192–194 (Hebrew). Version 1 is originally found in B. Nedarim 50a and version 2 in B. Ketubbot 62b–63a. The wife is first identified as Rachel in *Avot D'Rabbi Natan*, chap. 6. I am indebted to David Ellenson for reminding me how the Baal Shem Tov's marriage echoes this story. Like Akiba, he weds an aristocratic woman who lives in great poverty with him and works to support him. *In Praise of the Baal Shem Tov [Shivḥei Ha Besht]*, trans. and ed. Dan Ben-Amos and Jerome R. Mintz (Bloomington: Indiana University Press, 1970), 18–27.

24. B. Nedarim 50a; B. Ketubbot 62b–63a.

25. The account in *Avot D'Rabbi Natan*, chap. 6 also emphasizes the golden reward of Rachel.

26. Louis Finkelstein, *Akiba* (Philadelphia: Jewish Publication Society, 1962), 135.

27. David Biale, *Eros and the Jews: From Biblical Israel to Contemporary America* (New York: Basic Books, 1992), 33–36.

28. Although it does not appear in several of the original versions of the story, I am using the name Rachel as a convenient way of referring to a sometimes nameless female character.

29. Version 2. This proverb is also her response when the wicked neighbor in the Nedarim account asks why she is going with the rest of the town to welcome Akiba.

30. This descent from the powerful giver to the humble beseecher thrust away by an underling is reminiscent of the scene in 2 Kings 4 where the great lady of Shunem, now humbled and desperate, throws herself at Elisha's feet to plead for her dead child and is thrust aside by his disciple Gehazi.

31. Mikhah Yosef Bin-Goryon (Berdishevski) *MiMekor Yisrael*, 197. The earliest reference to a Natan D' Tzutzita (1B. Shabbat 56a) mentions him as the paradigmatic repentant sinner. In his commentary to B. Sanhedrin 31b, Rashi recounts a version of the story that he says he found in a book of aggadah. Neither of these references mentions the role of the woman, however. The earliest references to her are late medieval. The early brief references are particularly concerned with Natan's status as a penitent, a *ba'al teshuvah*. Hence, either the story of the woman was known but not deemed germane or it was a medieval elaboration perhaps reflecting changes in the status of women in the societies in which the story was retold. The earliest source in which the woman's story is elaborated is Nissim Ben Jacob Ibn Shahin, *An Elegant Composition Concerning Relief after Adversity [Ḥibbur Yafeh Min Ha-Yeshu'a]*, trans. and with an introduction and notes by William M. Brinner (New Haven, CT: Yale University Press, 1977), 127–131 (translated from Arabic, eleventh century).

32. B. Megillah 14a and b.

33. I am including such behaviors as self-shaming and penitential fasting as mutilations for the restoration of integrity. For example, in B. Kiddushin 81a, R. Amram, overcome by temptation, calls out the fire department, so to speak, crying, "A fire at R. Amram's!" In B. Kiddushin 81b, there is an acccount of the life-long penitential fasting of R. Ḥiyya bar Abba, after failing a test of his chastity. His wife, with whom he had ceased to be sexually intimate, disguised herself as a notorious courtesan, presented herself in his garden, and asked him to pluck a pomegranate for her. R. Ḥiyyah hastened to do so and then was struck with remorse.

34. I am indebted to Maeera Shreiber for observing how different this is from the classical Western tradition in which the woman is the text.

35. A description of the origins, dates, and provenances of the two rescensions of this collection can be found in Moses Gaster, *The Exempla of the Rabbis* (New York: Ktav, 1968), 7–8. I cite and summarize from text A, which Gaster identifies as the fuller version.

36. A psychomachia is a war within the soul. The externalized representation of psychomachia was a favorite dramatic device of medieval morality dramas; the good and bad angels perch on Everyman's shoulders alternately urging "don't do it" and "do it, Everyman."

37. See, for example, some of the texts in the Babylonian Talmud regarding the beauty of Yoḥanan ben Nappha: B. Berakhot 5b, 20a; B. Baba Metzia 84a.

38. Milan Kundera, *The Book of Laughter and Forgetting*, trans. Michael Henry Heim (Middlesex, England: Penguin Books, 1981), 209.

39. Regarding the connection between power and the objectifying male gaze, see Laura Mulvey, "Visual Pleasure and Narrative Cinema," *Screen* 16, no. 3 (1975): 6–18, and John Berger, *Ways of Seeing* (London: British Broadcasting Company and Penguin Books, 1972), 45–64.

40. See, for example, the burlesque resurrection story in Megillah 7b.

41. Avraham Finkel, *The Essence of the Holy Days* (New York: Jason Aaronson, 1993), 130–131. Finkel attributes this saying to the Ari and also quotes the observation of Simḥa Bunim that the affliction of Purim is greater than that demanded of us on Yom Kippur, because the commandment to drink *ad shelo yad'a* afflicts our reason and judgment, the loss of which is the greatest possible catastrophe. I am indebted to Chaim Seidler-Feller for this citation.

42. Regarding the carnivalesque and its grotesquerie, see Mikhail Bakhtin, *Rabelais and His World*, trans. Helene Iswolsky (Bloomington: Indiana University Press, 1984).

43. Arnold Band "Swallowing Jonah: The Eclipse of Parody," *Prooftexts* 10 (May, 1990): 177–195.

44. Ismar Elbogen, *Jewish Liturgy: A Comprehensive History*, trans. Raymond Scheindlin (Philadelphia and Jerusalem: Jewish Publication Society and Jewish Theological Seminary, 1993), 148. Elbogen notes that this is the only afternoon service Haftarah (prophetic reading) that can be proven to exist from the time of the Talmud.

45. Ricoeur, "The Hermeneutical Function of Distanciation," 139.

46. Michael Lerner, *Jewish Renewal* (New York: G. P. Putnam Sons, 1994). Lerner sees liberation from the repetition compulsion to abuse as the central ethical theme of Judaism.

47. B. Baba Metzia 59b.

Chapter 2

1. This debate among Jewish feminist scholars will be discussed at length later in the chapter. Some representative positions are: Rachel Adler, "The Jew Who Wasn't There: Halakha and the Jewish Woman," *Davka* (summer 1971), reprinted in *On Being a Jewish Feminist*, ed. Susannah Heschel (New York: Schocken, 1983), 12–18; Blu Greenberg, "Judaism and Feminism," in *The Jewish Woman*, ed. Elizabeth Koltun (New York: Schocken, 1976), 179–192; Cynthia Ozick, "Notes Toward Finding the Right Question," in *On Being a Jewish Feminist*, 120–151; Rachel Adler, "I've Had Nothing Yet, So I Can't Take More," *Moment* 8 (September 1983): 22–26.

2. Judith Plaskow, "The Right Question Is Theological," in *On Being a Jewish Feminist*, 223–233.

3. One essay written after this chapter was completed that raises these issues is Tikva Frymer-Kensky, "Toward a Liberal Theory of Halakha," *Tikkun* 10 (July/August 1995): 42–48, 77.

4. On the distinction between memory and history, see Yosef Hayim Yerushalmi, *Zakhor: Jewish History and Jewish Memory* (New York: Schocken, 1989), 8–22, 94–96, 108–110.

5. Alasdair MacIntyre, *After Virtue*, 2nd ed. (Notre Dame, IN: University of Notre Dame Press, l984), 216.

6. Narrative ethicists would argue that even nonstoried principles such as Kant's categorical imperative or Mill's utilitarianism implicitly contain the germ of an unarticulated story. For an illustration, see my discussion of Seyla Benhabib later in this chapter.

7. Beatrice Weinreich, ed., *Yiddish Folktales*, trans. Leonard Wolf (New York: Pantheon with YIVO, 1986), 103. I thank Rabbi Lynn Gottlieb, who first called this story to my attention.

8. B. Weinreich suggests that Skotsl is a contraction of *dos ketzl*, the little cat. Uriel Weinreich, *Modern English-Yiddish Yiddish-English Dictionary* (New York, McGraw-Hill with YIVO, 1968), simply lists the expression, glossing "Well, look who's here! Welcome." Alexander Harkavy, *Yiddish-English Dictionary*, 22nd ed. (New York: Hebrew Publishing Company, 1928), lists the expression under *kotsl* and suggests that it is a contraction of *Gotts vill*, "God's will," as in the traditional morning blessing for women: "Blessed are you who made me according to your will." Professor Mikhl (Marvin) Herzog observes, "The phrase is probably derived from something like MHG *bis gote (unde mir) willekommen* 'be welcome to God (and me).' Whenever it occurs it is associated with someone's arrival, but rarely does it retain the implication of welcome and nowhere one of blessing. Initial *s* is generally interpreted as the brief form of the neuter definite article *dos* and consequently *kocl* is taken to be a designation for the visitor (generally one who visits infrequently); thus 'the *kocl* is coming.'" Marvin Herzog, *The Yiddish Language in Northern Poland: Its Geography and History*, IJAL Publication No. 37 (Bloomington: Indiana University Press, and The Hague: Mouton, 1965), 66–67. Professor Chana Kronfeld has suggested to me that a *skots* is a tale, but I have been unable to document this. Most authorities concur that the greeting is usually ironic and usually addressed to a woman.

9. Arnold M. Eisen, *The Chosen People in America: A Study in Jewish Religious Ideology* (Bloomington: Indiana University Press, 1983).

10. Thumbing through a popular Judaica catalogue recently, I noticed that Howard Eilberg-Schwartz's book *God's Phallus* was listed under Modern Jewish Thought, whereas Judith Plaskow's *Standing Again at Sinai* (San Francisco: Harper and Row, 1979) was listed under Women's Issues. Both works deal with the theology of gender. "Gender and Judaism," dealing with the depiction of masculine and feminine roles in Jewish history and texts, is still rather an avant-garde category.

11. Heschel, "Introduction," in *On Being a Jewish Feminist*, xxiii.

12. Riv-Ellen Prell, "The Vision of Woman in Classical Reform Judaism," *Journal of the American Academy of Religion* 50 (1983): 575–589.

13. Martha Minow, "The Supreme Court 1986 Term: Forward: Justice Engendered," *Harvard Law Review* 101 (1987): esp. 31–70.

14. See, for example, MacIntyre, *After Virtue;* Michael Sandel, *Liberalism and the Limits of Justice* (Cambridge: Cambridge University Press, l982); Martha Minow, *Making All the Difference: Inclusion, Exclusion and American Law* (Ithaca, NY: Cornell University Press, 1990).

15. For an account of the relationship between stories and praxis in law, see Robert Cover, "The Supreme Court 1986 Term: Forward: *Nomos* and Narrative," *Harvard Law Review* 97, no. 4 (1983): 4–68.
16. Michael Goldberg, *Jews and Christians: Getting Our Stories Straight* (Nashville: Abingdon Press, 1985), 13–19. Michael Goldberg, "The Story of the Moral: Gifts or Bribes in Deuteronomy?" *Interpretation* 38 (January 1984): 15–25, demonstrates how an underlying story may be detected in a specific law.
17. My use of the term "praxis" has obvious kinships with the Marxian use of the term "revolutionary praxis," on which see Anthony Giddens, *Capitalism and Modern Social Theory* (Cambridge: Cambridge University Press, 1971), 6–8, 20; with the notion of Christian liberation praxis, on which see Gustave Gutierrez, *A Theology of Liberation,* trans. and ed. Sr. Caridad Inda and John Eagleson (Maryknoll, NY: Orbis, 1973), 6–18; and with the reappropriation of Aristotelian *phronesis,* practical wisdom, by narrative ethicists. See, for example, Alisdair MacIntyre, *After Virtue,* chap. 15.
18. Michael Meyer, *Response to Modernity: A History of the Reform Movement in Judaism* (New York: Oxford University Press, 1988), 16–27, 210–211. See also the practices of Abraham Geiger and Samuel Holdheim in David Rudavsky, *Modern Jewish Religious Movements: A History of Emancipation and Adjustment* (New York: Behrman House, 1967), 177–183, as well as his account of the Pittsburgh Platform, 298–302.
19. A daunting catalogue of such dissonant elements is provided by John D. Rayner, "Between Antinomianism and Conservatism," in *Dynamic Jewish Law: Progressive Halakha: Essence and Application,* ed. Walter Jacob and Moshe Zemer (Tel Aviv: Rodef Shalom Press, 1991), 126–127. He says, "Considering that whole, vast areas of its contents relate to sacrifices and priesthood, and ritual purity and male superiority and polygamy and yibum and halitzah and mamzerut and corporal punishment and capital punishment . . . for Progressive Jews to affirm such a system, subject only to a few cosmetic changes, is so bizarre that I can only understand it as either self-deception for the sake of the emotional comfort or else propaganda for the sake of the political advantage to be gained from a traditionalist posture."
20. *The Talmud of the Land of Israel: A Preliminary Translation and Explanation,* vol. 2, *Pe'ah,* trans. Roger Brooks (Chicago: University of Chicago Press, 1990), 128.
21. Yosef Hayim Yerushalmi, *Zakhor,* 81–103 discusses the problems Jewish historiography poses For Judaism as a religious committment.
22. The following are examples of eminent liberal halakhists and their works: Eliezer Berkovits, *Not in Heaven: The Nature and Function of Halakha* (New York: Ktav, 1983); Elliot N. Dorff and Arthur Rosett, *A Living Tree: The Roots and Growth of Jewish Law* (Albany: State University of New York Press, 1988); Louis Jacobs, *A Tree of Life: Diversity, Flexibility and Creativity in Jewish Law* (Oxford: Oxford University Press for the Littman Library, 1984); Joel Roth, *The Halakhic Process: A Systemic Analysis* (New York: Jewish Theological Seminary of America, 1986). An excellent book, which I discovered too late to include in my discussion, is Moshe Zemer, *Halakha Shefuya* (Israel: D'vir, 1993).
23. The following discussion summarizes my article "I've Had Nothing Yet, So I Can't Take More," *Moment* 8 (September 1983): 22–26. See also Plaskow, "The Right Question Is Theological," 223–233.
24. Mary Daly, *Beyond God the Father* (Boston: Beacon, 1973), 11–12.
25. Jacob Neusner, "The System as a Whole," in *The Mishnaic System of Women,* part 5: *A History of the Mishnaic Law of Women,* 5 vols. (Leiden: E. J. Brill, 1980), 13–42. This point is made particularly on 14.

26. Ibid., 13–21.
27. Judith Wegner, *Woman in the Mishnah: Person or Chattel* (New York: Oxford University Press, 1988), 186–191.
28. Neusner, "The System As a Whole," 16.
29. Adler, "I've Had Nothing Yet, So I Can't Take More," 24.
30. For an introduction to new ritual concerns expressed by women, see Rebecca Alpert, "Our Lives Are the Text: Exploring Jewish Women's Rituals," *Bridges* 2 (spring 1991): 66–80. For a simplified account of a feminist Jewish hermeneutics, see Rachel Adler, "Talking Our Way In" *Sh'ma* 23 (Nov. 13, 1992): 5–6; and William Cutter, "What the Teacher Learns—and Ponders," *Sh'ma* 23 (Nov. 13, 1992): 6–8.
31. Such analyses are ultimately indebted to the postmodern philosopher Michel Foucault. See in particular his *Power/Knowledge: Selected Interviews and Other Writings, 1972–1977* (New York: Pantheon Books, 1980).
32. Mark Washofsky, "The Search for Liberal Halakhah," in *Dynamic Jewish Law*, 27–51. Washofsky criticizes both Berkovits and Roth for underestimating legal consensus as a systemic principle. However, his own recommendation that liberal halakhists directly confront the halakhic consensus by demonstrating poor reasoning or the existence of equally valid alternatives is itself a formalist solution that undermines the power of consensus.
33. In Judaism, legal formalism can be made to undergird legal realism. The classical system enunciates a legal principle from which judicial discretion can plausibly be derived: *ein lo ladayyan ella mah she-einav ro'ot*, "a judge can only rely on what his own eyes see." This principle is invoked by Eliezer Berkovits as a rational principle, which is necessarily applied contextually, 53–57, and by Joel Roth, who elevates it to a "quasi-ultimate systemic principle," 86–113.
34. Eliezer Berkovits, *Not in Heaven*, 1–2, 47–48, 71–73.
35. Ibid., 19–22. Eliezer Berkovits, *Crisis and Faith* (New York: Sanhedrin, 1976), 97–121. Berkovits makes this argument on Maimonidean grounds.
36. Jacobs, 236–247.
37. Ibid., 245.
38. Ibid., 246.
39. S. M. Passamaneck, "Reflections of Reasonable Cause in Halakhah," in *Jewish Law Association Studies VI: The Jerusalem 1990 Conference Volume*, ed. B. S. Jackson and S. M. Passamaneck (Atlanta: Scholars Press, 1992). In the case of the *moser* informer, medieval responsa permit even execution without talmudic standards of proof. Shoshanna Gershenzen, "When Jews Kill Jews: Communal Integrity vs. Judicial Ethics in Medieval Jewish Responsa" [unpublished paper].
40. Alexander Pope, "An Essay on Man," in *Eighteenth Century Poetry and Prose*, 2nd ed., ed. Louis I. Bredvold, Alan D. McKillop, and Lois Whitney (New York: Ronald Press, 1956), 370–384, esp. line 294.
41. Roth, *The Halakhic Process*, 10.
42. Ibid.
43. Ibid., 81–113.
44. Joel Roth, "On the Ordination of Women As Rabbis," in *The Ordination of Women As Rabbis: Studies and Responsa*, Moreshet Series vol. 9, ed. Simon Greenberg (New York: Jewish Theological Seminary, 1988).
45. Roth, *The Halakhic Process*, 81–113.
46. David Ellenson, "The Challenges of Halakhah," *Judaism* 38 (summer 1989): 362.
47. Roth, *The Halakhic Process*, 151. Although Roth gives both theistic and nontheistic bases for the *grundnorm*, rabbis must subscribe to the theistic version.

48. This paragraph summarizes Robert Cover, *"Nomos* and Narrative," 4–18.
49. Ibid. 13n.
50. Robert Cover, "The Folktales of Justice: Tales of Jurisdiction" *Capital University Law Review* 14 (1985): 181.
51. For the most precise description of the modern self, its nature, its moral sources, and its historical context, see Charles Taylor, *Sources of the Self: The Making of Modern Identity* (Cambridge, MA: Harvard University Press, 1989), esp. 3–107.
52. Peter L. Berger, *The Sacred Canopy* (New York: Anchor, 1969).
53. Franz Kafka, "The Problem of Our Laws," in *Parables and Paradoxes* (New York: Schocken, 1961), 155.
54. A major defense of rabbinic authority turns upon this very prooftext. It is related in a dramatic midrash (B. Baba Metzia 59b) how a Tannaitic majority rules against the minority opinion of the powerful and influential Eliezer ben Hyrcanus, refusing to be swayed by the miracles he performs or even the heavenly voice that proclaims his opinion correct. Once Torah has entered history, the midrash seems to argue, authority is transferred irrevocably from its divine giver to its human receivers. They must make sense of it for themselves and determine how it must be practiced, even though, from the transcendent perspective, some of their decisions may be wrong. The addenda to the narrative of the rabbinic confrontation render its interpretation even more ambiguous. In one addendum, the prophet Elijah relates to Rabbi Natan how God laughed and exclaimed, "My children have defeated Me!" In another, the subsequent excommunication of Eliezer ben Hyrcanus is sympathetically described. The making and remaking of Torah are experienced simultaneously as occasion for divine laughter and for human tragedy. Law's tragedies arise out of the inevitable conflicts between the coercive force by means of which law is stabilized and standardized in communal praxis and the conscientious resistance of differing individuals. On this point, see Robert Cover, "Violence and the Word," *Yale Law Journal* 95 (1986): 1601–1629.
55. Feminists are not the only scholars to have rediscovered narrative. We have already seen its importance in the work of Robert Cover. Ethicists and theologians who use it extensively include Alasdair MacIntyre, Stanley Hauerwas, and Michael Goldberg.
56. Seyla Benhabib, "The Generalized and Concrete Other: The Kohlberg-Gilligan Controversy and Moral Theory," in *Women and Moral Theory*, ed. Eva Feder Kittay and Diana T. Meyers (Totowa, NJ: Rowman and Littlefield, 1987), 154–177. Another version of this essay can be found in Seyla Benhabib, *Situating the Self: Gender, Community and Postmodernism in Contemporary Ethics* (New York: Routledge, 1992), 148–177, but I will cite the version in *Women and Moral Theory.*
57. Narrative and contextuality are also distinguishing themes of critical legal studies. This account of context is indebted to Roberto Mangabeira Unger, *Passion: An Essay on Personality* (New York: Free Press, 1984), 5–15.
58. For a lucid explanation of the distinctions among essentialist, social constructivist, and poststructural feminisms, see Linda Alcoff, "Cultural Feminism Versus Post-Structuralism: The Identity Crisis in Feminist Theory," *Signs* 13 (spring 1988): 405–436.
59. Kenneth Karst, "Woman's Constitution," *Duke Law Journal*, no. 3 (1984): 447–508, esp. 499–500.
60. See in particular Robin J. West, "Jurisprudence and Gender," *University of Chicago Law Review* 55:1 (winter 1988): 1–71; and Robin J. West, "Authority, Autonomy and Choice: The Role of Consent in the Moral and Political Visions of Franz Kafka and Richard Posner," *Harvard Law Review* 99 (December, 1985): 384–428. In the latter,

West concludes, "It may be true, as Bentham thought, that 'all men calculate.' It is not true as Posner blithely assumes that all men calculate all of the time" (425).

61. Jean Bethke Elshtain, "Feminist Discourse and Its Discontents: Language, Power, and Meaning," in *Feminist Theory: A Critique of Ideology*, ed. Nannerl O. Keohane, Michelle A. Rosaldo and Barbara Gelpi (Chicago: University of Chicago Press, 1982), 127–145.

62. Minow, "Engendering Justice," 35–36.

63. Robin J. West, "The Difference in Women's Hedonic Lives: A Phenomenological Critique of Feminist Legal Theory," in *At the Boundaries of Law: Feminism and Legal Theory*, ed. Martha Albertson Fineman and Nancy Sweet Thomadsen (New York: Routledge, 1991), 115–134.

64. Minow, "Engendering Justice," 11–14.

65. John Rawls, *A Theory of Justice* (Cambridge: Belknap Press of Harvard University Press, 1971).

66. Ibid., 136–142.

67. Ibid., 60–83.

68. Susan Moller Okin, *Justice, Gender and the Family* (New York: Basic Books, 1989), chap. 5.

69. Ibid., 101–109. In her review of Okin's book, Martha Nussbaum objects that Okin's desire to eradicate all gender distinctions and remove all social significance from sexual differences minimizes the importance of constitutive experiences of self as male or female and of human sexual desire. Martha Nussbaum, "Justice For Women," *New York Review of Books* (October 8, 1992): 43–48.

70. Okin, *Justice, Gender and the Family*, 101–102.

71. Rawls's writings after *A Theory of Justice* take history into account.

72. Benhabib, "The Generalized and Concrete Other," 163–167.

73. Ibid., 162–163.

74. This point is also made by Sandel, *Liberalism and the Limits of Justice*, 131–132.

75. Joseph B. Soloveitchik, *Halakhic Man*, trans. Lawrence Kaplan (Philadelphia: Jewish Publication Society, 1983). For Soloveitchik's halakhic man, "the essence of the Halakhah, which was received from God, consists in creating an ideal world and cognizing the relationship between that ideal world and our concrete environment in all its visible manifestations and underlying structures. There is no phenomenon, entity, or object in this concrete world which the a priori Halakhah does not approach with its ideal standard" (19–20). These "entities and objects" implicitly include women, just as the descriptions of halakhic man implicitly exclude them.

76. David Ellenson, "Halakhah for Liberal Jews," *Reconstructionist* 52 (March, 1988): 30.

77. Carol Gilligan, *In a Different Voice* (Cambridge, MA: Harvard University Press, 1982), 24–63.

78. Nell Noddings, *Caring: A Feminine Approach to Ethics and Moral Education* (Berkeley: University of California Press, 1984).

79. Wicca is a feminist reconstruction of the religions of pre-Christian Europe. It utilizes "witchcraft" and worships the goddess and the horned god who is both her son and her consort. See Starhawk, *The Spiral Dance* (San Francisco: Harper and Row, 1979).

80. Annette Daum, "Blaming Jews for the Death of the Goddess," in *Nice Jewish Girls: A Lesbian Anthology*, ed. Evelyn Torton Beck (Watertown, MA: Persephone Press, 1982), 255–261.

81. Plaskow, "Blaming the Jews for the Birth of Patriarchy," in *Nice Jewish Girls*, 250–254. Susannah Heschel, "Anti-Judaism in Christian Feminist Theology," *Tikkun* 5 (May/ June 1990): 25–28, 95–97.

82. Carol P. Christ and Judith Plaskow, eds., *Womanspirit Rising* (San Francisco: Harper and Row, 1979), 134.
83. For example, Blu Greenberg, *On Women and Judaism* (Philadelphia: Jewish Publication Society, 1981), 39–71, and Cynthia Ozick, "Notes Toward Finding the Right Question," 210–161. For the term "hermeneutics of suspicion" as employed by feminist theologians, see Elisabeth Schussler-Fiorenza, *Bread Not Stone* (Boston: Beacon, 1984), 15–18.
84. Greenberg, *On Women and Judaism*, 40.
85. Ibid., 43.
86. Ozick, "Notes Toward Finding the Right Question," 148–150.
87. Ibid., 150
88. Ibid. The academy founded at Yavneh by Rabbi Yoḥanan ben Zakkai is the birthplace of rabbinic Judaism.
89. Judith Plaskow, *Standing Again at Sinai*, 65–67.
90. Plaskow, "The Right Question Is Theological," 231.
91. Plaskow, *Standing Again at Sinai*. The foregoing discussion relies on Plaskow's section on "Torah as Law in a Feminist Judaism," 60–73.
92. Ibid., 71.
93. It is interesting that the communal basis of halakhic authority is regarded as a given by Rachel Biale. In the epilogue to her survey volume, *Women and Jewish Law* (New York: Schocken, 1984), she comments upon my recommendation in my earliest article, "The Jew Who Wasn't There," that women form their own halakhic community and give decision-making authority to women decisors. Biale calls this "one of the most radical proposals ever made," but observes that because "recognized halakhists draw their authority from the fact that their followers accept their opinions," the proposal is not halakhically problemmatic (264). She could not have anticipated that the very year her book was published, Rabbi Herschel Schachter would publish an antifeminist responsum *"Tz'i Lakh B'Ikvei Ha Tzon,"* Bet Yizḥak 17 (5745) [1984]:118–134, in which he would adduce traditional sources to argue that all authority, even the authority to innovate custom *(minhag)*, belongs exclusively to *vatikin*, experienced Torah scholars, defining this category in such a way that women can never qualify (122–127).
94. Robert Cover, *Justice Accused* (New Haven, CT: Yale University Press, 1975). Robert Cover, "*Nomos* and Narrative," 34–40.
95. Ellen M. Umansky, "What are the Sources of My Theology?" *Journal of Feminist Studies in Religion* 1 (spring, 1985): 126. See also "Beyond Androcentrism: Feminist Challenges to Judaism," *Journal of Reform Judaism* (winter 1990): 25–35.
96. Umansky, "Beyond Androcentrism," 25–35.
97. Rosemary Radford Ruether, *Sexism and God-Talk* (Boston: Beacon, 1983), 19.
98. For a description of the prayer group's distinctive Torah service, see Rivkeh Haut, "From Women: Piety Not Rebellion," *Sh'ma* 15 (May 17, 1985): 110.
99. Alisdair MacIntyre, *After Virtue*; and *Whose Justice? Which Rationality?* (Notre Dame, IN: University of Notre Dame Press, 1988). Stanley Hauerwas, *Character and the Christian Life* (San Antonio: University of Trinity Press, 1975), and with Richard Bondi and David B. Burrell, *Truthfulness and Tragedy* (Notre Dame, IN: University of Notre Dame Press, 1977). Taylor, *Sources of the Self*, addresses the problem explicitly in his discussion of hypergoods, 62–75. Michael Walzer, *Exodus and Revolution* (New York: Basic Books), 75, 83, and *Spheres of Justice* (New York: Basic Books, 1983). For a critique of MacIntyre's and Walzer's reliance on traditions, see Okin, *Justice, Gender and the Family*, chap. 3.

100. Elizabeth Say, *Evidence on Her Own Behalf: Women's Narrative as Theological Voice* (Savage, MD: Rowman and Littlefield, 1990).

101. Okin, *Justice, Gender and the Family,* chap. 3.

102. Ibid., 56.

103. MacIntyre, *After Virtue,* 222.

104. Okin, *Justice, Gender and the Family,* 66.

105. Carol Christ, *Diving Deep and Surfacing: Women Writers on Spiritual Quest* (Boston: Beacon, 1980).

106. Okin, *Justice, Gender and the Family,* 60–62.

107. Audre Lorde, "An Open Letter to Mary Daly," in *Sister Outsider* (Trumansburg, NY: Crossing Press, 1984), 68.

108. "Feminist Reflections on Separation and Unity in Jewish Theology," *Journal of Feminist Studies in Religion* 2 (spring 1986). See in particular the responses of T. Drorah Setel, 113–118, and Marcia Falk, 121–125.

109. Marilyn Friedman, "Feminism and Modern Friendship: Dislocating the Community," in *Explorations in Feminist Ethics: Theory and Practice,* ed. Eve Browning Cole and Susan Coultrap-MacQuin (Bloomington: Indiana University Press, 1992), 89–97, points to an analogous failure on the part of communitarians to consider the complex interplay of bonds with voluntary, chosen associations and communities of place and ethnicity. Although I give more weight to communities of peoplehood than Friedman, I would agree that the interplay between the two kinds of associational commitments sparks movement and adaptation in both.

110. Gloria Anzaldua "La Prieta," in *This Bridge Called My Back: Writings by Radical Women of Color,* ed. Cherrie Moraga and Gloria Anzaldua (Watertown, MA: Persephone Press, 1981), 205.

111. Robert Cover, *"Nomos* and Narrative," 23.

112. Ibid., 19–25.

113. Ibid., 18.

114. For a discussion of the instability of context, see Roberto Mangabeira Unger, *Passion: An Essay on Personality,* 5–15.

115. The term "thickness" refers to multiple layers of meaning that an act or story may possess. The term was popularized by Clifford Geertz, "Thick Description: Toward an Interpretive Theory of Culture," in *The Interpretation of Cultures* (New York: Basic Books, 1973), 3–30.

116. Robert Cover, "Folktales of Justice," 183. See also David Schulman, "AIDS Discrimination: Its Nature, Meaning and Function," *Nova Law Review* 12 (spring 1988):1117–1119, for an example of the way in which a re/revisioning of civil rights can account for a place in society for people with AIDS. Schulman refers to law's re-membering those who are dismembered from society because of the stigma of their status.

117. Read, for example the disapproving thumbnail biography of Yalta in Adin Steinsaltz's commentary on B. Berakhot 51b.

118. Berakhot 51b. My translation.

119. See, for example, Maharsha and Ein Yaakov commentaries to Berakhot 51b. Yaakov bar Shlomo N. Haviv, *Ein Yaakov,* vol. 1 (New York: Avraham Yitzhak Friedman, n.d.), 158.

120. Certain ancient metaphysical biologies propound such views. Aristotle claims that only fathers are true parents, and mothers, themselves deformed beings, contribute not form but only passive matter toward the creation of a child: Aristotle, *Generation of Animals,* 2; 2.735A1–10. David Feldman, *Marital Relations, Birth Control and Abortion in Jewish Law* (New York: Schocken, 1974), argues that "the talmudic commentators" espoused a

popular variation of Aristotelian biology in which "a foetus is formed from female blood and male seed prevailed," 133–134. A brilliant feminist analysis of Aristotle's "motherless metaphysics of the monstrous female" can be found in Catherine Keller, *From a Broken Web: Separation, Sexism and the Self* (Boston: Beacon, 1986), 48–50.

121. On the thesis that the sexual and procreative capacities of women are regarded as patriarchal property, see Judith Wegner, *Woman in the Mishnah: Person or Chattel*, 168–181.

122. B. Niddah 20b. My translation.

123. Cover, "The Folktales of Justice."

124. "Trickster," *Funk and Wagnalls Standard Dictionary of Folklore, Mythology and Legend*, vol. 2 (New York: Funk and Wagnalls, 1950), 1123–1125. For application to biblical narrative, see Susan Niditch, *Underdogs and Tricksters* (San Francisco: Harper and Row, 1987).

125. Hebrew speakers will note that in biblical and Tannaitic Hebrew, all these verbs of communication and relation sometimes serve as euphemisms for sexual intercourse. What I envision is a world in which "intercourse," in its literal sense of "interaction," is truly communicative. This theme is explored further in Chapters 4 and 5.

CHAPTER 3

1. Italics mine. My translation.

2. Rashi, glosses *amitti as maskim al ha-emet v'sonei et ha-sheker*, "assenting to the truth and hating falsehood."

3. Laura Geller, "Symposium: What Kind of Tikkun Does the World Need?" *Tikkun* 1:1 (1986): 17.

4. Paul R. Mendes-Flor and Jehuda Reinharz, *The Jew in the Modern World: A Documentary History* (New York: Oxford University Press, 1980), 162.

5. Isaac M. Wise, "Women as Members of Congregations," in *Selected Writings of Isaac Mayer Wise*, ed. David Philipson and Louis Grossman (New York: Arno Press and the New York Times, 1969). See also David Ellenson, "Reform Judaism in Nineteenth Century America: The Evidence of the Prayerbooks" in *Between Tradition and Culture: The Dialectics of Modern Jewish Religion and Identity* (Atlanta: Scholars Press, 1994), 184.

6. The ceremony was not identical to a bar mitzvah. She had to read from a Bible, not a scroll, and not during but after the Torah service. Azriel Eisenberg, ed., *Eyewitness to Jewish History*, part 4 (New York: Union of American Hebrew Congregations, 1982), 32.

7. Riv-Ellen Prell, "The Vision of Woman in Classical Reform Judaism," *Journal of the American Academy of Religion*, 575–589.

8. Milton Himmelfarb, "Going to Shul," in *Understanding Jewish Prayer*, ed. Jakob J. Petuchowski (New York: Ktav, 1972), 156.

9. Adrienne Rich, "Invisibility in Academe," in *Blood, Bread and Poetry* (New York: W. W. Norton, 1986), 199.

10. The Israeli Supreme Court directed in 1994 that a governmental commisssion be established to determine how to accommodate the right of groups such as Women of the Wall to pray together without offending other worshippers. When by May 17, 1995, the commission failed to meet its exended deadline for issuing recommendations, the International Committee for Women of the Wall filed a new lawsuit against the government, the prime minister's office, and the Ministries of Religions, of the Interior,

and of the Police. At this writing, the Supreme Court has ordered that its directive be implemented promptly. However, the *Shas* party has introduced a bill in the Knesset to designate the Western Wall as a syngogue and forbid all deviations from Orthodox prayer on the site.

11. The literature on women and liturgy is too vast to be contained in a single citation. Much of it is cited during the course of this chapter. The suggestion that women's sins have less to do with pride and aggression than with self-negation is offered by Judith Plaskow, *Sex, Sin, and Grace: Women's Experience and the Theologies of Reinhold Niehbuhr and Paul Tillich* (Washington, DC: University Press of America, 1980).

12. The issue of whether mitzvot require *kavvanah* is debated throughout the Talmud. See, for example, B. Berakhot 13a regarding *kavvanah* for *Shema* and Berakhot 5 regarding *kavvanah* for the *Tefillah.*

13. B. Berakhot 31a. Whereas Conservative and Orthodox prayerbooks use the term *Amidah,* "the prayer said standing," the Reform prayerbook *Gates of Prayer* has resumed use of the classic term *ha-tefillah.* In this chapter, I use whichever term is preferred by the prayerbook I am citing.

14. See, for example, Edward Greenstein, "To You Do I Call: A Critique of Impersonal Prayer," *Reconstructionist* 52 (June 1988): 13–16.

15. Rita M. Gross, "Steps Toward Feminine Imagery of Deity in Jewish Theology," in *On Being a Jewish Feminist,* ed. Susannah Heschel (New York: Schocken, 1983), 245.

16. Renato Rosaldo, *Culture and Truth: The Remaking of Social Analysis* (Boston: Beacon, 1989), 202–204.

17. We tend to forget that other versions of Judaism coexisted with rabbinic Judaism.

18. Bernadette J. Brooten, *Women Leaders in the Ancient Synagogue: Inscriptional Evidence and Background Issues,* Brown Judaic Studies 36 (Chico, CA: Scholars Press, 1982).

19. Lawrence Hoffman, "Women's Prayer and Women Praying" [unpublished paper].

20. An important contribution to this project is *Four Centuries of Jewish Women's Spirituality,* ed. Ellen M. Umansky and Dianne Ashton (Boston: Beacon, 1992).

21. Laura Geller, "Symposium: What Kind of Tikkun Does the World Need?" 17.

22. Chava Weissler, "Women in Paradise," *Tikkun* 2:2 (n.d.): 43–46, 117–120.

23. Professor Shoshanna Gershenzon informs me that a book of *tkhines* passed down in her family contains prayers on such events as the sinking of the *Lusitania.*

24. Chava Weissler, "Mizvot Built into the Body," in *People of the Body: Jews and Judaism from an Embodied Perspective,* ed. Howard Eilberg-Schwartz (Albany: State University of New York Press, 1992), 108, citing *Seder Tkhines U-Vakoshes,* 1762, no. 91.

25. Monique Wittig, *Les Guerilleres* (New York: Avon, 1973), 89.

26. For an introduction to new ritual concerns expressed by women, see Rebecca Alpert, "Our Lives Are the Text: Exploring Jewish Women's Rituals," *Bridges* 2 (spring 1991): 66–80. For collections of various new ceremonies, see *A Ceremonies Sampler: New Rites, Celebrations and Observances of Jewish Women,* ed. Elizabeth Resnick Levine (San Diego: Women's Institute for Continuing Jewish Education, 1991), and *Lifecycles: Jewish Women on Life Passages and Personal Milestones,* vol. 1, edited and with introduction by Debra Orenstein (Woodstock, VT: Jewish Lights, 1994).

27. The first such ceremony is Savina J. Teubal, "Simchat Hochmah," in *Four Centuries of Jewish Women's Spirituality,* 257–265. See also Marcia Cohn Speigel, "Becoming a Crone: Ceremony at 60," *Lilith* 21 (fall 1988), 18.

28. Penina Adelman, *Miriam's Well: Rituals for Jewish Women Around the Year* (Fresh Meadows, NY: Biblio Press, 1986).

29. E. M. Broner, *The Telling* (San Francisco: Harper, 1993). Most of these haggadot are unpublished. For an analysis, see Lee T. Bycel, "To Reclaim Our Voice: An Analysis of Representative Contemporary Feminist Passover Haggadot," *CCAR Journal* 40 (spring 1993): 55–71.

30. Riv-Ellen Prell, *Prayer and Community: The Havurah in American Judaism* (Detroit: Wayne State University Press, 1989), 292–294.

31. For example, classical halakhah has no interest in and hence no information about women's prayer behavior with other women, as long as they do not usurp the liturgical prerogatives of the male minyan. This information vacuum has allowed Orthodox women to create an independent institution, the women's prayer group, over which Orthodox authorities are having difficulty establishing jurisdiction. See Rachel Adler, "Innovation and Authority: The 'Women's Minyan Responsum' and the Battle for Women's Ritual" [unpublished paper presented at the American Academy of Religion Annual Conference, Kansas City, Missouri, Nov. 1991].

32. David Ellenson reminds me that this strategy of radical reinterpretation by means of translations has been favored by liberal liturgists for the past two centuries. See David Ellenson, "The Mannheimer Prayerbooks and Modern Central European Communal Liturgies: A Representative Comparison of Mid-Nineteenth Century Works," in *Between Tradition and Culture*, 59–78.

33. *Gates of Prayer: The New Union Prayerbook* (New York: Central Conference of American Rabbis, 1975), 37, 134, 169.

34. *Siddur Sim Shalom*, trans. and ed. Jules Harlow (New York: Rabbinical Assembly, United Synagogue of America, 1985), 107, 210, 354.

35. *Siddur Sim Shalom*, 292. Note that feminine simile is followed by the term Lord, reestablishing the masculinity of the Deity.

36. *Gates of Prayer*, 97.

37. *Siddur Sim Shalom*, 232.

38. A responsum of the Law Committee of the Rabbinical Assembly now permits addition of the matriarchs to the recitation of the *tefillah*. Joel Rembaum, "Regarding the Inclusion of the Names of the Matriarchs in the First Blessing of the Amidah," 1990, available from the Rabbinical Assembly upon request. See also the summary paragraph in *Summary Index of the Committee on Jewish Law and Standards: The Rabbinical Assembly*, December, 1993, sect. 9, p. 19.

39. For other examples in classical liturgy, see Lawrence A. Hoffman, *The Canonization of the Synogogue Service* (Notre Dame, IN: University of Notre Dame Press, 1979).

40. I have used my own translations here, because literal translations highlight what the rabbinic liturgists were responding to in the biblical text. The euphemism is discussed in B. Berakhot 11b.

41. Lawrence Hoffman, *Beyond the Text: A Holistic Approach to Liturgy* (Bloomington: Indiana University Press, 1987), 157.

42. For example, the Chief Rabbinate of Israel has composed a prayer for the state of Israel included in most prayerbooks and a prayer for airplane travelers replacing an older prayer in which the traveler prays to be protected from highwaymen and wild beasts.

43. For example, Berakhot 29b. For discussions of the creative tension between *keva* and *kavvanah*, see Jakob J. Petuchowski, "Spontaneity and Tradition," in *Understanding Jewish Prayer*, 3–25 and Riv-Ellen Prell, *Prayer and Community*, 183–187.

44. George Steiner, *Real Presences* (Chicago: University of Chicago Press, 1989), 10.

45. Prell, *Prayer and Community*, 313.

46. Ibid.

47. T. S. Eliot, "Burnt Norton," in *Four Quartets* (New York: Harcourt, Brace and World, 1943), 14.
48. George Eliot, *Middlemarch* (New York: New American Library, 1964), 191.
49. Hoffman, *Beyond the Text*, 1–19.
50. The importance of the fixed place for prayer is mentioned in B. Berakhot 6b, 7b. The worshipper in a fixed place, especially a worshipper who provides a model of some sort, also serves as an orienting point. At the synagogue I attended in Minneapolis, I was fascinated to be shown a map of the congregation drawn for bar and bat mitzvah celebrants indicating the route of the Torah processionals on which I and other worshippers were signposts.
51. Lawrence Hoffman, *The Art of Public Prayer: Not for Clergy Only* (Washington, DC: Pastoral Press, 1988), discusses the impact of both custom and personal associations upon prayer.
52. Hoffman, *Beyond the Text*, 150–151.
53. Clifford Geertz, "Religion as a Cultural System," in *The Interpretation of Cultures* (New York: Basic Books, 1973), 87–125.
54. Prell, *Prayer and Community*, 30–111.
55. Ibid., 30–111.
56. Ibid., 159.
57. Barbara G. Myerhoff, "A Death in Due Time: Construction of Self and Culture in Ritual Drama," in *Rite, Drama, Festival, Spectacle*, ed. John J. MacAloon (Philadelphia: Institute for the Study of Human Issues, 1984), 149–178.
58. Ibid., 151–153.
59. Lawrence A. Hoffman, *The Canonization of the Synogogue Service*, 101–102. See also Ismar Elbogen, *Jewish Liturgy: A Comprehensive History*, trans. Raymond P. Scheindlin (Philadelphia and Jerusalem: Jewish Publication Society and Jewish Theological Seminary of America, 1993), 128.
60. Hoffman, *The Canonization of the Synogogue Service*, 101, quoting *Seder Rav Amram Gaon*, ed. Daniel Goldschmidt (Jerusalem: 1971), 162–163.
61. Lawrence A. Hoffman, *Gates of Understanding 2: Appreciating the Days of Awe* (New York: Central Conference of American Rabbis, 1984), 117.
62. *Gates of Repentance: The New Union Prayerbook for the Days of Awe* (New York: Central Conference of American Rabbis, 1978), 252. The same message is impressed upon the worshipper in a headnote in the old Conservative *High Holiday Prayerbook*, trans. and ed. Morris Silverman (Hartford: Prayerbook Press for United Synagogue of America, 1951), 207, and in a thick footnote extending over four pages in the Orthodox *High Holyday Prayerbook*, trans. and annotated Philip Birnbaum (New York: Hebrew Publishing Company, 1951), 489–492. It is more briefly and discreetly incorporated into the translation in the new *Mahzor for Rosh HaShanah and Yom Kippur*, 2nd ed., ed. Jules Harlow (New York: Rabbinical Assembly, 1978), 353.
63. Lawrence A. Hoffman, *Gates of Understanding 2*, 117.
64. Jakob J. Petuchowski, *Prayerbook Reform in Europe: The Liturgy of European Liberal and Reform Judaism* (New York: World Union for Progressive Judaism, 1968), 323–333.
65. For example, Deborah E. Lipstadt, "And Deborah Made Ten," in *On Being a Jewish Feminist*, 207–209; E. M. Broner, *Mourning and Morning: A Kaddish Journal* (New York: HarperCollins, 1994).
66. Marcia Falk, "What About God?" *Moment* 10 (March 1985): 32–36. Labeling ritual repetition "conditioning" seems inadequately nuanced.
67. Some of the stories with which such prayers are associated are not historically accu-

rate. Lawrence Hoffman makes this point regarding the popular association of *Kol Nidre* with *Marrano* rites. In fact, the prayer long predates the Spanish persecutions and *Marranos* neither composed it nor popularized it. Hoffman, *Gates of Understanding 2*, 114–115. Another example of a folk tradition attached to a prayer involves the liturgical poem *U'netaneh Tokef*, which was said to have been taught to its putative author, Kalonymus ben Meshullam, in a dream by a scholar martyred by the Christian rulers of Mayence. Philip Birnbaum, ed., *High HolyDay Prayerbook*, 359f–360f.

68. J. L. Austin, *How To Do Things With Words* (Oxford: Oxford University Press, 1962). Austin subsequently revised his theories. However, his original and simpler formulation regarding performatives is a handier way to understand liturgical language.

69. *Gates of Prayer*, 240.

70. Lawrence A. Hoffman, "Blessings and Their Translation in Current Jewish Liturgies," *Worship* 60 (1986): 136–161.

71. Ibid., 156.

72. According to classical halakhah, although God has created the minimal boundaries of the Sabbaths and holidays, human beings have the power to extend these boundaries on either side by reciting *kiddush* earlier than sundown or by reciting *havdalah* later in the evening.

73. This second class of future commitments Austin terms commissives. J. L. Austin, *How To Do Things With Words*, 150.

74. An enormous body of halakhah discusses espousal. See, for example, B. Kiddushin 1; Maimonides, *Mishneh Torah Hilkot Ishut;* "Ishah," in *Encyclopedia Talmudica*, vol. 1 (Jerusalem: Talmudic Encyclopedia Institute, 1969).

75. Tosafot, at B. Berakhot 454b; Shulḥan Arukh, Oraḥ Ḥayyim 55:1.

76. Mishnah Sotah 7:1; B. Berakhot 13a.

77. Jakob J. Petuchowski, "Hebrew and Vernacular Prayer," in *Understanding Jewish Prayer*, 43.

78. Ibid., 44.

79. Marcia Falk, *Book of Blessings* (San Francisco: Harper, 1996).

80. Hoffman, *Beyond the Text*, 161–163.

81. Prell, *Prayer and Community*, 189.

82. Hoffman, *The Canonization of the Synagogue Service*, 60–62.

83. The prayer is attributed in B. Berakhot 16b to Rav, founder of the Talmudic acadamy at Sura, active c. 220–250 C.E.

84. The hymn *L'kha dodi* was written by Rabbi Solomon Alkabetz of Safed. Ismar Elbogen, *Jewish Liturgy*, 92.

85. Barbara G. Myerhoff, "Sanctifying Women's Lives Through Ritual" [tape of workshop], Shekhina Conference, Los Angeles, 1985: Infomedix K316–IV, Garden Grove, CA 92643.

86. Victor Turner, "Liminality and Communitas," in *The Ritual Process* (Chicago: Aldine, 1969), 94–130.

87. Victor Turner, "Social Dramas and Ritual Metaphors," in *Dramas, Fields, and Metaphors: Symbolic Action in Human Society* (Ithaca, NY: Cornell University Press, 1974), 23–59.

88. Barbara G. Myerhoff, "Sanctifying Women's Lives Through Ritual" [tape of workshop].

89. Barbara G. Myerhoff, "A Death in Due Time," 151–153.

90. Turner, "Social Dramas and Ritual Metaphors," 23–59, infra 25. Turner quotes a striking definition from Robert A. Nisbet, *Social Change and History: Aspects of the Western Theory of Development* (Oxford: Oxford University Press, 1969), 4:

"Metaphor is our means of effecting instantaneous fusion of two separated realms of experience into one illuminating, iconic, encapsulating image."

91. This observation draws upon Karsten Harries's statement that "Metaphors speak of absence" and upon Richard Schiff's characterization of metaphor as "a bridge enabling passage from one world to another." Karsten Harries, "Metaphor and Transcendence" in *On Metaphor*, ed. Sheldon Sacks (Chicago: University of Chicago Press, 1979), 82. Richard Schiff, "Art and Life: A Metaphoric Relationship," in *On Metaphor*, 106.

92. Harries, "Metaphor and Transcendence," 82.

93. I have used the masculine pronoun because, historically, theological language has been controlled predominantly by men.

94. Rita M. Gross, "Female God Language in a Jewish Context," in *Womanspirit Rising*, ed. Carol P. Christ and Judith Plaskow (San Francisco: Harper and Row, 1979), 171 [italics Gross's].

95. Geertz, "Religion as a Cultural System," 93–94.

96. Judith Plaskow, "The Right Question is Theological," in *On Being a Jewish Feminist*, ed. Susannah Heschel (New York: Schocken, 1983), 227–228; Judith Plaskow, *Standing Again at Sinai*, (San Francisco: Harper and Row, 1979), 126–127. Plaskow, *Standing Again at Sinai*, 127. This point is made by many feminists. See, for example, Rita M. Gross, "Female God Language in a Jewish Context," and Tikva Frymer-Kensky, "On Feminine God-Talk," *Reconstructionist* 69 (spring 1994): 48–55.

97. Paul Ricoeur, *The Symbolism of Evil*, trans. Emerson Buchanan (Boston: Beacon, 1967), 2–18, 347–357.

98. Nelle Morton, *The Journey Is Home* (Boston: Beacon, 1985), 152.

99. Covenants as constructions of power relations will be discussed in Chapters 4 and 5. The dialogic theology of Martin Buber, the existentialism of Franz Rosenzweig, and the writings of modern covenant theologians such as Eugene Borowitz present some modern evolutions of the covenant metaphor.

100. A thorough explanation of this point is found in Sallie McFague, *Metaphorical Theology: Models of God in Religious Language* (Philadelphia: Fortress, 1982), 15.

101. Tikva Frymer-Kensky, "On Feminine God-Talk," 53.

102. Mordecai Kaplan, *Judaism as a Civilization: Toward a Reconstruction of American Jewish Life* (New York: Schocken, 1967), 391–405.

103. Ibid., 343–349.

104. Richard Hirsh, "Spirituality and the Language of Prayer," *Reconstructionist* 59 (spring 1994): 21–26.

105. Arthur Green, *Seek My Face, Speak My Name: A Contemporary Jewish Theology* (New York: Jason Aronson, 1992).

106. See, for example, the discussion of Eastern and Western forms of unitary mysticism in Rudolf Otto, *Mysticism East and West*, trans. Bertha L. Bracey and Richenda C. Payne (New York: Macmillan, 1932).

107. William James, *Varieties of Religious Experience* (New York: New American Library, 1958), 306–307.

108. Sigmund Freud, *Civilization and Its Discontents*, vol. 21, in *The Standard Edition of the Complete Psychological Works of Sigmund Freud*, trans. and ed. James Strachey in collaboration with Anna Freud, assisted by Alix Strachey and Alan Tyson (London: Hogarth Press and the Institute of Psycho-Analysis, 1930), 72.

109. Falk's theology is in implicit agreement with contemporary Reconstructionism, as the Reconstructionist prayerbook's use of her work attests, but she does not identify herself as a Reconstructionist liturgist.

110. Personal communication from Marcia Falk, July 26, 1995.

111. For example, Tikva Frymer-Kensky, "On Feminine God-Talk," 49.
112. Marcia Falk, "Toward a Feminist Jewish Reconstruction of Monotheism," *Tikkun* 4 (July/August 1989): 53–56. In the same issue, see Lawrence Hoffman, "A Response to Marcia Falk," 56–57.
113. That a blessing must mention God's name is the opinion of Rav. That it must mention God's kingship is the opinion of R. Yoḥanan, B. Berakhot 12a, 40b. These are Amoraic dicta that postdate the invention of the blessing formula by several hundred years.
114. Ismar Elbogen, *Jewish Liturgy*, 5–6. Lawrence A. Hoffman, "Blessings and Their Translation in Current Jewish Liturgies," 136–138.
115. Falk, "Toward a Feminist Jewish Reconstruction of Monotheism," 53–56.
116. Emanuel Levinas, *Ethics and Infinity: Conversations with Phillippe Nemo*, trans. Richard A. Cohen (Pittsburgh: Duquesne University Press, 1985). For a discussion of Levinas's metaphor of face, see Susan A. Handelman, *Fragments of Redemption: Jewish Thought and Literary Theory in Benjamin, Scholem, and Levinas* (Bloomington: Indiana University Press, 1991), 208–225.
117. B. Berakhot 6a.
118. Genesis 3:9.
119. A beautiful use of this metaphor of God as parent of grown offspring can be found in Margaret Wenig, "God Is a Woman And She Is Growing Older," *Reform Judaism* (fall 1992). A liturgical adaptation of this piece can be found in the Feminist Center Sliḥot Service of the American Jewish Congress, Los Angeles region, ed. Rachel Adler and Yaffa Weisman [unpublished].
120. Plaskow, *Standing Again at Sinai*, 128–134. Falk, "Toward a Feminist Reconstruction of Monotheism," 53–56.
121. In Taylor's terminology, equal respect is a "hypergood." Charles Taylor, *Sources of the Self: The Making of Modern Identity* (Cambridge, MA: Harvard University Press, 1989), 62–75.
122. Marcia Falk, "Notes On Composing New Blessings," in *Weaving the Visions: New Patterns in Feminist Spirituality*, ed. Judith Plaskow and Carol P. Christ (San Francisco: Harper and Row, 1989), 132.
123. *Kol Haneshama* (Wyncote, PA: Reconstructionist Press, 1994).
124. These are listed in a section at the beginning of each service. See, for example, 5, 247.
125. Richard Hirsh, 25.
126. Ibid., 24.
127. Linda Alcoff, "Cultural Feminism Versus Post-Structuralism: The Identity Crisis in Feminist Theory," *Signs* 13 (spring 1988): 405–436.
128. Social scientists make a distinction between sex, a biological condition, and gender, the social constructions upon sexual difference. Judith Butler argues convincingly that sex itself is in part socially constructed. Judith Butler, *Gender Trouble: Feminism and the Subversion of Identity* (New York: Routledge, 1990), esp. chaps. 1 and 3.
129. An effective counterargument to this temptation to oversimplify gender symbolism is a nuanced and temperate account of the multivocality of gender symbols by Caroline Walker Bynum, "Introduction: The Complexity of Symbols" in *Gender and Religion: On the Complexity of Symbols*, ed. Caroline Walker Bynum, Stevan Harrell, and Paula Richman (Boston: Beacon, 1986), 1–20.
130. "Grace After Meals," in *Ha-Siddur Ha-Shalem*, trans. and annotated by Philip Birnbaum (New York: Hebrew Publishing Company, 1977), 762.
131. Lynn Gottlieb, "Spring Cleaning Ritual on the Eve of Full Moon Nisan," in *On Being a Jewish Feminist*, 278–280. Margaret Wenig and Naomi Janowitz, *Siddur nashim* [unpublished]. *Siddur Birkat Shalom* (Somerville, MA: Havurat Shalom Siddur Project, 1992).

132. Sue Levi Elwell, "Reclaiming Jewish Women's Oral Tradition? An Analysis of Rosh Hodesh," in *Women at Worship: Interpretations of North American Diversity*, ed. Marjorie Proctor-Smith and Janet Walton (Louisville, KY: Westminster/John Knox Press, 1993), 111–126.

133. To the question, "Are there women?" poststructuralists answer "no." They "attack the category and the concept of woman through problematizing subjectivity." Alcoff, "Cultural Feminism Versus Post-Structuralism," 407. Some political feminists have argued for the elimination of gender. Shulamith Firestone suggests the freeing of women from their reproductive biology through artificial reproductive technologies. *The Dialectic of Sex* (New York: Bantam, 1971), 205–242. Susan Moller Okin argues that to eliminate injustice in the family, it cannot be gender structured. *Justice, Gender and the Family* (New York: Basic Books, 1989), 3–24.

134. Theoretically, concepts such as animus-anima mitigate Jungian gender polarities and account for variation and complexity in human personalities. However, to see Jungian psychology's tendency to reinscribe gender stereotypes one need only open a book like M. Esther Harding, *Women's Mysteries, Ancient and Modern* (London: Rider, 1971).

135. Arthur Waskow, "Feminist Judaism: The Restoration of the Moon," in *On Being a Jewish Feminist*, 261–272.

136. Virginia Ramey Mollenkott, *The Divine Feminine: Biblical Imagery of God as Female* (New York: Crossroads, 1984).

137. Gross recommends borrowing from Eastern religions. Rita M. Gross, "Steps Toward Feminine Imagery of Deity in Jewish Theology," *Judaism* 30 (spring 1981).

138. Frymer-Kensky, "On Feminine God-Language," 50.

139. Ellen M. Umansky, "Creating a Jewish Feminist Theology," in *Weaving the Visions*, 192.

140. Plaskow, *Standing Again at Sinai*, 165–166.

141. Frymer-Kensky, "On Feminine God-Language," 50.

142. Umansky, "Creating a Jewish Feminist Theology," 191.

143. This name was coined by Miriam Bronstein and Shifra Lilith Klibansky Fielding in the early 1980s when they were students at Oberlin College. Both became members of Havurat Shalom in Boston. Bronstein participated in the Siddur Birkat Shalom project.

144. Frymer-Kensky, "On Feminine God-Language," 50–51.

145. Steiner, *Real Presences*, 211–227.

146. This seems to be what Marcia Falk achieves in her interpretive *Amidah*, which is a mosaic of Jewish women's poetry. *Book of Blessings*, 177–259.

147. Cynthia Ozick, "Notes Toward Finding the Right Question," in *On Being a Jewish Feminist*, 120–122. Samuel Dresner, "The Return to Paganism," *Midstream* 34 (June/July 1988): 32–38.

148. Naomi Janowitz, "God's Body: Theological and Ritual Roles of Shi'ur Komah" in *People of the Body*, 183–201. A parasang is equivalent to 8000 cubits, according to Adin Steinsaltz, *The Talmud: The Steinsaltz Edition, A Reference Guide*, trans. Israel V. Berman (New York: Random House, 1989), 284.

149. Maimonides, *The Guide of the Perplexed*, vol. 1, trans. Shlomo Pines (University of Chicago Press, 1963), chaps. 55–59. Judith Plaskow adds that in these very chapters Maimonides refers to God in the masculine without acknowledging the language of maleness as anthropomorphic. *Standing Again at Sinai*, 127. *The Guide* is written in Arabic, which, like Hebrew, has no neuter gender, but the omission suggests that Maimonides was blind to his attribution of maleness to the Deity.

150. Gershom Scholem, *Major Trends in Jewish Mysticism* (New York: Schocken, 1961), 268–272.

Chapter 4

1. Robert Alter, *The Art of Biblical Narrative* (New York: Basic Books, 1981), 181–188.
2. Francis Brown, S. R. Driver, and Charles A. Briggs, *Hebrew and English Lexicon of the Old Testament*, reprinted with corrections (Oxford: Clarendon Press, 1968). They specifically identify *ednah* as sexual. Compare also *adin*, "voluptuous," in Isaiah 47:8, and associations with luxury, and delicacies for eating such as Genesis 49:20.
3. That the speaker is the angel representing God, rather than God directly, is attested by his promise to return "when life is due."
4. The question of precisely what occurs in the interaction between the reader and the text has occupied hermeneutical theorists for several hundred years. A full account would require not a footnote, but a book. The view that, in reading a work of art, the reader empathically recreates the artist's experience comes from the Romantic theorist Wilhelm Dilthey. The notion of understanding implicit in this view is challenged by the modern philosopher Martin Heidegger, who claims that understanding is an existential category that reveals itself in connection with our own involvements and perspectives. When we understand, we are determining how the thing we understand helps us, hurts us, or in some other way matters to us. Another challenge to Dilthey is Hans-Georg Gadamer's insistence that historical and cultural contexts constrain and indeed determine the experiences and reflections of individual subjectivities. Brief selections exemplifying these perspectives may be found in Kurt Mueller-Vollmer, ed., *The Hermeneutics Reader* (New York: Continuum, 1988), 148–164, 214–240, 256–292.
5. I have used the more tentative form "may offer" in regard to psychological theories because, as a generation's worth of feminist critique has demonstrated, the categories of classical theorists such as Freud and Jung were often employed to categorize women as less psychologically healthy than men and to condition women to accept submissive roles, thus reinforcing male dominance. On the other hand, various schools of feminist psychological theory have developed that I consider promising. See, for example, feminist family therapy: Marianne Walters, *The Invisible Web: Gender Patterns in Family Relationships*, The Women's Project in Family Therapy (New York: Guilford Press, 1988); feminist psychoanalysis: Dorothy Dinnerstein *The Mermaid and the Minotaur* (New York: Harper and Row, 1976); feminist object-relations theory: Nancy Choderow, *The Reproduction of Mothering: Psychoanalysis and the Sociology of Gender* (Berkeley: University of California Press, 1978), and Jessica Benjamin, *The Bonds of Love: Psychoanalysis, Feminism and the Problem of Domination* (New York: Pantheon Books, 1988).
6. For instance, David Biale, *Eros and the Jews: From Biblical Israel to Contemporary America* (New York: Basic Books, 1992).
7. Steven Fraade, "Ascetical Aspects of Ancient Judaism," in *Jewish Spirituality*, vol. 1, ed. Arthur Green (New York: Crossroads, 1988).
8. This sentimentality greatly distorts the work of the great Yiddish writers, many of whom document the class struggle, the impact of the Enlightenment, and the collusion of traditional Judaism in the sufferings of the poorest.
9. This section incorporates much of my article "A Question of Boundaries: Towards a Jewish Feminist Theology of Self and Other," in *Tikkun Anthology*, ed. Michael Lerner (Oakland, CA: Tikkun Books, 1992) 465–471.
10. A separate book would be needed to catalogue and analyze traditional patriarchalist interpretations such as 1 Timothy 2:11–14 or B. Berakhot 61, as well as their reuse in later, more systematized theologies. For summaries of male supremicist translation and commentary, see Carol Meyers, *Discovering Eve* (New York: Oxford University

239

Press, 1988), 72–121; Phyllis Trible, *God and the Rhetoric of Sexuality* (Philadelphia: Fortress, 1978), 73; Merlin Stone, *When God Was a Woman* (New York: Dial Press, 1976), 5–8, 198–233; and Elaine Pagels, "The Politics of Paradise," *New York Review of Books* (May 12, 1988): 28–37.

11. For a summary of six representative views, see Ilana Pardes, *Countertraditions in the Bible: A Feminist Approach* (Cambridge, MA: Harvard University Press, 1992), 13–38. Catherine Keller, *From A Broken Web: Separation, Sexism and the Self* (Boston: Beacon, 1986), 33–36, 78–92. Mieke Bal, *Lethal Love: Feminist Readings of Biblical Love Stories* (Bloomington: Indiana University Press, 1987), 104–130.

12. Rosemary Radford Ruether, "Motherearth and the Megamachine," in *Womanspirit Rising*, ed. Carol P. Christ and Judith Plaskow (San Francisco: Harper and Row, 1979), 43–52; Rosemary Radford Ruether, *New Woman/New Earth: Sexist Ideologies and Human Liberation* (New York: Seabury Press, 1975); Carol P. Christ, *Diving Deep and Surfacing: Women Writers on Spiritual Quest* (Boston: Beacon, 1980), 120, 130; Susan Griffin, *Pornography and Silence: Culture's Revenge Against Nature* (New York: Harper and Row, 1981) 156–199; Judith Plaskow, *Standing Again at Sinai* (San Francisco: Harper and Row, 1979), 121–169, 192–194. In her later writing, Ruether gives a more nuanced account that recognizes that all dualisms are not alike either conceptually or in their effects upon women's lives. For example, in *Sexism and God-Talk* (Boston: Beacon, 1983), 72–82, she points out that Greek thought represents a more radical mind/body, male/female dualism than Hebrew thought. A consequence of Gnosticism's dualistic cosmology was a kind of egalitarianism. It invited women along with men to renounce body and sexuality and to become pure spirit.

13. Catherine Keller, *From a Broken Web*, 7–46.

14. Ibid., 11–15.

15. Ibid., 33–38.

16. Ibid., 78–92.

17. Mary Douglas, *Purity and Danger* (London: Routledge and Kegan Paul, 1966). Howard Eilberg-Schwartz, *The Savage in Judaism* (Bloomington: Indiana University Press, 1990).

18. Jessica Benjamin, *The Bonds of Love*, 126–127.

19. Ibid., 127.

20. Ibid., 126.

21. This first dividing of the waters is paralleled by the splitting of Tiamat "like a shellfish" in the Enuma Elish. "Akkadian Myths and Epics: The Creation Epic," trans. E. A. Speiser, in *The Ancient Near East: An Anthology of Texts and Pictures*, vol. 1, ed. James B. Pritchard (Princeton, NJ: Princeton University Press, 1958), 35.

22. These translations of Genesis 1 and 2 are adaptations of the JPS Tanakh. I have left *adam* and YHWH untranslated, because by translating *adam* as "man" and YHWH as "Lord," the JPS attributes gender and hierarchical status that these Hebrew terms do not imply. Another problem for translators is that Hebrew has no neuter gender. Every noun is either masculine or feminine, although grammatical gender assignment may be arbitrary. Thus, in one quotation from Genesis 1, I have bracketed "it" next to the literal translation "him." I have also chosen not to capitalize masculine pronouns referring to God as the JPS does. The capitals predispose readers to regard masculinity as a divine attribute even where a particular text may not image God as masculine. There are no capitals in the original.

23. Ludwig Kohler and Walter Baumgartner, *Hebraisches und Aramaisches Lexikon Zum Alten Testament*, 3rd ed., with contributions from B. Hartmann and E.Y. Kutscher, fasc. 1 (Leiden: E. J. Brill, 1967), s.v. ADM, 13; DM, 215. Kohler-

Baumgartner's lexicon, incorporating the latest philological research maintains that *adam* and *adamah*, "soil," are derivatives from this primary root meaning concerning redness, and that *dam*, "blood," is a related root. These conclusions differ from the conjectural derivation proposed by the older lexicon of Brown, Driver, and Briggs that the primary meaning of ADM, "humankind," is "make or produce," cognate to an Assyrian root, whereas ADM, "red," is separately derived from an Arabic root meaning "tawny." See I. ADM and II. ADM.

24. There is a complex constellation of wordplays in Genesis 1 and 2 involving the words *adam, adamah* (earth), *dam* (blood), and *domeh* and *d'mut* from the root DMH, "to resemble." Genesis 1 emphasizes kinship with God with puns on *adam* and *domeh*, whereas Genesis 2 emphasizes earthiness with the pun on *adamah* (2:7). *Tardemah*, from RDM, the deep sleep during which *adam* has a rib extracted in Genesis 2, may also participate in this wordplay.

25. Although some indisputably metaphorical meanings for *tzelem* can be documented, they are rare. See, for example, Psalm 39:7: "Man walks about as a mere shadow *(tzelem)*," where contextually it is indisputable that *tzelem* means a semblance without substance.

26. Hebrew has no neuter gender. Whether the grammatical masculine gender of God or *adam* also confers actual masculinity is a matter of debate among translators and commentators. I am going to argue that, in Genesis 1, there is insufficient evidence to prove that God and *adam* are narratively portrayed as masculine, whereas they are clearly masculine in Genesis 2.

27. Trible, *God and the Rhetoric of Sexuality*, 13–21.

28. Ibid., 21.

29. This is also a gnostic argument, although with strikingly different corollaries than mine. Elaine H. Pagels, *The Gnostic Gospels* (New York: Random House, 1979).

30. The theme of God's need for the other is found in the midrashic tradition, in classical mysticism, and in hasidism. Modern theologians who utilize the idea include Abraham Joshua Heschel and Martin Buber.

31. Because its Masoretic voweling is plural, the rabbis do not contest the word's plurality as scripture. Its missing vav functions for them merely as *remez*, an exegetical hint that the word could also be read as *kibshah*, "[you, masc. sing.] master her/it."

32. B. Yebamot 65b. It can be inferred that the rabbis are not satisfied with this proof because another prooftext is proposed that restates the commandment in the singular (Gen. 35:11). However, that it is not the first statement of the obligation weakens this second proof. Ultimately, argument, rather than prooftext, is conclusive in establishing the law. A probably unintended side effect of this ruling is that it provides a strong argument for women's freedom to use birth control, leaving men to fulfill their obligation on their own. Centuries of legal controversy focus upon this dangerous loophole. David M. Feldman, *Marital Relations, Birth Control, and Abortion in Jewish Law* (New York: Schocken, 1974), 53–56, 123–131, 169–248.

33. Bereshit Rabbah 8:12.

34. Rashi on Genesis 1:28.

35. This issue is addressed in ecofeminist theologies. A classic example is Rosemary Radford Reuther, *New Woman/New Earth*. A more current collection is *Ecofeminism and the Sacred*, ed. Carol J. Adams (New York: Continuum, 1993).

36. Permission to eat flesh is not given until after the Flood, when the disharmony between humanity and the other creatures is intensified (Gen. 9:1–5).

37. Carol Meyers, *Discovering Eve*, 47–71.

38. Ludwig Kohler and Walter Baumgartner, *Hebraishes und Aramaishes Lexikon*, s.v.

ZKhR. The noun meaning "male member" and the verb "to remember" are listed separately. Their etymologies do not preclude the possibility of a single root, although this is not proposed by the lexicon. It therefore seems plausible to suggest that the two terms *zakhar/zakhor* reflect a social fact confirmed by the Hebrew Bible's patrilineal genealogies and inheritances, its predominantly male subject matter, and its assignment of authorship almost exclusively to males. I am indebted to Professor Bruce Zuckerman for access to this lexicon and for his assistance in interpreting its entries.

39. I have followed Speiser's translation here. *Genesis,* vol. 1 of *The Anchor Bible,* trans. and with introduction and commentary by E. A. Speiser (Garden City, NY: Doubleday, 1964), 16n.

40. I have changed one word in the JPS translation. JPS has "clings to his wife," where I have put "clings to his woman." The word *ishah* was introduced in the previous verse, where it clearly means woman and not wife. Clearly, he clings to her not because of the social rules pertaining to marriage, but because these rules enact the reincorporation of a derivative part of man. The translation is problematic because *ishah* means both woman, generally, and wife. In Chapter 5 I discuss the implications of Hebrew's lack of a specific term for wife.

41. That the text itself does not express normativity is a central point of Carol Meyers's *Discovering Eve.*

42. One arguable exception is B. Berakhot 61a, an aggadic passage from which the rabbis derive rules forbidding men from walking behind a woman from man's original antecedence of woman. It is debatable, however, whether these rules have the force of law.

43. See Adrienne Rich, *Of Woman Born* (New York: W. W. Norton, 1976), 162–165.

44. Dorothy Sayers, "The Human-Not-Quite-Human," in *Are Women Human?* (Grand Rapids, MI: William B. Eerdmans Publishing, 1971), 17–47.

45. Otto Eissfeldt, *The Old Testament: An Introduction,* trans. Peter R. Ackroyd (New York: Harper and Row, 1965), 233–239. The Holiness Code is considered to extend from Chapters 17 to 26. It is characterized by the formula "You shall be holy, because I the Lord your God am holy." Eissfeldt observes, "With a very special insistence, it holds before the people the idea of holiness in the sense of cultic and ethical cleanness" (233).

46. The following discussion summarizes a Durkheimian approach to classification systems as reflections of societal values, drawing upon the work of Mary Douglas, *Purity and Danger,* Jacob Neusner, *The Idea of Purity in Ancient Judaism* (Leiden: E. J. Brill, 1973); Howard Eilberg-Schwartz, *The Savage in Judaism,* 177–234. See also *Leviticus 1–16,* vol. 3 of *The Anchor Bible,* trans. and with an introduction and commentary by Jacob Milgrom (New York: Doubleday, 1991), 719–742. Milgrom also critiques Mary Douglas's treatment of Leviticus, charging that she has confused the notions of purity/impurity with holiness/secularity (21).

47. Exodus 20:23, 28:42.

48. Documentary scholarship notes extensive linguistic and substantive parallels between Ezekiel and the Holiness Code. Otto Eissfeldt, *The Old Testament,* 238.

49. I include the references to the nakedness of the land in Genesis 42:9, 12, because land is conventionally imaged as female through the Bible. Of the remaining citations, three refer to both sexes (Lev. 18:6, Deut. 23:15, and Isa. 20:4). The other term, *erom,* "male," is associated with being unsocialized or desocialized, for example, the presocial state in the Garden of Eden or the desocialized state of being stripped for slavery or captivity.

50. Rashi follows the opinion of R. Judah in Sanhedrin 54a analogizing Leviticus 18:7 to 20:11. The proposal that *ervat avikha* refers literally to homosexual relations with the

father is disputed in Sanhedrin 54a: one view holds that Leviticus 18:22 already covers such a case, the other that there is a dual penalty because of consanguinity.

51. After the rebellion was put down, the polluted concubines were confined "in living widowhood until the day they died" (2 Sam. 20:3).

52. Leviticus 18:10 does prohibit grandfather-granddaughter incest.

53. Rava, citing R. Yitzhak ben Abudimi, derives the prohibition by analogizing Leviticus 18:10 with Leviticus 18:17. The *gezerah shavah* is quoted in both B. Sanhedrin 51a and 75b and in B. Yebamot 3a. In these texts, the daughter is viewed as equally culpable. But see also M. Ketubbot 3:2, which seems to acknowledge the possibility of incest-rape. See also Ilona N. Rashkow, "Fathers and Daughters in Genesis . . . Or What Is Wrong With This Picture?" in *The New Literary Criticism and the Hebrew Bible*, ed. J. Cheryl Exum and David J. A. Clines, Journal for the Study of the Old Testament Suppl. Ser. 143 (Sheffield: JSOT Press, 1993), 250–265.

54. JPS has "let no woman lend herself to a beast to mate with it." The root RB' means "four." A passive participle of the verb means "squared." Brown, Driver, and Briggs define our verb *rb'a* as "lie stretched out," but they note that, with the exception of the difficult passage "my journey and my resting You have measured," *'orhi v'riv'i zereta* (Ps.139), the verb describes copulation: "chiefly unnatural." In this sense, the verb occurs only in Leviticus. Leviticus 18:23 and 20:16 refer to the copulation of women with animals. Leviticus 19:19 contains the only occurrence of the verb in the *hiphil*, a prohibition against causing animals to cross-breed. Brown, Driver, and Briggs suggest that this verb *rb'a* is an Aramaic form of RBTZ, "to lie stretched out." But it seems at least plausible that the verb means "to copulate crouched on all fours like an animal."

Regarding the question of address, in *The JPS Torah Commentary: Leviticus*, commentary by Baruch Levine (Philadelphia: Jewish Publication Society, 1989), Levine observes, "This is the only instance in Chapter 18 where a commandment is addressed to the woman" (123). Levine might also have noted that it is the only instance in Chapter 18 where a commandment is phrased in the jussive rather than in the masculine singular imperative. This construction is not a direct address.

55. For example: Jacob has two wives (Gen. 39). Abraham and Jacob sire children by their wives' maids (Gen. 19, 39). Samuel's father has two wives. (1 Sam. 1). David and Solomon have numerous wives. (1 Chron. 3 and 1 Kings 11).

56. Isaiah M. Gafni, "The Institution of Marriage in Rabbinic Times" in *The Jewish Family*, ed. David Kraemer (New York: Oxford University Press, 1989), 13–30. Yebamot 65b: "Raba said, 'A man may marry wives in addition to his wife, as long as he has the means to support them.'" However, Gafni maintains that polygyny was frowned upon by Palestinian Jews, influenced, perhaps, by Roman ideals of monogamy (22–23).

57. Stories relate that both Rav and Rav Naḥman, upon traveling to another city, asked "Who will be my wife for the day?" (B. Yebamot 37b). Gafni argues that this demonstrates the influence of the surrounding culture: marriage for a specified period was a known institution in Sassanian Persia, *The Jewish Family*, 23–25.

58. Mordecai Friedman, "Marriage as an Institution: Judaism Under Islam" in *The Jewish Family*, 31–45, quotation on page 39.

59. Ze'ev Falk, *Jewish Matrimonial Law in the Middle Ages* (Oxford: Oxford University Press, 1966), see chapter on monogamy.

60. Recently, some Orthodox fathers have revived the practice of contracting *erusin*, the first stage of marriage for their minor daughters, with a new twist. They deliberately keep secret the identity of the groom, to blackmail wives who obtain civil divorces into returning home. In order to marry anyone else when they grow up, these girls have to

discover the identity of their grooms and obtain divorces. "New Leverage in Divorce for Orthodox Fathers," *New York Times*, Saturday, May 27, 1995, 21–22.

61. Exodus 21:15.

62. Judith Wegner, *Woman in the Mishnah: Person or Chattel* (New York: Oxford University Press, 1988), 24. I would add that the statement in B. Kiddushin 4b that slavegirls cannot be acquired by sexual intercourse because they are not acquired for sexual purposes does not rule out the possibility of sexual use in addition to the functions for which the slave was acquired.

63. According to the Talmud, eligibility to receive the fine ends at the girl's legal maturity *(bagrut)* at age twelve and a half (B. Ketubbot 29b).

64. In Exodus 22:16, the girl's father may refuse her hand to the man who seduced her. In talmudic law, either the girl or her father may refuse either the rapist or the seducer (B. Ketubbot 39b).

65. M. Ketubbot 3:4. The ruling means that he must tolerate the woman he violated, however flawed or unattractive she may be. Jastrow defines *atzitz* as "a common earthenware vessel used for refuse." The possible repugnance of the victim regarding the rapist is not discussed. Marcus Jastrow, *Dictionary of the Targumim, Talmud Babli, Yerushalmi and Midrashic Literature* (New York: Judaica Press, 1971), s.v. *atzitz*. Hereafter cited as Jastrow, *Dictionary*.

66. In rabbinic law, the death penalty is incurred only if she is not a minor, that is, over the age of twelve years and one day.

67. Deuteronomy 22: 23–27. If she is in the town, she is considered guilty unless she was heard to cry for help.

68. Susan Estrich, *Real Rape* (Cambridge, MA: Harvard University Press, 1987); Catherine MacKinnon, *Feminism Unmodified: Discourses on Life and Law* (Cambridge, MA: Harvard University Press, 1987); Kristin Bumiller, "Fallen Angels: The Representation of Violence Against Women in Legal Culture," in *At the Boundaries of Law: Feminism and Legal Theory*, ed. Martha Albertson Fineman and Nancy Sweet Thomadsen (New York: Routledge, 1991), 95–111.

69. Andrea Dworkin, *Intercourse* (New York: Free Press, 1987), maintains that dominance and submission continue to characterize all heterosexual intercourse. This requires invalidating the intimate experience of those who disagree by accusing them of false consciousness.

70. Howard Eilberg-Schwartz, *The Savage in Judaism*, 182–185. David Biale, *Eros and the Jews*, 28–31.

71. David M. Feldman, *Marital Relations, Birth Control and Abortion in Jewish Law*, 81–105.

72. John Boswell, *Christianity, Social Tolerance, and Homosexuality* (Chicago: University of Chicago Press, 1980), 92–102. Bradley S. Artson, "Judaism and Homosexuality," *Tikkun* 3 (March/April 1988): 52–92. See also his "Gay and Lesbian Jews: A Teshuvah," submitted to the Committee on Jewish Law and Standards of the Rabbinical Assembly, March 1992 [unpublished].

73. Howard Eilberg-Schwartz, *God's Phallus* (Boston: Beacon, 1994).

74. The Talmud also distinguishes between the penetrator and the one penetrated and, therefore, must find a textual basis for reading the submissive participant into the violation. Two sources are proposed: Rabbi Ishmael proposes Deuteronomy 23:18, which forbids male cult-prostitition, whereas Rabbi Akiba proposes that both can be included in the prohibition in Leviticus 18:22 by a dual voweling of the verb "to lie" so that the active *pi'el* form *tishkav* is also read as a passive *nif'al* form *tishakev* (B. Sanhedrin 54b).

75. Robert Cover, "The Folktales of Justice: Tales of Jurisdiction," *Capital University Law Review* 14 (1985): 181.

76. Rachel Adler, "A Stumbling Block Before the Blind: Sexual Exploitation in Pastoral Counseling," *CCAR Journal* 40 (spring 1993): 13–43.

77. See, for example, Deuteronomy 21:15. "If a man has two wives, one beloved and one hated *(senua)*." The JPS translates *senua* more restrainedly as "unloved," but, the narrative of Leah suggests that the woman's experience is less temperate. Leah's names for her first three sons all refer to the pain of rejection: Genesis 29:31 and 29:33. "She named him Reuben, for, as she said, 'Now God has seen (R'H) my anguish and now my man will love me'"; and Genesis 29:33: "She said, 'God has heard *(sham'a)* that I am hated *(senu'ah)* and has given me this child,' and she called him Simeon."

78. I have translated as literally as possible to emphasize the reiterations of the words love and hate in the Hebrew sentence.

79. Marvin H. Pope, *Song of Songs,* vol. 7C of *The Anchor Bible,* (New York: Doubleday, 1977), 40–89. Henceforth cited as Pope, *Song of Songs.* See also Harold Fisch, *Poetry With a Purpose: Biblical Poetics and Interpretation* (Bloomington: Indiana University Press, 1988), 148–149.

80. See T. Drorah Setel, "Prophets and Pornography: Female Sexual Imagery in Hosea," in *Feminist Interpretation of the Bible,* ed. Letty Russell (Philadelphia: Westminster Press, 1985), 86–95.

81. Pardes, *Countertraditions in the Bible,* 124.

82. M. Yadaim 3:5; Megillah 7a.

83. We do not know any specifics about Rabbi Akiba's interpretation. However, allegorical interpretations of the song are pervasive in talmudic literature. The Targum's interpretation is also allegorical. Pope, *Song of Songs,* 93–101.

84. A partial list would include Marcia Falk, *Love Lyrics from the Bible: A Translation and Literary Study of the Song of Songs,* Bible and Literature Series, ed. David Gunn (Sheffield: Almond Press, 1982); Pardes, *Countertraditions in the Bible*; Trible, "Love's Lyrics Redeemed," in *God and the Rhetoric of Sexuality,* 144–165; Juanita J. Weems, "Song of Songs," in *Women's Bible Commentary,* ed. Carol A. Newsom and Sharon H. Ringe (London and Louisville, KY: Westminster/John Knox Press, 1992), 156–160.

85. Trible, *God and the Rhetoric of Sexuality,* 144–165.

86. Ibid., 161.

87. Falk, *Love Lyrics from the Bible,* 87.

88. For example: Song of Songs 2:4, the lovers at the winehall, 3:6–11, depicting King Solomon's wedding procession, and 7:1, the Shulamite at the Maḥanaim dance.

89. This is my translation, a clumsy attempt to solve a translator's dilemma. Literally, the preposition *l'* of *ani l'dodi* indicates many kinds of relation other than possession: membership as in a tribe or family, favor or support, tendency or obligation. Although I am in complete agreement with Falk's refusal to translate *ani l'dodi* to indicate a passive state of possession, i.e., "I am my beloved's," her translation, "turning to him who meets me with desire," sacrifices the inversion of Genesis 3 that I particularly wish to preserve. Falk, *Love Lyrics from the Bible,* 118–119. Bloch and Bloch also note the reversal of the Genesis 3 reference, but their rendering of 7:11, "I am my lover's, / he longs for me, / only for me" does not convey the allusion. Ariel Bloch and Chana Bloch, *The Songs of Songs: A New Translation* (New York: Random House, 1995), 103, 207–208.

90. In English it is particularly difficult to convey the subjectivity of both partners. As Luce Irigaray observes, conventionally in English the term "lover" is assigned to the

245

male and the term "beloved" to the female, making her an object of desire rather than a desirer herself. Luce Irigaray, "Questions to Emmanuel Levinas on the Divinity of Love," trans. Margaret Whitford, in *Rereading Levinas*, ed. Robert Bernascon and Simon Critchley (Bloomington: Indiana University Press, 1991), 115–116. Luce Irigaray, "The Fecundity of the Caress," trans. Carolyn Burke, in *Face to Face with Levinas*, ed. Richard Cohen (Albany: State University of New York Press, 1986), 231–256.

91. The technical term for this catalogue, drawn from the conventions of modern Arabic poetry, is *wasf.* See Marcia Falk's chapter, "The Wasf," in *Love Lyrics from the Bible,* 81–87.

92. This point is made by Trible, Pardes, and Landy.

93. In Avodah Zarah 2:5, Rabbi Yehudah and Rabbi Yishmael debate whether "Your love is better than wine" (Song of Songs 1:2) is more appropriately voweled as a masculine or feminine possessive.

94. Falk also makes this point repeatedly, passim. To give just a few examples, 8:11–12, "Solomon had a vineyard / in Baal-hamon. / He had to post guards in the vineyard: A man would give for its fruit / A thousand pieces of silver. / I have my very own vineyard: You may have the thousand, O Solomon, and the guards of the fruit two hundred" could be assigned either to the woman or to the man. In 1:6, she has complained of her brothers, "They made me guard the vineyards. My own vineyard I did not guard." It would be symmetrical, because the brothers' threatening voices are heard, in 8:8–9, for the sister to claim her power to confer or withhold her own vineyard. However, one could also make a case for assigning 8:11 to the male lover, on analogy with 4:12 and 13 or 5:2 where she is imaged as his orchard and his garden. This would be particularly plausible if the subsequent verse, 8:13, is assigned to him. Similarly, 2:15, "let us catch the foxes, the little foxes that ruin the vineyards, for our vineyard is in blossom" could be assigned to the male lover who has been speaking, to the two lovers in chorus, or, if one viewed the Song as a continuous performance piece rather than as a collection of disparate lyrics, to the daughters of Jerusalem or to the woman's suspicious brothers. The lyrics about the equipage of Solomon could be assigned to the male lover or to the daughters of Jerusalem.

95. My more literal translation emphasizes the peekaboo game. JPS has "one [glance] of your eyes," and Falk "one flash of your eyes."

96. Shula Abramsky, *"Ha-Ishah ha-Nishkefet ba-Halon," Bet Mikra* 80, no. 2 (January/March 1980):114–124. In *Telling Queen Michal's Story: An Experiment in Comparative Interpretation,* ed. David J. A. Clines and Tamara C. Eskenazi, Journal for the Study of the Old Testament Suppl. Ser. 119 (Sheffield, JSOT Press, 1991). The male lover, like Abimelekh, who catches Isaac and Rebecca in bed, is on the outside looking in. The women (Sisera's mother, Michal, Jezebel) are all on the inside looking out.

97. Pardes, *Countertraditions in the Bible,* 129–143.

98. Falk, *Love Lyrics from the Bible,* poems 1, 13, corresponding to Song of Songs 1:2.

99. Francis Landy, *Paradoxes of Paradise: Identity and Difference in the Song of Songs* (Sheffield: Almond Press, 1983).

100. Sigmund Freud, *A General Introduction to Psychoanalysis,* rev. ed., trans. Joan Riviere (New York: Liveright, 1935), lectures 20 and 21. Most feminist discussions of polymorphous sexuality are ultimately indebted to the discussion in Herbert Marcuse, *Eros and Civilization: A Philosophical Inquiry into Freud* (Boston: Beacon, 1966). Marcuse envisions polymorphous sexuality as a transformative Eros that enhances rather than undermining civilization. See also Audre Lorde, "Uses of the Erotic: The

Erotic as Power," in *Sister Outsider* (Trumansburg, NY: Crossing Press, 1984), 53–59.

101. Benjamin, *The Bonds of Love*, 130.
102. Michael Fox, "Love, Passion and Perception in Israelite and Egyptian Love Poetry," *Journal of Biblical Literature* 102/2 (1983): 219–228.
103. Pardes, *Countertraditions in the Bible*, 126.
104. For an introduction to the literature of this allegory, see *Shir haShirim*, compiled by Rabbi Meir Zlotowitz, allegorical translation and overview by Rabbi Nosson Scherman, the ArtScroll Tanach commentary (Brooklyn, NY: Mesora Publications, 1979).
105. Eilberg-Schwartz, *God's Phallus*. See esp. 163–196.
106. Rachel Adler, "The Virgin in the Brothel and Other Anomalies: Character and Context in the Legend of Beruriah," *Tikkun* 3 (November/December 1988): 28–32, 102–105. Footnoted and expanded version in *Vox Benedictina* 7 (January 1990): 7–29.
107. Daniel Boyarin, "The Great Fat Massacre: Sex, Death and the Grotesque Body in the Talmud," in *People of the Body: Jews and Judaism from an Embodied Perspective*, ed. Howard Eilberg-Schwartz (Albany: State University of New York Press, 1992), 69–100. Boyarin points out that the relationship between Resh Lakish and Rabbi Yoḥanan inverts the Greek pairing of dominant virile *hoplites* and effeminate young *ephebe*.
108. Emmanuel Levinas, *Ethics and Infinity: Conversations with Phillippe Nemo*, trans. Richard A. Cohen (Pittsburgh: Duquesne University Press, 1985).
109. Landy links the voices of the birds of spring and the voices of the lovers themselves: *Paradoxes of Paradise*, 43.
110. Ibid., 178.
111. Ibid., 179.
112. Regarding *kumaz*, which the JPS translates as "pendants," it notes "meaning of Hebrew uncertain."
113. Jastrow's *Dictionary* lists as one of the meanings of BYT "euphemism for pudenda" (168), which seems more appropriate contextually than his translation of *beit ha-rehem* under RḤM, "sides of the womb" (1467).
114. Jastrow's *Dictionary* lists both meanings, and as I have previously established, laughter and the erotic or pornographic are related.
115. Jastrow, *Dictionary*. See entries under ZIMA, ZMM, ZUM, ZHM.
116. In Job 33:20.
117. See Isaiah 55:12. Regarding God playing with Leviathan, see Psalm 104:26 and B. Avodah Zarah 3b.
118. Mieke Bal, *Death and Dissymmetry: The Politics of Coherence in the Book of Judges* (Chicago: University of Chicago Press, 1989).
119. Ilona N. Rashkow, *Upon the Dark Places: Anti-Semitism and Sexism in English Renaissance Biblical Translation*, Bible and Literature Series 28 (Sheffield: Sheffield Academic Press, 1990), 141. Rashkow notes this etymology but argues that the Bible reserves this term for widows who are destitute, and the absence of the term from the Book of Ruth indicates that Naomi and Ruth do not fit into this category. But this is not tenable. Neither Tamar living in widowhood in her father's house (Gen. 38:11) nor the sequestered concubines of David violated by Absalom (2 Sam. 20:3) are destitute. That the High Priest is forbidden to marry a widow, a divorcee, or a prostitute (Lev. 21:14, Ezek. 44:22) is best explained as a stipulation about the woman's marital and sexual, rather than economic, status.
120. Moshe Greenberg, *Biblical Prose Prayer as a Window to the Popular Religion of Ancient Israel* (Berkeley: University of California Press, 1983), 30–37.
121. Ibid., 35.

122. JPS translates "taken note of his people." But this misses the connotation of making good on a promise, as in Genesis 21:1: "YHWH *pakad* fulfilled his promise to Sarah, as he had said."

123. Danna Nolan Fewell and David M. Gunn, "'A Son Is Born to Naomi': Literary Allusions and Interpretation in the Book of Ruth," *Journal for the Study of the Old Testament* 40 (1988): 99–108.

124. The biblical root 'GN is a *hapax legomenon*, meaning "to be left fettered or imprisoned." In rabbinic Hebrew, it acquires the specific legal meaning "to be tied to a husband who has deserted." Naomi seems to be saying that the widows would be barred from marriage until the new sons would be old enough to assume the levirate obligation. Unless she is proposing her own hypothetical redemption by an eligible levir miraculously transported to Moab, Naomi is making the dubious assumption that her sons by another man would be eligible to redeem the wives and property of her sons by Elimelekh. This passage illustrates the difficulty of extrapolating Israelite inheritance law from the Book of Ruth.

125. Danna Nolan Fewell and David M. Gunn, "'A Son Is Born to Naomi'," 104. Phyllis Trible also notes Naomi's failure to acknowledge Ruth but without condemning her: *God and the Rhetoric of Sexuality*, 174.

126. Trible, *God and the Rhetoric of Sexuality*, 176.

127. Rashkow's explanation that Ruth has not been gleaning but standing around waiting for Boaz's permission to collect grain from among the sheaves rather than following the reapers seems implausible. The servant seems to be saying that she has been on her feet working. Rashkow's Ruth, plotting to gain a landowner's favor, standing about demanding special privileges, and fawning exaggeratedly seems unattractively manipulative. Boaz's offer of access to the water jars is not necessarily a trifling concession. The water, after all, did not gush out of a faucet. The more drinkers, the more energy has to be transferred from reaping to pumping. *Upon the Dark Places*, 146–151.

128. Peter W. Coxon, "Was Naomi a Scold? A Response to Fewell and Gunn," *Journal for the Study of the Old Testament* 45 (1989): 28.

129. Pardes, *Countertraditions in the Bible*, 114.

130. Trible, *God and the Rhetoric of Sexuality*, 177.

131. For a summary of scholarship on the term *ivri*, see Speiser, *Genesis*, 102–103. See also Nahum Sarna, *The JPS Torah Commentary: Genesis* (Philadelphia: Jewish Publication Society, 1989), 377–379. I consider the moral implications of the term *ivri* more fully in Adler, "A Question of Boundaries," 465–471.

132. Marge Piercy, "The Book of Ruth and Naomi," in *Tikkun Anthology*, 471.

133. JPS Ezekiel 16:8n.

134. *Midrash Rabba Ruth*, 3rd ed., trans. L. Rabinowitz (London: Soncino Press, 1983), 2:14.

135. Carole Pateman, *The Sexual Contract* (Stanford: Stanford University Press, 1988), argues that this misrepresentation is a primary characteristic of contracts and serves in particular to disguise the operation of patriarchal sex-right in contracts made by men with women qua women, such as marriage or prostitution.

136. Information in this paragraph is based on the following sources: George E. Mendenhall, "Covenant," in *Interpreters' Dictionary of the Bible* (Nashville, TN: Abington, 1962); Moshe Weinfeld, "Covenant," in *Encyclopedia Judaica* (Jerusalem, Keter, 1972); George E. Mendenhall, "Covenant Forms in Israelite Tradition," in *The Biblical Archeologist Reader 3*, ed. Edward F. Campbell and David Noel Freedman (New York: Anchor Books, 1970), 25–53.

137. Elaine J. Adler, "The Background for the Metaphor of Covenant as Marriage in the Hebrew Bible," Ph.D. Dissertation, University of California at Berkeley, 1989.

138. A conjectured allusion to such a ritual is discussed in note 167.
139. These laws are explained in detail in Chapter 5.
140. Elaine J. Adler argues convincingly that the marriage metaphor is also found latently in the Pentateuch itself, "The Background for the Metaphor of Covenant as Marriage in the Hebrew Bible," 93–111.
141. See, for example, Setel, "Prophets and Pornography;" and Gracia Fay Ellwood, *Batter My Heart* (Wallingford, PA: Pendle Hill Pamphlets, 1988).
142. David Blumenthal, *Facing the Abusing God: A Theology of Protest* (Louisville, KY: Westminster/John Knox Press, 1993), 245–246.
143. I use the masculine pronoun because David Blumenthal images the abusing God as masculine—a battering husband or abusive father. See my "Response to *Facing the Abusing God*," paper delivered at the Association for Jewish Studies Conference, December, 1994 [unpublished].
144. Carol P. Christ, *The Laughter of Aphrodite* (San Francisco: Harper and Row, 1987), draws precisely this conclusion. See especially 61–63, 73–81.
145. H. W. Wolff, *Hosea: A Commentary on the Book of the Prophet Hosea*, trans. G. Stansell Hermaneia (Philadelphia: Fortress, 1974), 17.
146. It is impossible to convey my meaning in the appropriate academic "language-about" sexuality. I have had to violate this code.
147. H. H. Rowley, "The Marriage of Hosea," in *Men of God: Studies in Old Testament History and Prophecy* (London: Thomas Nelson, 1963), 66–69.
148. Renita J. Weems, "Gomer: Victim of Violence or Victim of Metaphor?" *Semeia* 47 (1989): 87–104.
149. Elaine J. Adler, "The Background for the Metaphor of Covenant as Marriage in the Hebrew Bible," 383.
150. Regina M. Schwartz, "Nations and Nationalism: Adultery in the House of David," *Critical Inquiry* 19 (autumn 1992): 131–150. See also Regina M. Schwartz, "Adultery in the House of David: The Metanarrative of Biblical Scholarship and the Narratives of the Bible," in *Poststructuralism as Exegesis in Semeia* 54, ed. David Jobling and Steven D. Moore (Atlanta: Scholars Press, 1991), 35–55.
151. Regina M. Schwartz, "Nations and Nationalism," 149.
152. Ibid.
153. Elaine J. Adler, "The Background for the Metaphor of Covenant as Marriage in the Hebrew Bible," 383, argues that the marriage metaphor does not endow YHWH with an erotic nature, but this is clearly untenable. See, for example Hosea 2:16, in which God plans to seduce Israel and coax her to respond.
154. See Chapter 5 for a discussion of the various connotations of *ba'al*.
155. Carole Pateman argues that property right over women is also foundational in liberal political theory, existing even in the state of nature. It is men who enter into the social contract because, by that means, men's natural right over women is transformed into a right in civil society. *The Sexual Contract*, 1–18.
156. The marriage metaphor is not the context of this discussion, perhaps because some degree of coercion of brides was not uncommon, and indeed, fathers, in contrast to mothers or brothers, have the prerogative of giving minor daughters in marriage without their consent (M. Yebamot 13:2).
157. *Moda'ah raba l'oreita.* A *moda'ah* is an advance notice in the presence of witnesses that a party to an agreement is being compelled to sign under duress. The evidence of the *moda'ah* invalidates the contract. Adin Steinsaltz, *The Talmud: A Reference Guide* (New York: Random House, 1989), *Moda'ah*, 211.
158. Rava's prooftext for this contention is Esther 9:27: *kimu v'kiblu ha-yehudim*, "the

Jews upheld and accepted." Two terms, "upheld" and "accepted," are used to indicate that the Jews now voluntarily upheld what they had previously accepted only under coercion.

159. Family-systems theory views affairs as attempts to relieve intolerable stress in the dyad by forming a triangle to redistribute the stress; hence Carl Whittaker's comment, "An affair is an amateur's attempt at therapy."

160. Jeremiah explicitly acknowledges the legal problem in Jeremiah 3:1: "If a man divorces his wife, and she leaves him and marries another man, can he ever go back to her? Would not such a land be defiled? Now you have whored with many lovers: can you return to me?" R. Yohanan, quoting this text in B. Yoma 86b, observes, "Great is *teshuvah* (repentance/return), for it supersedes a prohibitory Torah commandment." If the rabbis had not conferred upon *teshuvah* this radical power to supersede law, they would have no response to the Christian polemic that the Jews had been discarded as a chosen people because of their sins.

161. *Hosea,* vol. 24 of *The Anchor Bible,* vol. 24, trans. and with an introduction and commentary by F. I. Anderson and David N. Friedman (New York: Doubleday, 1980). Weems, 97n, suggests that the pronouncement cannot be a divorce formula because it is ineffective, but this presumes that law is automatically efficacious.

162. The main source for the establishment of this principle is B. Berakhot 53–54. For an insightful discussion of law-violating or law-abrogating powers that the rabbinic system accords its jurists, see Joel Roth, *The Halakhic Process,* 169–204.

163. Robert Cover, "The Supreme Court 1986 Term: Forward: *Nomos* and Narrative," *Harvard Law Review* 97, no. 4 (1983): 34–35.

164. Tamara Eskenazi. "Strategies for Restoration: Hosea 1, 2, 3" [unpublished paper].

165. The *hiphil* or causative form of the verb God uses in Hosea 2:16 is also used in the punning blessing to Noah's son Japhet in Genesis 9:27: *yaft elohim l'yefet,* "may God make wide for Japhet," i.e., give him a spacious inheritance. Here, PTH is used exactly like the more common root meaning width, RHB. There, its moral linkages are with freedom and relief, while narrowness is associated with being distressed or trapped. For example, a literal translation of Psalm 118:5 would read: "From the narrow place *(met-zar)* I called upon God. He answered me with spaciousness *(merhavya)*." Genesis 9:27 indicates the blessing of width with a rare usage of PTH rather than the common RHB in order to make the pun with the name Japhet *(Yefet).* Granted, the ameliorative uses of the root are outnumbered by the pejorative ones. My point is that, because there are occasions when the term is used in a good sense, that possibility cannot be ruled out if the context will support it. To give some other instances, Brown, Driver, and Briggs's conjecture that *poteh* in Job 5:2 means open-minded seems dubious, given its pejorative context, but it is credible that, in Psalm 116:6, *shomer pet'aim YHWH* is probably a tender reference to God's protection of the innocent or the guileless rather than a contemptuous reference to lucky simpletons.

166. The root PTH has to do with opening. JPS translates *petah tikva* as "a plowland of hope," connecting *petah* with *pitah* "to plow," citing Isaiah 28:24. This seems less probable than the common term *petah* meaning "doorway." The image of "doorway" also allows for more female initiative, as, I will argue, the chapter goes on to reinforce. Whereas, as Tamara Eskenazi has pointed out to me, plowing is an agricultural image for sexuality and fertility, it portrays a male doer and a female "done-to," whereas a doorway is a place of meetings.

167. Mordecai Friedman, "Israel's Response in Hosea 2:17b: 'You are My Husband'," *Journal of Biblical Literature* 99/2 (1980): 199–204. If there had been a biblical text explicitly depicting the ceremony Friedman describes, it would have constituted a seri-

ous challenge to the Babylonian rabbinic tradition's definition of marriage as unilateral acquisition and hence also challenged the male's unilateral right to divorce. This is discussed further in Chapter 5.

168. It euphemizes the verse to "I will take you to my worship and you will not bow down any more to the abominations of the gentiles" (Hosea 2:18, loc. cit.).

169. The only verses where females are the subject of YD', "to know," in its sexual sense are a few in which it is asserted that they are virgins and thus have not known any man. See Genesis 19:6 and Judges 11:39. Although he acknowledges the analogy with sexual union indicated by "you shall know," Abraham J. Heschel seeks to distance the knowledge of God in Hosea from the sexual. Indeed, he argues that, even where the term is sexual, as in "Adam knew Eve his wife and she conceived," a more accurate translation would be "Adam attached himself to Eve his wife," meaning that they had a total relationship in which emotional experiences were shared. Why the only noteworthy consequence of this reciprocal sympathy mentioned by such texts should be conception, Heschel does not explain. Abraham J. Heschel, *The Prophets* (Philadelphia: Jewish Publication Society, 1962), 57–60.

170. This is not the only instance of gender reversal in the covenant-marriage metaphor. See Malachi 2:14: "Because YHWH is a witness between you and the wife of your youth with whom you have broken faith although she is your partner *(haveratkha)* and your covenanted spouse *(eshet britkha)*." Jacob Milgrom, *Cult and Conscience: The Asham and the Priestly Doctrine of Repentance* (Leiden: E. J. Brill, 1976), 134, argues that covenant *(brit)* here is "a literary metaphor with no legal value" (134) because it is the husband who violates the covenant in Malachi, whereas legally it is the wife who is subject to the laws of adultery. This view tried to code the covenant marriage-metaphor by gender. What is so interesting here is that God is the wife, not the husband, in this metaphor. In this differently gendered variation, God is compared with the wife who has been put aside for the foreign woman.

171. Roberto Mangabeira Unger, *Passion: An Essay on Personality,* 7–10.

Chapter 5

1. For example, Genesis 20:3, 24: 48, 28:6; Exodus 2:61, 6:25; Leviticus 21:7; Numbers 12:1; Deuteronomy 21:11, 22:13–14, 24:4, 25:8; 1 Samuel 25:39–40; 2 Samuel 12:9; 1 Kings 7:8; Ezekiel 16:61; Hosea 1:2; Nehemiah 6:18, 7:63.

2. Ze'ev Falk, *Jewish Matrimonial Law in the Middle Ages* (Oxford: Oxford University Press, 1966), translates *erusin* as "inchoate marriage," rather than "betrothal," because, unlike an engagement or promise to marry, *erusin* marks the woman as appropriated by a particular man (38). Although I agree that "betrothal" is a misleading term, "inchoate marriage" is rather a mouthful. I prefer to term this initial stage of marriage "espousal."

3. For instance, the archers in Genesis 49:23 are called *ba'alei ḥizim,* masters of arrows. Other usages include creditor (Deut. 15:2) and citizen of a city (Josh. 24:11; Jud. 9:2).

4. Exodus 22:7.

5. Exodus 21:34.

6. Exodus 21:28.

7. Exodus 21:4.

8. Elaine J. Adler, "The Background for the Metaphor of Covenant as Marriage in the Hebrew Bible." Ph.D. dissertation, University of California at Berkeley, 1989.

9. For example, Jeremiah 2:32, 7:34, 33:11; Isaiah 49:18; 61:10, 62:4–5; Joel 2:16.

10. Falk, *Jewish Matrimonial Law in the Middle Ages*, 42.
11. Judith Wegner, *Woman in the Mishnah: Person or Chattel* (New York: Oxford Unversity Press, 1988), 6–8; 175–180.
12. There are indeed halakhic limitations on a husband's use of a wife's sexuality. However, these limitations are determined by male legislators and are enforced at the discretion of male judiciaries. See, for example, Mordechai Frishtik, "Physical and Sexual Violence by Husbands as a Reason for Imposing a Divorce in Jewish Law," *Jewish Law Annual*, vol. 10. The Institute of Jewish Law, Boston University School of Law (Chur: Harwood, 1991).
13. Jacob Neusner, *A History of the Mishnaic Law of Women: The Mishnaic System of Women, Part 5* (Leiden: E. J. Brill, 1980), 268.
14. Ibid., 266. Wegner, *Woman in the Mishnah: Person or Chattel*, 10–39. As Wegner observes, it is the minor who is most like chattel. Her consent to marriage is unnecessary, and she can even be sold as a slave. In contrast, Wegner declares that the emancipated daughter *(bogeret)* who has total personal autonomy is "largely hypothetical," because most girls were married off at puberty (14–15). Goitein, *A Mediterranean Society: The Jewish Communities of the Arab World as Portrayed in the Documents of the Cairo Geniza*, 4 vols. (Berkeley: University of California Press, 1978), vol. 3, *Family*. Goitein claims that, in these sixth- through thirteenth-century documents, marriage of children under the age of puberty was rare. However, even the consent of legally adult young women was often pro forma:

    > near absolute paternal authority . . . was operative with regard to the mature virgin who was legally independent. There must have been countless cases in which the teenaged girl was shocked when her father communicated his choice to her. But I have searched the *Geniza* in vain for a complaint lodged by a daughter against a Jewish court, a Muslim authority or even only a relative. A father's decision was like a decree of God (vol. 3, 79).

15. James Joyce, *Ulysses*, 9th ed. (New York: Random House, 1961), 783.
16. B. Kiddushin 2a.
17. This deed should not be confused with the *ketubbah* or marriage contract, which merely stipulates expectations for the conduct of the marriage.
18. B. Kiddushin 2b Tosafot, at D'asar.
19. Eugene Mihaly, *Teshuvot on Jewish Marriage with Special Reference to Reform Rabbis and Mixed Marriage* (Cincinnati: Hebrew Union College, 1985), 36–38, explicitly identifies *kiddushin* as a metaphor. However, Mihaly conflates metaphor with analogy, depriving it of polysemy and dynamic capacities.
20. The continuing presence of acquisition in the sacred ceremony is illustrated by a note of Ze'ev Falk on the seventh-century Nestorians whose church espousal ceremony parallels *kiddushin*. In their ceremony, the bridegroom gave a ring, the couple drank from a cup of wine that had been blessed, and a marriage bond was declared. Significantly, the ceremony was called *mekhiruta*, sale or property conveyance. Falk, *Jewish Matrimonial Law in the Middle Ages*, 68n.
21. Adin Steinsaltz estimates the value of a *peruta*, the academy of Hillel's minimum, at 24 milligrams of silver, or one United States cent. Adin Steinsaltz, *The Talmud: The Steinsaltz Edition: A Reference Guide*, trans. Israel V. Berman (New York: Random House, 1989), 291.
22. Two sums were promised by the husband: the erstwhile bride price *(mohar)*, now the *ketubbah* money, and the *tosefet* or addition, which replaced the *mattan* or bride gift.
23. This is more the case in the talmudic period than in the medieval period. Talmudic sources emphasize the sum in the *ketubbah* as a debt that will fall due at some later

time and that, in the *ketubbah*, the husband pledges to mortgage all his possessions to redeem. However, the Cairo *Geniza* documents indicate that a bridegroom's wedding gift *(mohar)* included a substantial sum that had to be delivered up front. Goitein, *A Mediterranean Society*, vol. 3, 118–123.

24. Falk, *Jewish Matrimonial Law in the Middle Ages*, 39.

25. Elliot N. Dorf and Arthur Rosett, *A Living Tree: The Roots and Growth of Jewish Law* (Albany: State University of New York Press, 1988), suggest that "the rabbis went out of their way to justify that form of betrothal [money] because money was used to bind other contracts (at least morally) and therefore it should be applicable to the contract of betrothal too" (450). They add, "Jewish marriages . . . obviously include love, passion, hopes, and all the other emotional components of marriage, but Judaism assumes that those will follow if the material conditions are straightened out first" (451). The authors seem oblivious, however, to the possible impact of economic power allocations on "emotional components." See also Kopel Kahana, *Theory of Marriage in Jewish Law* (Leiden: E. J. Brill, 1966), 30–33, and Maurice Lamm, *The Jewish Way in Love and Marriage* (San Francisco: Harper and Row, 1980).

26. Kopel Kahana, *Theory of Marriage in Jewish Law.* Its explanation is tautological: "Words may seem the same, but the meaning is different. We may use the same terminology in two institutions, but the concepts of the underlying ideas may be entirely diverse. In a figure of speech we say one acquires property, and also one acquires a wife. In the first it is acquiring ownership; in the second it is an act of marriage" (33).

27. As I explain later in the chapter, mutual exchange is viewed as a swap; that is, if I give you a dollar bill, and then you give me a dollar bill, then nothing has happened because the second transaction canceled out the first one.

28. According to Maimonides, the acquisition of women before witnesses is a positive commandment. It replaces a primitive pre-Sinaitic form of marriage that relied solely upon mutual consent. *Hilkhot Ishut* 1:1, Mishneh Torah

29. Polygyny was banned by Ashkenazic authorities during the eleventh century C.E. It would appear that pressure and disapproval from the church and from the governments of lands where Jews resided contributed to this decision, combined with increasing resistance from Jewish women to the practice. See Falk, *Jewish Matrimonial Law in the Middle Ages,* chap. 5.

30. Lamm, *The Jewish Way in Love and Marriage*, 150.

31. These are discussed in Chapter 4.

32. Ketubbot 7a; "Marriage Ceremony," Birnbaum *Siddur*, 753.

33. In the rabbinic period, a *huppah* was a decorated tent into which the bridegroom brought the bride: B. Baba Batra 146a; B. Kiddushin 50a. The portable bridal canopy came into use in Renaissance Europe and, according to Joseph Gutman, was borrowed from Church ritual. Joseph Gutman, "Jewish Medieval Marriage Customs in Art: Creativity and Adaptation," in *The Jewish Family*, ed. David Kraemer (New York: Oxford University Press, 1989), 47–62.

34. Kiddushin 12b.

35. Rachel Biale, *Women and Jewish Law* (New York: Schocken, 1984), 53–59.

36. Isaiah M. Gafni, "The Institution of Marriage in Rabbinic Times," in *The Jewish Family*, 14–16.

37. B. Yebamot 65b.

38. Gafni, "The Institution of Marriage in Rabbinic Times," 14. However, Lawrence A. Hoffman, *The Canonization of the Synagogue Service* (Notre Dame, IN: University of Notre Dame Press, 1989), 140–144, suggests that Hai Gaon's objection to the ending *(hatima), mekadesh Yisrael al y'dei huppah v'kiddushin*, "who sanctifies Israel by

means of *huppah* and *kiddushin*," defends the halakhic insistence that *kiddushin (erusin)* effectuates marriage independent of and prior to consummation, a point disputed by the Karaites. He argues that the word "this" *(kakh)* in Hai Gaon's statement, "the sanctity of Israel is not dependent upon this," refers specifically to *huppah*. This reading is less persuasive than Gafni's, however. Had Hai objected to only one element of the blessing's compound predicate, would he not have named that element in the interests of clarity?

39. Martha T. Roth, *Babylonian Marriage Agreements 7th–3rd Centuries B.C.* Alter Orient und Altes Testament. Veröffentlichungen zur Kultur und Geschichte des Aten Orients und des Altes Testament, Band 222 (Kevelaer: Butzon & Bercker; Neukirchen-Vluyn: Neukirchener Verlag, 1989), see especially 24–27.

40. Tal Ilan, "Premarital Cohabitation in Ancient Judea: The Evidence of the Babatha Archive and the Mishnah (Ketubbot 1.4)," *Harvard Theological Review* 86 (1993): 247–262.

41. For an account of the discovery and contents of this archive, see Yigael Yadin, *Bar Kokhba* (New York: Random House, 1971), 222–253. This source contains quotations from, but not transcriptions of, the documents. Exact transcriptions are found in Naphtali Lewis, ed., *The Documents from the Bar Kokhba Period in the Cave of Letters*, vol. 1 (Jerusalem: Israel Exploration Society, 1989), 130–133.

42. For example, see B. Berakhot 4b, where a *baraita* attempting to establish the evening service as mandatory rather than optional concludes, "And all who violate the words of the rabbis deserve to die."

43. Mordecai Friedman, *Jewish Marriage in Palestine*, 2 vols. (Tel Aviv: Jewish Theological Seminary, 1980).

44. Goitein, *A Mediterranean Society*, vol. 1, introduction. For those unfamiliar with the term, a *geniza* is a document morgue. One of the richest ever discovered, the Cairo *Geniza* contains a variety of court records on business, debts, loans, sales, marriage, and family matters from the Jews of medieval Old Cairo.

45. Friedman, *Jewish Marriage in Palestine*, vol. 1, 19.

46. The following discussion summarizes material from Mordecai Friedman, *Jewish Marriage in Palestine*, vol. 1, chap. 5.

47. Friedman, *Jewish Marriage in Palestine*, vol. 2, document no. 20:6, 212–217.

48. Friedman, "The Ethics of Medieval Jewish Marriage," in *Religion in a Religious Age*, ed. S. D. Goitein (Cambridge, MA: Association for Jewish Studies, 1974), 83–97, see especially 85.

49. Friedman, *Jewish Marriage in Palestine*, vol. 1, 19–30.

50. This is often translated "the bridegrooms' blessing," or "the blessing of bridegrooms." But the blessings were never recited by the bridegroom, and, as two blessings explicitly state, they refer both to the bridegroom and to the bride. However, Gesenius notes (124a), that the plural form in Hebrew may be used to indicate an abstract noun of the sort that in English usually ends in y, ness, hood, or ship. Because this noun qualifies "blessing," I have translated it with an adjective, as "bridal blessing." E. Kautzsch, ed., *Gesenius' Hebrew Grammar*, 2nd ed., trans. A. E. Cowley Coxford (Oxford: Clarendon Press, 1910), No. 124a.

51. Hoffman, *Canonization of the Synagogue Service*, 147.

52. Hebrew blessings characteristically address God in the second person and then use the third-person masculine for the appositive clause. I have used second person throughout.

53. The translation of this blessing presents special difficulties, which I discuss later.

54. I have followed Jules Harlow's translation of the seventh blessing (*Siddur Sim*

Shalom, 773), with some divergences. I have translated *ditzah* as dance, following Jastrow's definition of the Aramaic verb *dutz.* I have also translated *ḥuppah* as bridal chamber rather than bridal canopy, because canopies did not begin to be used until the medieval period. I have not distinguished between *sos* and *sameh* because the meanings seem to be interchangeable.

55. The signatures or eulogies of blessings six and seven vary slightly. The first reads "bridegroom *and* bride," whereas the second most literally is "bridegroom *with* the bride."

56. The rules stipulate that only the first blessing in a series should open with the complete *berakhah* formula. Strung onto this opening blessing, the remainder require only the short form of the blessing, the *ḥatima,* or eulogy, to conclude. Rashi and Tosafot (at Ketubbot 8a) offer various post-facto explanations to justify these irregularities.

57. Tosafot at B. Ketubbot 8a argues that the purpose of the structural anomaly is to maintain the distinctness of these two *berakhot.*

58. Each consists of an infinitive absolute followed by a jussive: *sos tasis,* may she exult, and *sameaḥ tesamaḥ,* may you cause [them] to be joyful.

59. A variant text found in a talmudic manuscript signs the sixth blessing "Blessed are You who gladden Your people and build Jerusalem." This variant signature, which also appears in the prayerbook of Saadia Gaon, may represent a Palestinian custom. Hoffman, *The Canonization of the Synagogue Service,* 145.

60. I have used my own more literal translation, "the whole earth is full of his glory," rather than the JPS Tanakh, "His presence fills all the earth," to underline parallels with the wedding blessing.

61. Hoffman, *The Canonization of the Synagogue Service,* 62.

62. Joseph B. Soloveitchik and Abraham R. Bestin "As A Bridegroom with His Bride," in *Man of Faith in the Modern World: Reflections of the Rav,* 2 vols. (Hoboken, NJ: Ktav, 1989). Soloveitchik observes that, structurally, the third blessing resembles both *birkot ha-nehenin,* blessings for enjoyment, and blessings for the performance of a mitzvah, vol. 2, 57.

63. For *tavnit* meaning an idolatrous representation, see Deuteronomy 4:16–18, Isaiah 44:13, Psalms 106:20.

64. Other references include the altar at Shilo (Joshua 22:28) and the Damascus altar replicated by King Ahaz (2 Kings 16:10).

65. Birnbaum, *Siddur,* 753.

66. Jastrow, see entry for *binyan,* p. 177.

67. See Rashi in reference to, Ketubbot 8a *vhitkin,* as well as Maharsha and R. Nissim. Ritba suggests that the first phrase, "who shaped *adam* in his image," refers to man, and "in his image patterned after his likeness" refers to woman who is, consequently, a copy of a copy. Meiri also identifies the third blessing with the making of Adam and the fourth with Eve. Menahem ben Shlomo ha-Meiri, *Bet ha-Beḥira Al Masekhet Berakhot,* ed. Avraham Sofer (Jerusalem: n.p., 1968), 38.

68. The same pericope with minor variations occurs in B. Berakhot 61a and B. Eruvin 18a. Reference is made to the pericope and its content in B. Ketubbot 8a with regard to the fourth wedding blessing.

69. The association of Genesis 1:27 with an original androgenous *adam* is a Tannaitic tradition. See Bereshit Raba 55 and Avot D'Rabbi Natan 8:1.

70. It could be argued from this passage that the fourth blessing is of Babylonian origin. In the two cases cited in B. Ketubbot 8a, a Palestinian authority does not recite the blessing at the wedding of R. Yehudah ha-Nasi's son (c. 220–250), whereas a Babylonian authority does recite it at the wedding of R. Ashi's son (c. 375–425). A vari-

ant cited by Albek, *Mavo La-Talmudim* (Tel Aviv: D'Vir, 1969), identifies this Babylonian authority as R. Iti, although most editions read "R. Assi." But it is most unlikely that R. Assi, who moved to Israel to study with Yoḥanan ben Nappha (c. 290–320), would have attended a wedding that took place in Babylonia between 375 and 425!

71. The Tosafist, citing Rashbam, identifies this unitary creation not as the double-faced male-and-female *adam*, but as a single-face *(partzuf)*. B. Ketubbot 8a, Tosafot, at *ḥada yetzira havei*.

72. The prooftext for the masculine singular *adam* is Genesis 5:2, but it could just as well have been the end of Genesis 1:27, where a similar usage occurs.

73. *The Schocken Bible*, trans. Everett Fox (New York: Schocken, 1995). I will use Fox's translation for all the Genesis citations in this section, because it is the most faithful to the exact language of the Hebrew.

74. Hence, both in the Eruvin and the Berakhot versions, the discussion ends with a series of rules enforcing the literal precedence of men: they must always precede women rather than following them.

75. This exegesis occurs in both the Berakhot and Eruvin versions, where it is attributed alternatively to the second-generation Amora R. Ḥisda, or, according to some, a *baraita*.

76. This unit appears in B. Shabbat 95a, B. Eruvin 18a, B. Berakhot 61b, and B. Niddah 45b, as well as in Avot D'Rabbi Natan 4. Kohelet Rabba 7:2.2 and Bereshit Rabba 18:1.

77. Thanks to Tamara Eskenazi for reminding me of these points. The *banim/bonim* pun occurs in Genesis 16:2. A rabbinic *banim/bonim* pun is found in B. Berakhot 64a.

78. My adaptation of JPS Tanakh translation.

79. My translation.

80. Examples of *re'a* as a synonym for lover occur in Song of Songs 5:16 and Jeremiah 3:20.

81. The bridal blessings' connection with grief is of antique origin. According to Y. Ketubbot 8:12, *birkat ḥatanim* was parallel in form to a no longer extant mourner's blessing *(birkat avelim)*.

82. These vows are not confined to liberal ceremonies. The Orthodox Hertz prayerbook, compiled by the former Chief Rabbi of England, offers a set of "unofficial" questions that could have been lifted straight out of the Anglican rite. Joseph H. Hertz, *Daily Prayer Book* (New York: Bloch, 1948), 1009–1010nn. Institutional innovations in non-Orthodox wedding liturgies are recorded not in prayerbooks but in rabbis' manuals, thereby limiting couples' independent access to the ceremony.

83. Ceil Skydell, "Renegotiating an Old Contract," *Moment* 17 (October 1992): 48–53. Shalom Sabar, *Ketubbah* (Philadelphia: Jewish Publication Society, 1990).

84. For a brief account of these laws, see "Partnership" in *Encyclopedia Judaica*.

85. For an overview of this legal concept, see Menachem Elon, ed., *Acquisition: The Principles of Jewish Law* (Jerusalem: Keter, 1975), 206–210.

86. For "putting into one pouch," see M. Ketubbot 10:4. For lifting as a sign of the acquisition of movable property, see B. Baba Batra 84b.

87. *Kinyan sudar* is still used in halakhic wedding ceremonies to ratify the bridegroom's acquisition of the *ketubbah* he will give the bride. When the bridegroom takes the handkerchief out of the hands of the officiating rabbi, it signifies his acquisition of the obligations of the *ketubbah*. Witnesses then sign the document.

88. I am aware that I am using this rabbinic term in a contemporary sense. Too many books to mention specify what this task requires in the contemporary world, but for two notable discussions, see Judith Plaskow, *Standing Again at Sinai*, 211–238, and Michael Lerner, *Jewish Renewal* (New York: G. P. Putnam Sons, 1994).

89. For an analysis of the Levitical prohibition of homosexuality, see Chapter 4.

90. The question of children is sensitive. Many panicky articles extrapolate the eventual extinction of the Jewish people from the falling Jewish birthrate. Nevertheless, I would decline to obligate all couples to have children. As mounting evidence about child abuse indicates, no good can come of forcing people who do not love and value children to have them anyway. Social punishment for childlessness also falls painfully upon couples who long for children and have not been able to have them. The real communal responsibility should be to support all families, heterosexual and gay, who contribute a new generation to the Jewish people.

91. For those who have forgotten freshman rhetoric as quickly as they learned it, metonymy is the figure of speech in which the part represents the whole. For further enlightenment, see James Thurber's immortal essay, "Here Lies Miss Groby," in *The Thurber Carnival* (New York: Harper and Row, 1945), 52–54.

92. I thank my husband, David Schulman, for this brilliant and lawyerly solution to the ring problem.

93. Barbara Myerhoff, "Sanctifying Women's Lives Through Ritual Workshop" [tape], Shekhina Conference, Los Angeles, 1985. Infomedix K316–IV, Garden Grove, CA 92643. See the discussion of ritual in Chapter 4.

94. Originally, the custom seems to have represented a carrot-and-stick approach to the management of demons. The wine in the glass served as a bribe, while the shattering of it would hurt them or frighten them. Joseph Gutman, "Jewish Medieval Marriage Customs in Art: Creativity and Adaptation" in *The Jewish Family*, 49–50.

95. See, for example, Brooklyn Aramaic Papyri 2 in Emil G. H. Kraeling, *The Brooklyn Aramaic Papyri: New Documents of the Fifth Century B.C.E.. from the Jewish Colony at Elephantine* (New Haven: Yale University Press, 1953). For further discussion, see Falk, *Jewish Matrimonial Law in the Middle Ages,* 120–121.

96. As we saw in the Palestinian *ketubbot*, however, he can be bound to confer the divorce upon the wife's request.

97. In the passage that follows, Miriyam Glazer vividly captures the humiliation of this gesture:

> "Stand face to face," they said. "You, *g'veret* [ma'am], put up your hands, no, not like that, your thumbs are up, you see they show eagerness that way, they mustn't show eagerness, yes like that, absolutely flat they have to be flat. Now *adoni* [sir], say the words, '*ha-ray aht megurehshet lee*—Behold you are divorced from me,'" and echoing in my ears were the words of marriage, "*ha-ray aht mekudehshet lee*— Behold you are sanctified to me," and the Rabbi said, "Now *adoni*, drop the *get* into her hands, keep your thumbs down, *g'veret*, absolutely flat, *g'veret*," and he dropped the *get* into my hands. Still I was silent, still I said nothing, and the Rabbi said, "Now you, *g'veret*, hold the *get* up high, you are showing it to the world, good, now walk to the four corners of the room holding up the *get*, to that corner and to that corner."

> Miriyam Glazer, "Exorcising the *Get*: a Ritual of Healing," in *A Ceremonies Sampler,* ed. Elizabeth Resnick Levine (San Diego: Women's Institute for Continuing Jewish Education, 1991), 63. It should be noted, however, that, for an additional fee, a woman can receive the *get* before a separate rabbinic court through the agency of a messenger rather than directly from her husband.

98. For a detailed comparison of divorce and manumission documents, see Daniela Piattelli, "*Get* and *Get Shihrur,*" in *Jewish Law Association Studies,* vol. 1, ed. B. S. Jackson (Atlanta: Scholars Press, 1985), 93–100.

99. According to the views of later halakhic authorities, only in extreme cases should a husband be compelled to divorce. In Western countries, religious courts have no coer-

cive power, but even in Israel, where recalcitrant husbands can be jailed, coercion may prove ineffective. In 1994, an 81-year-old man who had refused his wife a divorce finally died after 32 years in an Israeli prison. His wife, who had been married to him when she was 12, was by this time 66. "Jailed Man Keeps His Word Until the End," *Los Angeles Times* (Dec. 6, 1994), 2.

100. Moshe Zemer, "Purifying Mamzerim," in *Jewish Law Annual*, vol. 10 (Boston: Institute of Jewish Law, Boston University School of Law, 1992), 99–114. Zemer notes that the tendency of halakhic precedent is precisely the inverse of these genealogical inquisitions. Using such fictions as the twelve-month pregnancy, it labors mightily to uphold the presumption of legitimacy.

101. These proposals include Eliezer Berkovits, *Tenai B' Nesuin U'Get* (Jerusalem: Mossad Ha-Rav Kook, 1967), who proposed placing a condition upon the *kiddushin* itself, as follows: The husband says, "You are hereby acquired by me (or sanctified to me), on condition that I am never unable or unwilling to grant a *get* upon the demand of a rabbinic court." If subsequently the husband refuses or is unable to grant the *get*, no divorce is necessary. The marriage is retroactively annulled because the basis on which it was contracted is now seen to be invalid. This proposal was rejected by most authorities. A clause drafted by Professor Saul Lieberman of the Jewish Theological Seminary has been added to the *ketubbah* of the Conservative movement. In it, the husband acknowledges the Conservative rabbinic court's authority to take action regarding any marital difficulty and authorizing the rabbinic court to levy a fine for noncompliance. To collect this fine, the court would turn to the secular courts, arguing a breach of contract, and thus place financial pressure on the husband to deliver the divorce. See Isaac Klein, *A Guide to Jewish Religious Practice* (New York: Jewish Theological Seminary, 1979), 393. Antenuptial contracts whereby the secular courts can be used to force the giving of a *get* have been proposed by some Orthodox rabbis. Most secular courts in the United States do not enforce such contracts, on the grounds that they conflict with First Amendment rights. Shlomo Riskin, *Women and Jewish Divorce* (Hoboken, NJ: Ktav, 1989), 139–142.

102. *Jewish Law Annual*, vol. 4 (Leiden: E. J. Brill, 1981), is entirely devoted to the subject of the wife's right to divorce. See particularly, E. Lipinski, "The Wife's Right to Divorce in the Light of an Ancient Near Eastern Tradition," 9–27, which traces a West Semitic tradition embodying this right and points to its influence upon Palestinian custom and upon the customs of the Jews of the Elephantine colony, and Friedman, "Divorce Upon the Wife's Demand as Reflected in Manuscripts from the Cairo Geniza," 103–127.

103. The first systematic argument that marriage and divorce for Jews could be effectuated by civil courts was made by the nineteenth-century Reform rabbi Samuel Holdheim. He argued that marriage is a civil transaction, no different from any other acts of *kinyan*, and as such falls under the rabbinic principle *dina-d'malkhuta*, which stipulates that the law of the secular state applies in monetary matters. David Ellenson, "Samuel Holdheim on the Legal Character of Jewish Marriage: A Contemporary Comment on His Position," in Walter Jacob and Moshe Zemer, eds., *Marriage and Impediments to Marriage in Jewish Law*, Freehoff Institute of Progressive Halakhah (Tel Aviv: Rodef Shalom Press, 1997). A full account of the history and reasoning of this position in to be found in Solomon Freehoff, "Civil Divorce," in *Reform Jewish Practice* (New York, Union of American Hebrew Congregations, 1974), 99–110.

104. Boaz Cohen, "Appendix on Civil Marriage," in *Law and Tradition in Judaism* (New York: Jewish Theological Seminary, 1959), 239–243.

105. Rachel Adler, "Feminist Folktales of Justice: Robert Cover as a Resource for the Renewal of Halakha," *Conservative Judaism* 45 (spring 1993).

106. Thus, B. Kiddushin 13a: "one who does not know the particularities *(tiv)* of *gittin* (divorces) and *kiddushin* should not be involved with them."
107. B. Kiddushin 13a.
108. Peter Berger, *The Sacred Canopy*, 4, uses the term "objectivation" to describe the process by which human beings "forget" that they constructed nomic worlds and project them outward, so these constructions attain a reality separate from the human beings who constructed them—an "objective" reality.
109. The most comprehensive analysis of this halakhic controversy is found in Eliakim G. Elinson, *Nesuin She'lo K'dat Moshe v'Yisrael* (Tel Aviv: D'vir, 1975). However, see also David Friedman, "The Status of Non-Halachic Marriage," *Journal of Halakha and Contemporary Society* 8 (fall 1984): 118–128.
110. David Novak argues convincingly that such an interpretation is much broader than the text warrants. David Novak,"'The Marital Status of Jews Married Under Non-Jewish Auspices," in *Jewish Law Association Studies*, vol. 1, ed. B. S. Jackson (Atlanta: Scholars Press, 1985), 61–77, see especially 63–69.
111. Eliakim G. Elinson, chap.9.
112. Even Ha-Ezer 26:1.
113. Louis M. Epstein, "The Institution of Concubinage Among the Jews," in *American Academy for Jewish Research*, vol. 6 (n.p., 1934–1935), 153–187. Epstein contends that talmudic legal discussions of concubinage have been hampered by their conflation of two very different institutions. The first is concubinage as it appears in biblical narratives, a socially and economically inferior form of wifehood within the ancient Near Eastern family. The second, Greco-Roman concubinage, is described by Epstein as a "legally recognized unmarried state of enduring sex companionship between a man and a woman who could not or would not be legally married" (179).
114. Louis M. Epstein, "The Institution of Concubinage Among the Jews," 179.
115. Maimonides, *Hilkot Melakhim* 4:4, Mishneh Torah. This is disputed by Radbaz, loc. cit., and by the Kesef Mishneh in his comments at *Hilkot Ishut* 1:4. In these comments, the Kesef Mishneh cites the responsum of Ramban permitting concubinage to commoners.
116. Some of these authorities cite Rashi because, in his commentary on Genesis 25:6, he says that a concubine lacks a *ketubbah* but does not mention *kiddushin*. Because Rashi cites B. Sanhedrin 21a, it is more reasonable to assume that he agreed that concubines lack *kiddushin* but addresses only their lack of *ketubbah* as justification for Abraham's sending away "the sons of the concubines" with gifts, rather than giving them shares in his inheritance. There is a lively wrangle among the commentators on the Mishneh Torah as to whether Maimonides believed that a concubine had *kiddushin*. Both Rabad and the Magid Mishnah make this claim regarding *Hilkot Ishut* 1:4. However, in rebuttal, the Kesef Mishneh cites Maimonides' word-for-word quotation of the talmudic distinction in *Hilkot Melakhim* 4:4.
117. Nahmanides, *Teshuvot HaRamban*, ed. Chaim Dov Chavel (Jerusalem: Mosad HaRav Kook, 1975), no. 105. R. Yaacov Embden, *She'elot u'Teshuvot Yabetz*, vol. 2 (New York: Rabbi Chaim Gross, n.d.), no. 15. The latter decisor not only permits but endorses concubinage as a means of keeping men from sexual sins.
118. Novak, "The Marital Status of Jews Married Under Non-Jewish Auspices," 76–77, quoting R. Toledano, *Otzar Ḥayim* 6 (1930): 209.
119. Moshe Zemer offers an extensive catalogue of these decisions in "*Ha-Halakha KeMa'arekhet Musarit Mitpatahat,*" in *Halakha Shefuya*, chap. 1, 19–39.
120. David Tracy, *Plurality and Ambiguity* (San Francisco: Harper and Row, 1987).
121. Tracy, *Plurality and Ambiguity*, 90.

122. My translation.

Epilogue

1. My translation.
2. Some earlier manuscripts have "Alas for me." This reading appears to have been censored by Christian authorities.
3. See, for example, Isaiah 38:14, 59:11; Ezekiel 7:16; Nahum 2:8.

Index of
Bible Citations

261

INDEX FOR BIBLE CITATIONS

General Index